To William J. Hiebert, S.T.M., *who has made the Rock Island Model a gift to thousands of families. Always ahead of his time, he helps us put one foot on a firm foundation and the other dangling out there on the cutting edge. Bill, thanks for years of inspiration from your genius and creativity!*

From the short-legged Japanese woman

Table of Contents

iv

The Practice of Family Therapy

Key Elements Across Models

FOURTH EDITION

Suzanne Midori Hanna
Loma Linda University

THOMSON ™

BROOKS/COLE

Australia • Brazil • Canada • Mexico • Singapore • Spain
United Kingdom • United States

THOMSON

™

BROOKS/COLE

The Practice of Family Therapy: Key Elements Across Models, Fourth Edition
Suzanne Midori Hanna

Editor in Chief: *Marcus Boggs*
Acquisitions Editor: *Marquita Flemming*
Assistant Editor: *Samantha Shook*
Technology Project Manager: *Julie Aguilar*
Marketing Manager: *Meghan McCullough*
Senior Marketing Communications Manager:
  Shemika Britt
Project Manager, Editorial Production:
  Christy Krueger
Creative Director: *Rob Hugel*
Art Director: *Vernon Boes*

Print Buyer: *Judy Inouye*
Permissions Editor: *Roberta Broyer*
Production Service: *Interactive Composition
  Corporation*
Copy Editor: *Victoria Thulman*
Cover Designer: *Ross Carron*
Cover Image: *© Leon Zernitsky/Images.com*
Cover Printer: *Thomson West*
Compositor: *Interactive Composition
  Corporation*
Printer: *Thomson West*

For more information about our products, contact us at:
**Thomson Learning Academic Resource Center
1-800-423-0563**

For permission to use material from this text or product, submit a request online at
http://www.thomsonrights.com.
Any additional questions about permissions can be submitted by e-mail to
thomsonrights@thomson.com.

Thomson Higher Education
10 Davis Drive
Belmont, CA 94002-3098
USA

Library of Congress Control Number:
2006904583

Student Edition: ISBN 0-534-52349-8

PART 2 | THE ASSESSMENT STAGE

CHAPTER 5
Starting Off on the Right Foot: Referral and Intake   112

PART 3 | **MATCHING INTERVENTIONS TO CLIENTS AND SETTINGS**

CHAPTER 8
Interventions for Beliefs, Behaviors, and Emotions   207

List of Cases

Preface

The fourth edition of this book comes at a time when clinical research continues to show that couple and family therapy are important and sometimes the treatment of choice for a variety of mental health symptoms and social problems (Sprenkle, 2002; Hardy & Laszloffy, 2005). Convincing evidence also shows that family therapy can have a positive impact on the management of obesity, diabetes, and hypertension. These findings suggest that it is increasingly important to prepare beginning therapists for practice in the real world, including nontraditional settings outside of mental health clinics.

Too often, students must find their own bridge to connect what they've learned in their coursework with the myriad clinical experiences they have in the community. Ironically, some of the best evidence-based models of family therapy are tested in the community but not fully accessible to instructors in academic settings. This edition of *The Practice of Family Therapy* helps instructors illustrate how the concepts and interventions from previous editions form the core of family therapy's most successful clinical research. It may come as no surprise that our best evidence-based approaches to family therapy are excellent examples of integration. They illustrate how foundational approaches to family therapy are strengthened with additional attention to therapeutic alliances, client strengths, and knowledge of human development.

This book provides practical guidance that acknowledges the breadth of the field while helping the student of family therapy integrate common elements of practice from first-, second-, and third-generation approaches to family therapy. It can be used as a text in entry-level courses or as a guide for students and supervisors in a practicum. Previous editions have also been used by busy clinicians who just want some new ideas for troubleshooting that are easy to implement. This book helps clinicians who are trained in one or two models of family therapy to integrate the latest in evidence-based practice.

This book summarizes 13 approaches to family therapy and provides suggestions for getting started by outlining in detail the beginning stage of treatment. I make the assumption that beginning students often want suggestions as to what to say or where to start, so each chapter contains many sample questions the therapist can ask, dialogues between therapist and client, and corresponding commentaries. The result is a mosaic of basic skills that form the core of many current mainstream approaches with families. As students proceed through each chapter, they are given rationales for how the strengths from these varied approaches can be most useful during different stages in therapy, for different cases, and in different settings.

NEW MATERIAL IN THE FOURTH EDITION

Chapters have been streamlined to represent movement in the process of family therapy, from hypothesizing and assessment through treatment. The book uses Marriage and Family Therapy Core Competencies (see Appendix F) and the concept of *developmentally appropriate practice* to show new therapists how to approach the task of integration. The emphasis on developmentally appropriate practice is unique in that it is borrowed from the field of early childhood education and might be foreign to the mainstream family therapist. Chapter 1 provides a definition of family therapy that is drawn from various stakeholders in mental health treatment. Chapters 2 and 8 have expanded coverage of the concepts and interventions of evidence-based models, including a beginner's guide to the models that places heavy emphasis on attachment in human development. Chapter 4 now contains material on a client's stage of change and explains how to troubleshoot the therapeutic relationship when clinicians get stuck with a case. To help the student bridge the study of family therapy with practicing in the real world, Chapter 6 pays more attention to the Global Assessment of Relational Functioning (GARF) in treatment plans. These plans illustrate how clinicians can integrate the world of the medical model with family and systemic thinking. Additional case studies throughout the book illustrate problems in social services and diverse client characteristics related to sexual orientation and race. Some cases are followed in multiple chapters to show how different approaches apply at different stages during therapy.

CLINICAL APPROACH

The approach to the practice of family therapy in this book views problems as embedded in multiple relationships that evolve through many transitions. The importance of inter- and intra-personal dynamics is illustrated in presenting problems, and strategies for tracking historical and day-to-day sequences of interaction are woven throughout the chapters. The theory of change in this work is strength-based and client-centered, drawing from those approaches that maximize the therapeutic alliance and realistically address the nature and severity of a problem. I think the field of family therapy continues to show a willingness to critique all prevailing practices of the day—even those of postmodern models. Therefore, this book has equal emphasis on modern and postmodern approaches. For example, the reader will find solution-focused suggestions for developing a genogram as well as narrative approaches to taking a family's history. Behavior management plans for children are used alongside family art therapy interventions. Because students in various settings are required to provide a treatment plan and manage the practical aspects of each case, I offer suggestions for organizing clinical work. As in other editions, the pragmatic elements of each client session are outlined as negotiating structure, exploring client experience, addressing relationships, and developing a shared direction.

ORGANIZATION OF THE BOOK

This edition contains three general sections that transition from common themes to the pragmatics of assessment and intervention. To help students grasp how the therapeutic process can begin in a simple fashion and then become more complex, the metaphors of driving a car and traveling are used. These images both illustrate similar multidimensional processes that make up the creativity and spirit of adventure in our practice.

Each chapter begins with an outline and a list of relevant core competencies. Tables summarize key points, and boxes contain basic questions related to certain critical approaches as well as steps for practice. Figures help students visualize how various approaches fit together and provide diagrams of case material. A summary at the end of each chapter pulls together main themes and desired outcomes. Appendices offer related material and are arranged in the order they are mentioned in the book.

Part 1: From Theory to Practice: Common Themes

Part 1 includes 4 chapters that cover 13 models and 3 generations of family therapy practice. Practical aspects of each model are illustrated through case discussions. In Chapter 1, the reader learns about how family therapy is defined within and outside the field. This chapter introduces the concept of *developmentally appropriate practice*, which provides a basis for clinical judgment throughout the book. An introduction to the developmental criteria of individual functioning, relational functioning, and problem severity helps the beginning clinician think about clinical priorities before he or she ever sits down with a client. There are "snapshots" of six first-generation approaches and hypotheses from each approach that provide a multifaceted picture of a single case. The models covered in this chapter are structural, MRI, strategic, intergenerational, experiential, and behavioral. This chapter also details a supervisory session, providing the reader with recommendations and rationale intervention for a particular client's circumstances. This chapter breaks down complex skills so that they can be easily learned. The chapter can also be used as a supervisory resource, because the skills taught can be used by the therapist to manage interactions as they occur in sessions. Other skills are taught to change behaviors, beliefs, and emotions. Taken together, these sections provide a foundation for integrating the most common interventions in the field. For each intervention, I provide step-by-step instructions and guidelines for implementation. The chapter summary underscores the therapeutic alliance as a crucial process underlying all interventions.

Chapter 9 provides material on types of collaborations that are becoming a growing part of our field. Sections on school-based work and medical family therapy build on basic principles of collaboration and are illustrated through case material. Sample outlines guide a clinician through school consultations. The traditional concept of mind-body is expanded to include mind-body-spirit and relationships in medical work. A project that combines family therapy and art therapy illustrates how professionals with different traditions can work together toward common goals. In addition, beginners receive guidelines for fostering successful teamwork in their communities and developing projects with other professionals.

INSTRUCTORS AND SUPERVISORS

The Instructor's Manual contains a conceptual overview of each chapter, points of interest to guide the learning process, learning objectives for each chapter, discussion and examination questions for personal growth and evaluation, and quizzes to assess recognition and comprehension of information.

ACKNOWLEDGMENTS

I am so grateful to my editors and their staff for talented guidance during the production of this edition: Marquita Fleming for her encouragement and organization of the review process, and Jill Traut for her skillful management as all the pieces fell into place. I thank the following reviewers for their helpful suggestions: Michael D. Reiter, Nova Southeastern University; Gene Mastin, Liberty University; Ruth Paris, Boston University; Gary Paquin, University of Cincinnati; Gonzalo Bacigalupe, University of Massachusetts, Boston; Linda Metcalf, Texas Woman's University.

There are important others who have been invaluable and generous with their experience and insights: Nancy Edwardson, my graduate assistant at Loma Linda University, made this project possible with her excellent research and organizational skills; Donna Smith-Burgess, Director of Behavioral Health, SAC Health System, San Bernardino, provided significant critique and suggestions regarding treatment planning; Vernon C. Rickert, Executive Director, Boys' Haven, Louisville, helped with several treatment suggestions and shared his clinical expertise.

Finally, I want to thank my colleagues in the larger community of marriage and family therapy who have inspired me with cutting edge work that comes from their passion for bringing the benefits of family therapy to more consumers of mental health treatment. They include Duncan Stanton, for his generous mentoring and deep commitment to advancing family therapy approaches for substance abuse; Doug Sprenkle, for his eloquent defense of research-based practice; Bill Northey, for his work on the Marriage and Family Therapy Core Competencies; Howard Liddle, for a program of research that turns the tide of detachment in adolescents; Bill McFarlane, for his courage to step outside the box with schizophrenia, and Sue Johnson, for her bravery and persistence in the face of a world that once minimized the importance of emotion in our work. These individuals have my deepest respect and appreciation. Their leadership inspires me as we pass the baton to another generation of marriage and family therapists.

Suzanne Midori Hanna

Family Therapy: From Diversity to Integration

CHAPTER 1

CHAPTER OUTLINE

What Is Family Therapy?

So, Where Do I Start? A Developmentally Appropriate Framework

Individual Functioning

Relational Functioning

Problem Severity

Overview of First-Generation Family Therapy

Structural Family Therapy

Mental Research Institute

Strategic Family Therapy

Intergenerational Family Therapy

Experiential Family Therapy

Behavioral Family Therapy

Case Integration

Getting Started

Toward Integration: "The Best of Us Always Learn from the Best of Others"

Summary

CORE COMPETENCIES

1.1.1 Conceptual Understand systems concepts, theories, and techniques that are foundational to the practice of marriage and family therapy.

2.2.3 Perceptual Develop hypotheses regarding relationship patterns, their bearing on the presenting problem, and the influence of extra-therapeutic factors on client systems.

The history of marital and family therapy has always been one of professional diversity. In the twentieth century, the early interests of clergy, physicians, and social workers came together around issues of family relationships and marital enrichment. Researchers across the United States began to study communication and behavior related to schizophrenia and the family. During the 1950s, collaboration among these groups led to an exchange of publications and joint presentations at major national conferences. As these parallel efforts evolved in different regions of the United States, the practice of these groups gained momentum to produce a dramatic shift in thinking: Rather than viewing an individual's problems as originating solely within that individual, therapists saw an individual's problems from a relational perspective. If a person was depressed, the clinician explored his or her relationships in depth. If a child displayed unusual behavior, the psychiatrist involved the parents in problem-solving discussions rather than merely addressing the issues by medicating the child. As family therapists understood more about human development, they invited traditional psychotherapists to view individual symptoms within an interpersonal context. This *interpersonal focus* ranged from analyzing subtle verbal and nonverbal exchanges to assessing the expression of emotions across three generations of a family.

From 1900 to 1970, many professionals began thinking about mental health problems "outside the box," expanding their ideas beyond the concepts of Freud to more relational and interpersonal perspectives. The ancestors of present-day family therapy, who ranged from professionals in anthropology and communications to clinicians practicing psychiatry and hypnosis, extrapolated the knowledge of their original discipline and integrated it with other knowledge bases. Table 1.1 summarizes the historical contributions of some early theorists who began looking at family and social systems. Regarding clinical practice, the developing field of family therapy represented a wide range of professional training and mental health settings. However, what these early practitioners had in common was the courage to critique prevailing practices of their day and the willingness to experiment with new theories. A creative synthesis occurred as this multidisciplinary network of innovators dialogued and debated across the country. Gradually, this experimentation gave way to new methods developed by various charismatic innovators. Table 1.1 outlines these early approaches.

Today, the field of family therapy uses numerous approaches, all claiming this common heritage. During nearly 30 years as a practicing family therapist, I have seen this field develop some of the most exciting trends in mental health treatment and relationship enhancement. However, beginning practitioners are often overwhelmed when marital and family therapy is taught to them. After learning about each model, they typically ask, "So, where do I start?" The answer to this question usually comes from the approach practiced by the student's first clinical supervisor and from the employing agency's administrative policies. Because the student can approach the clinical hour in so many ways, this book helps the student steer a course that provides safety for clients, confidence for the clinician, and success for both.

Table 1.1 | Early Theorists

Year	Theorists	Concepts
1911	Alfred Adler, MD	Departs from Freud. Believes psychotherapy should encourage more "social interest" in the individual. *Social interest* is the awareness individuals have of their relational world, the desire to belong and to make a contribution to it.
1948	Norbert Wiener	Coins the term *cybernetics,* referring to the science of communication and human control systems such as physiological nervous systems or complex electrical systems.
1949	Ludwig von Bertalanffy	Applies biological concepts of *systems as organisms* of interrelated parts, where each part is distinguished by its *boundaries* and all systems have higher and lower levels (*suprasystems* and *subsystems*).
1949	John Bowlby, MD	Developed *attachment theory,* which addresses family interactions and the emotional development of children and adults.
1951	John Ruesch and Gregory Bateson	*The Social Matrix of Psychiatry,* a book on the role of feedback and information in communication theory. Their work suggests that all communication has *report* (content) and *command* (process) levels.
1967	Paul Watzlawick, Janet Beavin, and Don Jackson	*Pragmatics of Communication: A Study of Interactional Patterns, Pathologies and Paradoxes,* a seminal work on communication theory that builds upon work from the Bateson projects at M.R.I. They describe all behavior as a type of communication and categorize specific interactions as either *symmetrical* (egalitarian) or *complementary* (opposite in some way).

This chapter begins by providing a description of family therapy and a developmental framework for prioritizing clinical issues. The framework illustrates how a group of family therapy models can collectively describe any case. Milton Erickson, a psychiatrist who inspired family therapists to see the importance of language and communication in therapy, once said, "I invent a new theory for each patient" (Lankton & Lankton, 1983). The case example

SO, WHERE DO I START? A DEVELOPMENTALLY APPROPRIATE FRAMEWORK

Early childhood educators are already very familiar with the term *developmentally appropriate practice*. This refers to educational practices based on the abilities of children as they develop rapidly during the first years of life. For example, in preschools, specific differences are apparent in many three- and four-year-old children. Their attention spans, physical development, and cognitive complexity change significantly from one year to the next. A three-year-old begins to speak in short sentences and may ask "What?" or "Why?" A four-year-old learns to take turns and begins to understand the concept of time.

Likewise, clients who come to family therapy differ. Their life journeys have resulted in a wide range of symptoms, abilities, motivations, and worldviews. Their relationships also present a range of characteristics, such as conflicted, stable, close, and distant. When beginning practitioners assess these developmental differences in light of problem severity, they can proceed step by step through a series of questions that will help them find a place to start working with clients. These developmental factors—individual functioning, relational functioning, and problem severity—provide a framework for beginning the clinical process. Before deciding on a treatment plan for a given case, the practitioner must assess these differences in a variety of sequences, because they will dictate the clinical direction.

Individual Functioning

Symptoms. In contemporary practice settings, most agencies adopt some aspect of a medical model (assessment, diagnosis, treatment, cure). As family therapists, the core competencies help us follow this general medical model and still maintain our systemic/relational focus. For example, most agencies require an individual assessment and diagnosis in order to bill for services. In Chapter 6, you will find some practical ways to include this process in a treatment plan. Sometimes, considering a person's stage of life is important before making a proper diagnosis.

Life Stage. A client's age is an obvious element that dictates how a clinical session will proceed. In addition, evidence-based models of family therapy address these issues and integrate research and knowledge about child and adult development into the treatment process (Liddle, Rowe, Diamond, Sessa, Schmidt & Ettinger, 2000; Szapocnik & Coatsworth, 1999; Johnson, 1996). For example, multisystemic therapy (MST) acknowledges research on the importance of peer groups for adolescents and includes this level of influence in treatment goals (Henngeler, Schoenwald, Borduin, Rowland, & Cunningham, 1998). Multidimensional family therapy (MDFT) addresses the life task of increased independence during adolescence by holding some separate meetings with the youth and parents (Liddle, 2000). Chapter 3 outlines more developmental considerations based on a client's life stage. In addition to these stage issues, the dimension of individual functioning also includes a person's motivation to change.

Motivation. Prochaska's transtheoretical model of change suggests that all people seeking help can be located along a continuum of readiness to change (Prochaska, DiClemente & Norcross, 1992). Chapter 4 summarizes the stages along this continuum and some of the recommended interventions for each stage. Later in this chapter, a case discussion illustrates how the clinician can assess readiness to change and use this assessment to decide on a model of family therapy. From a systemic/relational view, this initial assessment is an opportunity to inquire about the client's present level of functioning and that of significant others, even when a session includes only one person. This focus on the network of important relationships includes understanding each person's motivation to be engaged in a therapeutic process. This is a critical factor in deciding where to start. Quite often, readiness to be involved in traditional mental health treatment is influenced by a person's culture, values and goals, and worldview.

Worldview. Chapters 3 and 7 provide the beginning practitioner with tools to explore and understand a client's worldview. Many cultures are averse to mental health treatment. Families who seek help for a child's behavior problem want practical, focused problem-solving, not "therapy." In addition, some men have gendered views about the meaning and implications of attending therapy sessions (Brooks, 1998). Thus, some models are a better match than others for clients with a particular worldview. In addition, some models of family therapy do a better job of exploring client experience and understanding the complexity of a person's presenting problem. This complexity will always involve the nature and history of the client's relationships.

Relational Functioning

To alter a common cliche, a relationship is worth a thousand words. An assessment of individual functioning is equivalent to words on a page that describe one person in the present moment. However, once therapists understand the history and quality of a person's relationships, they have a picture of that individual in living color that breathes life into the story and gives the "big picture."

For the Diagnostic and Statistical Manual, 4th edition (DSM-IV) (American Psychiatric Association, 1994), family therapists developed a helpful instrument for quick and easy assessment of relationships—the Global Assessment of Relational Functioning (GARF). The GARF assesses three important areas: *problem-solving, organization,* and *emotional climate.* (See Appendix E.) These three relational processes receive primary attention in one or more models of family therapy. Once you become familiar with the GARF and these models, you can choose interventions based on your assessment of these relational processes.

Problem Severity

The chosen model of family therapy should address the level of crisis or stability. The beginning therapist who performs intake screening should have a working knowledge of which models fit best with the type of problem at hand. In most realms of mental heath practice, the first priority of treatment is to stabilize clients and foster a return to their prior level of functioning. Stabilization is very important when a client is suicidal or homicidal (lethality). After lethality is assessed, life-changing issues such as illness, divorce, acute symptoms, and any other debilitating condition (crisis) should be assessed. All initial assessments should attend to issues of lethality and crisis as the highest priority. In the next chapters, you will learn about the representative models that can be used along this continuum of safety/crisis.

In addition, the history of the problem provides a basis for choosing intervention within each model of family therapy. Some central questions for this dimension are: How long has this problem been going on? Has it always been this way? When did things change? The answers can help therapists determine whether the problem is situational, transitional, or chronic.

From my point of view, these developmental issues fill in gaps left by the pioneering models during the first generation of family therapy. This book is inspired by evidence-based family therapists who applied developmental theory to their work, providing a working knowledge of family therapy practices with a focus on individual functioning, relational functioning, and problem severity.

Now that you have an outline for decision-making, let's look at a case through the eyes of first-generation family therapists. By the end of this chapter, the observations of each model combined with the dimensions of development will show you where to begin.

OVERVIEW OF FIRST-GENERATION FAMILY THERAPY

Following our developmental framework, the ABCs of family therapy are those pioneering approaches that began to look at social and mental health problems though the lens of relationships. In this introduction, you will learn how each model explores a case problem and hypothesizes about the best place to start therapy work with a client. With respect to these first models, each innovator put his or her unique interpersonal style into what he or she developed. Sometimes the setting and population also brought out a unique style of practice. However, these personal differences are difficult to imitate and can be overwhelming to students. Thus, this review removes such idiosyncrasies and looks only at the basics. After understanding the basic components of each model, the beginning practitioner can find simple ways to implement them.

So, take a step back in time and imagine the various contexts and populations that stimulated this new thinking about relationships and interactions. By 1970, first-generation family therapists were organized into counseling centers, training institutes, and research groups. Table 1.3 at the end of this chapter summarizes these major approaches. *Mental Research Institute* (M.R.I.) approaches, through the work of Watzlawick, Weakland, and Fisch, came to be known as brief, pragmatic, and interactional. *Experiential* approaches, through the examples of Virginia Satir and Carl Whitaker, were known for their attention to human growth and development. *Structural and strategic* approaches, from the mentoring of Minuchin, Haley, and Montalvo, were known as directive and engaging therapy that focused explicitly on relationships surrounding the presenting problem. *Intergenerational* family therapists, led by Bowen and Boszormenyi-Nagy, targeted the *family of origin* (birth or childhood family), the extended family, and those developmental experiences related to a given problem. *Behavioral* approaches were started from the work of Gerald Patterson and others who developed systematic, research-based, problem-focused interventions.

Keep in mind how revolutionary these approaches were, given the world at that time. Psychoanalysis was the primary mode of treatment for mental, emotional, and relational problems, and these mavericks stood apart from the prevailing medical establishment. What did the first family therapists begin to see through the lens of general systems, communication, cybernetic, and human development theories? The following case discussions provide an overview of how each model addresses perceptual skills. In Chapters 7 and 8, beginning clinicians will learn more about specific interventions that are compatible with each model.

Case 1 | The Nelsons

Paul Nelson, age 14, was admitted to a residential group home for adolescent males when his truancy and behavior problems became so pronounced that his parents could no longer keep him at home. A caseworker was assigned through juvenile court, and Paul was placed in a local facility where parents were involved in parent education and family therapy. The adolescents had a structured school experience and could earn weekend visits home through good behavior.

Paul's parents—Roy, 45, and Lilly, 42—were a white, working-class couple who had three children: Ed, Janet, and Paul. Ed, 18, dropped out of high school two years prior and was working at a local gas station. His girlfriend, Roxanne, 17, was pregnant. Ed was living at home, trying to save enough money to support this forthcoming child. At the time of treatment, Ed was uncertain whether he would marry Roxanne, although they were currently seeing each other on a regular basis. Janet, 17, was in her senior year of high school. She was an A student and enjoyed such school activities as cheerleading and chorus. She hoped to finish high school and go on to college. Paul had been held back in the seventh grade because of absences and was in the eighth grade at the time of his placement. (Figure 1.1 shows a genogram of the Nelson family. For more information about genograms, see Chapter 7.)

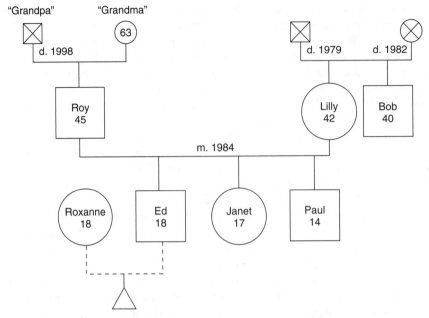

Figure 1.1 | The Nelsons' Genogram

Structural Family Therapy

In 1960, Salvador Minuchin, MD, a psychiatrist, began a project at the Wiltwyck School in New York to study the inner-city families of delinquent boys. He and his colleagues developed a structural approach to family therapy that relates patterns of delinquency to the degree of disorganization in the family (Minuchin, Montalvo, Guerney, Rosman, & Schumer, 1967). Minuchin took concepts from general systems theory and applied them to family organization. Therapists using this approach observe the interactions and activities of family members to determine the organization or structure of the family. Organization can be assessed by the quality of leadership, balance, and harmony that exists within the family (Breunlin, Schwartz & MacCune-Karer, 1992). Symptoms are regarded as a consequence of organizational difficulties. According to Minuchin, this organization must evolve to meet the developmental tasks for each stage of the family life cycle.

Organization. Within families, *hierarchy* is the type of leadership, often expressed by the pecking order, by shared perceptions of who "the boss" is, and by interactional patterns that indicate who gets the last word. The *parental subsystem* is supposed to provide leadership for growth and development of the child or *sibling subsystem*. In turn, children are influenced by leadership style and interpersonal patterns of parents. *Boundaries* are imaginary lines that describe who is included in an interpersonal event (i.e., who interacts with whom, for what purpose, and how often). They also denote the closeness of relationship on a continuum (i.e., too close, balanced, or too disengaged). The corresponding type of interpersonal boundary in a given relationship would be labeled as *diffuse*, *rigid,* or *permeable*. Sometimes parents develop complementary roles with their children (that is, one close, one distant). When this happens, the parental hierarchy is thought to lack balance.

Power is the "relative influence of each family member on the outcome of an activity" (Aponte, 1976b, p. 434). *Alignment* is the level of agreement or disagreement between members or subsystems in the family. A *cross-generational coalition* can occur when one parent joins in a coalition with one or more children against the other parent. Such a coalition is often indicated when the therapist notes critical discussions about a parent who is absent, when one parent confides in a child about marital discord, or when one parent openly sides with a child against the other parent. In structural terms, parent-child coalitions are thought of as a violation of the boundary between the parental and sibling subsystems because they change the role of the child from one of dependent to one of confidant or emotional peer.

Interactional Sequences.   The therapist discovers that when Mrs. Nelson is called by the school, she responds by leaving work and confronting Paul. When Paul refuses to interact with her and withdraws to his room, she reports to Mr. Nelson about the situation. Mr. Nelson confronts Paul about his behavior and threatens him with punishment if his behavior does not improve. When Janet becomes aware of the problem, she spends time with Paul, encouraging him to behave better. She has also become Lilly's *sounding board,* providing a listening ear as her mother worries out loud. The therapist asks Paul about his relationship with each member of the family. Of his parents, he spends the most time with Lilly and is uncomfortable with Roy. Of his siblings, he is closest to Janet and feels some disgust that Ed has gotten himself into "trouble." Roy and Lilly are asked about the time they spend together. Because they work different shifts, they have very little time together until the weekend. Recently, Roy was asked to work overtime at the meatpacking plant as a result of layoffs and employee reductions.

Hypotheses.   The structural family therapist hypothesizes from this information that the marital subsystem has become distant as a result of the family's economic situation. In addition, Lilly seems to be overinvolved with Janet and Paul in contrasting ways. By confiding in Janet, she has elevated Janet from the status of child to that of peer. By engaging in repetitive interactions with Paul, she is equally enmeshed with him, but in a way that produces opposition rather than peer status. Because Paul has been persistent in his misbehavior, he has rendered the parental subsystem ineffective at this time, obtaining a level of power that is inappropriate.

Mental Research Institute

In 1959, the psychiatrist Don Jackson, MD, organized the Mental Research Institute (M.R.I.) and applied the physiological concept of homeostasis to the family. As used in family therapy, *homeostasis* is the family's tendency toward stability through maintaining consistent patterns of thought, emotion, and interaction over time. Although the concept was originally thought of as a social force that resisted change within the family, later applications suggest that any family or social system has two balancing dimensions, one of maintaining *stability* during the threat of change and one of flexibility (*adaptability*) in the wake of change, whether it is normal, developmental, or a time of crisis. Another important concept addressed at M.R.I. was that of *circular causality,* which refers to the way in which any behavior is understood by seeing it as part of a cycle of interaction rather than as an isolated entity. The M.R.I. incorporated the work of Bateson, Erickson, Haley, Weakland, and others into creative theory and practice projects that continue to have a compelling influence on the practice of family therapy and psychotherapy.

Communication and Behavior.   Brief family therapists believe that symptoms in the family are messages about some aspect of the family system. This concept comes directly from communication theory. These therapists are also influenced by the work of Milton Erickson, who was pioneering hypnotic and paradoxical techniques that emphasized the uniqueness of the symptom and the importance of behavioral directives. This blend of communication, cybernetics, and Ericksonian influences results in a pragmatic approach to therapy that avoids any personal conflict with the client.

Because behaviors often communicate meaning on more than one level, the symptom can contain an explicit message ("I have a stomachache") as well as an implicit message ("I want more affection"). This is an example of the *report* and *command* levels of communication. Because these therapists view all behavior as communication, a symptom is a communicative act between two or more members that symbolizes some problem within the interpersonal network (Watzlawick, Weakland, & Fisch, 1974). Thus, any behavior can potentially be an attempted solution to some unidentified problem ("I want my divorced parents to reconcile"). In addition, family members' attempts to address problem behavior might become a vicious cycle in which the solution becomes a problem.

Hypotheses.   Therapists at M.R.I. explored which solutions had been tried to resolve the problem (Weakland, Fisch, Watzlawick, & Bodin, 1974). Often the attempt to solve the problem would worsen the original situation. In exploring the Nelsons' attempts at solving the problem of Paul's behavior, the therapist discovers that their primary solutions have been verbal (nagging, criticizing, and threatening), and Paul's responses have been nonverbal; furthermore, none of these attempted solutions has been successful. These would be considered first-order attempts at change, rather than second-order solutions that change the nature of the relationship. In first-order change, *the method changes slightly, but the category of the method stays the same (negative interaction).* Second-order change would require Lilly and Roy to identify options they could implement in order to be more action-oriented and less verbal and negative (the change in category leading to a more constructive relationship).

Strategic Family Therapy

In 1967, Jay Haley completed his research assistantship with Gregory Bateson and took a position at the Philadelphia Child Guidance Clinic, led by Salvador Minuchin. He joined Minuchin and Braulio Montalvo in developing a family counseling and training institute. For ten years, the three men drove in a car pool back and forth from work, developing their shared ideas about families and family therapy (Simon, 1992).

Many new students of family therapy are unaware that Haley took the unconventional ideas from M.R.I. and Milton Erickson and influenced Minuchin's evolving model on the east coast. Likewise, Minuchin influenced Haley with his applications of structure and function. With each refinement came different perspectives about the role and responsibility of the therapist. Haley's unique integration of these influences resulted in a model that conceptualized the family in terms of organization, but emphasized an unwavering focus on the presenting problem. For Haley, all therapeutic interactions should relate directly to the presenting problem. Otherwise, they are irrelevant (Simon, 1992). Like Erickson, strategic family therapists emphasize a unique approach or strategy for each presenting problem.

Systemic Meaning of Symptoms.   Symptoms often occur when a family is stuck at a particular stage in the family life cycle; that is, whereas Paul Nelson's behavior might be a metaphor for conflictual interactions between his parents, his behavior might also be saying something about the family's adaptation to a new stage in the life cycle (the launching stage). In this way, the symptom is often an attempted solution to some other problem that goes unacknowledged or unnoticed by others in the system. Such metaphorical messages help the therapist to conceptualize the relationship between symptoms and interactional patterns within the family. By targeting specific interactions that occur during the session, the therapist works on the premise that small initial changes will lead to greater changes over time (Weakland et al., 1974).

Hypotheses.   In a session with the family, the therapist asks about the sequence of interactions surrounding the presenting problem. Lilly is the first to speak. Roy remains silent. Both Roy and Paul wait to be spoken to by the therapist. When the therapist asks Roy to describe what happens when Paul gets stubborn, Roy outlines the usual sequence of interactions: his arrival from work, Lilly's complaints about Paul's truancy, Roy's questions to Paul about why he is behaving this way, and Paul's silence. At that point, in exasperation, Roy tells Paul that if he keeps up with his behavior, he will never amount to much of anything. Finally, Paul retreats to his room and begins to listen to his collection of heavy metal music.

The strategic family therapist would assume that Paul's behavior is a metaphor or nonverbal message about something else going on in the family. It might be related to the distance between his parents, challenges with Ed in entering the launching stage of the family life cycle, or some other aspect of the family's well-being that has not yet come to light. As strategic therapists explore opinions and interactions within the family, they will search for possible clues to clarify the message of the symptom.

Intergenerational Family Therapy

Several pioneers share an attention to family dynamics across several generations and a history in psychodynamic theory. They conceptualize families and their problems in terms of psychological dynamics passed from generation to generation. In 1954, Murray Bowen, MD, left the Menninger Clinic and began a project for the National Institute of Mental Health (NIMH) with Lyman Wynne. In the project, families and their schizophrenic children lived in a research inpatient unit. Bowen developed the set of concepts taken from biological systems called *family systems theory* that contributed to decades of therapists exploring their own families of origin. One of these concepts, *differentiation of self,* is the process by which adult children develop a balance of independence (autonomy) and connection with their families of origin and with other important social-emotional systems. This concept comes from Bowen's analysis of *family emotional process,* the balance of emotional reactivity (anxiety) and rationality that each family exhibits during times of change or stability. Through Bowen's work, therapists today often explore beliefs, values, and interactions that influence the emotional growth and maturity of family members.

In 1957, Ivan Boszormenyi-Nagy (the last syllable is pronounced *Nahzsh*), MD, began a family therapy project at East Pennsylvania Psychiatric Institute that included intensive psychotherapy of hospitalized psychotics. His work emphasized including the entire family, communication, and behavior patterns. However, he found that general systems theory ignored issues related to personal issues of entitlement and injustices (*fairness*) in family life. He developed a model called *contextual family therapy* that defines a person's context as *relational ethics,* or the dynamic balance of fairness, trust, and loyalty between people. The concept of the *parentified child* refers to children who have assumed so much responsibility for parental functions that they no longer trust that fairness will prevail. As this model developed, practitioners also recognized that issues of fairness and justice extended beyond the intergenerational family to society. They acknowledged the "societal background of ripped-off, overburdened, abandoned nuclear families" (Boszormenyi-Nagy & Ulrich, 1981, p. 161).

In 1958, Nathan Ackerman, MD, sometimes referred to as the grandfather of family therapy, published *The Psychodynamics of Family Life.* This was the first book describing the diagnosis and treatment of family relationships and bridging the gap between intrapsychic and interpersonal theories. Ackerman was a child psychiatrist, and his interest in the welfare of children took him into homes and stirred his interest in seeing the entire family. He noticed a "live type of history" emerging as families reviewed the history of a problem. Because these historical disclosures related to present emotional experience, he considered this "the *'live past,'* not the 'dead past' of family life" (Ackerman, 1981, p. 319). For him, the main tasks of the therapist became *reeducation* of the family, *reorganization* of family communication, and facilitation of growth through an exploration of the *emotional experience* of the family.

These early leaders saw the past as operating in the present and developed theories that helped them chart a therapeutic course across time. As a result of Ackerman's untimely death, the work of Bowen and Nagy became more widely known and carried forth. Only a few of the many concepts from their work are featured in this text. Although Bowen and Nagy developed various ideas that are unique to their separate approaches, together they represent the primary roots of most intergenerational therapy practiced today.

Unlike structural, M.R.I., and strategic therapists, the practitioners of this model consider information about past relationships to be a meaningful springboard from which to design interventions in the present (live past). Intergenerational therapists assume that parenting and marital patterns are influenced by experiences in each parent's family of origin. As parents pass on their level of differentiation to children, relationships are often fused (too close and too emotionally reactive). This model suggests that each member of the family acts impulsively out of emotion or tradition and is unaware of how the power of reason can generate improved relational patterns. This imbalance of emotionality over rationality is referred to as a *lack of differentiation.* The fact that the family members engage in repetitive interactions that bring about the same unsatisfactory results is an indication of the intense anxiety that motivates their behavior. In addition, this anxiety leads to a process of *triangulation,* in which one person enlists the support of another person against a third party in the family. This model suggests that when family members can discern the difference between the anxiety of their current behavior and the logic of alternative solutions, they can develop more healthy relationships in the future.

Hypotheses. Bowenians would assert that both Roy and Lilly respond out of emotion rather than rationality when addressing Paul's behavior. They would reason that Paul and his siblings are mirrors of a transmitted family process (*family projection process*) rooted in the historical evolution of previous generations. Paul's behavior would be thought of as coming from some gut-level instinct that manifests the same level of differentiation as his parents'.

The therapist discovers that Roy's mother lives in their neighborhood and has been widowed for five years. As family members begin discussing the loss of Grandpa, Paul becomes animated and talkative for the first time. He relates his memories of Grandpa, giving particular emphasis to the sadness that he can still vividly remember feeling on the day of the funeral. Other family members also describe family vacations that Grandpa organized and the great void his death left in the family. Since his death, there have been no family vacations. The year after his death, Lilly went to work outside the home for the first time. Paul was ten at the time.

The Nelsons can be seen as having not recovered fully from Grandpa's death. The void in the family was not filled by anyone else taking on the planning of family vacations. For Paul, the void might have widened when Lilly went to work and Janet graduated from elementary school, leaving him to attend his school alone for the first time.

The historical development of the Nelsons illustrates how a lack of differentiation can be passed down through the generations and also how it can be exacerbated through traumatic life events. It emerges that Paul's behavior did not become problematic until the sixth grade, approximately one year after Grandpa's death. This was also the year that Lilly went to work. During the early parts of the interview, Roy and Lilly describe the first years of their marriage as very happy. Lilly's parents died when she was young, and she was happy to be adopted into Roy's family.

Boszormenyi-Nagy (1987) might assume that each person in the family is motivated, in part, by a subjective sense of fairness that can be understood only from his or her unique development (*relational ethics*). This *ledger system* provides a framework by which the family therapist discovers each person's subjective justification for his or her current behavior (Boszormenyi-Nagy & Krasner, 1986). Paul's motivation for skipping school could come from an unspoken sense of *entitlement* based on some contribution that he perceives himself to be making to the family. For example, having seen his brother drop out of school at age 16 (a perceived privilege), Paul might think he is entitled to the same privilege in return for the loyalty he manifests to his mother against his father. Understandably, Roy and Lilly might also be motivated by a sense of justice that comes from their experience in their own families. ("We were expected to obey our parents unconditionally, and we are entitled to the same obedience from our children.")

Experiential Family Therapy

Although Virginia Satir and Carl Whitaker are both described as experiential in their approach to family therapy, each evolved from different traditions. Satir came out of the communication tradition at M.R.I. and later aligned closely with the human potential movement. In 1964, Satir, a social worker, published the first edition of *Conjoint Family Therapy*, a pioneering work in family therapy that highlighted her beliefs about human beings as evolving and capable of growth, change, and intimacy with each other. As a founding member of M.R.I. and one of the few women recognized as making pioneering contributions to family therapy, she became a leading figure in the human growth movement. While she was associated with M.R.I., she became "a kind of living legend as family therapy's most celebrated recruiter and goodwill ambassador ... perhaps the most imitated family therapist of her time" (Simon, 1981, p. 168). She emphasized the development of positive *self-esteem* through self-acceptance and family relationships that fostered the *individuality* of each member.

Whitaker came from a psychiatric background in which he worked with families of schizophrenics. He developed his ideas of family therapy in psychiatric settings where he had the authority to work in novel and creative ways. However, unlike Satir, he was difficult to imitate because of his challenging and controversial personal style. Throughout his career, students flocked to him because of his wisdom and forthright opinions.

These pioneers share an investment in "spontaneity, creativity and risk-taking ... a commitment to freedom, individuality and personal fulfillment" (Nichols & Schwartz, 2001, p. 175). Both believed that when the therapist is open and spontaneous, family members will learn to behave in the same way.

Human Growth and Development. Experiential family therapists focus on subjective needs of the individual in the family and facilitate family interactions that address the *individuality* and *self-esteem* of each member. These clinicians believe that all individuals have the right to be themselves; however, family and social needs might often suppress the individuality and self-expression by which a person becomes fully understood and known in the family (*intimacy*). As parents are the architects of the family (Satir, 1972), they are responsible for providing sufficient structure and nurturance so that the individuality of each child can be fostered. However, parents often manifest their low self-esteem through embarrassment, helplessness, criticism, or hostility that they feel regarding their children's struggles.

With empathy and support from the therapist, the parents come to accept their own emotional experience, thereby becoming more intimate and caring. As *self-awareness* increases, the quality of communication improves, fostering self-esteem and growth in family members. By fostering *self-acceptance,* the experiential family therapist helps parents to become who they want to be. They can learn to forgive themselves for not being perfect parents or marital partners. As they do this, they can also risk more intimate self-expression with each other. As they learn to tolerate intimacy (and the accompanying risk of conflict), their acceptance of themselves and each other generalizes to their children. Interactions become opportunities for family members to be heard and understood, rather than contests to control or judge.

Hypotheses. The therapist discovers that Ed does not see himself like either parent. He dropped out of school with his parents' permission. He felt discouraged about his school performance and did not want the continued humiliation of failure. Thus, he has low self-esteem and lacks confidence about his abilities. He never exhibited behavior problems at school or at home. However, as the family discussed ways in which they tried to help Ed with his studies, it emerged that both Lilly and Roy thought Ed was like them because they had no understanding of the math techniques being taught at the high school and they felt intimidated and helpless in the process. They are viewed as discouraged and feeling powerless about how to help their children. However, they would usually become angry and embarrassed when Ed received his report card, telling him he should ask his teachers for more help. When Ed announced that he wanted permission to drop out of school, Roy had few words to say and Lilly was relieved. This pattern indicates fear of expressing the most personal of emotions and an inability to respond to the discouragement and vulnerability of another.

Behavioral Family Therapy

In 1971, Gerald Patterson published the first edition of *Families: Applications of Social Learning Theory to Family Life*. In 1975, he published *A Social Learning Approach to Family Intervention*. Both of these works showed the effective and positive contributions of *parent training* and *behavior modification* on family relationships. The influence of social learning theory spawned a number of prominent family therapists who brought research training from their degrees in psychology and from their close studies of the minute details of *interactional sequences* in family life. These family therapists used their findings to develop intervention strategies for child problems and marital distress.

Because Patterson began to consider the cost-effectiveness of the treatment of children, he paid increased attention to employing the child's parents as agents of change. As he began to help parents with the behavior of their children, he also observed and noted the interactional patterns of other family members (Patterson, 1971). Research began to shift from investigating the child's inappropriate behavior to studying patterns of interaction between family members (i.e., how two family members influence each other in ways that maintain the behavior).

Behavioral Sequences and Reinforcements. This approach focused on the behavior of individuals and the events in the social environment that trigger their behavior (*antecedents*) and that shape and maintain their behavior. Clinicians using this approach conduct a *functional analysis* that explores the *consequences* of behaviors (what follows) that are considered *goals* and *reinforcements* to them. (See Box 9.1 in Chapter 9 for an example of a functional analysis.) The social learning approach views family dysfunction as the result of infrequent *positive reinforcement* between family members (i.e., not enough rewards for positive behavior). Thus, positive behavior is consistent when it is rewarded accordingly. Often an *aversive stimulus,* or punishment, is used by one family member to control the behavior of another. Social learning theory views family conflict as the use of aversive control rather than the use of *positive reinforcement*. The eventual outcome is a low rate of positive reinforcers exchanged over an extended period of time.

Hypotheses. Before skipping school, Paul reports getting up in the morning and wishing that he didn't have to face his teacher, Mr. Rawls. He is self-conscious about being held back a year in school, and he's jealous that Ed doesn't have to get up as early. When he goes in the school door, he feels a heaviness in his chest. Out of his mother's view, he walks down the hall and out the other door. He walks through the neighborhood and sometimes goes to the gas station where Ed works.

The remaining sequence of these events appears in the earlier section on structural family therapy. Although the questions are similar, note the antecedent information that comes from a functional assessment. The therapist can hypothesize that Paul's interactions with his teachers serve as an aversive stimulus, signaled by the heaviness in his chest. This might be a phobic reaction (fear). His visits to the gas station may serve as positive reinforcement. After school, his mother's reaction might be a negative reinforcement and his sister's attention might be a positive reinforcement.

CASE INTEGRATION

What follows is a summary of how these early therapeutic models can be used to describe the Nelsons' situation:

- **Structural.** Parents' teamwork may have eroded due to life stressors; relationships are uneven with the children.
- **M.R.I.** Attempted solutions appear ineffective.
- **Strategic.** Paul's behavior may be a symptom (or message) for life-stage adjustments, marital conflict, and so on.
- **Intergenerational.** Unresolved losses may be underneath the family's emotionality; Paul may feel a sense of entitlement due to his brother's dropping out of school.
- **Experiential.** Paul's humiliation and failure at school may be a reflection of parents' low self-esteem and intimidation in the educational system. Parents' responses to Ed may stem from a lack of intimacy.
- **Behavioral.** Paul is faced with aversive stimuli from school, positive reinforcements from trips to the gas station and from his sister, and negative reinforcement from his mother.

In contrast to the traditional lens of psychoanalysis, these perspectives were radical for their day—hard to imagine, given how practical and obvious some of them may seem to us now. This is because our society has become more attuned to these levels of analysis and theories of development.

Now, let's take these initial hypotheses and combine them with the developmental dimensions outlined in the beginning of this chapter. Box 1.1 illustrates an initial assessment. Box 1.2 provides a blank form to copy and use for future assessments. In Chapter 6, this assessment will develop into a treatment plan. However, here, let's look at an example of how to put different approaches in a certain order.

| Box 1.1 | **Initial Family Assessment: The Nelsons** |

Individual functioning	Symptoms	Many family members are despondent and discouraged. Screening for depression is warranted. Paul's humiliation and failure at school may be a reflection of parents' low self-esteem and intimidation in the educational system (experiential).
	Life stage	This is a family in the launching stage with adolescents, thus, issues of autonomy are central. Paul's behavior may be a symptom (or message) for life-stage adjustments, marital conflicts, etc. (strategic).
	Motivation	The family wants help, but therapy is a process foreign to their day-to-day life. They know something needs to change, but they fear criticism and guard themselves due to their fears (see Chapter 4).
	Worldview	Rural, working class family with here-and-now orientation to time and a cognitive-rational, pragmatic approach to individual functioning (see Chapter 3).
Relational functioning	Problem solving	Attempted solutions appear ineffective. Repetitive interactions end without resolving the problem (M.R.I.).
	Organization	Parents' teamwork may have eroded due to life stressors; relationships are uneven with the children (structural).
	Emotional climate	Unresolved losses may be underneath the family's emotionality; Paul may feel a sense of entitlement due to brother's dropping out of school (intergenerational).
		Parent's responses to Ed may stem from a lack of intimacy (experiential).
Problem severity	Lethality	No one is suicidal or homicidal.
	Crisis	The point of crisis was when Paul was placed in residential treatment (a life-changing action). See Chapter 2 for descriptions of MST and MDFT, family therapy approaches that might have prevented an out-of-home placement.
	History	Given the current situation, the goal is to return Paul and family to the best prior level of functioning. This appears to be the stage before Grandpa died (Intergenerational). Thus, problem severity is viewed as transitional. Chapters 6 and 8 have more information on how to assess problem severity.

Box 1.2	**Initial Family Assessment**

Individual
functioning

Symptoms:

Life stage:

Motivation:

Worldview:

Relational
functioning

Problem
solving:

Organization:

Emotional
climate:

Problem
severity

Lethality:

Crisis:

History:

GETTING STARTED

Based upon this initial assessment (taken over two or three sessions), the following steps are recommended:

1. Start with the goal of returning the family to their best prior level of functioning.
2. Explore Grandpa's death, his role in the family, and what is necessary for the family to assume the tasks of his role (intergenerational and structural).
3. Create a family history timeline (see Chapter 7) to help the family productively grieve and develop a plan to carry on Grandpa's legacy.
4. Provide an environment of brainstorming to help the family reorganize and engage in problem-solving the tasks of launching (strategic).
5. Encourage and coach Dad and Mom to assume leadership in the directions just listed (structural).
6. Through the intergenerational exploration, create conversations in which family members can encourage, support, and bond with each other (experiential).

In many cases, the components of each model might be equally relevant. Therefore, these recommendations suggest an order of therapeutic perspectives rather than an exclusion of one particular perspective based on developmental factors. In cases where lethality or crisis are pressing issues, the therapist might begin with structural, behavioral, and M.R.I. approaches, because these can be used effectively to stabilize an unsafe situation. This approach to making clinical decisions, coupled with the core competencies established in the profession (and discussed earlier in the chapter), help beginning practitioners find a place to start working with a case.

TOWARD INTEGRATION: "THE BEST OF US ALWAYS LEARN FROM THE BEST OF OTHERS"

The models presented in this chapter discussed the Nelson family using many different perspectives. Table 1.3 at the end of this chapter summarizes key aspects of the pioneering models. These are the characteristics that have withstood the test of time. Although each model provides different concepts and language, *the therapist's ability to integrate the family's developmental reality with a given theoretical direction may really be at the heart of successful family therapy.* As the field of family therapy has developed over the past several decades, the movement toward distinct schools of thought has given way to integration of these major modes of thinking. As Nichols and Schwartz (1991) note:

> Theoretical positions tend to be stated in doctrinaire terms that maximize their distinctions. While this makes interesting reading, it is somewhat misleading. The truth is that the different systems of family therapy are more alike in practice than their theories suggest. Moreover, each new approach tends to become more eclectic over

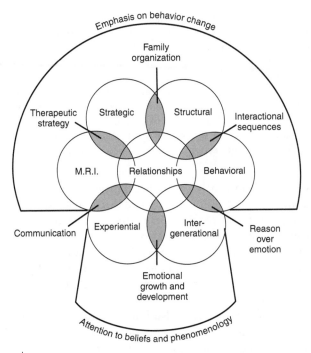

Figure 1.2 | Common Factors Across Early Models

time. Practitioners start out as relative purists, but eventually discover the validity of theoretical concepts from other approaches and the usefulness of other people's techniques. (pp. 512–513)

This quote suggests that contemporary family therapists integrate some or all of these perspectives when they assess a case. Figure 1.2 illustrates the commonalities among the theories, even in the early years. The old phrase "All roads lead to Rome" suggests that some general outcomes can be achieved in a variety of ways. In the world of families and relationships, this is especially true. Perhaps the earliest example of integration occurred when Stanton (1981) coined the term *structural-strategic* and then, with Todd, applied that model in their groundbreaking work on drug addiction (Stanton & Todd, 1982). This term is now used frequently to describe those who attend to structural themes while using strategic interventions.

In an additional move toward integration, Stanton (1992) developed the use of a "Why now?" question, integrating it into his structural-strategic approach. This question incorporates elements of family transitions and development into the process that might be overlooked by a more present-focused orientation. Another example is Minuchin (1987), reflecting on the factors that shape his practice:

Recently, I was working with a family with three adult children whose mother committed suicide 20 years ago. I surprised myself by asking them to watch family movies and to mourn the mother's death. I thought Norman Paul might be proud of me. Another day I was seeing a family with an anorectic child. I found myself remembering some of the writings of Hilde Bruch. I didn't know she was one of my voices, but so it seems. Naturally pulling many voices together usefully demands an organizing frame. Briefly, the business of family therapy is change. Within this framework the possibilities are many and varied, as are the voices that speak to me. Within the possibilities open to us, the best in us always learns from the best of others. I am pleased to acknowledge that when I say to a man, When did you divorce your wife and marry your office?, it is Carl [Whitaker]'s voice speaking. He might not recognize it in my accent, but it is there, as are all the others. (pp. 13–14)

Perhaps if Minuchin's early career had brought him in contact with hundreds of mid-life families whose mothers had died tragically, he would have pioneered a therapy different from his structural approach. On the other hand, one might also imagine, in the latter case, that his personal style, insight, and daring would still be inspiring to us today. In 2005, at age 84, he reported that when he reads his early writing from the 1980s, he can hardly identify with it. "If that is structural family therapy, maybe I'm not a structural family therapist!" (Minuchin, 2005).

Other models of practice have also built upon the work of these pioneers to account for gender, race, culture, life-cycle issues, and individual experience. This suggests that family therapy is a field organized around systemic/relational concepts, but is continually open to new and creative refinements in practice. Chapter 2 reviews these second-generation models and demonstrates how the first two generations led to a group of evidence-based models.

SUMMARY

From the beginning of the twentieth century, worldwide changes in thinking led to the development and refinement of mental health practice. Those changes continue today. In the United States, practitioners listened to innovative thinkers at home and abroad, developing a more holistic and interpersonal approach to understanding human problems and resolving them. This led to the development of family therapy, first as early practice and research, and then as diverse approaches used with different populations. Now an institutionalized profession, marriage and family therapy is regulated (licensed) and practiced in most of the United States and in many other parts of the world.

Reflecting this integration of ideas and approaches, this book describes family therapy by using state laws, accreditation standards, core competencies, and research. A developmental framework guides the decision-making process so that practitioners can tailor a treatment plan to individual cases by assessing individual functioning, relational functioning, and problem severity. The models presented in this chapter and summarized in Figure 1.2 and Table 1.3 are the basis of this integrative approach for beginning practitioners.

As Minuchin suggests, perhaps the therapist is on a journey of discovery as much as the client is and must be open to shifting directions as new information comes forth. With this goal of openness in mind, take on a spirit of discovery and see what happened to the practice of family therapy as the twentieth century came to an end. Now let's move from observing first generation models to understanding the contribution of postmodern family therapy and evidence-based family therapy, both of which lead the family therapist to some very innovative choices.

Table 1.3 | Early Models of Family Therapy

Therapy Model	Theory	Goals
Structural	Hierarchy Subsystems Proximity Boundaries Coalitions	Effective leadership of parents Balanced relationships
M.R.I.	Levels of communication Behavior as communication Solutions as problems	Successful solutions Disruption of vicious cycles
Strategic	Adaptation to life stages Symptoms as metaphors Small changes lead to greater changes	Effective leadership of parents Successful solutions
Intergenerational	Level of differentiation Past affecting the present Triangulation Relational ethics	Differentiation Detriangulation Resolving losses Restore trust and fairness
Experiential	Individuality Self-esteem Intimacy Self-awareness	Acceptance Creativity Interpersonal competence Family unity Healing
Behavioral	Antecedents of behavior Consequences of behavior Reinforcements Aversive stimuli	Pro-social behavior

Role	Assessment	Intervention
Director Stage manager Narrator	Quality of leadership Interactional sequences related to health and wellness Coalitions	Joining Enactments In-session interactions
Consultant	Behavioral descriptions Attempted solutions Description of the desired change	Out-of-session tasks Paradoxical interventions Reframing
Leader Director	Quality of leadership Interactional sequences related to problem-solving	Out-of-session tasks Direct and indirect directives
Coach Multidirected partiality	Genogram Family ledger (perceptions of trust and fairness) Triangles Emotional process	Addressing nodal events Tracing transitions over time Decreasing emotional reactivity Encouraging adult to adult relationships Crediting each member's contribution
Use of self Modeling Self-disclosure Directing flow of communication	Nurturing behavior Conflict Location of pain	Directives toward clear communication Empathic responses Nurturance Confrontation
Educator Coach	Behavioral descriptions History of the problem Functional analysis	Parent training Cost-benefit analysis Time-out Token systems Modeling

2 CHAPTER | Family Therapy Models in the Twenty-First Century

CHAPTER OUTLINE

Second-Generation Family Therapy: Postmodern Models

The Milan Team

Solution-Focused Family Therapy

Narrative Family Therapy

Third-Generation Family Therapy: Evidence-Based Models

Cognitive-Behavioral Family Therapy

Multisystemic Therapy

Multidimensional Family Therapy

Emotionally Focused Couples Therapy

Summary

CORE COMPETENCIES

3.1.1	Conceptual	Know which models, modalities, and/or techniques are most effective for presenting problems.
4.1.1	Conceptual	Comprehend a variety of individual and systemic therapeutic models and their applications, including evidence-based therapies and culturally sensitive approaches.
4.1.2	Conceptual	Recognize strengths, limitations, and contraindications of specific therapy models, including the risk of harm associated with models that incorporate assumptions of family dysfunction, pathogenesis, or cultural deficit.

The evolution of marriage and family therapy involved the addition of new dimensions to pioneering approaches, moving family therapy practice from more technical to more human terms. During the 1970s, the heavy influence of the M.R.I. led to continued critiques of mental health practices in general, and of those practices developing within the field. Under the broad umbrella of *constructivism*, family therapists began to question the limits of their early models and propose alternative views of the therapeutic process. Constructivists believe that a given situation can be interpreted in many different ways. For example, they argue that traditional approaches to family therapy represent many different ways of viewing the same case (as approached in Chapter 1).

The question of which view is most correct becomes irrelevant. Instead, constructivists ask which view is most helpful to the family. They also suggest that the family's view of the problem may be the most important to consider because it may be restraining the family from discovering more effective solutions. Constructivists emphasize Bateson's idea that, if brought forth, information that provides a contrast to the family's dominant mode of thinking is information that moves the family toward the change process. As Goolishian and Anderson (1992) point out, individuals are thought of as a "storehouse of maps and lenses" (p. 11). Constructivists try to capitalize on this human capacity for change by shifting a client's attention to alternative ways of thinking.

As its history reveals, the field of family therapy started with task-oriented strategy and evolved into the practice of reflection and questioning. This questioning led to dialogues, and established family therapists across the United States became more open to considering the importance of gender, race, and culture, that is, to new ways of viewing people and their problems. With increasing frequency, family therapists assumed that any problem could be seen through multiple lenses. Practitioners began to look not only at the possibility of alternative perspectives but also at the interactional process that leads to adopting new perspectives.

An extension of constructivism, *social construction theory* considers a person's view to be the product of conversations, dialogues, and interactions. The meaning a person assigns to a situation comes through social process, not an isolated internal process (Goolishian & Anderson, 1992). This view of the therapeutic process places more emphasis on developing collaborative dialogues with and among clients, rather than on searching for a given reality that is assumed to be flawed. Language, from this perspective, is highlighted as a critical element in therapy because the choice of words has influence over what attitudes are formed. Social constructionists often encourage the use of words based in human experience (e.g., stories and conversations) and in the language of the clients (e.g., metaphors from their relationships, work, and neighborhood) to downplay the influence of the therapist.

Some family therapists, such as Minuchin (a Russian-Jewish immigrant raised in Argentina), had always worked with disadvantaged families. However, many second-generation family therapists were from the middle class, so the voices of those marginalized within American culture (e.g., women and people of color) and those from outside this culture (Europe, South America, and Australia) were heard as different and innovative. Their influence made the study of family therapy more inclusive and personal. Tied to this developmental trend was a growing interest in how life transitions related to common presenting problems.

During the 1980s, constructivism (the view that there are many ways to look at a problem) and social construction theory (a theory of how multiple views develop) were gaining more attention in the field. These schools of thought are part of the *postmodern* era in the history of philosophy in the Western world. This era is known as one that challenges traditional thought and questions authority. This transition included changes in thinking about how the therapist should be a better listener and collaborator. In addition, pioneering concepts continued to be integrated, resulting in greater sensitivity to the resources of diverse people evolving in their relationships. Attention turned from an emphasis upon behavior change alone to the beliefs and values that influenced a family's interaction patterns. Present-day adaptations emphasize the client's personal wisdom and the egalitarian aspects of therapy (i.e., collaborative, narrative). In this book, these approaches are referred to as *second-generation* family therapy, and they are discussed in more detail later. They include work of the Milan team, solution-focused family therapy, and narrative family therapy. These approaches took some aspects of early models and added reflection, questioning, and more attention to meaning and story.

Finally, other developments in the field came from clinical research. A number of family therapists created outcome research to compare family treatment with other approaches, and to apply family therapy to a specific problem area such as adolescent conduct disorders, substance abuse, adult depression, domestic violence, and marital conflict (Sprenkle, 2002). The result has been very exciting. Analyses of the reports from this research show positive results and a clear advantage to using family approaches. Because of these research efforts, government agencies are paying more attention to the development of family interventions. I think this is a sign of growing maturity for our field. These integrative, research-based models are a bridge between past and future family therapy. They represent the cutting edge and demonstrate the utility of family therapy practice across many populations and settings. In this chapter, these integrative approaches are considered *third-generation:* cognitive-behavioral family therapy (CBFT), multisystemic therapy (MST), multidimensional family therapy (MDFT), and emotionally focused couples therapy (EFT).

SECOND-GENERATION FAMILY THERAPY: POSTMODERN MODELS

An important difference between first- and second-generation family therapy is the attention that each gives to theories about relationships. In first-generation models, theories and concepts about family process were an important perspective that led to therapeutic priorities. However, with the postmodern tendency to question authority, second-generation approaches avoided the idea of theory related to normal or healthy families. Such theories were thought to encourage negative labels. Therefore, their concepts are related to theories about the process of change and what will bring about the most positive and hopeful outcomes.

The Milan Team

In 1967, Mara Selvini Palazzoli organized the Milan Center for Family Studies, and was joined by Luigi Boscolo, Giuliana Prata, and Gianfranco Cecchin. This group developed a systemic approach for treating the families of anorectic, encopretic, and emotionally disturbed children that was informed by work at M.R.I. They combined the directives of strategic therapists, the theory of structural therapists, and Bateson's ideas on communication and knowledge systems. Their book *Paradox and Counterparadox* (Selvini Palazzoli, Boscolo, Cecchin, & Prata, 1978) provides a comprehensive description of their early therapy, which ushers in an emphasis on changing meaning and beliefs, not behaviors alone. Their work had a dramatic influence on the field.

In their early strategic work, the Milan team pursued research and practice in Haley's area of cross-generational coalitions. They developed the *invariant prescription,* which is a standard directive given to every family. (See Chapter 8 for more examples of directives.) The directive instructs parents to continue therapy secretly without their children knowing. Their early research suggested that when parents did this successfully, symptoms in the children remitted. However, if the secret was broken, symptoms would recur (Selvini Palazzoli, Cirillo, Selvini, & Sorrentino, 1989). Thus, they addressed a number of structural issues, but added to their approach careful questioning about beliefs and perceptions of each family member.

Through the systematic use of questions, they had a direct and indirect impact on family dynamics. Termed *circular questions,* these questions explored family interactions, the history of the problem, and emotional issues still influencing the family. "Circular" was used as a synonym for "systemic," assuming circular causality related to the problem. Circular questions start with present concerns, shift to an interest in the relevant past, and evolve toward future transitions. Today, many family therapists add these questions to their work.

The questions are of four types: problem definition, sequence of interaction, comparison/classification, and intervention. (See Table 2.1.) Their intent ranges from exploratory to provocative. When the intent is exploratory, the Milan team emphasizes the usefulness of questions that draw comparisons, whether between people, points in time, or definitions of the problem. This direction relates the problem to current interactions and significant events in the family history. When questions are provocative, therapists use them as an indirect intervention to make some implicit family dynamic explicit and verbalized.

Table 2.1 | Circular Questions

Present	Past	Future
	Problem Definition	
What is the problem in the family now?	Has it always been this way?	What will happen if things don't change?
What other concerns does the family have now?	When have things been different?	
	Why do you think things changed?	
	Sequences	
What happens when the problem starts?	Who first noticed the problem?	What would happen if (a family member) did ____ instead of _____?
Who does what?	What was happening in the family at that time?	
What happens next?		What would each person do?
Who else has a reaction to the problem?	How did you try to solve the problem?	
	Comparisons	
Who agrees and disagrees about the problem?	Who else was different back then?	If (the problem) improves, who will be the most/least relieved?
Who is in the most pain in the family?	Who was close to whom?	
Then who? (Rank order.)	Compared to (a family member), what do you remember back then?	How would each person adjust to the changes?
	Intervention	
From whom did your son learn to be so persistent and caring (positive connotation)?	When did you first think that your father needed your support in dealing with your mother?	How will your parents get along without you?
How would you like to teach your son about being independent?	What led you to conclude that he needed your help?	What would you need in order to adjust to the change of allowing your parents to settle their own disagreements?
What do you think your parents need to learn to improve their relationship?		

Once patterns, comparisons, and relevant history are identified, the therapists look for opportunities to provide a positive connotation for problematic behaviors. This is a positive explanation of why a family member's behavior might be useful for oneself or others in the family. Going beyond the strategic idea of positive labeling, these clinicians used *positive connotation* to elucidate how and why family members might be covertly cooperating with the problem (Boscolo, Cecchin, Hoffman, & Penn, 1987). For example, if a son seems to be taking the side of one parent over another, the therapists may describe the child as "sympathetic and soft-hearted; one who is very sensitive to the father's feelings." The therapists might suggest that the son wants his father to be happy and can't stand to see him uncomfortable (the solution becomes the problem). The father might be described as one who had taught his son about the virtue of loyalty, and the therapists would suggest that perhaps the son should continue standing up for the father, in case the father would see him as disloyal if he did not.

Once positive connotations are identified, they are used as a rationale for the paradoxical argument to go slowly for fear of the stress from too much change too quickly (i.e., "We don't want Father to feel abandoned by his son"). In addition to this in-session intervention targeting changes in thinking, the Milan team might also create a ritual for the family (see Chapter 8 for a description) or prescribe other interactions that might help the family reorganize its behavior with the goal of accommodating developmental transitions. For example, in the same case of the father and son, a ritual might be developed to help the son to express his loyalty in other ways. The father and son might decide upon some activity that would become a substitute for the previous pattern.

The Milan team remained open to multiple interpretations of any problem. As the team members analyzed and changed their work, they decided to "approach the family in a far less arrogant, far more collaborative spirit" (Selvini Palazzoli et al., 1989, p. 250). Confrontation gave way to normalization, in which the team would empathize with family dilemmas and suggest that "it could have happened to anyone in the same circumstances, including me" (Selvini Palazzoli et al., 1989, p. 250). They considered indirect interventions to be the most appropriate for difficult cases, because they are more respectful of the client's reality and minimize resistance to change. Paradoxes indirectly legitimize client ambivalence toward change and provide an atmosphere that is accepting and respectful of these client dilemmas. As a result of their influence, family therapists developed an increasing emphasis on the use of questions as a way to be "curious, yet hopeful" (Fleuridas, Nelson, & Rosenthal, 1986; Penn, 1982; Tomm, 1984).

Solution-Focused Family Therapy

Solution-focused therapy is often practiced in individual psychotherapy. However, many family therapists integrate solution-focused strategies into their relational work. This branch of Milton Erickson's work describes therapy as changing "the viewing" or "the doing" related to a problem (O'Hanlon &

Weiner-Davis, 1989). Following Erickson's early ideas that people learn limitations that can be bypassed, these models recognize the therapist's role in
assisting a family to identify its resources, to build on what is working, and to
manage its problems. The therapist accomplishes this through the liberal
use of questions as interventions. This is representative of a trend toward
competency-based treatment, in which strengths and successes are systematically investigated and highlighted as a central element in the treatment
process. Similar to structural family therapy and the Milan team, these inves-
tigations often take the form of tracking interactions between family members
or significant others (Lankton, 1988; O'Hanlon, 1982).

In this model, therapists do not see problems as signs of failure, but rather as
an inevitable part of family development. The relationship between the therapist
and the family becomes less hierarchical and moves closer to a collaborative
problem-solving consultation. In this model, a collaborative stance is thought to
help clients adopt a more hopeful attitude about solving their problems. In fact,
when a solution-focused therapist assesses clients' motivation, the clients are
considered either "visitors or customers" (Berg & Gallagher, 1991). A visitor is
often someone who does not see the presenting problem as a problem or who has
become defensive when discussing the problem, particularly when a previous
history with public agencies exists from which he or she has felt criticism. A customer is a person who wants some change to occur and believes therapy could
be a means to that end. However, this model also assumes that client motivation
can be mobilized through client-therapist interaction and that visitors can become customers through careful interviewing (Lipchik, 1987).

Consider the sequence and its analysis in Table 2.2. Because solution-focused
therapists do not adopt a position of pathology, client perceptions about helping
professionals often begin to change in solution-focused interactions. This does
not mean that therapists normalize violent or abusive behavior. Rather, the practitioner acknowledges the family's point of view and addresses problem behavior
within the context of the family's perceptions. The therapist wants to know what
a child does when a parent behaves in a certain way and what happens to the
child's behavior when the parent behaves in an unexpected way. Problem-free interaction sequences are elicited, and these exceptions become the basis for future
solutions. Thereafter, assignments, tasks, or questions are designed to maintain
and highlight positive changes that are already occurring.

I think the popularity of solution-focused approaches has come from at
least three directions. First, therapists recognize the benefits of a positive approach that breaks from the pathologizing traditions of mainstream mental
health practice. Second, managed care companies find the notion attractive
that common problems can be resolved in only a few sessions. Third, students
have found the step-by-step instructions of solution-focused workshops easy to
learn. However, as solution-focused work has become popular, there has been
a trend toward expanding solution-focused practice to include attention to
emotion (Kiser, Piercy, & Lipchik, 1993), not just behavior alone. In addition,
beginning practitioners are cautioned to consider the client's worldview—not
just about the problem, but also about therapy. For example, when working

Table 2.2 | Sample Solution-Focused Sequence

Therapist Questions	Explanation
So, you'd like to get your probation officer off your back. Should I list that as one of your goals?	This type of interviewing includes accepting (not necessarily agreeing with) the clients' view of the problem and using their language.
What will convince your probation officer that you're really a changed person? What will you have to do to make that happen? What exactly will you have to do or say?	Once the family's goals are accepted and listed, each goal is recast in specific behavioral descriptions of what will be different. Clients begin to think in action-oriented terms. Thus, goals become action-oriented.
What is life like for you when the probation officer isn't on your back? What are you doing when that happens? How do you get that to happen?	As this hopeful and collaborative pattern continues, behavior change occurs from a discussion of behaviors related to exceptions, or times when the problem is not occurring. This highlights client strengths and downplays the authority of the therapist.
On a scale from 1 to 10, with 10 being the best, where would you say you are with respect to getting your probation officer off your back?	Scaling questions help the client focus on a situation as part of a continuum.
What do you have to do to move from a 3 to a 4?	Exploring the problem in terms of small steps of progress makes goals reachable.

with victims of trauma, a traditional solution-focused approach may be premature if individuals need an opportunity to review and retell their story of trauma as part of the healing process. Rickert (2006) suggests matching the client approach to the therapeutic approach. If clients are problem-oriented, the therapist should be problem-oriented. If clients seem to be searching for answers rather than understanding or empathy, the therapist can be more solution-oriented. Exploring directly with the client to determine the best pace and timing for the client's situation is most desirable. Is she ready to move from the time of trauma to a time of healing? Does he need more time in one stage than another? A helpful suggestion comes from Berg and Gallagher (1991): "Discover what matters to the client the most" (p. 97).

Narrative Family Therapy

As one who has continued the constructivist tradition in family therapy, Michael White has also integrated processes that illustrate social constructionist thinking.

He evolved from structural-strategic approaches to a Batesonian emphasis on the beliefs that could limit families from pursuing new solutions to their problems. He has been successful in integrating the search for competencies with an analysis of interactional cycles and assignments that instill hope in his clients. Although his therapeutic process is quite different from that of the Milan team, he is also successful at helping families find a face-saving way out of their present difficulties. In an early article (White, 1983), he indicates how important it is to minimize those interactions in which family members might become defensive. Thus, he accepts multiple views of the problem (constructivist) and sees his role as one who is responsible for leading the family into hopeful and life-changing conversations about their lives (social constructionist).

In describing their work, Epston and White (1992) emphasize that they do not want to name their work or have it thought of as a school of family therapy. Instead, they expect to explore and change their work on a regular basis—hence, what they might write one year could drastically change the next. This is in keeping with the value they place on a "spirit of adventure" (p. 89) and how that spirit keeps their work vibrant and rewarding. However, White was the first to introduce narrative ideas to the field of family therapy and has continued as a leader in the narrative trend in family therapy. Experienced family therapists applaud his spirit of adventure and believe that this spirit keeps the profession of marriage and family therapy stimulating and creative. Beginning practitioners should strive to adopt this same spirit to keep their work inspiring and successful.

White most commonly addresses themes of oppression and liberation. This distinguishes his approach from other models covered in this chapter. In working with families, he assumes that the dominant view held by much of the mental health system has led to the *depersonalization* of his clients. He also assumes that the family is feeling oppressed by the influence of their problems. By using social justice theory regarding oppression and liberation, White helps families to notice their own expert knowledge, that is, to notice those times when the problem did not interfere with their lives. He uses a process described by Bateson (1972) that looks for small exceptions to their negative experiences. This increased awareness of successes is thought to help the family develop a new life story of victory, competence, and leadership.

Although his focus on exceptions sounds similar to solution-focused therapy, White emphasizes the importance of oppression and characterizes the problem as some influence outside the family. A cycle or pattern is often labeled as the culprit. This might be "a truant lifestyle" or "a tradition of bickering," or it might be a make-believe character that children can understand, such as a monster or a tiger. This process, called *externalization,* is one of White's distinctive contributions to family therapy.

A session with Michael White consists of a progression through various sets of questions (see Table 2.3). White adapts easily to the family's subculture. He carefully notes in writing their words and their language, incorporating these into his analysis and into the family's story of liberation. As therapy proceeds, the family is invited to think about their lives and problems as an old

Table 2.3 | Sample Narrative Sequence

Therapist Questions	Explanation
How does the problem influence or defeat the family?	Using a similar approach as that of structural, strategic, and the Milan team, White carefully tracks interactional sequences and learns how each person reacts and behaves related to the problem. Attention is on specific behaviors. What do the family members do? The family therapist must be able to visualize how people act and what people say when they are overcome by the problem and when they are overcoming the problem.
What are the times when things go well—when you are challenging the problem? Is it possible that coming here today is a challenge to the problem?	White would spend much time elaborating upon these few experiences as examples of the family's expert knowledge of how they have influenced and controlled the problem. If someone fails to recognize exceptions, White would use his own observations to begin creating a picture of competence and cooperation.
Would you prefer to be someone who is being held hostage by a truant lifestyle or someone who has battled the influences of a truant lifestyle and won?	White provides a benevolent confrontation with present destructive cycles while pointing toward a hopeful future.

story that they are rewriting together. He is the audience, director, and editor of the emerging work of art. Family members are the authors and principal characters in the production. His use of literary metaphors (i.e., a good story has a plot, characters, drama, intrigue, and so on) reframes family problems by placing the problem in an alternative knowledge base (Epston & White, 1992). His use of rituals, games, and assignments has led to such creative therapeutic goals as "monster taming" (childhood fears), "beating sneaky poo" (encopresis), and "going from vicious to virtuous cycles" (marital conflict). He prefers thinking of solutions in these terms rather than adopting the dominant language of traditional mental health practice. The goal is to liberate the family from the oppression of the problem and the oppression of larger systems that stereotype and label them.

White uses sessions as a time for the family to report on their successes, similar to session use in solution-focused models. When difficulties occur, these sessions are compared to situations that are even worse to help the family members maintain their sense of momentum. For example, if family members

Table 2.4 | Narrative Focus Upon Strengths

Therapist Questions	Explanation
How did you manage to lecture him for only 10 minutes instead of the usual 45 minutes, like in the old days?	Questions focus on how they were able to stop the old pattern so quickly and what they thought made the difference.
Even though you're feeling discouraged, I'm curious about how you were able to develop such insight about the old patterns.	Noticing that "the glass is half full" punctuates even the smallest bit of progress.
How did you decide to face this situation so directly?	Exploring and extending the progress.
What difference do you think it will make in your future if you are able to continue this type of awareness?	Highlighting the influence that small steps can have over time by exploring clients' beliefs about their own progress.
What would it say about you as parents if you are able to continue exercising this type of awareness?	Anchoring the new story in the future and in a person's own thoughts and language about self and others.
Who would most appreciate this story of progress and liberation?	After the family feels a sense of progress, a celebration, ritual, or meeting is planned to anchor the new story within the social network of the family by inviting others to witness and become part of the new story.

remain persistently discouraged about their lack of progress, a sequence might be similar to that in Table 2.4.

White's approach is known for the way it addresses societal oppression, empowers discouraged families, and diminishes family isolation by using their language, values, experience, and natural support system. He provides a counterpoint to existing cultural practices that label and categorize those who need help. He is very active in sessions and leads through his suggestive and interventive questions. His artistry lies in his balance between leading and following what a family brings to the experience.

These approaches emphasize a more indirect approach through using a series of questions. In addition, they seek to know about the past in a focused and productive way. For solution-focused and narrative family therapists, asking about past exceptions to the problem is important; resources emerge from asking about past successes in coping, relating, or functioning. For Milan-style therapists, past transitions and beliefs related to the development of the problem guide the clinician toward an assessment of problem severity and family process. To enhance understanding, consider a case from these three perspectives.

Case 2	Jerry

Jerry, a 19-year-old Caucasian man, enters a community agency with symptoms of severe depression. He was referred by his doctor because of his level of depression and his report of his recent rejection by family when he disclosed that he was gay. He was very close to his parents until this disclosure and has now been cut off from any meaningful contact. His father does not want to see him at all. The client reports difficulty sleeping, changes in appetite, and poor concentration. Though denying active suicidal ideation, he states several times that he wishes he could just go to sleep and never wake up. This client cries throughout the intake and reports a previous episode of depression two years ago. He fears that his plan to attend college in the fall is threatened, because his parents were going to pay tuition out of their savings.

During intake, the therapist determines that Jerry wishes to die but has no thoughts of killing himself, nor does he have a plan for such action. He also has no thoughts of harming family or others. He is the youngest of three children and has been living at home until a month ago when he disclosed his homosexuality to his parents. Now, he migrates from place to place, staying with friends. To his knowledge, none of his siblings know about the disclosure. There is a wide gap (five years) between him and his next sister. He says his siblings are "into their own lives." When his doctor suggested this referral, Jerry was afraid the doctor thought he was "crazy." The referral was explained as "maybe it would be good to talk to someone." The doctor wanted an assessment before prescribing medication for his depression. Jerry isn't sure "what good talking will do." He is unsure whether medication is necessary. However, he came for the first session to see what it was like, because he had never been to "a shrink" before.

The Milan Team

These were the first family therapists to write extensively about the referral process (see Chapter 5). Hence, questions from their tradition gather the above information and determine that Jerry's level of motivation to engage in therapy is a "wait and see" attitude. This is the contemplation stage maybe . . .). Because the doctor was concerned about Jerry's level of depression, exploring what Jerry considers to be the most pressing issue is important. Circular questions about the definition of the problem help the therapist learn that Jerry is most concerned about his parents' reactions and his future college plans. Because he doesn't mention his sexual orientation as a problem, the clinician explores his past close relationship with his parents and defines the problem as conflict resulting from disclosure to parents about his sexual orientation.

From a crisis perspective, a beginning goal can be to stabilize Jerry's mood and explore a plan to address parental rejection. He meets criteria for major depressive episode. This is discussed as a *result* of the presenting problem. Circular questions about sequences of interaction helped the therapist learn that Jerry had planned to tell his parents for some years. Compared to his siblings, he was considered the "model child" and felt pressure to live up to his father's ideals. A recurring subject of conversation had been about Jerry joining his father in his advertising business after college. He wanted to do this, but also wanted to be honest with his family about who he really is. His mother considered him to be a leader in their church. He decided to tell them when they kept encouraging his interest in certain female friends. His father was angry and stern. His mother was quiet and sad. He keeps in touch with his mother, but his father will not allow him to come home: "Maybe that will knock some sense into him!" This information addresses culture and beliefs.

Based on Jerry's level of motivation, the therapist educates Jerry as to what family therapy can do. She gives examples she knows of the ways in which other people in his situation have successfully overcome their challenges. Before making a recommendation about medication, she gathers more information about his previous episode of depression and finds it was related to rejection by another gay teen to whom Jerry was attracted. Because both episodes are tied to specific events with adequate functioning in between, she discusses the pros and cons of medication with Jerry and asks for his opinion. He doesn't see the need and the therapist is able to support his decision. However, his father's rejection is more dramatic and severe than he had anticipated, so the therapist suggests that they spend one additional session developing a plan for how Jerry can "get through to" his parents. The conservative recommendation from the therapist reassures Jerry that he isn't "crazy," and Jerry can see that the therapist is like a coach and a support to help him chart a course for coping with his challenges. He agrees to return.

In the second session, circular questions about comparisons uncovered information about how his parents and siblings felt about sexual orientation, gay life in general, and so on (i.e., Who might be most/least accepting?). The therapist learned that his oldest sister has a childhood friend who is lesbian. His older brother has made demeaning comments about a gay person. In addition, his extended family had beliefs that ranged from criticism to acceptance. This information is about structure and coalitions (i.e., Who might be on his side?).

Finally, circular questions about intervention asked Jerry to think about how his disclosure fit into his family's development and what the advantages might be to having told them now, rather than five years ago or five years later. Jerry had to pause and reflect. First, he was at a loss for words. Then, he began to think about how he disliked the pressure of living with family under false assumptions. He also thought his father depended on him for friendship and they often went to sports and car activities together, excluding his mother. Jerry thought his father and mother should spend more time together. Neither of them had many friends. (This addresses strategic hypotheses about the meaning of the problem in the family.)

At this point, the therapist explores family members and friends who Jerry has named as the most likely to be accepting (his mother, sister, and two friends). She learns that his father listens to his sister. Can Jerry consider inviting them to become part of his support network? Would he like to explore these possibilities in additional sessions? The therapist maintained a focus on what Jerry considered his most pressing problem. Jerry finds her style empathic and pragmatic. She doesn't treat him like he's crazy. He doesn't feel stigmatized. If she can be a help to him with his family concerns, the process will help his depression and lead him to trust her with additional issues that may be affecting his mental health. Eventually, other family members may attend; they may even invite Dad to attend and the therapist can work with his parents through the intense grief they suffer in the wake of Jerry's disclosure. With Jerry prepared for this direction, the therapist can become a consultant to his entire family as they negotiate this major transition.

Solution-Focused Family Therapy

Solution-focused therapists might define the problem in a similar way because customership is about treatment motivation. In addition, similar precautions about lethality and crisis would indicate Jerry's overall health and stability. Then, during a consultation, the process pursues descriptions of how each person acts when things are going poorly, steps that have been taken to improve things, and the predictable and unpredictable ways in which people might respond to each other. Since Jerry was surprised by his father's response, both parties are now responding in unpredictable ways during this time of crisis. The therapist might help Jerry think through hypothetical situations in which he can envision how he would be acting if things were resolved between them.

One technique for exploring hypothetical possibilities is the *miracle question*. The therapist asks, "Suppose you woke up tomorrow and things were back to normal with your parents. What would you be doing now? What would your behavior be from day to day?" The therapist can help Jerry choose what behaviors are still possible (i.e., "I'd still be calling Dad at work to tell him about the Dodgers' game. I'd still be telling Mom about my plans for vacation"). What support would he need from others to follow through with his plan? What can he do to cope if there is a backlash? (Developmentally, some options may be more realistic than others, because Jerry and his parents were close before his disclosure. If the relationships had been chronically critical or distant, the therapist might look to relationships in the family that are positive for Jerry, or to those who have a positive influence on his parents.) The tone of the sessions would be that of hopeful experimentation with support from the therapist and others.

Narrative Family Therapy

Similar to the two approaches just described, a narrative family therapist screens for lethality and crisis, but avoids labels or stereotypes in referring to Jerry's situation. The narrative family therapist makes an effort to adopt Jerry's language and the words he uses to describe himself and others. This approach might consider the problem to be the *effects* of "coming out" to his parents (externalization). Then, Jerry is invited to fight and challenge these effects so that he doesn't become oppressed or controlled by them. A specific line of questioning traces interactions during the rough times and the impact of those interactions. These are the *effects*. The therapist is careful to explore ways in which the client feels oppressed. There is empathy and validation for the ordeal

Jerry has experienced. Then, more questions search for ways Jerry has stood up to the effects (i.e., calling his mother, visiting with friends who can encourage him, etc.). He is cast in the role of hero in his own life drama. A significant emphasis in narrative family therapy is on the empowering behaviors and events that demonstrate how the client is already overcoming the problem. This happens in the form of questions that call attention to Jerry's positive virtues, such as his courage, strength, and persistence.

A narrative family therapist looks for additional people who can serve as an audience to witness and document Jerry's accomplishments, thus helping Jerry to feel the power of a collective in support of him. These people might be family, friends, or others whom Jerry says see him the way he wants to be seen. They are invited in to encourage and support him, largely through answering the therapist's questions about how they see Jerry's strengths and what they view as hopeful possibilities for his future as he works to overcome the effects of coming out. These signs of success and support are viewed as the new story, intended to replace the old *problem-saturated story* of depression and rejection.

The Milan team, solution-focused approaches, and narrative family therapy are some examples of how postmodern thinking influenced the philosophy and practice of family therapy. These innovative approaches to the process of change are popular trends that influence many family therapists today. They have been adopted by many currently working in the field but not to the exclusion of first-generation models. In fact, as postmodern approaches rose in popularity, other family therapists were also asking similar questions (What do we know? How do we know what we think we know?). However, their answers came from explorations in clinical research rather than from explorations in philosophy. This development, known as *evidence-based practice*, has influenced a number of integrative models that use foundational family therapy practices with postmodern enhancements. These integrative models have led to successes outside of the mental health field in areas such as juvenile justice, social service, and substance abuse. The discussion now moves from the 1950s to the years past 2000, and I consider these integrative models to be third-generation approaches to family therapy.

THIRD-GENERATION FAMILY THERAPY: EVIDENCE-BASED MODELS

Evidence-based practice is a trend that began with evidence-based medicine (EBM) during the 1990s and influenced many health and mental health professions. It developed from studying the practice patterns of physicians and how they made their decisions in patient care. Studies showed that many difficult decisions were made based on the advice of colleagues or from outdated textbooks because the information explosion during the twentieth century made research reports in scientific journals difficult to organize. The aim of EBM is to help doctors access research reports electronically so that they can integrate clinical judgment, patient values, and research evidence into sound decision making. For example, if Mrs. Adams has asthma and has side effects from one medication, the clinician may turn to EBM databases to review various medications and their utility, given that she is elderly. Then, in consultation with the patient about her personal priorities (i.e., a choice between experiencing one side effect vs. another), a decision is made. Since then, other professions have adopted an interest in the principles of EBM and how they might improve decision making.

In marriage and family therapy, the interest in EBM has grown out of an increasing interest in medical family therapy (see Chapter 9). As more family therapists work with and for physicians in health care settings, the need to speak "many languages" becomes evident. It might seem ironic, but it is also predictable that family therapy began as a revolution against the medical establishment and came full circle with an interest in the latest medical innovations. The therapists' knowledge of systems suggests that healthy adaptations often begin as polarities (e.g., adolescent rebellion) and evolve into a respect for difference that accepts what each person has to offer the other (differentiation). In this circle is the history of interactional paradigms and pragmatic successes; medicine brings to it a history of rigorous research and technological advances.

In 1995, the *Journal of Marital and Family Therapy* published a special issue as a monograph, "The Effectiveness of Marital and Family Therapy." This was a comprehensive review of outcome research in the field. It reviewed decades of family therapy research for a variety of therapeutic problems, highlighting the most favorable results and calling for continued research to develop the knowledge base in our field. In 2002, a sequel was published that provides a progress report on successfully researched models of practice. Four models from that report are outlined in this chapter.

Evidence-based practice in family therapy most often comes from specific approaches that are developed for a given research project. Sometimes the approach is easy for mainstream practitioners to implement, and sometimes it remains a successful report with scientific merit but without a following to implement it in real-world settings. Still at other times, separate elements from a given approach are taken and applied to improve clinical outcomes. For example, the successful work of Anderson, Reiss, and Hogarty (1986) with schizophrenia predated the labeling of social construction approaches as such. However, their model adopted a collaborative, nonblaming, sympathetic approach with family members that helped the family develop successful patterns of coping. As one of the many family psychoeducational approaches to the management of schizophrenia, this model, though rarely practiced in its entirety, influenced a host of family therapists to take a collaborative, sympathetic stance with those affected by mental illness. In addition, a very successful multifamily group approach to schizophrenia is based upon Anderson's single-family program (McFarlane, 2002).

Research in family therapy has produced entire models of therapy in which detailed instructions are given for replication, and individual components of models can be integrated informally into one's own work. The models highlighted here are cognitive-behavioral family therapy, multisystemic therapy, multidimensional family therapy, emotionally focused couples therapy, and multifamily psychoeducation. The following summaries provide a picture of how these approaches proceed in a given research project. However, in Chapters 6, 7, and 8, I will highlight aspects of each that the beginning practitioner can adopt as a first step toward using these advanced models.

Cognitive-Behavioral Family Therapy

In the second generation of practice, family therapists built upon Gerald Patterson's (1971) early work and applied behavioral principles to couples therapy, delinquency, schizophrenia, and bipolar disorder (Barton & Alexander, 1981; Falloon, 1991; Jacobson, 1991; Miklowitz & Goldstein, 1997). This section focuses primarily on the evolutionary trends within these approaches that expanded traditional behavioral family therapy into cognitive-behavioral family therapy, or CBFT (Weiss, 1984). This integration exemplifies a number of approaches to family therapy during the 1990s that are research-based and problem-focused, and that address multiple levels of the change process.

To cognitive-behavioral therapists, a person's internal process affects behavior (e.g., unspoken *self-talk* influences what one does). Unrealistic expectations of another (spouse, child) often produces undesirable behavior (e.g., anger, criticism). These behaviors may be viewed as a response to the expectations and not necessarily to the behavior of others. In such cases, the spouse or parent may need to develop more realistic expectations to adjust to the situation. Cognitive-behavioral therapists often use self-report inventories to assess the effects of these cognitions on a couple's relationship. For example, one spouse may think the other is trying to control him or her, and this may lead to arguments over who controls the finances or who should clean the house. Thus, the area of disagreement (finances, cleaning the house) might not be the problem. Rather, the underlying thought (the intent to control) might be the major issue. CBFT has demonstrated its effectiveness in improving couple relationships. Baucom, Sayers, and Sher (1990) found that cognitive restructuring produces meaningful changes in the way that a couple views their relationship and improves marital adjustment. It appears that when spouses alter their cognitions as well as their behavior, positive change in the relationship is more likely.

In 1996, behavioral family therapists Neil Jacobson and Andrew Christensen published their book, *Integrative Couple Therapy*, in which they integrate cognitive dimensions (e.g., thoughts, expectation, and images) that influence behavior. They expanded their model after examining their research and finding that only 50 percent of couples were improving from traditional behavioral couples therapy. Of particular interest was how thoughts and attitudes serve to both trigger and maintain behavior. As a model for close relationships (e.g., heterosexual, gay and lesbian, married, or common law), it addresses the issue of *acceptance* in working with couples. This model of family therapy attempts to balance traditional behavioral methods for change with an equivalent emphasis on the acceptance of elements that cannot be changed (e.g., developmental histories, traditions, and values). A sequence using this model might follow these steps:

1. **Define the primary conflict.** Look for themes such as closeness/distance, responsibility, and so on.
2. **Describe the negative interaction pattern.** Obtain a clear picture of behavioral sequences.
3. **Decrease blaming and increase vulnerability.** Teach communication of fears, inadequacies, uncertainties (i.e., "I'm afraid she'll leave me").
4. **Address other beliefs about significant others.** Explore beliefs about why certain situations occur in the family, how family life should be, and what is needed to improve relationships.
5. **Teach support and empathy for each partner.** Assign reading and provide practice time in sessions.
6. **Use behavioral contracting.** Ask each partner to make a list of what the other can do to please them. Ask each partner to choose items from the list to begin positive cycles. Assess the couple's ability to solve problems and spend time in pleasurable activities.

CBFT shares commonalities with the Milan, structural, and strategic approaches. First, these approaches share a functional view of problem behaviors and interactional sequences. This means problems are seen as serving some function within the family and as being maintained by family members' behavior. Next, CBFT focuses on the present interaction of family members rather than on past history. It also employs cognitive restructuring (reframing) and assigns tasks to facilitate behavior change at home. Finally, in increasing vulnerability, Jacobson and Christensen's model includes elements similar to Susan Johnson's emotionally focused couples therapy and Virginia Satir's approach to intimacy, self-acceptance, and communication.

Multisystemic Therapy

During the 1980s, various approaches emerged that deliberately included therapist interventions aimed at family-school, family-church, family-peer group, and family-agency relationships. Boyd-Franklin (1989) found that successful therapy for an African American family often involved a "multisystem" approach. Her approach expanded to address the role of the family therapist in nontraditional therapeutic settings such as schools, medical facilities, and churches (Boyd-Franklin & Bry, 2000). As part of this trend, Henggeler, Schoenwald, Borduin, Rowland & Cunningham (1998), through extensive research projects with juvenile crime and substance abuse, developed a multisystemic (MST) approach to child and adolescent problems. The model was derived from social-ecological, structural, strategic, and cognitive-behavioral theories (Bronfenbrenner, 1979; Haley, 1976; Kendall & Braswell, 1993, Minuchin, 1974). This home-based approach positions the therapist to significantly reduce crime and substance abuse.

The outcome results of MST have been impressive. In a review of multiple studies, it was found that 70–98 percent of inner-city families were successfully

engaged and completed the desired 4-month treatment protocol (Cunningham &
Henggeler, 1999). Success was the same for Caucasian families and families of
color. The authors suggest that their success comes from paying specific attention
to the barriers of engagement and to implementing the nine principles of MST.
When certain treatment principles are learned, therapists can be systematic and
consistent while still tailoring treatment to the family's culture. Emerging from
multiple projects with children and adolescents, the nine treatment principles of
MST are shown in Table 2.5.

The therapeutic process begins by linking the goals of the larger system
with the individualized goals of the family or guardian system that is caring for
the adolescent. For example, the court system has its goals (e.g., prevent reoc-
currence of crime and increase school attendance), and the family generally has
other goals (i.e., "get the system out of our life," "make him mind," "get money
to turn on the phone," etc.). These divergent goals are brought under a general
umbrella (e.g., help Jake succeed) that will enable each stakeholder to be part of
the same plan. Then, intensive time is spent building trust and credibility with
the family (Cunningham & Henggeler, 1999).

Next, goals of the family are broken down into behavioral goals related to
strengths of the family. Therapists are trained to be goal- and action-oriented.
In addition, weekly supervision by the therapist is aimed at individualizing the
process for each family using the concept of "fit" (Schoenwald, Henggeler,
Brondino, & Rowland, 2000).

MST is an excellent example of integration because it uses structural-
strategic family therapy, ecological case management, culturally sensitive practice, and systematic data gathering for practice improvement. It also has commonalities with the other models presented in this chapter, such as a focus on
behavioral sequences, concrete tasks, and respect for the uniqueness of each
family. The emphasis on strengths and the engagement process is compatible
with Michael White's approach and with solution-focused notions of inviting
the client to move from visitor to customer through careful interactions that
respect the client's worldview. Although the model does not cite social construction theory as one of its influences, the nine principles of MST are excellent examples of this trend in family therapy.

Multidimensional Family Therapy

This groundbreaking model has been developed and tested on adolescent
substance abusers (Liddle, 1995; 1999; 2002). Like MST, the population for
MDFT has been high-risk, low-income families who have a youth who is the
identified patient. In these studies, adolescents present a range of high risk substance behavior. Often, their parents have substance or mental health problems.
Studies have compared MDFT with adolescent groups, cognitive-behavioral
therapy, and multifamily education. Results show that adolescents improve in
all treatments, however, MDFT participants maintained better school performance and family functioning at one-year follow-ups (Liddle, Dakof, Parker,
Diamond, Barrett & Tejeda, 2001). These advantages have earned MDFT a

Table 2.5 | Treatment Principles of Multisystemic Therapy (MST)

MST Principles	Elaboration
1. The primary purpose of assessment is to understand the fit between the identified problems and their broader systemic context.	How does the problem make sense? What interactions between the child, family, peers, school, and neighborhood will explain the problem in a nonblaming way?
2. Therapeutic contacts emphasize the positive and use systemic strengths as levers for change.	Home-based contacts build trust, credibility, and a positive relationship upon which to develop goals and assignments.
3. Interventions are designed to promote responsible behavior and decrease irresponsible behavior among family members.	Therapists work positively and strategically to help parents increase or change parental supervision and to develop consequences for positive and negative behaviors of the youth.
4. Interventions are present-focused and action-oriented, targeting specific and well-defined problems.	Overarching goals are the family's long-term hopes for the child. Intermediate goals are day-to-day progress described in behavioral terms.
5. Interventions target sequences of behavior within and between multiple systems that maintain identified problems.	Interactional sequences within and between multiple systems are addressed hands-on way through the therapist's intensive involvement.
6. Interventions are developmentally appropriate and fit the developmental needs of the youth.	The needs of parents and children alike are considerations for tailoring tasks and goals that are realistic for each family's situation.
7. Interventions are designed to require daily or weekly effort by family members.	Intermediate goals are broken down into small, immediate tasks such as assigning chores, giving rewards, or having a meeting about consequences for incomplete chores.
8. Intervention effectiveness is evaluated continuously from multiple perspectives, with providers assuming accountability for overcoming barriers to successful outcomes.	Given the focus of interventions, their effectiveness can be assessed in a few weeks. The therapist monitors this standard and uses immediate feedback to make midcourse corrections.
9. Interventions are designed to promote treatment generalization and long-term maintenance of therapeutic change by empowering caregivers to address family members' needs across multiple systemic contexts.	MST emphasizes the skill development needed for success in the family's social ecology. Skills include assessing future challenges and adapting to forthcoming developmental changes as youth and parents mature.

reputation as an efficient, effective treatment for very troubled teens and their families. The four premises of MDFT are:

1. Problems are multidimensional.
2. Multidimensional problems require multidimensional conceptualizations.
3. Multidimensional conceptualizations yield multisystems interventions.
4. MDFT assesses and intervenes into multiple systems of development and influence.

The four dimensions of MDFT with their specific topics are:

1. Adolescent (self, family, peers)
2. Parents (overall functioning, stress and burden, individual humanity, parental love, guidance, and stance against drugs and delinquency)
3. Family (healthy functioning, new and positive communication, understanding their youth)
4. Extrafamilial (school, neighborhood, legal, social, medical, other important influences on youth or parent)

Two unique elements set MDFT apart from MST and other evidence-based models for adolescents. First, therapists are trained to hold initial joining sessions separately with teens and their parents. Once these sessions have cemented the therapist's bond with each part of the relationship, family meetings provide an opportunity for relational interventions to unfold. Second, family sessions are balanced between attention to the pragmatics of behavior management (structural-strategic) and that of the emotional bond between parent and adolescent (intergenerational attachment). In these sessions, *enactments* are implemented by the therapist. These are interventions that actually help family members walk through new and positive communication, step by step (Diamond & Liddle, 1996; 1999). Table 2.6 outlines how each of the four dimensions might be addressed in a case.

These two models of family therapy for adolescent problems are representative of a larger group of evidence-based treatment approaches that combine first-generation theory about relational functioning with second-generation sensitivities about diverse world views and motivation for treatment (Snyder & Ooms, 1992). They inspired this book's emphasis on developmentally appropriate practice. In Chapters 4 and 8, you will learn more details about the interventions from these models and how they have been refined for client engagement, rapport-building, cultural sensitivity, and conducting family sessions.

Emotionally Focused Couples Therapy

Although John Bowlby's work on attachment influenced a number of British and American family therapists, his work was not widely embraced during the early years of family therapy practice (Bowlby, 1969; Ainsworth & Bowlby, 1991). Perhaps because American society was caught up in social changes dominated by life-saving medical practices and time-saving technology, early family therapists were fascinated by problem development rather than human

Table 2.6 | Basic Tasks in MDFT

Adolescents	Help them talk about past hurts, disappointments, etc., with family.
	Help them talk about hopes and desired changes in their lives.
	Get the message across: "There's something in this for you."
Parents	Listen to their stresses and burden.
	Get the message across: "You're the medicine."
	Focus on self-care. What can they do to get support and improve their functioning?
Family	Help adolescents express their hurts, etc.
	Help parents listen and apologize.
	Help parents discuss what they can do to improve things.
	Negotiate and support house rules.
Extrafamilial	Guide parents to be more involved in school issues.
	Help parents access services to support youth's abstinence.

Adapted from http://www.miami.edu/ctrada/SASATE/Elda/SASATE_Elda_2005.ppt

development. However, as divorce, trauma, and violence rates persist, an awareness of the complexity of human development has also steadily increased in the field. Thus, family therapists are revisiting early interpersonal theories of development and finding important keys to therapeutic turning points.

Emotionally focused couples therapy (EFT) developed when Dr. Leslie Greenberg, professor of psychology at York University in Canada, began his training in client-centered therapy and witnessed the value of expressing respect, empathy, and genuineness for his clients. Utilizing this orientation as a foundation, he learned to practice authentically listening to and checking his understanding with his clients. He then ventured into several years of Gestalt training and learned more about awareness and the experiential method. Dr. Greenberg had a desire to create a system for mapping out the process-experiential approach to change. His goal was to integrate Gestalt active methods and client-centered relational conditions. He fostered this process during a seven-year period of couples and family therapy and then pursued writing a treatment manual for emotionally focused couples therapy with his former student Dr. Susan Johnson (Greenberg, 2005).

During this collaboration, they began watching videotapes of their work, analyzing the therapeutic process during times when clients seemed to have insights or breakthroughs that led to significant changes in their relationships. Their analysis led to research projects in which their techniques were compared with other models of couple therapy. These results led to the formal development of emotionally focused couples therapy, a treatment program that follows a manual that applies Bowlby's (1969) theory of *attachment, separation, and loss* (Greenberg & Johnson, 1988). In this model, secure interpersonal attachments are considered a primary human motivation. These are addressed in EFT. The main tasks in EFT are *accessing emotional experience* and *changing interpersonal patterns.*

Johnson, a professor of psychology and psychiatry at the University of Ottawa, is now a forerunner in continuing the development of EFT and integrating attachment theory. In 1998, she published an article, "Listening to the Music: Emotion as a Natural Part of Systems Theory." This title would almost seem to state the obvious were it not for the fact that many early approaches to family therapy ignored emotion all together. (See Figure 1.1 for a reminder.) Emotionally focused couples therapy was birthed out of a desire for a more clearly delineated and validated marital intervention with a more humanistic approach that viewed "emotion as a powerful agent of change, rather than as simply part of the problem of marital distress" (Johnson, 1996). As part of a growing awakening to the power of emotion (rather than thoughts or behavior) in relationships, Johnson's work brings together all the best that family therapy has to offer: sound interpersonal theory that explains complex problems, congruent interventions tied to theory, and research regarding therapeutic process and outcomes.

In this approach, special attention is paid to repairing *attachment injuries,* those turning points in a relationship when a given partner has felt emotionally abandoned by the other (Johnson, Makinen, & Millikin, 2001). These turning points may be times of transition or crisis, when one partner had a particular need for support from the other and the other was unavailable. Miscarriages, illnesses, accidents, joblessness, and deaths are examples of times when some attachment injuries occur. This conceptualization makes EFT very successful in cases of trauma and couple distress. The important contribution of this work is the attention to emotional impasses and to the power of emotion in the process of attachment, which directs the therapist in developing effective interventions.

An impressive array of empirical research shows favorable treatment outcomes for EFT in a variety of populations, including those suffering from depression and chronic illness (Johnson, 2002; Kowal, Johnson, & Lee, 2003). EFT is considered a brief intervention that generally consists of 10–12 sessions. If additional problems or trauma are involved, therapy may extend to 30–40 sessions (Johnson, 2002). Emotion and how it is expressed between couples and family members is a key component of EFT and is considered the "music of the dance" between people.

EFT comprises a structured three-stage process:

1. **De-escalation of conflict.** Problematic cycles and related emotional states are identified, and emotional experiences are explored in depth.
2. **Restructure attachment bond.** The cycle is viewed as the enemy instead of either partner.
3. **Consolidate gains.** New communication patterns are reinforced.

Table 2.7 outlines the nine steps that constitute the three stages of the treatment process.

Table 2.7 | EFT Treatment Process

EFT Process	Goal of Intervention
Step 1: Delineate conflict issues in the struggle between the partners.	Connect with both partners and create an alliance. Assess the nature of the relationship and each partner's goals.
Step 2: Identify the negative interaction cycle.	Enter into the experience of each partner and sense how each constructs his or her experience. Track recurring sequences and begin to hypothesize as to the emotional blocks to securing attachment and engagement (fear, hopelessness, sadness).
Step 3: Access unacknowledged feelings underlying interactional positions.	This represents the music of the dance, that is, the primary emotions that are excluded from individual awareness and not explicitly included in the partner's interactions.
Step 4: Redefine the problem(s) in terms of underlying feelings.	Through accessing emotional responses, the therapist begins to uncover the attachment needs reflected by these responses and then reframes the couple's "problem."
Step 5: Promote identification with disowned needs and aspects of self.	Disowned needs are addressed. The intense engagement with one's own emotions allows the therapist to begin to facilitate a new kind of emotional engagement with the other partner.
Step 6: Promote acceptance by each partner of the other partner's experience.	The therapist assists in supporting the other partner to hear, process, and respond to this sharing so that this new experience can become part of, and begin to reshape, the couple's interactions.
Step 7: Facilitate the expression of needs and wants to restructure the interaction.	Statements of needs are made from an empowered, accessible position, constituting a shift in interactional positions, which in turn challenges the other partner to engage in the same process.
Step 8: Establish the emergence of new solutions.	The change events that occurred in the previous steps now have a direct impact on the couple's ability to problem-solve and cooperate as partners in their everyday life.
Step 9: Consolidate new positions.	The therapist helps the couple construct a coherent and satisfying narrative that captures their experience of the therapy process and their new understanding of the relationship.

(Johnson, 1996)

MST, MDFT, and EFT have some similarities. First, their approaches are based upon some theory of development (ecological, structural, attachment, etc.). These trends in thinking about human development have added depth and understanding to a field that was already rich in creativity and innovation.

Second, they have clear steps or principles that provide a framework for developmentally appropriate intervention. Within these elements are many options for personalizing and individualizing treatment for each family. *In fact, the success of their programs depends on it*. These models focus emphatically on building rapport, so Chapter 4 outlines a number of issues related to this critical therapeutic process. Because of this emphasis, many collaborative, empowering elements exist in each model that are not labeled as postmodern but nonetheless are excellent examples of second-generation processes. In MST and MDFT, many of these have come about because the populations they target are disadvantaged and culturally diverse, requiring that therapists adopt an empathic, nonblaming stance.

Third, all three credit a structural-strategic model of family therapy in some way. This may seem an unlikely connection. However, all three explore interactional sequences in detail, a procedure that is central to the basic models (see Chapters 6, 7 and 8). In addition, all three use directives aimed at creating a new interaction pattern (see Chapter 8). In the cases of MDFT and EFT, those therapists specifically address the attachment bonds of family members.

These characteristics challenge most stereotypes about evidence-based work. The untrained eye may assume that if a program has a systematic, orderly approach, it will stifle therapist creativity and the "art" of family therapy. However, this is why I present these approaches as the third generation of family therapy. They bring integration to a new, creative level. Beginners can adopt

Table 2.8 | Major Characteristics of Family Therapy Practice

Models	Description
Structural-strategic	Directive, in-session interactions, out-of-session tasks
M.R.I.-Solution-Focused	Consultative, exploratory, pragmatic, out-of-session tasks
Experiential	Personal disclosure, in-session modeling
Intergenerational	Historical, in-session analysis
Behavioral-CBFT	Education in session, problem-focused
Milan-Narrative	Questioning, reflecting, empowering, in session
MST	Home-based, pragmatic, principle-oriented
MDFT	Pragmatic, flexible, stage-oriented
EFT	Exploratory, empathic, stage-oriented, in-session enactments

these methods knowing that they have been tested on hundreds of diverse families and their outcomes analyzed. The beginning practitioner can also be reassured that choosing between models isn't necessary. With an integrative approach, each element has worth. Chapters 5 and 6 present some ideas about how to find an order to the process.

However, before leaving the study of specific models, a final review is in order. Table 2.8 reviews these three generations, summarizing the characteristics of practice that are most associated with each. In the remaining chapters of the book, the beginning therapist will see how these attributes fit with different clients and problems. Greater focus will be placed on characteristics of the process and less attention paid to specific models. For example, Chapter 3 reviews conceptual themes that cut across all family therapy practice today. These themes are addressed with sample questions and ideas about when to explore certain themes.

SUMMARY

Toward the end of the twentieth century, the field of marriage and family therapy evolved in response to societal changes, creative practitioners, health care trends, and ongoing research. These changes included greater sensitivity to gender, culture, and race. A postmodern emphasis led to less technical and more personable interactions in family therapy practice, characterized by Milan, solution-focused, and narrative family therapies. After this, third-generation approaches developed as evidence-based clinical models. These include CBFT, MST, MDFT, and EFT. Today, first-generation models are rarely practiced in their original form. Instead, integrative models such as those highlighted in this chapter incorporate the best and most relevant aspects of first-generation approaches with flexible and collaborative frameworks. Integration within the field has led to an acceptance of practices that beginning clinicians can recognize in cutting-edge research-based models of practice. Next Chapters 3 and 4 review common themes and then help readers organize the treatment process to put these themes into practice.

3 CHAPTER | Integration of Theory: Common Themes

CORE COMPETENCIES

1.2.1	**Perceptual**	Recognize contextual and systemic dynamics (e.g., gender, age, socioeconomic status, culture/race/ethnicity, sexual orientation, spirituality, religion, larger systems, social context).
2.1.1	**Conceptual**	Understand principles of human development; human sexuality; gender development; psychopathology; psychopharmacology; couple processes; and family development and processes (e.g., family, relational, and system dynamics).
2.3.3	**Executive**	Apply effective and systemic interviewing techniques and strategies.

As shown in Chapters 1 and 2, family therapy has many conceptual models that guide practitioners and help organize their thinking. This diversity, however, can often be overwhelming for the beginner. The structural therapist might assess the boundaries, coalitions, and hierarchy of a family (Minuchin & Fishman, 1981). The intergenerational therapist might focus on family beliefs, conflicts, and losses transferred from one generation to another (Framo, 1981; Paul & Paul, 1975). The Milan team might search for different points of view related to a symptomatic impasse in family interactions (Selvini Palazzoli et al., 1978). Trainees must often incorporate concepts and techniques from various schools. This can be confusing—different theoretical models use different terms to describe similar concepts. For example, Bowen's concept of differentiation is similar to Minuchin's concept of boundary when speaking of emotional and interpersonal distance. Likewise, certain techniques have proved useful in a number of schools of family therapy. For example, several approaches (structural, strategic, experiential, and contemporary) clarify communication, direct enactments, and describe the symptom (Nichols & Schwartz, 1991).

Learning about these subtleties can challenge the new practitioner, but the pursuit of conceptual purity also has pitfalls of its own. I think the adoption of a rigid theoretical framework can limit a family therapist's effectiveness, encouraging a tendency to distort observations to conform to theoretical precepts. For example, practitioners who are interested in assessing structural boundaries might attend only to specific interactions (e.g., when family members talk for each other). These practitioners can easily organize their observations, but they might miss some important information because it does not fit within that structural boundary framework (e.g., a critical issue raised even though members are talking for each other). To use an old cliché, a person with a hammer starts to think everything is a nail.

In a review of family therapy approaches applied to later-life families (families with older parents and grown children), Hanna and Hargrave (1997) found most early models of family therapy in their pure form to be lacking:

> Structural Family Therapy tends to ignore longitudinal changes over time with a family, thus ignoring historical factors that play heavily into the development of legacies. Bowenian family therapy does not offer enough pragmatic thinking to intervene in crises brought on by chronic illness. Behavioral family therapy does not have a framework for addressing the phenomenology of losses experienced by elders. Experiential family therapy (EFT) may be too direct for some families who prefer to cope with changing family roles in silent, persevering ways. (p. 27)

Although this critique is given in light of the needs of later-life families, similar shortcomings of these various therapy approaches have been seen with respect to minority families, court-ordered cases, and families who are not "therapy wise." Given that the early approaches came from clinicians socialized according to certain norms in the culture of psychotherapy, it is not difficult to understand how those first approaches became the foundation, but not ultimately the entire structure, of the family therapy movement.

The majority of practicing family therapists do not draw from a single theory or school of techniques (Quinn & Davidson, 1984). Even therapists trained in a single theory eventually incorporate other theories and techniques (Todd & Selekman, 1991a). Therapists integrate their own blend of methodologies based on training, personality, and the population of families they are serving. To begin this process of integration, the beginning therapist must identify major themes that provide ways of thinking about relationships, interactions, and problems.

These themes can be organized along a continuum that proceeds from larger to smaller spheres of observation. These differences are sometimes referred to as macroviews or microviews of family process. The *macroview* includes broad social factors that affect the interpersonal process such as gender, race, and culture. As the view narrows slightly, intergenerational and extended family relationships become additional influences on the interpersonal process. In the immediate relationship, as understood by the *microview*, looking at relational transitions and structural interactions is possible. Finally, individuals can be studied as systems in their own right—as a combination of thoughts, feelings, behaviors, and intentions; and in tandem with their psychodynamics, as a collection of biological subsystems that operate at all times. Like a camera with a zoom lens, the family therapist must maintain a flexible viewpoint to assess from different angles and assess multiple levels of process. In addition, the problem-solving system may comprise formal family relationships, friendships, or other important associates that can be resources in problem solving. The following discussion focuses on common conceptual themes and when exploring them might be useful.

GENDER

In 1978, Rachel Hare-Mustin published a pioneering article in *Family Process,* "A Feminist Approach to Family Therapy." Her critique of the field and thoughtful suggestions for a more gender-sensitive approach to family therapy began decades of reflection on how to understand a problem as it relates to societal practices such as sexism. Other reviews and critiques followed, including those of the Women's Project in Family Therapy, a group of feminist colleagues who added their voices of support for changes in hierarchical practices in our therapy and in our professional organizations (Simon, 1992). At the most general level, the feminist movement in family therapy suggested that all families are influenced by patterns of socialization that lead to rules and roles governing family process (power). Gender-related roles and rules are the most fundamental of these patterns. Goldner (1988) argued that gender should not be a special topic in family therapy, but is "at the center of family theory" (p. 17). Because *gender influences structure* in the family, it should be a fundamental element in family assessment.

In her seminal article on the subject, Hare-Mustin (1978) offered suggestions for implementing gender-sensitive family therapy:

> My purpose in what follows is not to analyze family therapy techniques, per se, but rather to consider certain areas of intervention in which a feminist orientation is

important. These areas are: the contract, shifting tasks in the family, communication, generational boundaries, relabeling deviance, modeling, ownership and privacy, and the therapeutic alliance with different family members. (p. 185)

To begin a gender-sensitive assessment, the following questions pose hypotheses that address a number of areas:

- **Tasks** Could role inflexibility regarding tasks be related to the problem?
- **Communication** Are communication styles disempowering to the females in the family?
- **Boundaries** Have generational coalitions developed as a result of disempowerment in the marriage?
- **Relabeling** Can disempowering stereotypes ("nag," "passive-aggressive") be relabeled to account for the context of powerlessness?
- **Modeling** Can the female therapist model more egalitarian relationships with males in the family, and can male therapists affirm female strength within the family?
- **Privacy** What are family rules around females' personal development and autonomy outside the family?
- **Alliance** What will each family member need from the therapist in order to feel understood and accepted?

As family therapy proceeds from the initial interview to the assessment process, the therapist can consider these questions while exploring the definition of the problem in greater depth. Then, during the assessment process, exploring the individual family members' points of view regarding gender development and the way they arrived at their current positions might be useful. An initial set of questions posed to clients might be:

1. What are some of the differences between how you each grew up as a female or male in our society?
2. How does your family address the differences between females and males in our society?
3. Are certain traditions in your family more closely related to either women or men?
4. How do you feel about these traditions and practices?
5. Are there any ways you think these ideas and traditions might be related to _____ (the presenting problem)?

Such a line of questioning acknowledges gender differences in a neutral, exploratory way. Even though the ultimate goal might be to correct gender imbalances, beginning with neutral questions allows families to describe themselves without feeling any pressure to change. As exploration continues, family therapists can decide which issues might be targeted for change later in the process.

Some clinicians provide suggestions for therapeutic dialogue that combines assessment and intervention. For example:

1. "What best explains your not wanting to tell me too much: that I am white, female or highly educated?" (Goldner, 1988, p. 29)

2. "Should you accommodate to prescriptions for men's greed and expediency or defy these prescriptions and insist that wisdom influences your decisions?" (White, 1986, p. 15)
3. "Would you prefer a life where you are a slave to tradition, or would you prefer a life where you are free to develop new views of people and relationships?" (White, 1990)

These questions are generally employed after extensive groundwork to establish a relationship and develop empathy, but they illustrate the creative use of questions that not only assess readiness for change but motivate families to consider change.

How to Focus on Gender

General questions about gender differences should be incorporated into all assessments. Each person's experience should be heard. In cases of marital conflict, gender differences are often the core issue and should be identified. For example, Jacobson, Holtzworth-Monroe, and Schmaling (1989) found that women often complain more than men about their current relationship. Indeed, women often desire greater involvement and closeness from their husbands, whereas husbands prefer to maintain the status quo and create greater autonomy and separateness for themselves. Moreover, women are more likely to seek therapy and push for an egalitarian relationship, whereas men are less likely to seek therapy and are inclined to maintain traditional gender roles.

When any family member exhibits extreme masculinity or femininity, practitioners have an opportunity to explore issues of gender socialization. Although therapists always have subjective views from their own socialization, they can engage clients in discussions about their subjective gender experiences while acknowledging their own biases. Such modeling on the part of the practitioner can provide a new environment from which a person can explore unacknowledged influences. Hypermasculinity often contributes to domestic violence and child abuse. In such cases, exploring in detail both the survivors' and perpetrators' beliefs and traditions about gender is critical. Current trends in the treatment of abuse suggest a focus on both perceptual and behavioral change is effective. Exploring beliefs and attitudes about gender differences is an important step toward identifying which beliefs and behaviors are ultimately targeted for change.

Implications for Treatment

The client's understanding of how gender relates to the presenting problem should dictate whether the therapist addresses gender directly or indirectly. When families are not ready to address gender differences directly, the practitioner should refrain from confrontation and address the issues in more indirect ways. For example, child and adolescent problems may be an opportunity to explore the impact of gender on developing children, thus introducing parents more indirectly to their own limitations. Sheinberg and Penn (1991) list four categories of gender questions:

1. The "norm" the man or woman aspires to and the relational consequences of changing
2. Hypothetical questions about the relational consequences of changing these norms
3. Norms of the couple's parents and their effects on the couple and their parents
4. Future questions to explore the potential for establishing new norms as well as altering how the problem continues

Marital partners might be highly sensitive to discussions regarding gender when they feel criticized. For example, men might be sensitive to the label "chauvinistic" and women might be sensitive to the label "just a housewife" when a therapist begins to explore issues of sex-role stereotypes. Practitioners should maintain a curious but hopeful position as they explore and identify patterns of thought and behavior related to gender differences. A lack of readiness on the part of families to discuss gender directly suggests the need for a more thorough assessment of the family's experience before choosing an intervention strategy. Then, the therapist can develop indirect ways of addressing imbalances.

With respect to men's issues, Brooks (1998) suggests that the culture of traditional men and the culture of traditional psychotherapy are very different, and therapists will be more successful when they recognize some men's discomfort with therapy and explore what mode could be the most comfortable for a male client. Because the majority of work on gender issues addresses the oppression of women in relationships, his advice is rare insight into how men might be disadvantaged by their socialization, society's portrayals of psychotherapy on television, and the expectations of emotional expression that therapists implicitly hold. He encourages clinicians to remember that men's socialization involves the need to guard their vulnerable emotions to effectively compete with others. As such, it behooves therapists to emphasize concrete processes in therapy, such as building skills and setting goals. The assessment process in Chapter 7 that involves genograms and timelines is especially "male-friendly" because these tools add a concrete, visual representation of an abstract process.

RACE AND CULTURE

Whereas gender is undoubtedly the first element that distinguishes human beings from each other, race and culture must rank second. Although race is similar to gender in that both are biologically determined, race is considered with culture in this discussion because of its influence on social and family groups. However, noting that race is not synonymous with culture is important. For example, many cultural groups experience a sense of difference from other groups but do not experience racial oppression.

In 1989, Nancy Boyd-Franklin published *Black Families in Therapy: A Multisystem Approach* that called attention to the differential issues of race for African American families. Boyd-Franklin began a trend of family therapists speaking out about important racial differences. She lists the first five differences as these, which summarize the fundamental premises of her book:

1. There is a great deal of *cultural diversity among black families* that is often overlooked or misunderstood.
2. African American culture represents *a distinct ethnic and racial experience* that is unique for a number of reasons, including history; the African legacy; the experience of slavery, racism, and discrimination; and the victim system.
3. The illusion of *color blindness* or the "class not race" myth needs to be challenged as both misguided and counterproductive.
4. Many *myths about black families* in the social science literature paint a pejorative, deficit picture of black family functioning.
5. Clarifying and understanding the *strengths of black families* is necessary, which can serve as a foundation for therapeutic work. (p. 5) [emphasis added]

Adding to Boyd-Franklin's work, Hardy and Laszloffy (1995) punctuate the need for white therapists to learn that trust-building with people of color comes from seeing and acknowledging the existence of racial differences in a relationship, rather than trying to be color blind (minimizing differences). They believe that positive relationships develop from the common ground of acknowledging and discussing differences.

In 1982, McGoldrick, Pearce, and Giordano were the first family therapists to review ethnicity in a broad way. Their book *Ethnicity and Family Therapy* surveys diverse ethnic groups in terms of their history, values, and other distinguishing cultural characteristics. It explores the process of family therapy for each group, paying particular attention to ways in which therapy can be respectful of cultural norms and values. Often a family's cultural heritage was overlooked as an important resource and strength that might be at the center of the family's ability to overcome its current difficulties. Social class was also considered a critical factor in how therapists drew conclusions about the family. Spiegel (1982) summarized some typical therapeutic values:

> Middle-class therapists, no matter what their ethnic origins, have been socialized in terms of mainstream values. The therapist will be future oriented, expecting clients to be motivated and to keep appointments punctually. He or she will also expect families to be willing to work on therapeutic tasks (Doing), over reasonable periods of time (Future), with the prospect of change before them (Mastery-over-Nature). All this is to be done while taking a pragmatic view of moral issues (Neutral), and at the very least the therapist will expect to help clients to distance themselves from any overwhelming moral burden or intense feelings of shame. And clients will be expected to separate themselves from enmeshment in the family structure and to develop increased autonomy (Individual). (p. 46)

McGoldrick and Giordano (1996) surveyed diverse ethnic groups in terms of history, values, and other distinguishing cultural characteristics:

> Italians rely primarily on the family and turn to an outsider only as a last resort. Black Americans have long mistrusted the help they can receive from traditional institutions except the church. . . . Puerto Ricans and Chinese may somatize when under stress and seek medical rather than mental health services. . . . Likewise, Iranians may view medication and vitamins as a necessary part of treating symptoms. (p. 2)

Thus, ethnicity—a sense of shared identity developed over many generations— can be a critical variable in understanding client families and mobilizing their strengths. If clinicians are not aware of differing worldviews and values, they are apt to be critical rather than complimentary of differences exhibited by families out of the mainstream.

Culture-sensitive family therapy continues as an important topic in family therapy theory and practice today. Charles Waldegrave (1990), a family therapist in New Zealand, has a therapy of social justice, or "Just Therapy," that includes the native culture of Maori and other Pacific Island people in the therapeutic process. Harry Aponte (1994) highlights issues of spirituality for family therapists who work with low-income and disadvantaged families.

In addition to acknowledging differences between cultural groups, avoiding stereotyping is also important. The practitioner's intent should be to strike a balance between understanding the common ground of general patterns and clarifying distinctions and variations within the larger group. Boyd-Franklin provides valuable help in this area with African American families. Noting that negative stereotypes often generate a fear of black men or suggest most African Americans actually have issues of poverty, rather than issues related to race, she encourages white therapists to engage in "soul searching" to avoid conveying an unconscious belief that thwarts authenticity with the client. To move beyond the common challenges white therapists face in working with African Americans, Boyd-Franklin suggests certain guidelines to follow when learning about the client. Table 3.1 shows her guidelines with my suggestions for how to implement them. When family therapists serve minority families in the United States, they can prepare by referring to Boyd-Franklin (1989) and McGoldrick and Giordano (1996) for helpful specifics.

The questions in Box 3.1 can be used to develop an assessment process that accounts for the effects of culture. Whatever questions the practitioner chooses, acknowledging and respecting cultural differences between the family and therapist is important. Then, families can be invited to teach therapists about the significant parts of their cultural identity. As clinicians pursue this type of assessment, their role is similar to the anthropologist who lives with people and understands them while being a participant in their culture. Such a role contrasts with that of the physician or scientist who analyzes, categorizes, and treats people from a distance.

A critique of the social service system by Minuchin (1984) illustrates that cultural conflicts can often be central to the definition of a problem. In reviewing selected court cases from British social services, he describes the plight of

Table 3.1 | Suggestions for White Therapists

Guideline	Therapist Statement
Allow the family to express feelings of anger, rejection, mistrust, etc.	I've often found that families in your situation have some good reasons for feeling angry, upset, and frustrated. Does this fit your experience?
Raise the issue of race.	I know that some black families have had bad experiences with white therapists, so I hope you'll instruct me if I start going down a road that doesn't fit for you. I want to learn about things I don't know.
Invite the family to share their experience of being black.	When I begin working with a family, I like to start by sharing about how I've dealt with issues of race. Then, I wonder if you could share some of your experiences.
Do not expect family members to "air their dirty laundry."	I'll let you be the judge of how much information is necessary to share. I'm comfortable working with what you think is most important.

Box 3.1 | **Questions for the Assessment of Racial and Cultural Factors**

1. How does your racial/cultural/religious heritage make your family different from other families you know?

2. Compared to other families in your cultural group, how is your family different?

3. What are the values that your family identifies as being important parts of your heritage?

4. At this particular time in your family's development, are there issues related to your cultural heritage that are being questioned by anyone? What and by whom?

5. What is the hardest part about being a minority in this culture?

6. When you think of living in America versus the country of your heritage, what are the main differences?

7. What lesson have you learned about your people? About other people of other races?

8. What have you learned about disloyalty?

9. What are people in your family really down on?

10. What might an outsider not understand about your racial/cultural/religious background?

Mrs. Obutu, a Ghanian mother rearing her family in London. After her daughter, Sylvia, was arrested for shoplifting, Mrs. Obutu was summoned to the police station and was observed beating her daughter with a stick. Court proceedings determined that Sylvia should not return to the family home. After the mother's poignant objections, Minuchin (1984) provides this commentary:

> The magistrates return, looking upset. Not because Mrs. Obutu roared in pain; in their many years on the bench, pain has become a frequent witness in the chamber and they have learned how to deal with it. . . . No, they are upset because their sympathies are with Mrs. Obutu. They understood, because all of them are parents, that Mrs. Obutu is a Ghanian mother trying her best with her English daughter. Cultural gaps are familiar to them. But they were caught in their own legal structure. Nobody protected Mrs.Obutu from giving evidence against herself. Nobody defended her because nobody represented Mrs. Obutu. And certainly it didn't occur to anybody to have Mrs. Obutu and Sylvia talk to each other in the court to put in evidence for the magistrates the conflicting sets of loyalties, affection, care, frustration, and rage that characterized their relationship. Just as in all families. (p. 130)

The challenge of relating to diverse people is connected to how family therapists respond to conflict—their own and others'. Students of family therapy must explore their own patterns of thought and emotion in the face of interpersonal conflict. Identify those coping strategies most often chosen and critique them for their usefulness with different cultural groups. As one begins to gain awareness of this personal process, the next step involves exploring how these personal patterns might or might not fit with the inclinations of a given client group.

An interesting example of how personal process interacts with client process is illustrated by a study conducted by Gonzales, Hiraga, and Cauce (1995). In observing mother-daughter interactions in African American and Asian American families, the researchers discovered that non–African American coders rated the level of conflict higher for African American mothers and daughters than did the "in-group" coders or the mothers and daughters themselves. Applying this research to a family therapy experience suggests the possibility that the practitioner's experience can be quite different from that of the family. A number of therapists think that learning to account for these differences and developing the ability to step back from them in order to "go with the flow" of a family are defining elements of cultural competence.

How to Focus on Race and Culture

As the preceding example illustrates, cases that involve families of an immigrant or a minority culture invariably have cultural issues to which the clinician should attend. With these families, the focus on culture is an important part of the joining process. As clinicians invite families to teach them about their culture, the opportunity to join emerges in a context that is familiar and comfortable for the family. In this way, the family becomes the expert and the therapist becomes the learner.

If the joining process does not evolve into a comfortable collaboration, family therapists are encouraged to invite a native consultant to the sessions. This individual can provide support for the family and clarify the cultural differences between therapist and family (Waldegrave, 1990). This consultant might be a bilingual extended family member, a professional from the native culture, or anyone else of the family's choice who could serve as a bridge between cultures. Such an effort on the part of the practitioner nonverbally communicates an acknowledgment of differences, a respect for his or her own limitations, and a desire to tailor the therapeutic process to the family's unique circumstances.

With respect to families who appear "mainstream," it is recommended that family therapists still ask one or two basic questions about culture, race, or religion, because many subcultures in the western hemisphere are not set apart by physical or biological characteristics. For example, military families form a subculture in the United States characterized by certain patterns of mobility and a degree of patriotism not found in many nonmilitary families. Likewise, certain religious groups have histories of persecution that may leave members with a heightened sense of alienation from the dominant culture. Though on the surface such families might appear to be white, middle class, and Protestant, questions about the effects of military life or religion could alert the therapist to the family's uniqueness and relevant cultural differences. Chapter 7 provides questions for genograms that help clinicians to discover these subtle differences in families.

Implications for Treatment

As mentioned earlier, the therapist's inquiry into culture facilitates the joining process. When specific personalities clash or the clinician is struggling, attention to culture can overcome difficulties that might arise at the microlevel of the therapeutic relationship. This is because an inquiry into the world of the family moves the therapist away from a hierarchical position (i.e., do what I want you to do) and into a collaborative position (i.e., teach me what is important for me to know about you). This exploration shifts practitioners into a macrolevel of experience, and the new information broadens their perspective about the interpersonal impasse.

Therapists such as White (1990) use gender and culture as concepts to define the problem so that the family can be helped to externalize blame and minimize shame while assuming more responsibility for solving the internal experience. These practitioners come to understand interpersonal dynamics through the lens of socialized cultural practices. In addition, as therapists learn details of the client's culture, the client's rituals, tasks, directives, and rationale can be couched in language and practices that are comforting and empowering. Very often, seemingly mainstream clients feel alienated from some part of their world because of the problem that brings them into therapy. This alienation can be addressed as a cultural problem to acknowledge the family's pain and isolation. As treatment proceeds, the family therapist can assist the family members in feeling more connected to their world by a process known as normalizing (helping them see their similarities with others). One way of accomplishing this task is to explore intergenerational patterns.

INTERGENERATIONAL RELATIONSHIPS

Not only is the family the usual vehicle for socialization within a given culture, but it is also responsible for the evolution of more specific traditions, roles, rewards, and obligations that bind family members together. Each family's history shapes unique patterns of belief and interaction analogous to cultural practice. These patterns often take the form of nonverbal rules (what people should do) that shape attitudes, communication, and intimacy.

Many family therapists have recognized previous generations as a major influence on family life in the present. Bowen (1978) conceptualized multigenerational transmission as the process by which dysfunctional patterns of coping are passed from one generation to the next. Boszormenyi-Nagy and Spark (1973) focused on loyalties or transgenerational obligations, suggesting that these were represented by symptoms in various family members. Ferreira (1963) discussed the significance of family myths, which are beliefs that go unchallenged within the family and enable members to maintain a certain image of themselves. Other family therapists applied object-relations theory to family life, theorizing that we unconsciously attempt to change intimate relationships on the basis of those in our past either by making them familiar or by making them fit our fantasies of idealized relationships that would compensate for past rejection or abandonment (Framo, 1976; Jacobson, 1984; Sager, 1981).

Approaches in intergenerational family therapy address several issues. Williamson (1981) focuses on how an individual can develop a sense of *personal authority* within the family of origin. Kramer (1985) resolves generational conflicts through an emphasis on *acceptance of differences* rather than on approval or agreement about the issues. Boszormenyi-Nagy and Spark (1973) help family members to explore their *invisible loyalty* or debts and to find appropriate tasks by which to *balance the ledger* of indebtedness or *entitlement*. Anderson and Bagarozzi (1989) explore family and personal *myths* on the grounds that they give meaning to the past, define the present, and provide direction for the future. These developments represent attempts at integration that work to resolve historical conflicts in multigenerational families.

In assessing intergenerational dynamics, the therapist might ask questions regarding past family issues, current extended family relationships, and future hopes and expectations for these relationships:

1. What stories from your own life would best describe your development in your family of origin?
2. What stories from your family's history still influence the thinking of family members?
3. Which family members have strong feelings about this situation?
4. Have any family members tried to help you with this situation?

5. Does this situation seem similar to any other situation that you recall in your family of origin?
6. Have other family members had experience in resolving a similar situation for themselves?
7. With which extended family members do you feel most comfortable?
8. With which extended family members do you feel least comfortable?
9. What are the emotional debts in the family?
10. What are the issues of loyalty?
11. What past experiences trigger current problems?

For interviewing couples, Wamboldt and Wolin (1989) developed a structured interview that incorporates questions such as:

1. How did you meet?
2. What is the state of your relationship now?
3. What are some of the important challenges that the two of you have made it through?
4. What are some of the most important similarities and differences between you and your family members?
5. What do you most want to conserve from your family background?
6. What do you most want to change from your family background?
7. Given the family you grew up in, is there a reason that your partner is a particularly good or meaningful choice? Is your partner ever too much that way? What is that like?
8. What do your parents think about your relationship? How do they react?
9. Is there anything I haven't asked that you think is important?

How to Focus on Intergenerational Relationships

Unattached adults who are not in significant relationships can benefit from intergenerational exploration because the consciousness of family-of-origin influences has not been diminished by relationships in a family of procreation. For clients whose goal in therapy is to understand some aspect of their lives, an intergenerational assessment often lays a foundation for later discussions of self-understanding. Additionally, adults who would normally seek individual counseling for the healing of traumatic childhood experiences can benefit from an intergenerational perspective, which encourages reflection on past experience as a springboard for future change.

Frequently, clients seek family counseling for a marital or child-rearing difficulty. In these cases, questions about present extended family relationships may alert the therapist to historical family issues that could be restraining the change process in some way. For example, the therapist might assume that the family member has an internalized critical voice that keeps saying, "I am incapable of changing this problem or my perception of the problem." In addition, problems related to aging and the elderly must often be put in the context of relationships that have evolved through the generations to assist adult children in making necessary transitions with their parents.

Implications for Treatment

Erickson and Rossi (1979) suggest that change can be brought about in individuals by facilitating "an inner resynthesis of past experience." Analogously, families can change their views and behavior toward each other by identifying restraining myths, exploring unconscious patterns of communication, and detaching from their current experience to develop a broader and more hopeful perspective with positive possibilities.

Durrant (1988) illustrates such a case in which intergenerational messages are identified for a female client and used as an externalized influence over which she was helped to triumph. Because the intergenerational process was used as the definition of the problem, blame was not personalized to any one person but rather was assigned to tradition. In this way, motivation for change is facilitated, and clients do not need to feel disloyal to parents. Even in cases of painful abuse, an intergenerational perspective can often help families and individuals explore the historical issues without becoming weighed down by unproductive introspection. Because intergenerational therapy maintains a focus that is interpersonal, clients can be helped to focus on interactions rather than on internal pain alone and to discover important insights while also claiming the necessary strength to heal. By addressing stories, myths, rules, and roles from their family of origin, clients can also gain a sense of moving through time, just as the generations of their family have evolved. This opportunity for a sense of temporal movement can be enhanced by reflecting on family transitions that might have influenced the development of intergenerational dynamics.

TRANSITIONS AND DEVELOPMENT

In 1980, Betty Carter and Monica McGoldrick published the first edition of *The Family Life Cycle: A Framework for Family Therapy.* This book began a trend toward looking at the family as an evolving unit that progressed through many transitions, some as normative stages and others as nonnormative, life-changing events. These nodal events became focal points in family therapy as family therapists discovered that many presenting problems began during some nodal event in the family's history. Understanding the relationship between these events and the presenting problem gave new meaning to clients and family therapists alike. Carter and McGoldrick began their integration by building upon their own training in Bowen theory and adding a multigenerational approach to family development. As their work evolved, they added an emphasis on aspects of culture and gender that interacted with stages of development in the family.

The critical timing of traditional nodal events, or transitional periods for each stage of life, was first undertaken by Evelyn Duvall (1977). She conceptualized the family as passing through eight stages, with developmental tasks for each stage. Although many variations of Duvall's eight stages exist, all emphasize *nodal events*: entering and leaving the family, birth, parenthood, children leaving home, retirement, and death (Carter & McGoldrick, 1989b). Hiebert, Gillespie, and Stahmann (1993) paid particular attention to stages of marital relationships and the interactional and psychological nuances that occur during important nodal events. These events often require a reorganization of rules and roles for the family to remain functional. This reorganization can be thought of as a set of developmental tasks for each stage. Box 3.2 outlines assessment questions that can be used to understand family functioning at each stage of life. For some cases, only those questions from the current stage are needed. For other cases, a complete review, with a sampling of questions from each stage, is required to fully understand the family's experience.

All couples have the task of solidifying their commitment and placing friends and family of origin second to their relationship. When this task is not negotiated successfully, in-law conflicts can be chronic. In the next stage, many families renegotiate rules and relationships to allow for the entry of children. Parenting roles are established, and the relationship with the extended family might be redefined to include parenting and grandparenting. For couples without children, this stage may involve the establishment of shared values, interests, or goals that provide a sense of unity and identity for both partners. If children were desired, this stage might also be a time to resolve grief to create alternative stages of growth and development.

The adolescent stage begins when the first child enters puberty. The primary task during this stage involves increased autonomy for adolescents in the household. Parents must continually alter their relationships and rules to allow the adolescent to move in and out of the family system. At the same time, the parents are facing midlife decisions and emotions. The ways in which critical tasks of communication and boundary negotiation were resolved in previous stages affect the resolution of challenges in this stage. To the degree that previous developmental tasks were mastered, the family can move into the launching stage. At this stage, ideally the parents and the adolescent are in a position to attain greater independence from one another. Parents must develop adult relationships with their children and renegotiate their marital relationship without children. Stress occurs when parents are alone for the first time in many years and must renegotiate their time, new careers, and other issues.

If couples do not have children, stages four and five might still involve interpersonal tasks related to structure, discipline, dependency, and autonomy. However, these tasks surface in a variety of situations such as work, friendships, and the development of personal identities and competence through family and community relationships.

The later-life family must deal with its declining health. Family members must reassess their life structures and explore new ways of living. At this stage, they deal with the loss of a parent or spouse or the loss of vitality, and with that they also deal with fears concerning senility and death—both their own and others'. These developments affect all members of the family.

Box 3.2 | Questions for Developmental Interviews

Stage One: Forming Relationships

When did you meet? What year?

Who introduced you to each other?

Who initiated further dates?

Were you dating other people at the time?

When did this relationship become exclusive?

What did you like about each other?

What did you discover? How were you different from each other?

What didn't you like?

How did your families react to each of you during dating?

When did each of you say on the inside, "You're for me"?

When did each of you say to one other, "You're for me"?

When did you get engaged? How did that happen?

Did the relationship change after the engagement?

How did you determine the wedding date?

How did you determine who was to attend the wedding?

Were you sexually involved prior to marriage? Were you able to talk about sex?

Did you have any serious disagreements before marriage? How did each of you know the other was angry?

Stage Two: Commitment

How did the wedding go? What were your expectations?

How did the honeymoon go? What were your expectations?

When did the first difference of opinion come about?

What kind of social life did the two of you have at the beginning of this relationship? Who initiated it?

How were decisions arrived at in regard to what you would do?

Who were your friends? His, hers, both?

How did the two of you decide to handle your money? Who decided that?

Did anybody have veto power?

How much could each of you spend without asking the other?

When did the two of you begin your sexual relationship? Did you discuss it before it happened?

How did you each experience the first time?

(Continued)

Questions for Developmental Interviews (continued)

Who initiates sex now?

How did each side of the family feel about the marriage?

What were early relationships like between each of your families?

How were disagreements handled with in-laws in the early years?

How did you each define happiness?

Stage Three: Parenting, Values, Goals

How did the two of you decide whether to have children?

Did you talk about contraception and family planning?

What were your different attitudes and ideas about it?

How did your husband react to the pregnancy?

How did your wife react to the pregnancy?

How did the pregnancy go? How was the delivery?

What kind of changes took place after the child was born?

Did you notice any differences developing between you after the birth of the child? How did you resolve these?

What attitudes from your families of origin have influenced your child-rearing relationships?

What percentage of your time is spent taking care of your marriage as opposed to taking care of your children?

Who do the children turn to for support? If they want something fixed? If they want to play?

Stage Four: Adolescence

Who do the children think is stricter, more lenient, moodier, and so on?

How do Mom and Dad feel about school? Friends? Other issues?

What privileges do your teenagers have now that they did not have when they were younger?

How do you think your parents will handle it when your younger sister wants to date?

Will that be different from when you wanted to date?

Stage Five: Launching Children

How did your parents help you leave home?

What is the difference between how you left home and how your children are leaving home?

Will your parents get along with each other better, worse, or the same once you have left home?

(Continued)

Box 3.2 | **Questions for Developmental Interviews (continued)**

Who, between your Mom and Dad, will miss the children the most?

Did you confide in one or more of the children if you were having difficulties with each other?

What effect did the children's leaving home have on your marriage?

Have either of you thought about goals for yourselves after the children leave home?

What type of support do you need from each other to adjust to the children being away?

Are there any unresolved issues between you that can be traced back to an earlier stage of development?

Have you discussed this time as an opportunity to resolve those issues?

Stage Six: Legacies

As you see your child moving on with a new marriage, what would you like your child to do differently than you did?

If your parents are still alive, do you have any issues you would like to discuss with them?

When you look back over your life, what aspects have you enjoyed most? What has given you the most happiness?

About what aspects do you feel the most regret?

What was the one thing you wanted but did not get from the children?

Have there been any changes in the way you and your children relate since they have become adults?

How does your family deal with the effects of illness and advanced age?

How do you maintain a zest for life as you get older?

Have you discussed issues such as death, living wills, and life supports with your children and each other?

Do you have a plan for resolving conflicting feelings over any of the foregoing?

Source: Adapted from Hiebert, Gillespie, and Stahmann, 1993.

The divorced or remarried family goes through additional stages of development. Box 3.3 contains interview questions for divorced and remarried families. Like other stages of family process, the stages of divorce and remarriage include developmental issues that can guide the clinician and family toward the most beneficial adjustment. Divorced and remarried families can find completing developmental tasks more difficult than the original nuclear family. Remarried families might have role models for parenthood but lack

Box 3.3	# Questions for Divorced and Remarried Families

Questions for Divorced Family Development Interviews

Have you accepted your inability to continue this relationship?

How do you and your ex-spouse deal with the issue of custody? Visitation? Finances?

What do your parents think about the divorce?

What do you miss from your old family?

How are things different for you now?

What do you like about your new life? What don't you like about it?

Do you ever wish you were back together?

Have you developed any new relationships? Activities?

What kind of relationship do you have with your ex-spouse?

How did you tell your children about the divorce?

What have you learned about yourself in this process?

What kinds of problems are your children having?

How are you responding to those problems?

Questions for Remarried Family Development Interviews

When did your last marriage end?

Do you think you had enough time to finish your first marriage?

What kind of communication do you have with your ex-spouse?

How are each of your children getting along?

How do each of them feel about your marriage?

How often do they see their mother/father?

How do your children get along with your spouse?

What do you do to help them get along with your spouse?

Which of your children has had the most difficulty with the new marriage?

How do your children get along with their stepbrothers? Stepsisters?

Do your children accept your spouse?

How do you expect your spouse to relate to your children?

Who is mostly in charge of the children?

What kind of help do you get from your spouse for your parenting role?

Are each of you responsible for disciplining your own children?

such models for single parenthood or stepparenthood. Society's focus on the joys of family living is evidenced in advertising and television, but divorced and remarried families sometimes have difficulty finding joy in their new life together. Moreover, at the time of remarriage, spouses must deal with many of the issues unresolved in the previous marriage.

In addition to the traditional transitions and tasks of intact white middle-class families, each family and individual has a particular developmental path that evolves from the different settings in which development occurs (Falicov, 1988). Nodal events such as untimely deaths, chronic illnesses, or other unusual circumstances can affect the course of life and the completion of various stage-related tasks. Many other types of transitions can also occur for unmarried adults, gay and lesbian couples, adoptive families, and family groups from nonmajority cultures.

The level of stress is much greater for families today than for those of past generations. The increasing divorce rate, the women's movement, and sexual and technological revolutions have had a profound impact on family development. The vast amount of change produced by these events puts a great deal of stress on families today. Job loss or divorce often precipitates a crisis that sends the family to therapy. However, if therapy focuses only on the symptom or the interactional patterns at the time of crisis, the therapist can miss information gleaned from a macroview perspective that would help normalize the current difficulties and make them easier to overcome.

To trace a family's or individual's development over time, the family therapist must understand traditional and alternative patterns of evolution. Carter and McGoldrick (1989b) do this by expounding upon Duvall's work and discussing stages of divorce adjustment and remarriage. Howard (1978) researched related and nonrelated family groups. In her work, she surveyed individuals from all walks of life about what makes a "good" family. The consensus was that high satisfaction was related to the aspects of family life outlined in the following list. In diverse and nonrelated family groups, these aspects can be considered as developmental tasks that lead to relational satisfaction over time. The respondents to Howard's survey suggested that satisfied family groups:

- Have a chief, that is, someone around whom others cluster
- Have a switchboard operator, that is, someone who can keep track of others
- Are hospitable
- Deal squarely with directness
- Prize their rituals
- Are affectionate
- Have a sense of place
- Find a way to be involved with children
- Honor their elders

Landau-Stanton (1986) uses a practice known as *transitional mapping* to pinpoint the impact of social and cultural changes that can transform a family. Such issues as migration, changes due to illness or death, and shifts from rural to urban society have important effects on the family. These transformations begin as an event, such as a geographic relocation, but evolve gradually as a process of adaptation and change. Using transitional mapping, families can track their process in retrospect and begin to capture the complexity that contributes to their dilemmas (see Chapter 7).

In mapping transitions, the practitioner becomes aware of evolving sequences and processes. The result is a perspective that identifies family and individual problems according to their developmental place in time:

1. What stage of relationship are the family and individual members in now? What other major life transitions have they lived through? What is the next stage?
2. How did things come to be the way they are now?
3. Has the problem always been this way? When did it change?
4. When were things better than now? When were they worse?
5. Does the family view their current life situation as part of a temporary stage or part of a permanent problem?
6. Does the family therapist have a view of the problem that uses time as a dimension of hope or as an indictment of despair?
7. Does the use of parental control fit the developmental needs of the individual?
8. Does consideration of differences allow developmentally appropriate growth?
9. Are there signs that tasks of previous stages have not been successfully accomplished?
10. Is each person in the family attaining his or her needs in a fashion that helps the parents maintain control?

When to Focus on Transitions and Development

Many family therapy theorists focus on developmental issues in some way (Haley, 1980; Hoffman, 1983; Minuchin, 1974; Selvini Palazzoli et al., 1978). Most commonly, client populations with children, adolescents, and elders are best served by focusing on these issues because common life transitions can be easily implicated as part of the problem. In addition, individuals and nontraditional family groups can benefit from an assessment that helps them identify and label their unique developmental progression, giving them a sense of movement through time, which helps create a positive context for targeted changes.

Implications for Treatment

The advantage of a developmental perspective is that it offers the family therapist increased options for defining the problem. Rather than seeing a problem as a permanent condition, the therapist is able to view behavior and symptoms as a response to a unique transition in the person's life (Haley, 1980). If a couple's marital conflict became serious after the birth of their first child, that developmental stage can be explored for circumstances that might have prevented the couple from developing problem-solving strategies. These developmental circumstances (e.g., isolation, poverty, or in-law interference) can be labeled as the problem, and the couple can then be invited to join together to overcome this problem rather than blame each other and remaining adversaries (White & Epston, 1991).

When a person or a family does not proceed through traditional stages, the problem brought into therapy can be thought of as an opportunity for clients to pioneer a new societal pattern or as an opportunity for the therapist and the clients to collect information from their unique experience to share with others. In a developmental interview, the family therapist might ask participants to talk about what they perceive as the major stages of their life thus far and, more specifically, to reflect on perceptions of self and others and also the challenges and abilities that characterized each stage. By focusing on developmental milestones in family and individual history, the family therapist can conduct an assessment that invites the process of change to begin with affirmations of strength and resilience.

As the therapist assesses the developmental process, information begins to emerge about the interactional process between family members—that is, the microprocess that accounts for small, specific behavioral sequences in families, such as who started the fight or who stole the last cookie from the jar. Interactional process within the family is generally assessed as an indicator of family structure.

FAMILY STRUCTURE

The study of family structure is primarily concerned with interactions within the family that determine its organization. According to Minuchin, this organization must be modified to meet the developmental tasks for each stage of the family life cycle. He used the concepts of hierarchy, boundaries, subsystems, and coalitions in describing family structure. The family organism, like other social organizations, functions through an internal organization of subsystems (couple, parental, and sibling). When the functioning of subsystems breaks down, the family is unable to provide support and autonomy to meet the developmental needs of individual members.

Other family therapists refined Minuchin's pioneering concepts related to structure. Breunlin, Schwartz, and Mac Kune-Karrer (1992) refer to family organization, with related concepts of leadership, balance, and harmony. Their work illustrates the trend noted in Chapter 2, that of marital and family therapy moving toward concepts that are more human and less mechanistic. As this trend continues, it provides greater clarity for those who are learning to think systemically. Well-functioning systems have some form of leadership. Effective leaders use their influence judiciously in person-to-person interactions. As influence is exercised, members of the system have their needs addressed in tandem with the needs of the group. The intended outcome of these interactions is harmony. Questions to assess leadership, balance, and harmony include:

- How much time do you spend with each other? With whom does each family member spend the most time and what things do they do together?
- How do you decide what gets accomplished within the family?
- What is the process of decision making, and who is involved?
- Who is close to whom? Who are most alike and most dissimilar in the family?
- How are the mother and father different from each other?
- How is each sibling different from the others?
- Who agrees and disagrees with stated views about the problem?
- How do you decide the rules for your children?
- Who seems to be most upset by this problem?
- What are some things you have tried to do to solve this problem?
- Which of these seem helpful to you? How are they helpful?

The therapist assesses family interaction by observing various kinds of behavior. Useful nonverbal clues include tone of voice, facial expression, or eye contact with other family members. It is important to take careful note of who speaks for whom and when. The therapist might also probe other family members to assess their view of the family problem. Using these data, the therapist formulates hypotheses about the family problem and the underlying organization of the system.

The Importance of Family Structure

A basic practice in family therapy is to assess the pattern of leadership in each family and to develop a collaborative relationship with the family members who have the greatest ability to influence family life. Thus, a structural assessment is recommended for all cases, because treatment is maximized when it is aligned with the family's primary leaders. In addition, information about balance in relationships is important for assessment of specific interactions in the family and for determining who is actually involved in problematic sequences.

Implications for Treatment

Although structural assessment is most closely associated with the clinical work of Minuchin, Haley's strategic therapy also uses structural concepts to define child and adolescent problems. Structural-strategic forms of family therapy routinely emphasize the goal of strengthening the parental subsystem and addressing parent-child coalitions. These goals are often pursued by tracking interactional sequences in detail and intervening in these to change a targeted relationship. In addition, the Milan team and other practitioners developed circular questions designed to elicit information about family structure and family politics:

- Who is close to whom?
- How did family members come to their conclusions about the problem?

- Whose opinion has the most influence?
- What purpose might the symptom serve?
- What is the exact sequence of events when the problem is occurring?

As these questions are answered, the therapist can describe the structure of the family and note, in particular, how family interactions are influenced by the personal dynamics of each family member.

INDIVIDUAL EXPERIENCE

Despite the tendency in the field of family therapy to de-emphasize the analysis of intrapsychic dimensions within the individual, many approaches provide very helpful information related to how a family therapist would address individual concerns. In fact, even approaches that might overtly discourage attention to psychodynamics eventually reveal that the baby is not completely thrown out with the bathwater. For example, although Watzlawick has long been an advocate of analyzing failed solutions rather than analyzing people (in the traditional psychoanalytic sense), he suggests that in finding solutions, "the tactic chosen has to be translated into the person's own 'language'; that is, it must be presented to him in a form which utilizes his own way of conceptualizing 'reality'" (Watzlawick, Weakland, & Fisch, 1974, p. 113). Thus, without a framework facilitating empathy for each person's position, the family therapist is unlikely to be able to successfully elicit trust and cooperation from the significant parties involved. The following sections illustrate the variety of views related to understanding individuals from a systems perspective.

Self-Esteem

Experiential family therapists conceptualize self-esteem as the result of interpersonal processes. Virginia Satir (1972) was particularly interested in teaching others about the impact of family functioning on individual self-esteem. Satir was noted for therapeutic interventions in which she adopted a nurturing role with clients while coaching them toward more honest, open, and accepting communication with each other. In a statement that she called "My Declaration of Self-Esteem," Satir (1972) envisions the potential of every person to become an aware, self-responsible, growth-oriented person.

Satir also influenced other personal growth theorists who were interested in interactional models based on self-awareness and communication. One model of communication skills integrates the study of interpersonal interaction with humanistic psychology and family studies (Miller, Nunnally, Wackman, & Miller, 1988). Known as the *couples communication program*, this approach begins with five basic elements of self-awareness that can be taught to a student or family member to enhance the self-awareness and communication skills needed for personal satisfaction in relationships. These elements, as a set of interacting parts, are known as the *awareness wheel*. In family therapy, they can guide the practitioner toward an understanding of individual experience as it relates to significant relationships.

- **Senses** Information from the five senses is the initial link between the individual and the outside world. Sensory information is present at the beginning of all human life and continues to the end as part of an interactional cycle. Sensory data are regarded as factual; carefully assessed, they yield a limited but verifiable truth. For example, a wife hearing her husband's voice raised is an objective fact distinguishable from her subjective response, which may be the thought, "He's angry." Only her husband can really verify what his emotion is at that moment, even though family members commonly consider subjective information to be fact.

- **Thoughts** This category includes interpretations, assumptions, opinions, beliefs, and conclusions that an individual makes in response to sensory information. Often the result of history and experience, thoughts become a frame of reference that influences a person's actions, feelings, and intentions. In addition, assumptions are distinguished from objective facts in that they are constructed by the person in response to sensory data. The wife's statement "I think you're angry" legitimately communicates a fact about what she is thinking and distinguishes her thought process from what her husband's emotion might really be. In addition, self-esteem in individual family members is often related to their beliefs or thoughts about themselves as well as to what they perceive to be the beliefs of others about themselves.

- **Feelings** This category encompasses the physiological and behavioral responses associated with feeling a certain emotion. Common feelings include sadness, anger, happiness, fear, shame, and hurt. However, hundreds of words in the English language label an even wider range of emotional states. Self-awareness entails an individual's ability to label his or her own emotions, whether pleasant or unpleasant, and to accept them as part of being human. Self-esteem involves an acceptance of emotions as important information about the self and an ability to act responsibly on those feelings. When an individual is not able to tolerate his or her fears or anxieties, that individual develops controlling or addictive behavior that can numb unpleasant emotional states.

- **Intentions** These are personal and general goals, hidden and open desires, short-term and long-term needs, motivations, dreams, and hopes. They can involve both the self and others and are related to an individual's thoughts and feelings as they evolve. Behavior is viewed as always having a purpose; thus, intentions provide a personal context for actions. For example, when family members wish to please others as much as possible, they may develop behavior patterns that consistently accommodate others and do not assert on behalf of themselves. In other cases, intentions might underlie symptomatic behavior that serves a function in the family, as in the case where a child's problem interrupts parental conflict. Although the intention in young children may not be conscious, adolescent and adult family members are often able to identify their systemic intention when the therapist asks, "How might this problem actually be preventing something worse from happening in the family?"

- **Actions** These are behaviors that can be communicated with verbs. An individual can increase self-awareness by becoming aware of actions. Sitting, smiling, talking, shifting eye contact, listening, shouting, initiating, waiting, breathing, and walking are examples of actions that are related to the individual's feelings, intentions, thoughts, and senses. When the clinician begins to track interactional sequences, focusing on actions is helpful because family members often move quickly to their subjective experience before weighing the facts related to another's actions:

THERAPIST: Tell me exactly what happened.

CLIENT: He was trying to get me to do his homework for him. [statement of assumption: thoughts]

THERAPIST: No, I mean what was he actually doing when you had that thought?

CLIENT: Well, I guess he was sitting on the couch, watching TV. [sensory data: "I saw him sitting."]

THERAPIST: What else was he doing that made you think he was trying to get you to do his homework for him? [asking for more sensory data to inform assumptions]

CLIENT: He doesn't have to do anything else! He knows that if he hasn't already started working on his homework before I get home, I will do it when I come in! [statement of assumption: thoughts]

THERAPIST: Now, how do you think he knows that?

CLIENT: He knows because I've told him time and time again that I want his homework done before I get home so that I won't have to worry about it. [action and feeling statement: I tell him because I will worry.]

THERAPIST: So, aside from what your son may think, you have a desire that you put into action when you walk through the door. Is that right?

CLIENT: Yes, I want to know if he's done his homework, and if he hasn't, I want him to get busy right then. [statement of intention]

THERAPIST: Is this pretty predictable behavior for you? I mean, does it happen nearly every night?

CLIENT: Well, lately, yes, because he's been getting so bad. [statement of perception: senses]

THERAPIST: Well, we might want to start by seeing if we can help you to become more "unpredictable" in your son's eyes! Sometimes, surprising behaviors help kids change their minds about things.

Taken together, the five elements of self-awareness represent the individual as a system of interrelated parts. These parts interact with each other to form an individual's contribution to a relationship, regardless of whether the relationship is with self or others. Interactional patterns consist of sequences that use all five elements:

ACTIONS: Wife is fixing dinner in the kitchen.

SENSES: She notices her husband coming up the driveway.

THOUGHTS: "She wonders if he's still thinking about the argument they had this morning."

INTENTIONS: "She hopes he isn't still mad at her."

FEELINGS: "She's afraid he won't be happy."

ACTIONS: Husband comes in the door. He is frowning.

FEELINGS: He is tired and embarrassed about a traffic ticket just issued to him on the way home.

INTENTIONS: He wants to save face; he wants his wife to think well of him.

SENSES: Wife sees his frown.

ACTIONS: She asks, "Are you still mad about this morning?"

THOUGHTS: He thinks, "She's criticizing me and belittling my feelings."

ACTIONS: Husband says, "Why do you always think you can read my mind?"

By paying attention to all five dimensions of experience, the clinician is able to track a sequence while also understanding the individual's experience as it evolves in the interaction. Then, as the therapist helps the couple clarify and accept both partner's emotions, the couple is able to increase intimacy by understanding each other's intentions and emotions—especially their particular sensitivities. If each person had begun his or her part of the interaction with a statement of intent (e.g., "I want you to be happy" or "I want your approval"), or with a statement of feelings (e.g., "I'm afraid" or "I'm embarrassed"), the interaction might have taken a different turn. When family members feel most vulnerable, their intent is to protect themselves from anticipated psychological or emotional hurt.

The five dimensions of the awareness wheel are also useful with social construction models that focus on communication and personal belief systems. These new theoretical frameworks have been greatly influenced by theorists such as Jean Piaget (1952), George Kelly (1963), and Kenneth Gergen (1985, 1994). They posit that personal belief systems (thoughts) are an evolving set of meanings that continue to emerge from interactions (actions) between people. However, unlike traditional psychologists, who view the individual as a reactive being, the social constructionist asserts that personal meaning (beliefs) derives from the individual's perception (feelings and intentions) of what occurs in interactions with others (Mahoney, 1991). For example, a young unattached man might characterize himself as "weak" and "independent" because he has neglected those aspects of his life that are incongruent with his self-image of helplessness. The individual may have ignored times when he was able to overcome his helplessness (exceptions). Likewise, in his interactions with the members of his family, he may allow them to describe him as helpless, which likely influences the way they interact with him. In this case, personal narratives become an internalized set of conversations ("I must depend on others for help") that are consistent with our behavior (acting in ways that elicit help from others). Thus, for social constructionists, the meaning that family members attribute to an event determines member behavior. For constructivists, there is always the opportunity for each member to entertain a different view.

The work of Milton Erickson is related to this view, but Erickson's influence brought a new understanding of the unconscious. For Erickson, the unconscious was an untapped reservoir of positive resources, not a complex stockpile of repressed anguish (Erickson & Rossi, 1979). As he put his own belief system into operation, he was able to help his patients begin to use their perceived deficits as strengths and assets. Some of his techniques relevant to the practice of family therapy are reviewed later in this book. Although both the terms constructivist and social constructionist were not widely used in family therapy literature until the later 1980s, Erickson could be considered one. Evidence of his work being similar to these orientations can be seen in the way he views the formation of individual or family problems:

> Patients have problems because of learned limitations. They are caught in mental sets, frames of reference, and belief systems that do not permit them to explore and utilize their own abilities to best advantage. Human beings are still in the process of learning to use their potentials. The therapeutic transaction ideally creates a new phenomenal world in which patients can explore their potentials, freed to some extent from their learned limitations. . . . As the therapist explores the patient's world and facilitates rapport, it is almost inevitable that new frames of reference and belief systems are created. This usually happens whenever people meet and interact closely. (Erickson & Rossi, 1979, p. 2)

Thus, Erickson considered a critical factor in problem formation to be the importance of the patient's belief system and the meaning attributed to the on-going flow of the person's life. He then paid particular attention to the dialogues he shared with clients as a part of problem resolution.

An intergenerational approach that addresses personal beliefs in a slightly different way is the contextual family therapy of Ivan Boszormenyi-Nagy (Boszormenyi-Nagy & Krasner, 1986). In this approach, exploring a person's beliefs about the give-and-take in relationships helps the clinician understand how an individual experiences fairness and equity within the family. These family therapists suggest that human beings carry a subjective family ledger consisting of personal beliefs about how much they have contributed to family members and how much they are entitled to receive in return. According to Boszormenyi-Nagy and Krasner (1986), this concept of relational ethics is based on the premise that there is an innate sense of justice or fairness that exists within people. This approach proposes that dysfunction occurs within families when relational imbalances lead to a lack of trustworthiness or the development of "destructive entitlements" that involve individual symptoms (actions) developed in response to beliefs (thoughts) about unfairness within the family.

Attachment

With the growing interest in emotionally focused couples therapy, Bowlby's (1969) theories of attachment, separation, and loss have been revisited by an increasing number of family therapists. Attachment is considered an inborn process that promotes the survival of infants by prompting them to seek closeness and communication with caregivers. When attachment is secure, parental responses are emotionally sensitive to the child's nonverbal (and later, verbal) communications. To the extent that these interactions are soothing, the child develops a safe haven, referred to as a *secure base*. Adults continue attachment by seeking out connection with others during times of stress or anxiety. This tendency toward connection versus isolation is categorized in children as secure, avoidant, ambivalent, or disorganized attachment style. These are related to various parenting styles, patterns of intimacy between couples, and even response styles in the doctor's office and the therapy room (Johnson & Whiffen, 1999). Thus, there is a wide range of relevance in assessing quality of attachment. Siegel (1999) described the type of questions used in the assessment of attachment. Examples of such questions include the following:

- What was the person's early relationship with parents like?
- What was the experience of being separated, upset, threatened, or fearful?
- What was the impact of any loss upon the person and family?
- How did the person's relationship with parents change over time?
- How have these factors shaped the person's adult development and parenting practices?

In addition, EFT addresses attachment by tracking sequences with a couple and alternating questions that elicit the nature of their attachment. These questions can include a combination of elements from the awareness wheel:

- So, when he shuts you out, what is it like for you?
- I noticed you throw up your hands. Is that like helplessness?
- What would happen if you told her you're afraid of losing her?
- When you shake your head, are you saying how hopeless you feel?
- When you hear him saying that, what happens to you?

WHEN TO FOCUS ON INDIVIDUAL EXPERIENCE

Although many family therapy models address behavioral change before perceptual change, cases that do not respond to behavioral interventions most likely need a greater focus on personal dynamics that might be restraining behavioral change. Therefore, cases in which behavioral interventions are not successful can benefit from a shift to an exploration of personal dynamics (self-esteem, self-awareness, personal beliefs, or feelings of entitlement). In addition, when the joining process seems stalemated or the practitioner begins to notice subtle power struggles with clients, it is very important for the practitioner to step back from the normal operating procedure and explore personal dynamics to understand and affirm clients' beliefs about their process and about the process between therapist and the clients.

Too often, clinicians forget to focus on their own personal dynamics:

- How is my work related to my own self-esteem?
- Am I aware of my own hidden agenda, which might be incongruent with what my client has stated are his or her priorities?
- Do I have certain beliefs that could lead me to harbor critical or condescending views of my client?
- Is my sense of entitlement such that I pursue unrealistic goals for my client in family therapy?

A focus on individual motivations on both sides of the therapy experience often helps the clinician develop goals and expectations that match the developmental level of the family.

Focusing on individual dynamics is also important when the client goal is more process-oriented than problem-oriented (e.g., "I need help getting over the death of my daughter"). When the client goal is related more to coping, growth, or adjustment to some transition, focusing on individual dynamics also fits better with client expectations of the therapy experience.

Implications for Treatment

Although many models of family therapy have de-emphasized traditional Freudian views of individual psychodynamics, all models use some newer understanding of personal dynamics. Whether it is the structural therapist joining with the family, the strategic therapist looking for a directive that the client will accept, or the intergenerational therapist who seeks to help family members with unfinished business, the ability to understand personal dynamics is a clinical imperative in the practice of family therapy.

Falloon (1991) takes a strong position by suggesting that the individual goals of every family member should be targets for treatment:

> At times, these goals may be highly personal and inappropriate for intergenerational problem solving. For example, the resolution of sexual difficulties between parents, obsessive-compulsive rumination, or prophylactic drug therapy for schizophrenia. Such problems may be addressed in an individual or a marital context, where this seems most appropriate. (p. 79)

Increasing evidence seems to suggest that individually oriented strategies work best within a systemic framework. This is particularly so when the presenting problem involves major mental disorders, such as phobia, severe depression, or schizophrenia (Falloon, 1991).

Regarding the continuum of macroconcepts and microconcepts of family process, an emphasis on microdynamics facilitates therapeutic effectiveness as a complement to all other levels of assessment. By starting with a larger view of life and evolving to an exploration of personal dynamics, family therapists are able to fluctuate between macropositions that minimize personal shame and blame and micropositions that liberate clients to think of themselves and their relationships in new ways.

SUMMARY

Each conceptual theme presented in this chapter can be thought of as a different reality or lens from which to view families who seek treatment. Each perspective has its own set of issues and questions that range from larger societal views of human problems to smaller dissections of personal and interpersonal process. The beginning family therapist can learn flexibility by using different lenses to view panoramas or get to the heart of a matter, depending on the client's needs and the type of problem. Taken individually, each lens provides a sense of direction that is informed by theories of family functioning and social process. Sluzki (1992), drawing from narrative ideas, makes these observations about how any given model becomes a catalyst for effective family therapy:

> In order for new stories . . . to consolidate themselves in the therapeutic conversation, they must evolve from and yet contain elements of the old, "familiar" stories. The transformed stories are usually a recombination of the components of the old story to which new elements—characters, plot, logic, moral order—have been introduced either by the therapist, by the patient, or by the family. . . . (p. 220)

Chapter 4 explores common themes of practice that have developed in the field. In contrast to theories about families that center on gender, race, culture, transitions, and organization, practice themes center on theories of change as they relate to the therapeutic process as well as on factors associated with positive therapeutic outcomes. Family therapists often continue their tradition of innovation by adding other modes of thinking quite apart from family theories. With the same spirit of discovery that led us through innovation, integration, and consolidation, we now look at common themes of practice that have led marriage and family therapists to the forefront of creative and inspiring successes in their work.

Integration of Practice: Common Themes

CHAPTER **4**

CHAPTER OUTLINE

The Therapeutic Relationship: Joining

Developing an Alliance

Honoring the Client's Worldview

Highlighting Family Strengths

Instilling Hope

Reframing Resistance

The Self of the Therapist: Reflecting

Maintaining Flexibility

Troubleshooting the Therapist-Client Relationship

Tips for Self-Development

Summary

CORE COMPETENCIES

1.3.6 **Executive** Establish and maintain appropriate and productive therapeutic alliances with the clients.

1.3.7 **Executive** Solicit and use client feedback throughout the therapeutic process.

2.3.8 **Executive** Identify clients' strengths, resilience, and resources.

4.4.6 **Evaluative** Evaluate reactions to the treatment process (e.g., transference, family of origin, current stress level, current life situation, cultural context) and their impact on effective intervention and clinical outcomes.

Historically, family therapists focused on the interactional context related to the problem. Practitioners who emphasized the role of the family considered the goal to be the treatment of mental illnesses such as schizophrenia, as well as relationship change, and the treatment of choice was the involvement of family members with the symptomatic person. This placed the therapist in a traditional doctor-patient relationship but with a more active, directive role than typified traditional psychoanalysis, which encouraged the therapist to remain aloof and detached. As we showed in Chapters 1 and 2, family therapists continued to change the way they thought about the therapeutic relationship. Increasingly, they considered each encounter as an opportunity to develop egalitarian, collaborative working relationships in which both parties brought their individual expertise to bear upon the task at hand—that of solving problems. From this perspective, families are considered experts on their own experience, with special understanding about the complexity that comes from life's dilemmas. They teach practitioners about their culture and worldview. They know best what fits for them. Therapists are considered experts on the process of change and the type of process that might fit the family, given the family's unique circumstances. Together, the family and practitioner evolve a relationship, each dependent upon the contribution of the other for desired outcomes to occur.

Thus, the practice of family therapy has evolved from doctor-patient, to therapist-client, and now consultant-consultee. Early and integrative models of family therapy have a collection of elements that teach therapists to develop a *positive and productive relationship* with all clients, no matter how challenging these clients may be. Research has also continuously shown that the therapeutic relationship is one of the most critical factors in the effectiveness of outpatient psychotherapy (Hubble, Duncan, & Miller, 1999; Pinsof & Catherall, 1986). It is a key factor that is given priority in all models of family therapy, and the beginning practitioner must consider the development of this relationship as a top priority. To develop an authentic therapeutic relationship, practitioners must pay attention to their beliefs, values, worldviews, and coping styles. These personal attributes are often referred to as the *self of the therapist*. When these clash with any client, the chances of being helpful are limited. This chapter reviews how family therapists engage in the therapeutic relationship and how they foster personal growth in the self of the therapist. These elements form a bridge between the personal and professional sides of our practice.

THE THERAPEUTIC RELATIONSHIP: JOINING

First used by Minuchin (1974) as he developed structural family therapy, joining is probably the most universal—or the most borrowed—of family therapy terms. Not surprisingly, the personal rapport or empathy that therapists develop with those they are trying to help remains the single most proven variable determining the effectiveness of psychotherapy (Garfield & Bergin, 1978).

However, when a family therapist begins to grapple with this process within a larger systemic framework, the number of people involved may make this a significant challenge. Minuchin and Fishman (1981) view joining as an attitude:

> Joining a family is more an attitude than a technique, and it is the umbrella under which all therapeutic transactions occur. Joining is letting the family know that the therapist understands them and is working with and for them. Only under this protection can the family have the security to explore alternatives, try the unusual, and change. Joining is the glue that holds the therapeutic system together. (pp. 31–32)

This process begins with the first family contact and continues as the foundation for effective family therapy. Rather than an event, it is more a process of understanding and building rapport with each member of the family. Whereas some family members may be more central than others, an understanding of all members is often necessary if family therapists are to be successful. General psychotherapy models share the goals of empathy and positive regard for clients; however, family therapy integrates these goals with systemic thinking. The result is a type of *systemic empathy,* in which the clinician is able to identify and describe the unique roles and dilemmas experienced by each family member.

Thus, the joining process can best be conceptualized as an interactional pattern that is repetitive throughout the entire course of family therapy. When a family therapist first becomes acquainted with the family, a certain formal stage may exist, but ongoing sequences of therapy require an understanding that is continually expanded as new information challenges the original perceptions of therapist and client alike. Therefore, it is helpful to think of joining as a *characteristic that pervades all other stages of the therapy process.* At any time, the therapist is either well joined or poorly joined. The following list explains how different elements of the family therapy process contribute to the family therapist's ability to join with family members:

- Questions regarding the importance of ethnicity help family therapists join when they respond with an appreciation of the family's language, customs, heritage, or beliefs.
- Transitional mapping helps a family therapist join through identification of a family member's age, empathy with the family's stage of life, or understanding of the dilemmas the family faced with various transitions.
- Genograms (described in Chapter 7) help a family therapist join through a recognition of significant family members who may not be present in the session. Their nicknames, circumstances, and impact on present family members can lead the family therapist into the client's private world.
- Structural and strategic approaches help a family therapist join through assessing the family's hierarchy and making sure that those in authority are sufficiently engaged.
- Contextual family therapy encourages *multidirected partiality,* which is the art of consecutively siding with and showing an understanding of each member's position in order to develop trust and fairness in relationships (Bernal & Flores-Ortiz, 1991).

- Ericksonian and constructivist approaches are often noted for encouraging humor, playfulness, and creativity. Also, they view resistance in a positive light—as a helpful message about the client's uniqueness.

Although this is not an exhaustive list of elements, the descriptions are meant to stimulate the reader's creativity to find spontaneous and endearing ways of relating to family members that will contribute to trust and rapport. Many family therapists find it useful to join through the use of metaphoric comparisons from the client's world. Metaphors can tap into the client's worldview by using the client's language related to her or his interests. For example, a therapist who routinely obtains a genogram and a relationship history provides a rationale to each client for the necessity of such information gathering. A young couple who likes to go boating was provided this rationale for an assessment:

> In order for me to help you, it is important for me to get to know you and understand something about the important people and events in your life. Couple therapy is often like teaching someone how to sail. By gathering information on your extended family, I learn something about what kind of boat you each have—from the type of sail that it has, to its size and shape. Your families equip you with many skills for sailing through the waters of life. In addition, some of the experiences you have with your families help you to develop certain strengths in areas as you meet similar challenges along the way. By learning about your relationship history, I learn something about the weather conditions that you have sailed through in the past and in the present. In addition, the direction of the wind and the speed of the currents are important for the sailor to know about. A good sailor must learn to take many different factors into account while planning the journey. Once I understand something about the gusts of wind in your life and the many directions that your boats have taken you, I can help you to fine-tune your sailing skills for the current waters and your future life together. Your present complaint is likely to be a result of a coincidence between several of these elements, just as a storm might come up in the water and you must struggle to learn and master some new sailing technique.

In this example, the therapist took into consideration the couple's stage in the life cycle; this was a young couple in the first stage of married life. If the couple had been married 20 years, a different metaphor might have been more appropriate. A later stage in the life cycle would suggest that these people have been struggling with the same problems for a longer time. In that case, what they may need is some new way to address their conflict, if the old ways had not worked in 20 years. A more appropriate metaphor for such a couple might involve a new mode of transport: learning to canoe or deciding to take the train.

In an interesting study conducted at an agency emphasizing solution-focused brief therapy, researchers found that the espoused model had little to do with clients' reported experience (Metcalf, Thomas, Duncan, Miller, & Hubble, 1996). Miller, Duncan, and Hubble (1997) describe their final results:

> While therapists tended to attribute therapeutic success to the use of solution-focused techniques (e.g., specialized interviewing techniques, miracle quesions), the clients consistently reported a strong therapeutic relationship as the critical factor

in treatment outcome (e.g., therapist acceptance, non-possessive warmth, positive regard, affirmation, and self-disclosure). (p. 85)

The therapeutic relationship must be emphasized as a critical factor that organizes integration. As beginning family therapists analyze their process with clients, they should continually ask, "How will my position contribute to a positive relationship *from the client's point of view*?" Using our developmental model, the ABCs of joining are (a) developing an alliance (b) highlighting family strengths, (c) instilling hope, and (d) reframing resistance.

Developing an Alliance

The methods therapists use to join with a family are often just beyond their conscious awareness and appear to be much like those used in ordinary interpersonal relationships. The past few decades of pop culture have produced several expressions to describe the phenomenon—the slang expressions "on the same wavelength," "in the same groove," and "on the same track" all refer to joining. Family therapists place a high priority on being attentive and responsive to family members. Connecting with them is both an attitude and a skill. To connect with the family, the family therapist must convey *acceptance* of family members and *respect* for their way of seeing and doing things. It is critical to *validate* each family member and *acknowledge* his or her experience and effort. The therapist must let family members know that they are understood and their views are important. In addition to using the strengths from each model of family therapy, the following tips can be used to help the therapist join with family members:

- **Greet each member of the family by name and make friendly contact with each.** Ask each member about work, school, extended family, the place where he or she lives, and so on.
- **Respect family leadership and caregivers.** The therapist must begin with parents or caregivers when asking each member about his or her view of the problem.
- **Acknowledge each member's experience, position, and actions.** ("So, Ms. Brown, you think your son ran away because he was angry at you.")
- **Normalize experiences, views, and actions.** ("It is common for people in this situation to feel the way you do.")
- **Validate positive things you can say about a family member whenever possible.** ("Ms. Jones, I know you have tried your best to help your son. It shows how much you care about him.") Reinforcing or validating a family member will often confirm that individual and help other members to view the problem differently.

In some cases, the therapist may join with the family by connecting with one of its members. This process is called *selective joining* (Colapinto, 1991). The therapist may often choose to affiliate with the most peripheral member in the family; or in some cases, the therapist will make special efforts through using similar language and tone of voice to get closer to the family member who will most likely influence the outcome of family therapy. Boyd-Franklin (1989) has wisely pointed out that African American families often rely on their own perception of "vibes" given off by the therapist. This nonverbal and subjective element in the interaction will influence their level of trust versus mistrust in therapy. We can see that vibes are related to the level of candor, authenticity, and acknowledgment of the unique challenges of another racial or ethnic group.

When Boszormenyi-Nagy (1966) developed the strategy of multidirected partiality, one of his goals was to address the challenge of connecting with each member of the family. In his work, he systematically interacted with each family member in order to understand each position and to communicate that understanding for each member to ratify or clarify. As he did so, he was able to gain a clear picture of what each member thought about the presenting problem and what issues might become obstacles to change. In working with entire family groups or networks from the larger community, the skill of connecting with each member of the system will become a trademark of the evolving family therapist. To accomplish this, curiosity about the client's theory of change is often a critical component for success.

Honoring the Client's Worldview

Recent research highlights the importance of therapists honoring the client's view of the change process. This is a vital part of the client's worldview. Duncan and Miller (2000) suggest that client worldviews consist of ideas and opinions they bring into therapy about the nature of the problem, its cause, possible solutions, and the role of therapy in the process. Within these views lies the basis by which clients judge therapist credibility and treatment success. For example, Hayes and Wall (1998) found that treatment success was strongly related to a match between how client and therapist thought about who is responsible for the problem. The challenge for beginning practitioners is to suspend their personal views while they learn to understand and work from the client's point of view. We do not think of this as agreement. Instead, we see the client's theory of change to be similar to a person's body measurements if we were tailors or dressmakers. We gather measurements to make the best fit possible. Our own body measurements are irrelevant in the process, unless we make the mistake of trying our own clothes on the client! Instead, family therapists would assess who in the family is most influential to the change process and who is the customer for change. Then, using circular questions, we would explore their theories about change. Duncan and Miller (2000) offer these helpful questions:

- What ideas do you have about what needs to happen for improvement to occur?
- Many times people have a pretty good hunch not only about what is causing a problem, but also about what will resolve it. Do you have a theory of how change is going to happen here?

- In what ways do you see me and this process as helpful to attaining your goals? (p. 84)

In addition, these authors warn us to see the client's attitude about change as one that evolves *with* the therapist. Thus, these explorations begin the matching process but do not immediately produce a silver bullet. Instead, they generate "conversation structured by the therapist's curiosity about the client's ideas, attitudes, and speculations about change" (p. 84). These conversations become a foundation for the therapeutic alliance. It has been suggested that when assessing the client's worldview, the therapist might take notes in order to record the client's language and track her or his line of thinking. These therapists show their notes to the client and offer the client a copy if desired (collaboration). By carefully using client language to construct goals, family therapists can keep the process client-centered rather than therapist-centered. As these notes are taken, the clinician can also highlight important information about family strengths in spite of the severity of the problem (Karpel, 1986; Henggeler et al., 1998; Zeig & Lankton, 1998).

Highlighting Family Strengths

A good relationship with the family is not only characterized by having empathy, understanding problems, and honoring the worldviews of others, but also how the practitioner highlights family strengths. Knowledge of family strengths will help the therapist understand how families cope with problems and how they promote growth and development. Assessing a family as having virtues—rather than adopting a deficit (problem) model—gives the family hope that it can solve its own problems. Although this might seem obvious to most clinicians, it is frequently overlooked when family therapists become more intent on solving the family's problem than on developing a good relationship with the family. Focusing on the family's deficits without considering its strengths makes it difficult to establish a relationship where both the therapist and the family can be optimistic about change. Thus, careful use of language, deliberate explorations looking for strengths, acknowledging good intentions, and recognizing small steps of change are important factors in a strength-based approach.

Using Positive Language. Most family therapists use language that describes and labels competencies in clients. For example, Michael White (1986) suggests that clients are experts on themselves. This attitude emphasizes client strengths and downplays the authority of the therapist. Brief therapists such as O'Hanlon (1987) elaborated on the Ericksonian technique of looking for exceptions. For example, a brief therapist, after listening to a description of the presenting problem, might ask the client to describe the times when things are going well. This exemplifies the practice of competency-based treatment in which strengths and successes are systematically investigated as a central element in the treatment process. More traditionally, this same element was

found in early models of family therapy. Minuchin and Fishman (1981) outlined their own emphasis on client strengths as they integrated their values
with other leaders in the field:

> In every family there are positives. Positives are transmitted from the family of ori-
> gin to the new family, and from there to the next generation. Despite mistakes,
> unhappiness, and pain, there are also pleasures: spouses and children give to each
> other in ways that are growth-encouraging and supportive, contributing to each
> other's sense of competence and worth.... The orientation of family therapists
> toward "constructing a reality" that highlights deficits is therefore being chal-
> lenged. Family therapists are finding that an exploration of strengths is essential to
> challenge family dysfunctions. The work of Virginia Satir, with its emphasis on
> growth, is oriented toward a search for normal alternatives. So is the work of Ivan
> Nagy [Boszormenyi-Nagy], with its emphasis on positive connotations and his
> exploration of the family value system. Carl Whitaker's technique of challenging
> the positions of family members and introducing role diffusion springs from his be-
> lief that out of this therapeutically induced chaos the family member can discover
> latent strength. Jay Haley and Chloe Madanes' view that the symptom is organized
> to protect the family and Mara Selvini Palazzoli's paradoxical interventions all
> point toward family strengths. (p. 268)

In a different way, Whitaker (1982) considered the goals of family therapy
to be an increased sense of competency and self-worth. Symptoms were considered an attempt toward growth. Although each model executed this objective in
a different way, the practice of using positive language became the norm in family therapy. This approach is a key element found in all models.

Discovering Successes.   Focusing on the family's strengths and resources
contributes to the development of self-confidence, inspires hope, and enhances
growth within the family. Each family has unique strengths that can be buried
or forgotten. The therapist must explore and probe to discover these strengths.
Family members must be encouraged to discuss how they have coped with
problems. The following guidelines will help beginning clinicians to join with
the family by identifying the family's strengths:

- Emphasize positive statements reported by family members (e.g., "My
  mother listens to me when I have a problem"). Observing behaviors that
  reflect sensitivity, appreciation, or cooperation between family members is
  also important.
- Encourage family members to share stories about themselves. Spend extra
  time discussing those aspects of their stories that reveal how the family has
  coped successfully with problems.
- Note family interactions that reflect strength and competency (e.g., "I like
  the way you help your daughter find her own answers to the problem").
  Underscoring positive family interactions helps the interviewer to identify
  other strengths and competencies.
- Investigate times that family members enjoy together. What are they
  doing? What makes these experiences enjoyable? These questions offer
  opportunities to discuss strengths and capabilities.

- Reframe problems or negative statements in a more positive way (e.g., "Your anger shows how much you worry about him"). Reframing consists of changing the conceptual or emotional viewpoint so as to change the meaning of the problem without changing the facts—in other words, the situation doesn't change, but the interpretation does.
- Emphasize what families do well. All families have areas of strength (such as patience, certain skills, and coping behavior). By asking questions, the therapist can learn how families utilize these strengths to solve problems (e.g., "What works best with your child?" "Tell me about the times you were able to get him to _____. What did you do?" "How were you able to get him to _____?" "What does that say about your ability to get him to do that in the future?").

Acknowledging Effort, Caring, and Intent.   In addition, when family therapists have difficulty perceiving client competencies, a positive relationship can still include attention to positives. Using the analogy of whether the glass is half full or half empty, a beginning practitioner should always be prepared to see the glass as half full by commenting on the effort, sense of caring, and good intentions of family members. For example, the practitioner might try to interpret the family's definition of the problem in a different way, to give it new meaning. This new interpretation helps the family members get in touch with their own strengths. When a mother says, "I can't get him to do anything; he won't listen to me," the therapist shifts the focus to what she does out of her sense of "caring." If this makes it difficult for her to set firm limits, the therapist then can help her expand her sense of caring to include additional behaviors. The Milan team referred to this as *positive connotation*. Milton Erickson referred to this as bypassing a person's *learned limitations*. When the mother perceives herself as caring, rather than weak, she has a new way of thinking about the problem that lowers her defenses. When the therapist creates an environment based on strengths, family members are more likely to set goals that they can meet successfully.

MST (Cunningham & Henggeler, 1999) suggests that parents can always be validated for being part of the solution, regardless of their part in the identified problem:

> The therapist should strive to find "evidence" of client effort and improvement and positively reinforce such, regardless of how small. For example, a client should be reinforced for attending sessions, giving his or her best, and so on. During the initial phase of treatment, Maggie's mother felt considerable apprehension, frustration, and hopelessness. The therapist reminded the mother that she was making important progress in helping her daughter by meeting with the therapist and helping to plan for changes. (p. 29)

However, these authors warn that a focus on strengths need not be a Pollyanna approach. Instead, this focus can be a realistic assessment of challenges coupled with attention to the smallest attempts at improvement, regardless of their success. Sometimes those who are feeling discouraged just need to know that others recognize their good intentions and persistence. These efforts often reveal small steps of change.

Recognizing Small Steps of Change.   Miller, Duncan, and Hubble (1997) provide an excellent summary of how a therapist might be more aware of these very important factors. Their suggestions include "listening for and validating client change whenever and for whatever reason it occurs during the treatment process . . . highlighting the contribution to change made by the client . . ." (p. 80).

These suggestions can be seen operating in many integrative approaches to family therapy and reflect the growing trend that we have observed in which family therapists attend to the natural resources of the client. These resources may be (a) significant relationships or events, (b) daily routines or hobbies, (c) a history of challenges and successes, or (d) detailed descriptions of what life is like when family relationships are going well. Because many therapy services are offered outside the family's natural world, it is important for the family therapist to obtain a clear picture of life outside the therapy room. People, places, activities, thoughts, etc., are all important resources to ask about, especially as they contribute positively to the self-esteem of the client.

A good example of this direction comes from solution-focused models that adopt the following assumptions:

- Families have resources and strengths to resolve problems.
- Families are often aware of alternative ways to resolve a problem.
- Families will be more likely to implement a solution to the problem if they suggest it.

If therapists start treatment according to these assumptions, they can lead the discussion to focus on those areas that are working. The therapist will want to start by looking for small positive changes before examining bigger changes. When family members are able to make small positive changes, they are more hopeful about handling bigger changes (O'Hanlon & Weiner-Davis, 1989). This positive approach can be achieved by focusing on those aspects of the family that seem most changeable:

- What would be a small sign that things are changing?
- What might be one thing you could do to change?
- What are some things you could do now to handle the problem?

The therapist will also want to focus on times when the problem is not occurring:

1. When are you able to handle the problem?
2. Are there times when the problem isn't occurring?
3. What are you doing differently in these situations?
4. What seems to be different when things are going well?

Understanding when family members are able to manage the problem helps them get in touch with their strengths and resources. Because family members often feel hopeless, putting them in charge of deciding on changes (goals) is important. The clinician can also instill hope.

Instilling Hope

Repeated studies show that 40 percent of the variance in psychotherapy outcome is related to client attributes and factors outside the therapy process, 30 percent is related to the therapeutic relationship, 15 percent is related to the client's sense of hope, and another 15 percent is related to specific techniques and models of the therapist (Bergin & Garfield, 1994; Lambert & Bergin, 1994). Thus, amid this formula for success, increasing the sense of hope is an important function of the therapeutic relationship. The Milan team suggests that the therapist's stance should be "hopeful and curious" (Tomm, 1984). The therapist manifests these traits primarily through voice inflection, conveying positive intent, and conveying interest in what the family says. In MST, Cunningham and Henggeler (1999) borrow the term *gift giving* from Sue and Zane (1987) as a universal strategy.

Gift Giving.   This occurs when the therapist provides the client with some immediate and direct benefit, such as normalization of feelings, guilt reduction, and an understanding of the complexity of problems. Especially in the beginning stage of treatment, this practice provides relief, hope, and motivation to continue in the process. Examples of gift giving include statements such as:

- I'm amazed at how well you're coping with such a complicated problem. A lot of people in the same situation would have given up by now.
- I can see that you blame yourself for some of these problems, but I think you sell yourself short. I think you've done the best you could do under the circumstances. My role is to help you find some relief from some of your stresses so you'll have more energy. I know you don't want to give up on your son.
- You might be surprised to know how many people have the same challenges you do. These days, life can be hard for good parents who are just trying to survive. Many parents lose their temper when they don't mean to. That doesn't make them bad parents.
- I can see you really care about your daughter. If you didn't, you wouldn't be here. There are a lot of things I'll need to learn from you in order to understand how I can help. I'm looking forward to working with you.

Exploring Possibilities.   O'Hanlon (1999) calls his recent work *possibility therapy* to emphasize his focus upon positive possibilities. He describes possibilities as existing primarily in the future, but also finds positive possibilities in the past and present. His future orientation is one that uses careful language to help clients live in the future and to imagine the future that they desire. For example, when the clinician asks about exceptions to the problem and the family identifies one, client and clinician can explore in detail what life might be like if that exception was repeated. As these descriptions of the future unfold, the clinician identifies small steps of action that can be pursued in the present. If a family member stays focused on past events, the clinician might look for opportunities to offer a different interpretation of the events as the story is re-told. The new view might focus on the client's strengths and determination, or give credit for what the family has accomplished in spite of hardship. As small steps of action emerge as small steps of success, family members gain trust in the process and develop self-confidence and hope.

As practitioners gain experience developing therapeutic relationships, their journey of discovery will also contain small steps of action that lead to a sense of confidence and success. Because people are wonderfully unique and resilient, challenges to the relationship are often our best teachers. No clinician can be prepared to relate successfully to all people. The best preparation for beginning therapists is to embrace the element of surprise. On this journey of discovery, those who surprise us the most will be the most memorable and the most interesting, if we are open to the adventure. On the road to a positive and productive therapeutic relationship, the clinician must consider those cases that do surprise and challenge our abilities. Rather than blame or judge those clients for our challenges, think of traditional notions of resistance in more human, egalitarian ways.

Reframing Resistance

The term *resistance* has become a cliché in the field of psychotherapy. Most often, it connotes the client's lack of cooperation with the practitioner or a lack of progress in treatment. However, in family therapy, there is a strong bias toward the notion that resistance is an *interactional event* characterized by the professional's lack of understanding about what is important to the family. For example, battered women are often considered "resistant" when they fail to follow professional advice that places physical safety above psychological safety. Although agreement about the importance of physical safety as a human right is widespread, professionals are frequently guilty of blaming the innocent when they label clients as resistant or stubborn without understand-ing the history that has influenced their beliefs about themselves, others, and the world around them. Our observation is that in many difficult cases involv-ing elder abuse, domestic violence, and child sexual abuse, distinct perceptual patterns have a significant influence on the behavioral patterns that develop in family life. Thus, it is incumbent on family therapists to understand the unique thought processes of clients rather than to label them resistant or stubborn. As a therapist's skill develops in this area, client resistance diminishes.

It may be difficult to join with a family in which members manifest char-acteristics different from the therapist's (e.g., parents who abuse their children) or show hostile or detached behavior. These challenges are understandable and can usually be overcome by highlighting principles of Milton Erickson. He developed a process called *utilization* to address this issue (Erickson & Rossi, 1979). He learned to use, rather than challenge, a person's way of relating. For

Positive Connotation.   During a therapeutic impasse, one way to address family process is to search for a *positive connotation* to some element of the problem. For example, Selvini Palazzoli et al. (1978) describe a ten-year-old boy who exhibited psychotic symptoms following the death of his grandfather. At the end of the first session, the therapist told the boy that he was "doing a good thing" (p. 81). The therapist further noted that the grandfather was a "central pillar of the family" and kept the family together. The boy was told that he had assumed his grandfather's role to maintain balance in the family and that he should continue this role until the next session. In this case, the therapist used positive connotation to maintain homeostasis in the family rather than to challenge the behavior. The boy had taken the grandfather's place to maintain a gender balance in a family that, following the grandfather's death, was predominantly female. As this example illustrates, the use of positive connotation allows the therapist to join with the family at a time of crisis and to understand the problem in light of complicated systemic dynamics. Understanding these subtitles often requires clinicians to pursue personal growth and insight at several different levels.

THE SELF OF THE THERAPIST: REFLECTING

With respect to the therapeutic relationship, the most important knowledge a practitioner can have about family therapy might be that most models fail to supply. For example, many approaches fail to include a discussion of ethical considerations. All marital and family therapists should have a working knowledge of professional codes of ethics. Those published by the American Association for Marriage and Family Therapy (AAMFT) (2001) and the National Association of Social Workers (NASW) are included in Appendices A and B. Brock (1997) has also developed a questionnaire that helps family therapists assess their vulnerability for ethical violations (Appendix C).

Given these tools, practitioners should still become aware of how issues might emerge differently with different approaches. If a client is hesitant to involve certain family members, how does the clinician work systemically without becoming coercive? When seeing couples, what is the marital therapist's responsibility for confidentiality in the event that each partner is seen alone? These are examples of questions that are commonly addressed in many family therapy programs. The nature of ethical issues in family therapy can be different from that found in other professions because family therapists value working with relationships and consider the importance of the relational network closest to the problem. Because of this dimension, discussions . . . regarding . . . a code of ethics are important for all family therapists.

In addition to the application of ethical principles, all therapists should monitor their levels of stress and the emotional impact of their daily work. As Brock's assessment suggests, family therapy can have an unintended effect upon the well-being of the therapist and personal crises can have an unintended effect upon therapeutic work. The interplay of personal and professional stresses must be monitored continuously as part of professional development. These stresses can also be managed by developing a set of therapeutic attributes that lowers stress and makes the work rewarding and enjoyable.

continues regarding which attributes are essential to the
change, the general consensus is that certain personal
enhance therapeutic effectiveness. Here, we present a vari-
ectives on these qualities.

kton, Lankton, and Matthews (1991) suggest the following four therapist characteristics:

- A great pragmatic understanding of people and of coping with life's exi-
gencies (empathy).
- An ability to step outside of oneself into the world of another person while
at the same time retaining an awareness of that pragmatic understanding
of coping with life (sympathy).
- An excitement about learning.
- The ability to articulate, especially the differences between one's own
experience and that of the client. (p. 274)

In a national survey, Figley and Nelson (1989) asked family therapy
supervisors to list the most basic skills that should be taught to beginning family
therapists. Their results might be surprising to some, because personal characteristics were listed above specific skills.

> Our fellow educators/trainers seem to believe, based on these data, that the person of
> the therapist is as important as, if not more so than, the skill of the therapist. . . . It is
> probable that our respondents were aware that, for therapy training to be effective,
> a foundation of abilities, values, attitudes, and other traits is essential for effective
> family therapy. (p. 362)

In their survey, 5 of the top 16 ranked items were the following:

1. Possess integrity
2. Possess the desire to learn
3. Intellectually curious
4. Flexible
5. Take responsibility for mistakes

Finally, experiential family therapists are the best example of clinicians
who pay attention to the self of the therapist as part of their training. They are
described by Piercy and Sprenkle (1986) in the following way:

> Experiential family therapists participate actively and personally in therapy ses-
> sions; they do not attempt to hide behind a therapeutic mask. This means at times
> being vulnerable with family members and at other times being angry and upset. If
> the therapist expects the family to have the courage to be real, the therapist must
> also demonstrate that courage. (p. 53)

Because personal characteristics of the therapist determine how a particular intervention is delivered, therapists must be able to utilize skills that fit with
their own personality. Lebow (1987) suggests:

> The ability to feel and be hopeful, empathic, assertive, confrontative, and focused
> is all a part of being a therapist. To the extent possible, such skills should be

Case 3 | **Harvey**

Harvey, 65, was referred for home-based therapy by the Meals on Wheels program for older people. His angry, threatening behavior frightened the drivers away. He lived in a rented room in the part of town with many transient and homeless people. He had no phone, so the family therapist would drive by his home and hope to find him there. His conservator was part of a social service agency with responsibilities for homeless and mentally disabled adults. His room had been rented by the agency against his will. He preferred to be out on the street. However, his case manager, Sue, delivered his money to the room each week, and this practice helped Harvey to tolerate his new environment. Upon contacting Sue, the family therapist learned what times she would most likely find Harvey at home.

Sue provided some of Harvey's history to the family therapist: He was the third generation of Irish immigrants who had come to America and settled in the midwest. He had been diagnosed with paranoia and schizophrenia for 20 years. He was well-known in the social service community, and many were forced to terminate their relationships with him when he became uncooperative and demanding. He was viewed as being "manipulative," and numerous providers expressed their "burnout" from involvement with Harvey through the years.

The family therapist explored with Sue the usual ways that others had interacted with Harvey. Patterns of rational problem solving, communicating expectations, and encouragement seemed to characterize the start of most interactions. Then Harvey would enter into long, repetitive, angry tirades, blaming "the system" and stating, "You owe me! This city was built on my back!" At this point, providers would try to reason with Harvey, challenge his thinking, and redirect the conversation to no avail. Eventually, the agency and provider would pull away from him. In the case of residential facilities, they would ask him to leave. The clinician assessed these patterns as unsuccessful "attempted solutions." She decided to avoid these same interactions with Harvey.

To facilitate the joining process, the clinician learned about the things Harvey emphasized most in his speech. She thought his repetitions might contain clues that would help build rapport. During their first meeting in Harvey's room, his troublesome, disconnected interaction was even worse than she had predicted! To maintain some relevance in the process, she began to note his language patterns, both content and process. He rarely answered her questions, so she took his responses as a message that he was telling her what was more important to him. He was capable of rambling for 10–15 minutes with no break, seemingly unconcerned about her reaction or what she thought. She would interrupt him occasionally, but tried to stay focused on learning what seemed to be most important to him and what messages his nonverbal patterns might be sending. Because he had not sought her help, she clearly would have to earn his trust, motivation, and cooperation. His lengthy proclamations and allegations led her to summarize some goals for him. She finally interrupted him one more time and asked if this sounded right:

1. You've lost a lot in your life (i.e., job, family, money) and you deserve more than you have.
2. You've given a lot to this city and you want the care you deserve.
3. People don't listen to you and you don't get the respect you deserve.

(Continued)

| Case 3 | **Harvey** (continued) |

The next step was to propose some plan that would match his motivation.

> Harvey, I'd like to help you get more of what you deserve. If we're going to get people to respect you more, I think we'll need to change your reputation in town. I think that people don't listen to you because they think you're crazy. I want to change that. However, in order to help you, I may have to interrupt you when we start to get off track.

Harvey laughed, sat up, and talked about how psychiatrists never know what to do with him. He accepted the proposed goals. With this note of agreement, the clinician proposed a plan to "change his reputation." This involved looking at his previous records, talking to family, and so on, in order to understand the challenge ahead and what would be realistic. Harvey signed the release of information and the clinician spent a few weeks investigating his history before returning with a plan. In the second session, during his long rambling, Harvey invited the therapist to interrupt him, if she needed to.

---

personal process during the training experience of a family therapist. One way to focus on personal process is by troubleshooting therapeutic process *in detail* during training.

Troubleshooting the Therapist-Client Relationship

Because the therapeutic relationship is central to the facilitation of change, it should be monitored on many levels as family therapy progresses. This evaluation should include the perceptions of the practitioner and the family. Without feedback from each side of the interaction, clinicians, supervisors, and researchers find it difficult to account for strengths and weaknesses in the interpersonal process between therapist and family. What is the relationship like? Is it accomplishing the desired goals? Is it authoritarian, cooperative, or collegial? This assessment can focus on each person's role and expectations in the relationship as well as on the way these are manifest in therapeutic interactions. What type of communication patterns can be described in therapy sessions? Are therapist and family able to "communicate about their communicating" with each other? This type of evaluation is subjective in nature and should be used regularly to avoid misunderstandings. Such a review can troubleshoot when the clinician feels a lack of therapeutic progress. Now, let's look at both sides of the equation. First, how does the family view the process? Then, what is the therapist experiencing?

The Family's Evaluation.   Family members may be privately evaluating the therapist with respect to trustworthiness, empathy, safety, helpfulness, and so on. This level of evaluation is based on subjective criteria chosen by each person and is often related to first impressions of interpersonal comfort. At this level of evaluation, discussion must be initiated by therapists because the topic can be intimate and threatening for family and therapist. To ask families about how they are experiencing the process elicits information that might imply how therapists are doing their job.

Nevertheless, beginning family therapists can minimize their sense of threat in such an interaction by regarding the clients' perceptions as information about what is most comfortable for the clients. Therapist competence is then related to a willingness to ask the questions and not to worry about the content of the answers. Family therapists can conduct this type of evaluation in a spirit of reflection, communicating self-confidence and concern about the well-being of the client. Is the family feeling comfortable with the process? Does the process seem beneficial and hopeful? Is it too structured? Too unstructured? Too authoritarian? Relevant? Not relevant? This is an example of systematic inquiry that is part of sound clinical practice.

An interesting research project that addressed client perceptions of family therapists was conducted by Newfield, Kuehl, Joanning, and Quinn (1991) with families who had participated in family therapy as part of a study of adolescent substance abuse. In this qualitative study, independent interviewers asked participants to describe their experience of the family therapy process, their perceptions of the therapist, and their views of the outcome. The purpose of the project was to obtain qualitative information about therapy from a lay point of view. The investigators characterized professional clinicians as members of a culture (with a distinctive language and expectations) that was different from the culture of those who sought their services. This attention to the interplay of different cultures is borrowed from the field of anthropology. The main questions focused on what occurred in the process and what the implications of these occurrences were. The results of this research suggested that clients were most satisfied with treatment when therapy matched their conceptualizations of the problem. Consequently, an anthropological view of the therapeutic experience uses the natural language and expectations of clients to understand the process rather than technical theories that are rooted in the culture of the profession.

Often, beginning practitioners are most threatened by openly expressed anger, criticism, or despair from family members. However, we find it useful to help trainees anticipate their most feared stumbling blocks and develop a repertoire of questions and responses that encourages open discussion of client experience. For example, some clinicians give clients permission to express disagreement or discontent ("It's normal for family members to become upset over some aspects of the therapy process. Can you think of anything so far that has been upsetting or confusing for you?"). Family members may be uncomfortable with some part of the process (e.g., questions or responses from the therapist that inadvertently offend someone). When this is discovered, the therapist can legitimize their experience ("I'm sorry for the misunderstanding; you did the right thing to let me know about it") or put their feelings into a larger perspective ("I can understand how you would come to feel this way. You're not the only one who has had this type of experience, and sometimes we professionals need help in knowing how you're feeling about our work together").

Very often, anger can be reframed as pain, thereby alerting the practitioner to some aspect of the process that has become threatening for a family member. Dominance can be reframed as fear, which alerts the therapist to a covert sense of vulnerability. When clients express despair ("This isn't doing any good"), the therapist can inquire about expectations and priorities of the client that might need to be addressed more directly. Despair may also prompt the therapist to explain the process more fully and to shift the target of change—for example, from behavioral to cognitive or from cognitive to behavioral. Family members who are more literal or concrete (result-oriented) often want behavioral change to be manifest first. Family members who are more intuitive (process-oriented) often want emotional change that impacts their internal experience.

Practitioners need to ask for client perceptions of therapeutic process before and after various stages of assessment and treatment. For example, if a family agrees to cooperate with the construction of a genogram in an initial interview, the practitioner might still want to ask family members at the beginning of the second session if they feel comfortable proceeding in that direction (e.g., "On a scale from 1 to 10, how comfortable are you with our plan for today?"). By acknowledging that some families are uncomfortable with the process or do not think it is a relevant exercise for their particular problem, the therapist provides the family members with an opportunity to discuss their thoughts, second thoughts, or questions about the process. It also gives the therapist an opportunity to search for a rationale that makes sense to the family or to search for a different approach.

Careful observation of nonverbal messages is another important vehicle for gauging client perceptions. Many family members are too threatened to make direct disclosures about their experience. In that case, the observation of behavioral patterns and sequences over time provides useful information about how the process fits the clients. For example, family therapists might discover that clients respond to some direction, advice, or task with a "yes, but" pattern. This pattern can be interpreted as a nonverbal message that the direction or task does not fit. In addition, such a pattern should be thought of as a courteous power struggle between therapist and family member, which should be avoided through therapist flexibility. When the therapist can take a one-down position and state a desire to change the process so that the family feels more comfortable, the family is encouraged to trust the therapist more and to be more direct.

One way to learn from nonverbal messages involves noting how families respond to homework and out-of-session tasks. De Shazer (1985) lists five possible responses that clients could make to a given task assignment and five suggested responses from the therapist. Even when a family does something contrary to the task or fails to fulfill the assignment at all, therapists are encouraged to view the family's response as a message that the family members are instinctively doing what is best for the family. By such nonverbal observation, the therapist learns to understand messages that are sent through behavior instead of words.

As family therapists become skilled at eliciting microevaluations from family perceptions, they discover that such evaluations become interventions. These turning points of change in the therapeutic relationship become models for change in family relationships. In addition, the effectiveness of the therapeutic relationship is influenced by perceptions that develop within the therapist. These will now be examined.

The Therapist's Evaluation.   The therapist evaluates clients with respect to level of cooperation, severity of the problem, and so on. In addition to focusing on the family's perception of the process, clinicians must also pay attention to their own perceptions and misperceptions of the process. If a therapist is feeling stuck but finds that the client is satisfied with the process, what does that say about the theory that the therapist is using as a lens? By the same token, if both therapist and client are feeling dissatisfied with the process, blame can be centered on the process and not on either party. Then, both parties can work together to cooperatively resolve their dissatisfaction. Besides modeling problem-solving skills, the family therapist also demonstrates a willingness to admit mistakes and to explore misunderstandings. When the client is feeling dissatisfied, but the practitioner believes that all is well, clinicians must distinguish assumption from fact or, in constructivist terms, distinguish their personal reality from the reality of the client.

When reviewing their own perceptions, family therapists should remember that their behavior is often an extension of their beliefs and intentions. Using the awareness wheel from Chapter 3 (Miller et al., 1988), the clinician can identify what thoughts and intentions might have been operating during problematic interactions. A therapist who has chosen a specific model of family therapy may also compare his or her own perceptions with the assumptions adopted by the model. For example, suppose a therapist's goal is to address a client's weight problem from an intergenerational point of view. The fundamental assumptions of that model include an acknowledgment that past relationships and interactions affect present relationships and interactions, and the assertion that thoughts and intentions are often taught by one generation to another. If the therapist inquires about family and cultural values, significant intergenerational relationships, and the evolution of the client's experience in the family of origin, these behaviors reflect an intergenerational point of view. However, if the therapist becomes concerned with a client's weight problem without explaining how the weight is related to intergenerational dynamics, the therapist's conduct might fail to have an impact on the client's reality. This omission can lead to problematic interactions in which a client's reality may be based on one reality (e.g., "It's a problem of willpower") and a therapist's reality may be based upon a different reality (e.g., "It's a cultural and intergenerational problem that requires changes in the thoughts and emotions that underlie behaviors").

Therapists should also take the opportunity to evaluate their own perceptions when they leave a session feeling angry, defeated, or confused. At these times, reflecting on expectations for self, client, and the process itself is in order. Is the therapist expecting too much from the family? Is the therapist

becoming dependent on client behavior for a feeling of success? Has the therapist remembered to utilize strengths and idiosyncrasies of the family in the proposed solution to the problem? Has the therapist found a way to value the
unique and sometimes contrary style of a family? By means of these questions,
which constitute a form of self-supervision, clinicians are able to develop learning and process goals that can further their own cognitive and behavioral
development. The traditional supervisory process can also shed light on therapists' perceptions of the process. Objective evaluations can also provide an
external review of the therapeutic process.

Frequency of Process Evaluations.   In many instances, periodic evaluations
of the process prevent impasses from occurring. Coleman (1985) suggests that
treatment failures are often related to a variety of factors, including theoretical
issues, process issues, motivation and consumerism, goal setting, the therapeutic alliance, personal issues of the therapist, and relationships with larger systems. If an impasse has occurred, an evaluation of these factors might provide a
constructive resolution. For many beginning family therapists struggling to put
their nascent skills to work, initiating an evaluation is a challenge. Because negative evaluations make learning difficult, it is human nature to avoid the possibility of criticism until more confidence is gained. However, such evaluations
can be as simple as reviewing the history of therapy to date. Beginning practitioners can also use the outline from Chapter 6 to analyze the beginning stages
of therapy. Was any important topic skipped? Was the information about previous treatment history detailed? Was the discussion about goals and expectations candid? What might the client still be hesitant to disclose? What does the
family need for the therapeutic relationship to become more comfortable? As
clinicians begin to experiment with periodic evaluations of their own processes
through the eyes of the family, they discover the importance of such information
in facilitating therapeutic progress.

Discussions about the therapeutic relationship can often be informal and
impromptu, but evaluating therapeutic interaction in a formal way for supervision or research is also possible. Supervisors may observe therapeutic exchanges
firsthand to understand the nature of the therapeutic relationship. In some
training programs, sessions are recorded on audiotape to enable beginning
practitioners to review their communication patterns and to monitor their grasp
of various skills. For example, a formal evaluation might consist of the practitioner reviewing a tape of a family therapy session and counting how many circular questions were asked of the family. If the therapist felt stuck during a part
of the session, the evaluation could also include a review of circular questions
to see which ones could have been asked during the period of difficulty.

Thus, it is possible to conduct formal and informal evaluations of each person's experience in the therapeutic process, the nature of specific microinterac-
tions within the relationship, and the ongoing relationship and its effectiveness.
In focusing on therapeutic process in these ways, the beginning practitioner
begins to see that the process of family therapy is, indeed, a complex set of
interactions that accommodates multiple points of view and is experienced on

multiple levels. These interactions become the means used by the clinician to bring about change. However, take heart! Some of the ways you can foster your own growth and development are actually fun. Learning to accept different viewpoints can happen off the job in a number of recreational actitivities. Here are some recommendations to ease your stress and still encourage you to grow as a professional.

Tips for Self-Development

- **Learn as much about people as you do about models.** As one learns more about people, the practitioner must also learn more about him or herself in relationship to others. Learning about others from their points of view can be done in a number of ways. Movies, for example, might expose students to a world different from their own. In a multicultural environment, finding movies that portray life in a variety of cultures isn't difficult. For example, the filmmaker Spike Lee has become well-known for his depictions of African American life in America. Appendix D contains a list of movies used in teaching students how to empathize with diverse people who have diverse stresses and strengths. Fiction and nonfiction also provide trainees with views of the world that can be examined apart from professional jargon and scientific terminology.
- **Gain insight about the perspectives of others through exposure to diverse professions and cultures.** During a period of training, it is sometimes most helpful for the trainee to spend as much time as possible with nontherapists in order to remain connected to a broader culture. For example, one family therapist had friends in medical school and asked permission to join their work group in anatomy and physiology. While they dissected a cadaver, the therapist was allowed to work with them, seeing the heart and identifying veins, arteries, and nerves. At the same time, the therapist learned about the world of medicine—what is involved in becoming a doctor and how that professional culture is different from family therapy. The experience provided an adventure that led to increased flexibility in considering others' values, worldviews, and cultures.
- **Seek experiences outside the academic world, which can sometimes become an obstacle to the trainee's attempts to remain balanced and versatile.** It may seem an ironic paradox, but nonprofessional leisure activities can often be the best teacher in providing a trainee with exposure to a variety of people, cultures, languages, and metaphors. The use of metaphor is especially effective when clients differ dramatically from the therapist in stage of life, values, economic level, and ethnic background, to name a few. If the client is a farmer, the family therapist might want to be compared to the county extension agent. If the client is a physician, the family therapist might want to be compared to a medical specialist, perhaps a cardiologist. If the client cares a great deal about physical appearance, the therapist might want to be compared to a hairdresser. To get into the client's world, go to the beauty parlor and the auto repair shop,

spend a day in the country, or head downtown and "hang out" during a street festival. By visiting worlds that have different cultures, metaphors, and languages, the therapist has something to say that may be more connected to a client's experience.

SUMMARY

As noted in outcome research, the client's perception of the therapeutic relationship is an important factor related to successful outcomes. As the role of the family therapist has become more active and involved, there has been an accompanying shift in attitudes. Implicit in the more traditional doctor-patient relationship was the assumption that the therapist was the expert and authority who would pursue a cure for the client's distress. However, as interventions such as positive connotation have become popular, the therapist-client relationship has become more egalitarian and central to effective family therapy.

The therapeutic relationship can be maximized when the therapist is active in highlighting strengths, instilling hope, and reframing resistance, and when the therapist is flexible in accepting differences. This perspective requires sensitivity to the unique aspects of a client's life that can become resources. These unique aspects are discovered through the therapist's ability to relate comfortably to individual strengths and differences. To become "relationally versatile," the clinician must make a personal decision to respect and esteem diverse people.

In first-generation models, the therapist focused more upon behavior and less upon phenomenology. In integrative models, the role of cognition, personal experience, and individual meanings emerges as a critical factor in the process of change. Nevertheless, interesting parallels also remain between all models. For example, while the structural therapist is active in directing behavior, it seems that the collaborative therapist is also active. Collaborative activity may involve directing the thoughts of one person toward another or guiding a group toward a creative brainstorming process. Thus, certain activities remain universal in family therapy, even though the destination or purpose of the journey may vary. These activities are the foundation for a therapeutic style that will be effective in working systemically and relationally.

I like to think that the process of developing the therapeutic relationship in family therapy is similar to learning to drive a car. Driving a car is a process that involves a collection of actions, thoughts, and knowledge. The territory (types of cases) one drives through may be as different as Africa is to England; nevertheless, certain aspects of the activity are always the same (joining, highlighting strengths, etc.). In addition, driving is a series of separate but related activities like watching the road, estimating distances, and steering the vehicle (self-development). Each may happen in situations where one is a passenger rather than a driver (positive interactions or informal conversation). However, when the therapist is the one doing the driving, she or he must coordinate these activities in a certain way (positive therapeutic relationship). This review of the therapeutic relationship and self of the therapist has pointed to a variety of processes and personal characteristics that are encouraged across most models of family therapy. Just as driving a car has some universal elements, regardless of the roads, territory, or destination, systems and relational therapy has universal elements.

As this chapter concludes, let's leave the "parking lot" of training and proceed onto busy streets and highways. (Perhaps we can say that the rubber hits the road!) It is here that countless variations—from new surroundings to road construction—challenge the driver with endless surprises. Even the most routine drivers know that the roads of life never stay the same. Thus, adaptability and the application of skills over time provide the learner with a way to manage variety. The activity once referred to as driving a car can now be transformed into many different activities such as going shopping, traveling, or racing.

Chapter 5 will review the basic stages in the process of family therapy and provide a framework for integrating the themes of theory and practice that have been reviewed thus far. As we start the car and begin to move, we take along our theories, perceptions, and relational skills. We circle the parking lot—many times—and begin to see how each component interacts with the others, sometimes overlapping, sometimes proceeding in order. Our thoughts and actions become entwined as stages and interactions in the process. Now it is time to learn skills that apply to a variety of situations and driving conditions.

5 CHAPTER | Starting Off on the Right Foot: Referral and Intake

CHAPTER OUTLINE

The Referral Process: Understanding the Natural Environment
Assessing Client Motivation
Exploring the Relational Network
Working With Other Professionals
The Intake Process: Organizing the Therapeutic Environment
Identifying the Presenting Problem
Learning About Previous Help
Gathering Family Information
Including Others
Scheduling Information
Hypotheses: Using the Common Themes
Questions That Beginning Clinicians Often Ask
1. How Should I Handle the Issue of Alcohol If I Suspect It Is a Part of the Problem?
2. How Should I Deal With a Suicide Threat?
3. What Should I Do If I Discover Family Violence?
4. How Should I Handle Family Secrets?·
Summary

CORE COMPETENCIES

1.3.1 Executive   Gather and review intake information, giving balanced attention to individual, family, community, cultural, and contextual factors.

1.3.2 Executive   Determine who should attend therapy and in what configuration (e.g., individual, couple, family, extra-familial resources).

1.3.3 Executive   Facilitate therapeutic involvement of all necessary participants in treatment.

1.3.4 Executive   Explain practice setting rules, fees, rights, and responsibilities of each party, including privacy, confidentiality policies, and duty to care to client or legal guardian.

2.2.4 Perceptual   Consider the influence of treatment on extra-therapeutic relationships.

The first contacts with a family require the practitioner to be disciplined, deliberate, and wise. It takes great discipline to choose words and use language that will develop a positive relationship with those seeking help. It also takes discipline to manage the anxieties and uncertainties that come with starting any new endeavor. That's why a spirit of adventure is important to becoming a successful family therapist. With such a spirit, the practitioner approaches therapy with an openness to the unusual and a curiosity about challenge. Deliberately planning and organizing initial contacts is also critical so that families gain a sense of hope and trust in the process. All of this takes wisdom—the ability to choose the best course of action.

Some models of family therapy consider every contact, no matter how brief, to be a therapeutic interaction in which the therapist either prepares for or promotes change (Selvini-Palazzoli, 1985; Wright & Leahy, 1984). Thus, initial interactions in the course of seeking help are the beginning of the change process—even before meeting with a therapist. These first steps are known as the *referral process*. Once the referral is made and a family therapist is contacted, the therapist or agency gathers initial information through an *intake process*. If the clinician conducts the intake session as outlined in this chapter, assessment and treatment planning can proceed as described in Chapter 6. However, assessment can also occur in part of the intake session.

This chapter addresses intake as the first step of treatment to help clinicians explore each interaction in depth. Depending on the practice setting, these transactions may also be part of the initial interview. When this is the case, beginning professionals often approach their first session with some anxiety about how to address the tough issues. Thus, this chapter concludes by preparing for this meeting with a discussion of frequently asked questions.

THE REFERRAL PROCESS: UNDERSTANDING THE NATURAL ENVIRONMENT

The referral is an interactional process in which, generally speaking, someone decides that a problem exists and someone initiates the idea that therapy is a possible resource and should be sought. Generally, there are two types of referrals. *Self-referrals* are those in which the intended client (either individual or family) makes the first contact to seek help. Other referrals are those in which someone other than the intended client makes the first contact. Exploring the interactions leading to the first contact provides key information for understanding client motivation and the family's problem-solving process.

The appropriate time to gather this information varies across practice settings. For example, sometimes an agency's process includes an initial contact with one agency representative via telephone, an intake interview with a different staff person, and finally the initial interview with the assigned family therapist. When intermediate contacts are involved, detailed referral information is often overlooked. Thus, in these situations, family therapists should be prepared to explore the referral process during the initial interview.

However, when the practitioner is fully involved with either the first contact or the intake process, referral information can be gathered in detail during one of these earlier stages. This introductory exploration can convey interest and caring on the part of the therapist. The referral process often includes interactions within the family and between the family and other systems. Learning about these interactions can help the clinician to answer the following questions:

1. What relationship should be the central focus?
2. Who is most relevant to a successful outcome?
3. Who is the most motivated participant in the therapy process? Who is most reluctant?

These questions, which can be answered indirectly through conversation with the family, focus the family therapist on an exploration of the referral process. When the practitioner is interviewing individuals alone, he or she must assess whether the client's motivation for counseling is internal or external, that is, they may be sent by family or friends who want them "fixed."

With the frequency of court-ordered therapy in the United States, it is important for the therapist to explore and understand the sequence of interactions that leads the client to schedule an appointment or make a telephone inquiry. At the very least, the family therapist obtains information about who has taken the initiative. Ideally, the family therapist obtains crucial information about the family members' level of motivation, the family's influential external relationships, and whether therapy is even appropriate in some circumstances. Obviously, a court-ordered case has implications for the motivation of the client to participate in therapy. Many models rarely address this aspect of the therapeutic process, but my opinion is that to understand puzzling superficiality or courteous compliance without personal involvement, the beginning family therapist must assess the nature of the referral process.

In other circumstances, such as occurs in private-practice settings, relatives, family members, clergy, and service providers recommend or even initiate counseling while excluding themselves from the process. For example, the parents of a young married couple may send them to marriage counseling and even pay for the process. The Milan team has consistently addressed the referral process in the case where therapy is initiated by someone who claims to be uninvolved in the life of the problem, such as a member of the clergy or a sibling (Selvini Palazzoli, 1985; Selvini Palazzoli, Boscolo, Cecchin, & Prata, 1980b). The Milan team found that examining the relationship between the referring person and the family must take precedence over traditional therapy—that is, over merely examining relationships within the family or even exploring the problem itself. In this way, differences in motivation are addressed during early stages of the therapeutic process. By tracking the perceptual and interactional process, the therapist gains information for subsequent use in developing mutually satisfying goals that are sensitive to individual needs.

Assessing Client Motivation

Like the Milan team, O'Hanlon and Weiner-Davis (1989) address referral concerns by establishing who is the "customer" of therapy—that is, who is actually requesting a change. Questions such as these can aid in establishing who is the customer:

1. Who first noticed that this was a problem? (This identifies the pattern of perception.)
2. Who agrees or disagrees that this is a problem? (This explores the "politics" or the issues of power surrounding the definition of the problem.)
3. Whose idea was it to seek therapy? (This identifies the pattern of initiation.)
4. How was it brought to your attention? (This identifies the interpersonal process involved in seeking help.)
5. When you began to think about seeking help, who or what gave you the thought that coming here might help? (This helps the therapist understand how familiar the family may be with the "culture" of therapy and what it involves.)

When the therapist discovers that an outside party has suggested counseling, it is likely that the definition of the problem will have to focus initially on the relationship between those being interviewed and the referral source, for example, the family versus another system or the individual versus family, friends, or employer. Thus, if a family seeks therapy because the school is concerned about Johnny's behavior, the family therapist must decide how much the family agrees or disagrees with the school's perception of Johnny. When the family disagrees with others who believe a problem exists, the practitioner should follow the family's lead in developing client-driven goals (see Chapter 6).

When couples appear to be seeking help together, if one partner is more motivated and the other more reluctant to pursue therapy, the questions posed might be something like these:

- (To the woman) When you thought about coming to counseling, how did you talk to him about it?
- (To the man) When she talked to you about counseling, what was your reaction? Did you get "dragged" here against your will?

If a husband comes alone for counseling because his wife has given him an ultimatum, the therapist must determine who has defined the problem and whether the husband agrees or disagrees with her point of view. He may want to save his marriage, but he may be unable to fully represent his wife's point of view. The intricate politics that have led to her exclusion from the session must also be investigated:

1. Does she have her own therapist and feel that he should take his turn?
2. Has she already privately decided on divorce and identified the therapist as someone her husband can turn to when she "lowers the boom"?
3. Does she think he is totally to blame for the marital problems?

4. Has he been violent so that she has had to separate in order to capture some degree of control over her life?

Exploring the Relational Network

When callers are family members, the therapist should determine what role the referral source might have in the definition of the problem. Do other family members agree or disagree with the caller's view of the problem? When discovering that someone besides those in attendance actually developed the definition of the problem, the family therapist must try to clarify the relationship between the family and the parties defining the problem. This remains the therapist's focus until a shared problem definition emerges. As the Milan team discovered, when the problem is defined by a sibling, an in-law, or a service provider, the defining party or the person's perspective should be included in the session to provide the interpersonal context for the referral (Selvini Palazzoli, 1985). Because the family might disagree with the referring person but still initiate therapy, the family may believe that the real problem is a difference of opinion with this person of influence. With a difference of opinion defined as the problem, family therapists can then suggest that their role be that of helping both parties reach a shared goal that will transcend their differing opinions (Why don't we look for something you can both agree upon?).

Working With Other Professionals

Family therapists often receive referrals from various sources, including school counselors, psychologists, social workers, previous clients, and family members involved in the problem. When a family is referred by an outside agency (for example, a court or school), the family may be suspicious and less willing to attend the initial session. This is particularly the case when families are forced to attend therapy by a probation officer or the court (Boyd-Franklin, 1989). If professional referral sources (for example, social workers or school counselors) make the first contact, the following guidelines will help the clinician to begin on a positive note:

- Explain the family therapist's role as one that can address disagreements and conflict between the family and others.
- Gain a clear picture of whether there is disagreement between the referring party and the family. Encourage the referring party to explain to the client that the family therapist will take a neutral position.
- Encourage the referral source to emphasize the family therapist's independence in order to minimize client defensiveness. In such cases, the role of the family therapist might involve resolving conflict between the family and the larger system. That role can be carried out effectively only when family therapists establish a stated position of both neutrality with respect to the referral source and support with respect to the family.

- Gather information about the problem and the referral source's attempts to alleviate it. Weber, McKeever, and McDaniel (1985) suggest that determining what the referring person requests is important (for example, consultation for self or therapy for the family).

The following dialogue illustrates these issues with professional referral sources:

CASE MANAGER: I need your help with a family our agency is involved with. Can I talk to you about the family?

FAMILY THERAPIST: Sure. What seems to be the problem?

CASE MANAGER: Well, the husband attends our Adult Day Center and has Alzheimer's. I've been trying to get his wife to start planning for his long-term care needs, but she says they're doing fine and she doesn't need anything like that. She's really in denial.

FAMILY THERAPIST: What type of help did you have in mind? Are you looking for a consultation for yourself or therapy for them?

CASE MANAGER: I really think they need therapy. We just haven't gotten anywhere with them.

FAMILY THERAPIST: Have you discussed this idea with them?

CASE MANAGER: Yes. The wife said she would be willing to talk to you.

FAMILY THERAPIST: OK. Tell me what you said to her and the reasons you gave for recommending that she come here.

CASE MANAGER: I told her that I was concerned about her future coping with her husband's illness, and that I thought it would be a good idea if she talked to someone about her options.

FAMILY THERAPIST: How did she respond to this?

CASE MANAGER: She said, if I thought it was necessary, she would be willing to come.

FAMILY THERAPIST: Did you mention earlier that you don't think you've gotten anywhere with them?

CASE MANAGER: Yes, but she just won't look at the future.

FAMILY THERAPIST: Well, I wonder if we could think of this as a difference of opinion between the two of you. You want her to look at the future, and it seems like she doesn't want to.

CASE MANAGER: Yeah, I guess you could say that.

FAMILY THERAPIST: If this is the case, she may respond to me in the same way she has been responding to you, unless I'm able to establish a position with her that is independent of yours. Do you think you could raise the issue of this difference between the two of you and explain that I will be a neutral third party?

CASE MANAGER: Yes, I can do that. I told her I'd call her back after I talked to you.

FAMILY THERAPIST: Good. Why don't you describe me as someone who is interested in her point of view? Then, you and I should come to an understanding about my role. I've found that I can often help people reach a resolution by increasing their understanding of each other. Would you be open to additional information that might help alleviate your present concerns?

CASE MANAGER: Oh yes. If you can just get her to open up, that would really help.

In this instance, the family therapist should be prepared for the client to be cooperative but not necessarily motivated to pursue the case manager's agenda. However, because the case manager has been prepared for a new agenda—that of increasing their understanding of each other—the family therapist will not be hindered by the previous misunderstandings between the referral source and client. Very likely, the goal that the client will be most motivated to pursue is one that enables her to feel more support from the case manager and more freedom to manage her life as she wishes. The family therapist can be prepared to suggest that the purpose of the meeting is to help the case manager understand the client's needs.

Once information about the problem is gathered from the professional, an agreement should be reached about how treatment information should be shared. School counselors and teachers may want to know, for example, how a child is progressing so that they can support these changes. In many cases, families may request a report or evaluation of the progress. Court referrals often require periodic reports summarizing the progress of treatment. If the case is court-ordered, the family must be informed regarding the therapist's responsibility to the court. However, in cases in which there is no legal obligation to report, the intake worker should advise the referral source that the family has legal control over what information is shared. The intake worker should make a note of this issue, instructing the therapist to discuss these questions with the family.

The beginning practitioner can think of the referral process as having an important influence on the therapeutic relationship, goals, and ultimate outcomes. The suggestions for exploration presented in this section can alert the practitioner to important elements in the natural environment of families that can be overlooked. When these elements are addressed, the clinician establishes a thoughtful and realistic basis from which to begin direct contact with families during the intake process.

THE INTAKE PROCESS: ORGANIZING THE THERAPEUTIC ENVIRONMENT

As mentioned earlier, different clinical settings vary in how they organize referral calls and intake interviews. Wright and Leahey (1984) pay specific attention to the telephone contact preceding the first interview, suggesting that this first contact can have great impact on the future course of subsequent contacts. The first telephone contact has also been an issue of note for other clinicians, many of whom have developed guidelines and strategies for addressing systemic dynamics with the earliest possible contact (Brock & Barnard, 1988; Napier & Whitaker, 1978; Selvini Palazzoli et al., 1978). In agency settings, an intake process may already be established over which the practitioner has little control. However, sometimes the clinician can make a preliminary telephone contact after the agency intake and before the first session; the family therapist can then provide important direction before the first meeting. For others who have the discretion to structure client contact according to their own preference, this chapter may serve as a step-by-step guide to the beginning stages of family therapy.

Identifying the Presenting Problem

Getting a concise statement of the problem is important. When family members call, they are giving their view of the problem. Often family members express concern through the use of labels. For instance, they might state feelings of "depression" or "anxiety," or refer to a child as "out of control." These labels do offer a general indication of the problem area, but they have different meanings for different people. Therefore, asking for concrete examples of each label is important. For example, "out of control" might mean that the child "doesn't come home on time" or "punched a hole in our wall." Likewise, the intake person should ask how the problem is affecting family members. For example, if a mother calls and reports that her teenage son is "out of control," determining how his behavior is affecting her or other family members is critical. For instance, she may report that she and her husband "disagree about how to handle this problem"; she may report that her husband is "the only one who can handle him." Finally, the practitioner must summarize the referring family member's view of the problem ("So, you see the problem as your son being out of control, that he won't come home when you tell him, and that you and your husband don't agree about how to handle him"). The following dialogue illustrates how intake information can be gathered from a potential client:

INTAKE WORKER: Can you give me a brief description of the problem?

MARY: My husband and I are not getting along.

INTAKE WORKER: Can you tell me what is going on that makes you feel that way?

MARY: We never go out. We just don't seem to have anything in common since Laura, our daughter, left for college.

INTAKE WORKER: How long ago did your daughter leave?

MARY: She's been gone for two years.

INTAKE WORKER: Have you sought any help for this problem in the past?

Note that the intake worker questioned Mary immediately following her description of the problem. By asking specific questions early in the process, the interviewer guides the process and can move on to the next important topic.

Learning About Previous Help

Assessing previous therapy experiences helps determine what works and what does not work with a particular family. Prior requests for help are part of the client's problem-solving history and enable the therapist to determine how the family viewed previous therapy. Information such as whether if a family left therapy because the therapist wanted to focus on the marriage rather than on the child assists the therapist in avoiding the same mistakes. In such cases, therapists learn not to focus on the marriage until the parents raise the issue. Also, work with other therapists may be related to this current request for help, but even if previous therapy seems unrelated, the current therapist should always explore the effects of these other experiences on family members:

1. What was your experience like with _____?
2. Was there anything uncomfortable about that experience?
3. What things do you remember being helpful?
4. Why didn't you return there for help with this problem?

These questions often facilitate the joining process with families by providing an opportunity for empathy. Do the family members think their current therapist will be just like the last one? Are there certain things that make them drop out of therapy? Can the current therapist discover what fits for this family by listening to the family members' descriptions of past therapy? This information is often crucial to future successes with any client who has had previous helpers. In addition, if any family members are currently in therapy, the therapist can ask the family to sign a release so that information and services can be coordinated.

The same questions can be asked about informal helpers with equally fruitful results. Sometimes, informal helpers become unrecognized influences on the course of therapy unless they are identified during such a discussion. They may be those who have offered help or opinions about the problem in the past—friends, neighbors, clergy, or extended family members. What suggestions have they made? How does the family feel about these informal helpers? If such parties have significant influences with the family, asking about their inclusion in the first session is probably wise. These discussions help the therapist understand the family's pattern of seeking help and solving problems.

Gathering Family Information

Family information includes names of the principal client and partner or spouse, names of children, birth dates, level of education, and place of employment or school. The therapist must determine who is living in the home as well as who is related to the problem. Obtaining information about previous marriages, divorces, recent deaths, illnesses, and any other significant changes that have occurred in the family system is also helpful. This information can be useful in formulating hypotheses about transitions—particularly if a marriage has followed soon after a divorce or if other significant changes have occurred in rapid succession—as well as help determine who will attend the first session.

Including Others

All family members who live in the household should be asked to attend the first session. If the contact person is unwilling to bring the whole family, the therapist can meet with the family members who are most concerned about the problem. However, when significant others are excluded from the process, family therapists must ask questions during the assessment process to bring to light information about the missing parties' point of view and how much influence they have on other family members. Doing so increases understanding about each person's position in the system, and the therapist can look for opportunities to address key family members and negotiate their subsequent inclusion (see Chapter 6).

The therapist or intake worker should listen closely to how the contact person describes the problem. For example, a wife may say, "We just don't communicate," or "We don't get along." In some cases a parent might describe the problem in triangular terms: "She won't listen to us," or "He minds everyone but me." In such cases, the therapist needs to clarify to whom the contact person is referring and what that person's relationship is to the problem.

When the contact person is hesitant to invite others to the first session, the person may report that her or his spouse's work schedule prohibits attendance, or the person may explain that she or he is reluctant to impose upon extended family members not living in the home. As mentioned previously, some clients may have an adversarial relationship with the referral source, and as a result, refuse to include that person. In these instances, family therapists should prioritize the various parties who could be included. All family members living in the household are the highest priority, the next priority is the influential extended family, and the least necessary attendees are the referral sources. If the client has objections to all three possibilities, positive sources of support (friends, neighbors, etc.) might be included to highlight the person's support system.

The following intake dialogue illustrates how the interviewer might address the reluctance to include other members of the household:

INTAKE WORKER: Is your husband willing to attend the first session with you?

WIFE: Well . . . I don't know. He told me that he is perfectly happy and that it's my problem.

INTAKE WORKER: What do you think about his assessment?

WIFE: He's probably right. He usually is.

INTAKE WORKER: So, what do you think would happen if you asked him to come?

WIFE: I don't think he would come.

INTAKE WORKER: Have you ever been afraid that he would become violent with you?

WIFE: Oh, no! He would never do anything like that. He's just stubborn.

INTAKE WORKER: Let's think about some other issues for a moment. Even if he agreed to come, can you think of some ways that you might be more uncomfortable if he was included?

WIFE: Well . . . I guess I would probably clam up. I don't like to make him mad, and every time I bring up how I feel, he gets mad.

INTAKE WORKER: So you're afraid that things would go just like they do at home?

WIFE: Yes.

INTAKE WORKER: I see. . . . You may be right. I'm wondering if you might be able to tolerate that possibility in order to get the very best help.

WIFE: What do you mean?

INTAKE WORKER: Our family therapists generally find their greatest success when they are able to hear all sides of the story. Even if your husband thinks the problem is yours, it would help the therapist to understand your husband's point of view. That way, because you plan on staying married, she could give you the kind of direction that would be good for you and your relationship. Sometimes, therapists give suggestions that seem good for the person but ultimately turn out to threaten the marriage in some way.

WIFE: But I don't know how to make him come in.

INTAKE WORKER: Would it be possible for you to simply quote me? You could tell him, "The intake worker at the agency says your opinion is important to the process, to help me with my feelings. He knows you're not seeking any help right now, but he'd like to know if you would attend a session and give your opinion about what you think my problem is. He says it's customary for the therapist to meet the person's spouse before proceeding with individual work. Would you be willing to attend the first session with me?"

WIFE: OK. I'll try. What if he still won't come?

INTAKE WORKER: Let us know what happened, and we'll ask your assigned therapist to contact you for further direction.

In this dialogue, the intake worker explores the reluctance from the husband's and the wife's point of view. Although the wife was focused more on her husband's reluctance, her own unspoken reluctance may be a significant factor as well. Without trying to change the husband's mind (something the wife might do repetitively), the intake worker suggests a rationale that meets her overall goal (help) without escalating the conflict between them. If the intake process reveals the presence of violence in the relationship or the wife's intention to follow through with divorce, the initial interview may be conducted individually. Once this is accomplished, it may be possible to engage violent men in individual counseling for themselves using the strategies of Jenkins (1991).

When the client is a single adult living alone, proceeding with the initial interview individually is often best. During this interview, the clinician can determine who the significant others are and how they might be successfully included (see Chapter 6).

Scheduling Information

The therapist needs to know what the scheduling requirements are and who will be attending the first session. Then an appointment date, the time, and the location of counseling can be set and communicated to the family. Families should be told about the intake procedure and fees, and also made aware of any cancellation policy.

Hypotheses: Using the Common Themes

Information gathered from referral and intake helps the therapist formulate hypotheses for the initial interview or for additional assessment sessions that follow. Hypothesizing has been used by the Milan team as a formal part of their strategic plan. Specific theories often encourage family therapists to bring certain ideas with them to the therapeutic experience. However, these assumptions may limit their ability to see other possible realities. Just as data gathering can become theory-specific, so can the hypotheses generated by the therapy. Therefore, we want to encourage a style of hypothesizing that is creative and flexible rather than limiting and rigid. Instead of being told what to hypothesize, the beginning family therapist should learn to formulate a hypothesis and then test it through an organized set of questions such as those found in Chapter 3. By asking the right questions, students and trainees can examine and test hypotheses rather than transform their hypotheses into unquestioned truths that might not fit their families' experiences.

The process of hypothesizing is also related to the therapist and client co-creating a definition of the problem. Certain theories generate certain definitions of problems. However, family members often have their own definitions, whether private or public, which have a bearing on how the family responds to therapy. More important than what the therapist thinks is what the *family* thinks and how the therapist interacts with the family around these variant definitions. Thus, I think brainstorming about questions that can guide the clinical interview is important, but it is important for the therapist to stay flexible. How a definition of the problem becomes shared by the therapist and the family is an important step toward a positive working relationship.

Most schools of family therapy share a basic hypothesis about physical and emotional problems. Hanna (1997) suggests that "all problems have a relational component" (p. 104). This hypothesis assumes that some relationship within the family or with some significant other (even a teacher, an employer, or a neighbor) is a relevant part of either the problem or the solution. This hypothesis leads to the identification of relationship conditions that are important to consider. The following case illustrates this relational concept.

The following case about Frank, the hypotheses of the couple were included in an expanded definition of the problem, which grew to include

Case 4 | Frank

Frank, a husband in his mid-50s, sought therapy for depression. His wife agreed to accompany him and be helpful. In pursuing a relational hypothesis, the therapist explored the client's own description of his internal process and the couple's description of how each responded to his depression. Instead of attempting to convince them that depression is really an interactional problem rather than an individual problem, the therapist chose to acknowledge the internal reality of the husband's depression while exploring the couple's attempted solutions and their own interactional process. This discussion led to the identification of perceptual and behavioral sequences that all agreed were problematic. The wife thought of her role as his emotional caregiver. Each time he expressed his despair ("I feel lousy"), she tried to make him feel better ("Cheer up and look on the bright side"). To him, these responses were implicit disagreements with his internal experience. Feeling misunderstood, he became more entrenched in his own position. As the therapist helped them examine and change this interactional pattern, the husband was not robbed of his internal experience, and his wife was not blamed for his depression. Instead, they were directed toward a plan that could facilitate the healing process. In this instance, the husband's depression lifted as the spouses began to cooperate in a new way. However, had the depression persisted, the couple, equipped with new relational skills, could pursue additional solutions with their relationship strengthened rather than strained.

---

relational factors. Because the couple's hypotheses about the depression had included such issues as the husband's job change (transition) and a strained relationship with his only daughter (intergenerational), the couple could easily incorporate and more effectively address these issues using by their new relational process (structure, roles).

Another example of a relational hypothesis deals with a universal concern for all therapists: what some call resistance. As mentioned in Chapter 4, *resistance* is often described as client rigidity or lack of cooperation. However, a relational hypothesis of resistance suggests an interactional definition that involves the therapist as a participant in the problem. Such a hypothesis helps the beginning family therapist examine his or her own interactional process with the client rather than indict the client. Interactional hypotheses can help the practitioner change perceptions and behaviors that may have unwittingly elicited resistant behavior. Like the wife of the depressed husband in Case 4, many family therapists can learn how to be more helpful by examining and changing their own part in a problematic sequence.

Hypotheses are the beginning but not the end of how the therapist will view a problem. Those themes shared by most models of family therapy appear in Chapter 3. These themes are a good place to start when generating hypotheses from intake and referral data. Selected questions from each category can guide the initial interview. For example, a young couple seeks therapy, each complaining that the other places his or her career above their marriage.

The following hypotheses are all possible views of the problem that lead to corresponding questions:

- **They did not learn to negotiate closeness or distance in their relationship—a major developmental task of the beginning family (structure).** How much time do you spend together? When you first married, how did you decide about the use of time?
- **They did not successfully clarify beliefs, roles, and expectations—a developmental task of courtship and mate selection (individual experience).** Before you married, what discussions did you have about the type of relationship you wanted?
- **Over time, their relationship has experienced some structural change that they cannot understand or resolve (transitions).** Since you married, what major events have occurred in your lives?
- **Their communication and problem-solving styles have not brought about successful conflict resolution (more of the same or the solution becomes the problem).** When this disagreement comes up, how do you handle it? What happens when you try to talk about it? Who first brings up the subject?

The therapist can develop questions like these from intake forms or from intake interviews and then pursue these hypotheses until concrete information eliminates or verifies their relevance. In addition, the therapist can assess the situation as to whether interactional change (the way they behave) or cognitive change (the way they think) will be the focus of the interventions.

Box 5.1 is a sample intake interview form. Box 5.2 presents sample case material on the intake form. From the information in Box 5.2, the following hypotheses can be generated prior to the first session:

1. A rapid remarriage may have left no time for the new marital subsystem to successfully organize parenting responsibilities or for the biological parents to resolve custody and visitation issues.
2. There may be divorce-adjustment issues and grief issues lingering for Robert and his mother.
3. There may be conflict between Jerry and Robert.
4. There may be some historical interactions between Robert and his mother that have become an ongoing pattern.

After the initial interview, the therapist should present these hypotheses to the family and either eliminate or expand them based on the family's response. In the practice of MST, reviewed in Chapter 2, Cunningham and Henggeler (1999) suggest that this presentation process is a form of "scientific mindedness." That is, therapists check out their assumptions with the family before taking them as true for the family, and in this way learn to be flexible and stay tentative about assumptions. For example, in the first session, the therapist might discover that Jerry works many evenings, leaving little opportunity for conflict with Robert. However, when he is home, Robert seems to respond more obediently to Jerry than to his mother. This information may eliminate hypothesis 3 and strengthen hypotheses 1, 2, or 4.

Box 5.1 | Intake Form

Date _____

Referral information

Client of record   Last _____ First _____ M.I. _____

Parent/Partner/Spouse   Last _____ First _____ M.I. _____

Parent/Partner/Spouse   Last _____ First _____ M.I. _____

Street _____ City _____ State _____ Zip _____

Phone #s: Home _____ Work _____ Cell _____

Referral source: Org. _____ Name _____ Phone _____

Clinical information

Problem description _____

_____

_____

_____

Previous relationships: Client of record _____ Dates _____

Partner/Spouse _____ Dates _____

Current marriage date: _____

Previous therapy

Name	Org.	Address	Dates
_____	_____	_____	_____
_____	_____	_____	_____
_____	_____	_____	_____
_____	_____	_____	_____

Family information

Last name	First name	Birth date	Ed.	Employ/School
_____	_____	_____	_____	_____
_____	_____	_____	_____	_____
_____	_____	_____	_____	_____
_____	_____	_____	_____	_____

Scheduling information

Appointment date _____ Time _____ Therapist _____

Box 5.2 | **Completed Intake Form**

Date 5/13/95

Referral information

Client of Record   Last Starks   First Robert   M.I. _____
Parent/Partner/Spouse   Last Russell   First Barbara   M.I. S. _____
Parent/Partner/Spouse   Last Russell   First Jerry   M.I. L. _____
Street 2553 Hawthorne Ave.   City Batesville   State IN   Zip 47006
Phone #s: Home (812)451-8484   Work (812)276-3533   Cell (812)647-5989
Referral source: Org. Hawthorne Elem.   Name M. Briggs, Counselor
Phone 821-4793

Clinical information

Problem description Mrs. Russell stated that her son, Robert, is failing the 4th grade. He also resists rules at home. This started after her remarriage last year. She thinks Robert is depressed about being away from his biological father who moved out of state last year.

Previous relationships: Client of record widowed Dates spouse died 3 yrs ago

Partner/Spouse divorced   Dates married 1980, div. 1991

Current marriage date: October 1994

Previous therapy

Name	Org.	Address	Dates
Mrs. Russell	The Family Ctr.	1337 W. Main St.	May, 1990
			2–3 sessions

Family information

Last name	First name	Birth date	Ed.	Employ/School
Russell	Barbara	9-1-43	H.S.	Sec., Ford Motors
Russell	Jerry	10-5-40	H.S.	Sales, Lincoln Ins.
Starks	Robert	10-10-85	4th gr.	Hawthorne

Scheduling information

Appointment date 5-20-95   Time 4 pm   Therapist Jim Austin

Now let's look at another case, from referral through intake, to see how the process produces hypotheses and an initial treatment plan. This sequence places current relationships as most important, but doesn't lose sight of important life transitions that may be relevant in understanding Ellie's worldview, stage of change, and psychosocial development over time. With a chronic problem, these pieces of the puzzle help to address one of the central questions in MST: How does the problem fit into the larger context of a person's life? Chapter 7 shows how the themes of Ellie's life story lead the clinician toward certain family therapy models. In addition, the caseworker's referral included two previous psychological assessments, which the therapist can review in light of the initial sessions to evaluate their fit with her current circumstance. The exploration of these elements—a) individual functioning, b) relational functioning, and c) problem severity—will help the clinician prioritize which family therapy approaches will be most effective.

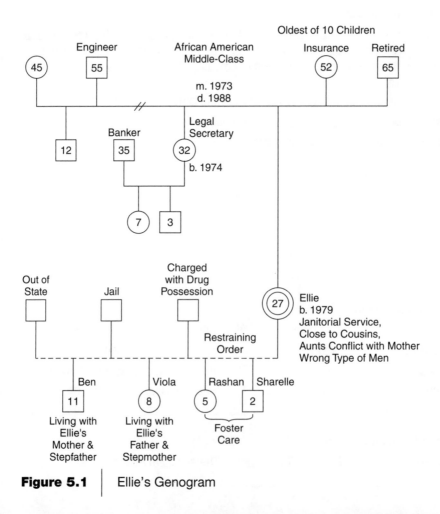

Figure 5.1 | Ellie's Genogram

| Case 5 | **Ellie** |

Ellie, 27, was a single mom who was court-ordered for counseling through Child Protective Services (CPS). The referral requested that a therapist help Ellie to implement her family care plan as specified in her family reunification plan. Her two youngest children, Rashan, 5, and Sharelle, 2, had been removed from her home when neighbors reported unsafe conditions in her home (no food, no supervision, partner prosecuted for drug possession). Her two older children, Ben, 11, and Viola, 7, had each been placed with different grandparents some years earlier. She was upset with her caseworker and was in the process of requesting a new caseworker on grounds that the caseworker "doesn't like me" and "isn't fair." That request was under review by CPS.

Joining
The tone set by the therapist during beginning discussions was friendly and informal, to match Ellie's personal style. The therapist began by telling the client about herself so that the client could "check her out." She mentioned aspects of her work and life that involved African American women and explored areas of black culture to see how Ellie saw herself in relation to her race and cultural heritage. The clinician had recently seen a Spike Lee movie (Appendix D) and spoke about it. This led Ellie to describe an experience when racial slurs were aimed at her when Ben was a baby and she was a teen mother, carrying him home from the bus stop. This sharing provided an early opportunity for the clinician to respond to Ellie with sympathy. Upon learning that Ellie was faithfully attending all her supervised visitations, the therapist highlighted Ellie's hard work and her effort regarding her children. Ellie had a sense of humor, and the therapist could see that they could form a personal, warm relationship over women's issues and the welfare of her children.

Referral and Intake
The therapist and Ellie discussed the goals of her Family Care Plan:

1. Address previous psychological assessments, "deeper issues," and DSM-IV diagnosis.
2. Develop a prevention plan to address the relationship of "deeper issues" to safe parenting.
3. Develop a prevention plan for high-risk situations in parenting.
4. Address high-risk situations and warning signals as part of her "feeling plan."
5. Use her "feeling plan."
6. Discuss difficulties in utilizing her "feeling plan."

The referral was made by Ellie's caseworker as part of the Adoptions Opportunity Act, in which parents are given 18 months to regain custody of children before an adoption is finalized. The law requires that every effort be made to help parents regain custody. At the time of Ellie's intake to demonstrate the progress required by the court. In the meantime, her children had been placed with a foster mother who received encouragement from CPS to pursue adoption because of her excellent parenting and ability to address the children's special needs.

Client Motivation
Ellie spoke about wanting to work on her family care plan, but her speech patterns over time showed how preoccupied she was with her perception of the caseworker as critical and unfair. Thus, before developing a treatment plan, the therapist suggested that they

(Continued)

| Case 5 | **Ellie** (continued) |

set some goals related to their relationship and that of the caseworker. The clinician acknowledged that she couldn't predict whether the outcome of the counseling would be to recommend custody, as Ellie wanted. However, because Ellie had experienced the pain of many injustices, she stated her goal as that of helping Ellie to have "a fair hearing" in court. Although she had little control over the caseworker, she also agreed to attend as many quarterly case review meetings as possible to foster good communication between all relevant parties. She also suggested that all reports be discussed with Ellie to maintain a high level of respect in the relationship. Ellie was pleased with these suggestions.

Family and Others
Figure 5.1 is a brief genogram of Ellie's family. In Chapter 7, we will see how a basic genogram can be transformed into an intervention in its own right, with another layer of questioning. However, at this point in the case, the clinician begins with just the basics. With middle-class parents and an older sister who was married and financially success-ful, Ellie's circumstances were significantly different from those of her immediate family. Although she did not accept public assistance and had her own health insurance, she did not have a driver's license and could not afford a car. However, she suggested that her "deeper issues" related to her family, especially to her mother, as well as "codepen-dency" on the wrong type of men. When asked, she said she thought her mother and stepfather might be willing to come to some sessions.

Hypotheses: Using Common Themes
1. Race and gender discrimination may affect Ellie's stress level, coping style, and self-esteem.
2. Social class issues may contribute to conflict between Ellie and her mother and to Ellie's lack of financial resources.
3. Ellie has a large extended family that may be an important resource.
4. Divorce may have affected Ellie's early development.
5. Ellie's ability to provide leadership, balance, and harmony for her children may be hampered by her individual functioning in relationships with men.
6. Injustices, disapproval by family, and Ellie's desire to prove to those in authority that she is legitimate (respect) may have come from long-standing developmental experi-ences, thus problem severity may be rated as chronic.

Initial Treatment Contract
The therapist suggested that Ellie return for two sessions to discuss her relationship with her mother and the fathers of her four children. This would help the clinician understand the current significant relationships in her life. Thereafter, her parents would be invited to attend and reflect upon Ellie's life story.

Thus far, the joining and intake processes have included nonlabeling, non-judgemental approaches that are common in all forms of family therapy. In this case study, a particular emphasis was placed upon the joining instructions of MST (Cunningham & Henngeler, 1999) and the suggestions of Boyd-Franklin (1989) for working with African American families.

As the referral and intake stage comes to a close, beginning family therapists often ask certain questions as they prepare for the initial interview. These represent common clinical situations that can have a significant impact on the course of therapy. In preparing for the first interview, the following section provides some guidelines to help practitioners think about these questions.

QUESTIONS THAT BEGINNING CLINICIANS OFTEN ASK

1. How Should I Handle the Issue of Alcohol If I Suspect It Is a Part of the Problem?

When family members identify alcohol as part of the presenting problem, the issue of alcohol must be addressed if therapy is to be successful. The therapist must assess the function of alcohol and its relationship to the problem in the family. Is the family concerned that one of its members is abusing alcohol? How has the family dealt with this problem? How are family members affected by the alcohol abuse? Do those affected family members have a plan for addressing the issue? Treadway (1989) suggests that if the therapist and family are therapeutically joined, family members may raise concern about the chemical abuse of another member. He emphasizes the importance of the twin objectives of remaining allied (joined) with the alleged substance abuser and remaining neutral about the chemical dependence problem. The beginning therapist should understand that discussion of the alcohol use provokes defensiveness on the part of the client unless those two objectives have been achieved.

Terms such as *problem drinking* or *alcohol use* are preferred to *alcoholic*. Treadway also suggests that the therapist and client develop a controlled-drinking contract (e.g., time-limited abstinence). If clients are unable to comply with this plan, they should be referred to Alcoholics Anonymous (AA) and obtain a chemical-dependence assessment. If other family members object to this type of plan, the clinician can use their objections as an opportunity to intervene with the family and begin encouraging the new patterns of thought and behavior necessary for successful recovery.

When the therapist suspects alcohol is contributing to the problem but family members do not identify it as part of the problem, the issue should be considered as a preliminary hypothesis that must be explored and validated before focusing treatment in that direction. Tracking interactional sequences and exploring the referral process can elicit information about the evolution of the presenting problem. As this is done, the practitioner can assess alcohol use by asking if any member was using alcohol or drugs before, during, or after the sequences described. Steinglass, Bennett, Wolin, and Reiss (1987) encourage clinicians to make a distinction between families who have become organized with an alcoholic identity and those who happen to have an alcoholic member. Their research sheds much light on various types of alcoholic families, suggesting that the stereotype of a dysfunctional family does not represent the diverse levels of competence and strength that may exist among families affected by alcohol.

2. How Should I Deal With a Suicide Threat?

A suicide threat brings with it tremendous responsibility. The first step in dealing with a suicide threat is to understand the extent of the client's thinking. Does this client have a well-thought-out plan for conducting the suicide? What keeps him or her from completing this plan? What effects does the suicide threat have on the family? What message is the client trying to send by expressing this threat? Is the suicide threat linked to other losses in the family? Is the client attempting to help another family member avoid a painful transition? Beginning therapists may be tempted to offer the person advice or argue against suicide. At the beginning of a conversation about suicide, exploring and asking the preceding questions with concerned curiosity is important. If the therapist takes too strong a position, the determined client may decide to go underground and withhold information to maintain personal control. If the therapist remains concerned and exploratory at the outset, the client is more likely to share fully regarding the extent of his or her progression toward an actual attempt.

Once the therapist has listened to and explored the client's experience, she may proceed toward an intervention strategy. If the danger of suicide presents itself during an individual session (because of previous attempts or the presence of a specific plan), the therapist should discuss a no-suicide contract that will stay in force until a family or network intervention can be organized. Family members and significant others should be notified immediately. The family and others (e.g., referral person, agency personnel, or physicians) should be convened to build a coalition that will cooperate around therapeutic goals. One group of family therapists developed an in-home crisis intervention strategy that avoided hospitalization in 42 of 50 cases (Pittman, DeYoung, Flomenhaft, Kaplan, & Langsley, 1966). Madanes (1981) provides guidelines for addressing suicidal adolescents, and Scalise (1992) reports the successful structuring of a family suicide watch in the case of a suicidal adolescent. In the case of suicidal adults, the family therapist should engage spouses, significant others, or extended family members in discussions regarding any significant life-cycle transitions or changes in family roles that might assist in understanding how the suicide threat could be a response to some unrecognized problem (Pittman et al., 1966). Efforts should be made to involve the network in treatment. Making sure that all the members of the therapeutic system (family, friends, caseworkers, etc.) commit to the goals and the successful completion of treatment is a critical feature of this therapy (Landau-Stanton & Stanton, 1985).

3. What Should I Do If I Discover Family Violence?

Increased awareness of family violence has drawn the attention of family therapists to their responsibilities in this area. The therapist must be aware of behaviors that indicate physical abuse. For example, a mother may appear depressed although seeking help for her children rather than for herself. Families often feel shame, so members find it difficult to discuss the abuse. Some therapists are legally bound to report violence to the appropriate agency (e.g., Adult Protective Services) if they suspect it. Informing clients properly of any legal responsibility early in the initial interview is important so that if abuse or violence becomes apparent, clients do not feel betrayed by the therapist.

As the issue of reporting is addressed with clients, family therapists should explain the procedure as it is carried out in the given community. In some communities, if clients are already voluntarily seeking therapy, the consequences of reporting may be minimal, with little disruption to the family or the therapy. However, in other cases, more formal involvement with the legal system might be necessary. In view of this diversity, beginning practitioners should thoroughly investigate local procedures under a variety of circumstances to be as accurate as possible when explaining the process to families. In addition, practitioners must understand the legal definition of abuse in their community to avoid unnecessary reports.

In all cases, maintaining a position of partnership with all family members is best, with special emphasis on maintaining an empathic bond with the abuser. The process of reporting can then be an opportunity to join with the family by highlighting the courage it takes to discuss the violence and by suggesting that many people are never able to muster the courage to do so (Jenkins, 1991). By emphasizing what courage has already been shown, the therapist can lay a positive foundation for the reporting process.

In some cases, therapists are able to persuade clients to personally make the call in the office as a manifestation of their commitment to improving the relationship. By speaking directly with authorities, clients are able to take greater control over their lives, and correspondingly, they often feel empowered and respected. They receive information directly from social services and do not have to be dependent on the therapist for interpreting the process. Therapists can help families who remain reluctant to participate in reporting by encouraging them to make an anonymous telephone call for information, and then the actual report. If danger is not imminent, the clinician and family might also be able to delay the report until they can agree on how the report will be made. In these cases, however, the issue should not be confused—the question is not whether a report will be made, but rather how the report will be made, that is, who will call, what will be said, and so on.

In defining the problem, the therapist must view the violence as the problem rather than as a symptom of something else. Whereas other dynamics such as gender socialization, communication patterns, or faulty belief systems may encourage violence, family therapists must remain firm in defining the initial problem as violence, with the hope of creating a safe foundation for examining the related dynamics. Without addressing the safety issues first, a climate for further growth cannot occur.

4. How Should I Handle Family Secrets?

Family secrets usually become an issue in two ways: first, when family members or referral sources want to disclose information about other people to the therapist prior to the first session (thereby forming a covert coalition); and second, when family members in individual sessions disclose information about others that they are unwilling to discuss in their presence.

Such revelations need not be disruptive if the therapist takes a few precautions. One is to decide how such information might affect the therapist's relationship with other family members. For example, Keith and Whitaker (1985) give an account of a young practitioner who received a telephone call between sessions about a family member's alcoholism. He decided to share the information with the family. Subsequent sessions were preempted by a suicide attempt on the part of the identified patient. Keith and Whitaker suggest that families have their own wisdom about how much information they can tolerate.

In this case, they argue, the clinician violated the family's threshold for emotionally charged information. These professionals suggest that revealing secret information might be unnecessary if the therapist abides by the family's intuitive judgment on such issues. They make the assumption that there is no such thing as a secret in families because members know at some covert level and have merely agreed not to address it openly.

The Milan team has chosen to avoid receiving disclosures altogether (Selvini Palazzoli & Prata, 1982). Instead, the team maintains a strict rule that if the discloser must share the information, that information is not kept confidential, and he or she must be willing to be exposed as the source of the information. In receiving between-session phone calls, the team begins by stating that anything disclosed must be discussed in the next session. Then, callers have the opportunity to decide how much to say. If family members are unwilling to change their rules of communication, the Milan team is unwilling to become part of a covert coalition. With this approach, maintaining the neutral position of the therapist (process) takes priority over gaining additional information (content).

These examples illustrate issues of context and therapist bias. However, in cases where individuals share personal information that is difficult to share in group sessions, family therapists must make decisions about structure that depend on the stage of the therapeutic process. Because we are discussing the initial interview, the therapist should take into account whether a client's spouse will eventually be engaged and how the therapist will delay the potential alignment with the client until both parties are present. The order of the initial interview presented here is designed to help the therapist stay away from detailed and intimate content when individuals come in without other family members until the structure of the individual's significant relationships can be identified. It is also helpful for the therapist to explain to the client that the order of the initial interview leaves the most detailed information for last so that the therapist can obtain a general picture of the client's relational world.

Then, if an individual is willing to invite a partner, the therapist can suggest that the details of problem definition be saved for the next session. In later stages of the therapeutic process, clients might request individual sessions in which they begin to disclose information on a different level from that shared of group sessions. The therapist must assess family and couple dynamics to determine how these disclosures should be handled given the current goals of the therapeutic process.

When the information disclosed concerns abuse or safety issues in the current relationship, therapists must assess whether his or her relationship with the abuser is strong enough to confront the abuse directly without escalating danger for the spouse. In the worst case, more individual sessions with the victim might be required to develop an initial safety plan. Sheinberg (1992) has addressed treatment impasses at the disclosure of incest by integrating constructionism and feminism into strategies that respect all sides of three major dilemmas: social control versus therapy, pride versus shame, and loyalty versus protection. Her work makes an important contribution to addressing secrets of this nature.

If the information disclosed is important but not related to physical safety, the therapist is wise to go slowly, taking the time to understand the complex issues of secrecy, privacy, and confidentiality. In particular, family therapists should consult a collection edited by Imber-Black (1993), who makes a detailed study of the topic. In this work, she encourages clinicians to understand their own biases about the sharing of information and to grapple with the complexities that make many unique situations call for careful understanding by the professional. For example, people who are HIV positive must develop strategies for maintaining their privacy that minimize potential discrimination. Some choose never to disclose their diagnosis to certain family members. Others choose to deal with their shock and depression before disclosing the diagnosis to their children. This delay enables them to be more available to the needs of those children as they adjust to and cope with new circumstances. Understanding the dilemmas that accompany each circumstance is an important goal during the initial stages of treatment.

SUMMARY

Treatment has begun! The clinician has an introduction to the family. Whether in person or through intake, initial contacts should be guided by the common elements of the therapeutic relationship in Chapter 4. As treatment continues, the clinician moves forward with an assessment of client motivation, an introduction to significant others, a description of the problem, and beginning hypotheses. These elements become the foundation for a preliminary assessment in treatment.

As in driving a car, these issues are like weather and road conditions. Client motivation gives us a "read" on whether to move full steam ahead or take a side trip to find the right goals for motivation. Significant others may represent foul or fair weather. Early discussions may uncover resources and challenges within the client's relational world. Beginning hypotheses are based upon the themes in Chapter 3. They are like the roadmap that gives us a general idea about the route we take. They provide us with questions to assess individual functioning, relational functioning, and problem severity. Through this beginning assessment, we choose our route from key elements in the models from Chapters 1 and 2.

However, this is just the beginning! In Chapter 6, we add another layer to the process of assessment and treatment planning, exploring these themes further and working to organize treatment, explore client experience, address relationships, and develop a shared direction. These general tasks in family therapy are applied to the real world of diagnosis, treatment planning, and agency practice. As your road trip continues, you will find the heroism of clients inspiring when paired with your own creativity and compassion. We've found that this chemistry within the therapeutic system is what makes the entire process worthwhile. At the same time, the big picture of treatment planning, managed care, and getting paid are what make the process financially possible. Chapter 6 will help you make sense out of it all.

The Next Step: From Problem Definition to Treatment Plan

CHAPTER OUTLINE

Overview of Family Therapy Tasks

Organizing Treatment

Clarifying the Role of the Therapist

Describing the Therapeutic Process

Exploring Client Experience

Defining the Problem

Assessing Individual Functioning

Addressing Relational Functioning

Tracking Interactional Sequences: The "Microscope" of Family Therapy

Expanding the System: "There Is No Such Thing As a Person Without a Relationship"

Completing the GARF

Developing a Shared Direction

Setting Treatment Goals: Where Are You Going?

Setting Process Goals: How Will You Get There?

Starting a Treatment Plan: Academia vs. Real World

Summary

CORE COMPETENCIES

3.2.1	**Perceptual**	Integrate client feedback, assessment, contextual information, and diagnosis with treatment goals and plan.
3.3.2	**Executive**	Prioritize treatment goals.
3.3.3	**Executive**	Develop a clear plan of how sessions will be conducted.
3.3.4	**Executive**	Structure treatment to meet clients' needs and to facilitate systemic change.

As families and therapists begin their work together, the path followed by each is unique. As explained in Chapter 5, therapists explore the referral process to understand the natural problem-solving process of families before they enter treatment. We learn whether help-seeking has involved the family's informal (nonprofessional) relational network, a professional network, or both. As part of this learning process, we ask specific questions about interactions—the thoughts, feelings, intentions, behaviors, and perceptions of relevant parties—which teaches us about the client's potential motivation for therapeutic work.

In some cases, referral and intake leads to assembling a group of relevant individuals involved in the initial assessment process. One model of family engagement uses the term *concerned other* to refer to a variety of people who could potentially attend a problem-solving session (Garrett, Landau-Stanton, Stanton, Stellato-Kobat, & Stellato-Kobat, 1997). In other cases, however, the initial assessment is another opportunity to explore the relational network of an individual and develop a strategy for involving important persons.

In Chapter 4, we reviewed self-development and how beginning therapists might prepare to work with unusual situations that are new to their experience. During the initial assessment is usually when the worlds of the client and the therapist meet. This meeting of worlds is like two vehicles approaching each other—circumstances will lead to either a collision or a coordinated series of movements in different lanes of the highway. If the therapist has engaged in self-development and personal preparation, he or she has the option to follow (join), lead (intervene), or drive parallel with the other car (explore) on this journey that now becomes more complex than merely controlling a single vehicle. If clients and therapist quickly agree upon goals, two cars are reduced to one (it saves gas!). The terrain might entail traffic jams or isolated country roads, but using the resources that each rider brings regardless of the territory (e.g., identifying family strengths) is part of the adventure.

Let's revisit the developmental framework proposed in Chapter 1. A well-organized assessment helps the clinician plan an appropriate itinerary with clients. The purpose of the assessment stage is to:

1. Assess individuals and symptom severity (i.e., individual functioning, DSM-IV).
2. Assess the influences and impact of the problem (i.e., relational functioning, GARF scales).
3. Assess problem severity (situational, transitional, chronic).
4. Create a treatment plan that is developmentally appropriate.

We began gathering information related to these goals during referral and intake. In the next sessions, clinicians can discover more specific information that will help them chart a course of action. In practical terms, the topics of the next sessions will depend on what information was gathered during referral and intake. The assessment stage begins with intake and referral, but may evolve into *assessment as intervention*. The number of sessions for assessment is variable, but most managed care companies want a treatment plan and goals established by the third session. Thus, this chapter assumes between one and three sessions from intake through initial treatment plan. Box 6.1 provides a

I. Referral process (Milan Team)
  A. Step-by-step process that led to the appointment and who was involved
  B. Client's motivation for coming
II. Intake process
  A. Statement of the problem
  B. Family information
  C. Concerned others
  D. Schedule
  E. Hypotheses and relevant questions for first session (MST, Milan team)
III. Session outline
  A. Negotiate structure (structural, behavioral, experiential)
    1. Discuss organization, expectations, and purpose of the session
    2. Describe the therapeutic process
    3. Clarify the roles of those in attendance
  B. Explore client experience (solution-focused, narrative, Milan team)
    1. Join with the client according to their expectations and level of motivation
    2. Explore each person's opinion about the problem, *including those individuals who are not present*
    3. Explore history and onset of the problem (Milan team, intergenerational)
      a. Situational
      b. Transitional
      c. Chronic
    4. Explore exceptions, those times in which the problem does not occur (solution-focused)
  C. Address relationships (structural, intergenerational)
    1. Track interactional sequences related to the presenting problem
    2. Determine the views of other important people missing from the session
    3. Address the inclusion of important people
    4. Define the problem in relational terms
  D. Develop a shared direction
    1. Set treatment goals
    2. Set process goals
      a. Assess level of crisis
      b. Decide on the pace of intervention
        (1) Clarification (M.R.I.)
        (2) Exploration (narrative)
        (3) Experimentation (strategic, behavioral, intergenerational)
    3. Develop a treatment plan
      a. Presenting problem
      b. Relational goals and issues
      c. Intervention strategies matched to history/onset of problem
      d. Role of the therapist
    4. Highlight strengths and instill hope (narrative, solution-focused)
    5. Propose options and elicit feedback (strategic, M.R.I.)

summary of the entire assessment stage, including the four general tasks of family therapy that should be repeated in all sessions. These four tasks provide a step-by-step process that ends with a final treatment plan.

OVERVIEW OF FAMILY THERAPY TASKS

A review of family therapy literature reveals that several approaches to the initial interview share some common elements. Breunlin (1985) noted a beginning phase of family therapy in which the therapist organizes the referral system, convenes the family, begins the helping relationship, assesses the family, and develops a definition of the problem. Haley (1976) described the initial interview in four stages: social introductions, problem definition, interactional description, and goal setting. According to Segal and Bavelas (1983), the goal of the initial interview is to gather specific behavioral information regarding the nature of the complaint and the client's attempted solutions; this resembles Haley's interactional stage. The general pattern for many schools of thought involves the evolution of the therapeutic system in which family and therapist come together to determine the who, what, where, when, and how of family therapy.

As the trainee prepares to practice, developing a plan that provides a sense of direction is helpful. Some models have their own protocols for conducting each session. For example, Todd and Selekman (1991), in their work on adolescent substance abuse, provide a useful model for integrating structural-strategic family therapy with narrative and solution-focused approaches. They recommend starting with traditional structural-strategic approaches and implementing narrative, solution-focused, or paradoxical modes of practice when impasses occur.

The integrative approach in this book builds upon common themes that address family process (Chapter 3) and common elements from practice (Chapter 4). It is based upon a review of family therapy literature and personal experiences with minority and community-based populations. As previous chapters explained, the therapeutic relationship is an important element that should be monitored during each step of the process, and the referral process contains important clues to clients' motivation. The next step should include the tasks of:

1. Organizing treatment clearly and collaboratively.
2. Exploring experience and context from the micro to the macro level.
3. Seeking relational change.
4. Developing a direction that considers the needs of important family members.

As with other stages and interactions covered in the book thus far, each of these tasks may proceed in order or may overlap during complex exchanges with the family. These steps provide a map to integrate theory, practice, and the family therapy skills covered in the remainder of the book. With this in mind, let's see how these steps can guide an initial assessment and lead the therapist to a treatment plan.

ORGANIZING TREATMENT

During the assessment stage, the professional takes responsibility for exploring what family therapy will be for an individual or family—how it will be organized and how decisions will be made about the process. In subsequent sessions, organizing treatment will include discussions about previous assignments, expectations, and the purpose of each meeting. These expectations should be summarized at the outset to provide an avenue for the client or therapist to ask for changes in the process. For example, if certain family members are continually absent, the impact of this must be explored and a decision made about how the therapeutic process will proceed in light of this change in attendance. If a crisis has occurred between meetings, this initial organizing task provides an avenue to decide the relevance of information from the previous meeting. This task, at the beginning of each meeting, should be a mutual agreement about what will happen in that session.

Clarifying the Role of the Therapist

The family therapist and the family each bring a set of expectations to the therapy hour related to their roles, the procedures that will be followed, and the conditions to be met by each party. For example, perhaps the family has a media-related stereotype of a counselor, therapist, or social worker. Perhaps the family therapist also holds certain stereotypes or has a desire to maintain a certain image with the family. What if the two sets of expectations do not match? To use Bateson's terms, all communication has report (content) and command (process) levels: the report level is the verbal information transmitted; The command level is the nonverbal manifestation of how the sender is defining the relationship (Ruesch & Bateson, 1951). This means that the family therapist and family each define the nature of the relationship, but neither may be openly communicating their expectations to the other. For example, the family therapist may have chosen a role as neutral negotiator for the family. Meanwhile, the family may have defined the therapist as a referee or even an ally. As these implicit expectations unfold through nonverbal behaviors (process), the implicit conflict may interfere with explicitly stated goals (content).

Once the implicit information is brought forward, roles can be clarified in a way that enlists cooperation more fully, as illustrated in this example:

> A woman sought help from a family therapist, and a pattern developed in which she brought up a different problem each week. Puzzled and frustrated, the therapist wondered about how the woman might be defining the professional's role. In the next session, the therapist inquired about the pattern and what it could mean. After some hypothesizing by the therapist, the woman was able to explain that involvement was more important to her than problem solving. She thought that if she didn't bring in some problem to talk about each week, the therapist would discontinue treatment. Having clarified how she was defining the relationship (command level), the therapist could help the woman feel more in charge of therapy and how long it continued. Once the problem of involvement was clarified, they could decide which problem was most important.

As family therapists learn how to effectively clarify their role, reviewing Table 1.1 for examples of therapeutic roles that are adopted by various models of family therapy might be helpful. These examples can be used to reconcile differences in expectations and to explain the role the therapist decides to assume.

Describing the Therapeutic Process

Once the therapist begins the initial interview, he or she should orient clients to the process of therapy—that is, describe the staff involved and the specific techniques employed to pursue goals. Providing at least a minimal structure of the therapeutic process is important at the outset. Just as a travel agent might provide an itinerary for a family vacation, the therapist might provide an overview of the initial interview in the following way:

> Today, we'll talk about things that concern you (your family) and discuss what you want to do about them. I want to know what is important to you, and I assume you might like to know what I can do to help. We can pool our ideas and come up with some ideas about where to go from here. If you're not in the middle of a crisis, I usually spend a few sessions learning everything I can about what works best for you. If you are in a crisis, we can decide what you might need immediately. After that, we'll develop a plan of action. If you try something and it doesn't work, we'll talk about it and figure out what else might help.

The description of the therapeutic process will vary depending on the family's previous experience in therapy. Families who have not been to therapy or who are uncertain of what to expect will require more specificity. If families have had previous therapeutic contact, exploring their expectations for service will be important. After hearing about the family's previous experiences with counseling, family therapists might need to clarify how the current experience might be the same as or different from experiences with other practitioners.

One of the questions the client might ask is whether the therapist will reveal what is said in the session to others (for example, parents, a probation officer, or a social worker). Before the question arises, family therapists should say that what is discussed will be held confidential *except under certain conditions*. A promise without this qualification can undermine trust, and the therapist loses effectiveness. In certain cases (usually with children or adolescents), it is in the client's best interest to share information. Also, laws in many states mandate reporting under certain circumstances. Consequently, the confidentiality qualification should be included. For example, the therapist might say:

> I will try to keep what we talk about between the four of us, but if one of you said you were planning to do something that would be harmful to you or someone else, I would tell someone else and try to keep anyone from getting hurt. I promise that I'll let you know if I'm going to tell anyone what we've talked about. And sometimes, if I think it would be helpful for someone to know something you've told me, I may ask you if it's okay for me to mention it. For example, if you told me you were having trouble in school, I might ask you if you minded my discussing it with your teachers. It is also important for you to know that the law also requires that I disclose information in certain cases. These include . . .

Box 6.2	**Questions for Negotiating the Process of Therapy**

Who will attend? (Referral source, extended family, others)

What will each person's role be? (Consultant, client, provider of information)

What are the treatment goals? (Presenting problem and desired relational changes)

What are the process goals? (Assessment, then treatment; further exploration to define problem; brainstorming; experimentation)

When will sessions be held? (Frequency or pace)

How will sessions be conducted? (In-session directives, circular or systematic questioning, out-of-session tasks, genograms, specific interventions, psychoeducation)

When will the arrangement be renegotiated?

What fees, resources, space, time, and help are needed?

Who else needs to be made aware of the plan?

Are there any barriers or costs to the plan?

Other questions concerning the therapist's role or the therapeutic relationship might come up throughout therapy sessions and should be answered as they arise. What's crucial in explaining the therapeutic process is relieving anxieties that clients might have, giving them some idea about what is likely to happen when they come, and helping them feel at ease in the situation. Box 6.2 provides a series of questions to help the practitioner negotiate aspects of therapy with families.

EXPLORING CLIENT EXPERIENCE

Each session should afford all participants the opportunity to respond to questions about their thoughts, feelings, actions, intentions, and senses regarding the presenting problem. During the initial interview, the therapist should obtain descriptions of interactional sequences and of each person's perception of the problem over time. As therapy proceeds from session to session, systemic themes (i.e., transitions, intergenerational process, gender, etc.) can be chosen as the focus of these explorations (see Chapter 3). Discussions can also include reviews of attempted solutions, times when things went well, and the telling of stories about important experiences that form the basis for a client's worldview.

Defining the Problem

In the early years of family therapy, problem definition was a continual struggle. Clients would come in asking for help with a child's behavior or their own predefined mental illness, but family therapists, anxious to convert their client families to systemic thinking, were quick to persuade families to think of their child's behavior as a family problem or their own mental illness as a marital problem. This approach only served to communicate blame to other family members. Today, many constructivist approaches seek to "co-create" the definition of the problem (O'Hanlon & Weiner-Davis, 1989), and evidence-based models speak explicitly about avoiding resistance and respecting the family's uniqueness. These trends suggest a collaborative process. By asking families to clarify what they would like to see happen in family therapy, therapists have the opportunity to rid themselves of any hidden agendas that might define the problem in ways that conflict with the family's way of thinking (theory of change).

To begin a dialogue about the problem with a family or individual, the family therapist might ask the following circular questions as a way of exploring clients' definitions while obtaining relational information:

1. What brings you here?
2. What would be helpful for us to discuss?
3. Who first noticed the problem and how long ago was this?
4. What led you (or another person) to conclude that this was a problem?
5. Who else agrees or disagrees that this is the problem?
6. Who else (inside or outside the family) has an opinion about the problem?
7. Have you or anyone else thought of any other possibilities regarding what the problem might be?
8. Are there times when the problem isn't occurring? What is going on at those times?
9. What are the differences between times when the problem does and doesn't occur?
10. What would happen if things don't change?

As we have seen, families sometimes come to counseling with a definition that has been created by others in the system. Do clients agree or disagree with the views of these authorities? If clients disagree ("I don't think I have a problem"), the therapist may be able to influence the definition of the problem away from a pathologized view. Sometimes families are relieved at this and are able to express their hopes and fears. However, if families feel strongly about a certain view of the presenting problem ("I'm bipolar," or "My family is dysfunctional"), the family therapist must negotiate a cooperative relationship above all else, rather than one that unwittingly becomes subtly adversarial due to philosophical differences. An example of this is when a family comes in seeking help for a chemically dependent member. If the family therapist suggests that the problem is really a family problem, the family members are likely to leave the session thinking to themselves, "But we still think the problem is his drinking!" They may be reluctant to return. Instead, the therapist can develop a problem definition that unifies diverse opinions, such as "His drinking has affected your relationship, and you wish things could be better between you."

Thus, in the initial session, the therapist explicitly accepts the family's definition of the problem while implicitly exploring additional ways to describe it using relational terms. As the family members answer these questions, accepting their description of the problem without criticism or premature advice is important. Validating the importance of each member's contribution is also essential ("That's a very good point. You seem to have thought a lot about this issue"). If family members interrupt each other, remind them that they will each have an opportunity to express their views.

If an individual has come to the session alone, the definition of the problem might evolve from *questions not only about the individual's opinion but about those of his or her significant other* ("If your wife was here with us, what would she say?"). If a couple or family has come for family therapy, the definition might incorporate each person's opposing view of the problem. For example, if a husband says the problem is too little sex and his wife says the problem is too little communication, the family therapist might suggest that the problem is the couple's inability to meet each other's needs. The newly formulated problem definition must include the various positions within the relational network.

Once descriptions of the problem emerge, the practitioner should ask questions that bring about greater specificity. Clients will often express global concerns through the use of labels (depressed, angry, nervous, etc.). Whereas labels offer a general indication of the problem area, they often mean different things to different people. For example, a family member may say, "I don't want to go to school," which really means she is unhappy. A therapist might use the following questions to help each family member clarify the problem:

1. What do you mean by _____?
2. Give me some examples of _____?
3. Describe a situation when you _____?
4. How does this affect you now?
5. Tell me about the last time _____ happened.

The goal is to help each family member to be specific and concrete, so that the problem defined will become more solvable. As the family members share their views, therapists can build on this information to assess individual functioning.

Assessing Individual Functioning

As we continue our review of the assessment stage of treatment, it is important to reflect on mental health assessments in general and how family therapists fit into the larger culture of mental health treatment. As illustrated in Chapters 1 and 2, family therapy became an alternate approach to traditional mental health treatments as psychotherapy became more mainstream in the United States during the last half of the twentieth century. Today, traditional mental health treatment approaches use a *medical model* that involves *diagnosing* a problem using the Diagnostic and Statistical Manual of Mental Disorders, fourth edition (DSM-IV, American Psychiatric Association, 1994). This approach is accepted among healthcare providers, insurance companies and many community agencies. Although the profession of marriage and family therapy has remained unique in its relational/contextual views of mental health problems and their corresponding solutions, family therapists generally practice in environments where it is necessary to provide a DSM-IV diagnosis and assess mental status, suicidal ideation and other risk factors. As mentioned in Chapter 1, these settings often begin by seeking stabilization and a return to the person's previous level of functioning. Thus, mainstream family therapists learn what Bertram (2001) refers to as "walking the MFT walk while talking the DSM talk."

Describing Symptoms. In many settings, problem lists, mental status exams, and diagnostic report forms help the clinician to assess individual functioning. Table 6.1 lists some categories in a biopsychosocial assessment. Suggestions to the right stimulate the therapist to explore systemic/relational issues whenever possible, providing opportunities for the clinician to expand on each topic in a relational way. This table provides the practitioner with a thumbnail sketch of the main problems/symptoms and some of the relational resources/ challenges that exist for the person or family. In addition to considering the information generated by these standard sources, it is important to explore the client's motivation and worldview. Using our driving metaphor, motivation

Table 6.1 | Common Symptoms, Goals and Relational Issues

Type of symptom		Goal	Relational issues
Physical	Abuse	Food	Leadership
	Neglect	Clothing	Clarity of roles
	Poverty	Shelter	Protection
	Trauma	Safety	
Emotional	Depression	Self-esteem	Secure attachment
	Anxiety	Resilience	Belonging
	Mood swings	Hope	Differentiation
	Flashbacks	Confidence	Personal authority
	Confusion		
	Trauma stress		
Interpersonal	Conflict	Cooperation	Communication
	Trauma interference	Shared responsibility	Rules
	Betrayal	Balance of power	Beliefs
	Chaos	Productivity	Boundaries
		Intimacy	Adaptibility
			Roles
Societal	Attention deficits	Prosocial behavior	Isolation
	Defiance	Success with peers	Oppression
	Hyperactivity	Success with job, school	Justice
	Paranoia	Social support	Relational ethics
	Violence	Community support	

and worldview dictate whether to pull over at the rest stop or continue at the same speed.

Acknowledging Motivation and Worldview.   In Chapters 4 and 5, we discussed the skills of reframing resistance and exploring the referral process. The sections that follow prepare clinicians to identify the important issues related to motiviation and worldview. Quite often, clients have hidden agendas that they are unable to make explicit. These are unspoken intentions of which clients believe others might disapprove. In an earlier case example, a woman was afraid to express her perceptions of how she thought therapy was organized. In marital therapy, an unfaithful spouse may come to the first session simply to assuage his or her guilt, having already decided to leave the marriage. Without ever intending to salvage the relationship, this client might hope that the therapist will become someone for the abandoned spouse to lean on. However, the client might be unable to disclose that intention unless the family therapist raises the possibility first. Similarly, a single parent may seek family therapy for his or her child when the parent is still grieving the loss of the marriage.

In the case regarding infidelity, the hidden agenda will have a great influence on the course of therapy, especially if it remains unknown to the family therapist. If it can become known, it may become the focus of therapy because it is actually the primary motivation for seeking services. In the case of the single parent, the hidden agenda may not greatly affect the course of therapy because divorce-adjustment work can be done in a way that simultaneously benefits parent and child. If the parent does not validate a therapist's hunch, the therapist has nothing to lose in staying with the stated agenda.

In addition, families often have expectations regarding who will actually be seen in sessions (the child alone, each spouse separately, etc.), how the problem will be defined, and what topics will or will not be discussed. Although it is difficult to second-guess all the possible expectations, the therapist can try to join sufficiently so that families feel comfortable in disclosing even their most sensitive agendas (for example, "I'm hoping you can tell me if my marriage is worth saving"). Sometimes making some tentative guesses about what clients are expecting is helpful; other times the family therapist needs only to provide an atmosphere that is comfortable for sharing all possible responses. When the therapist shows an acceptance of the most unusual (i.e., "Sometimes people think I'm a little crazy, so you'll have to bear with me. . . ."), the family will be more forthcoming with hidden agendas. However, there will be additional opportunities to clarify these expectations as the therapist learns more about relevant relationships.

ADDRESSING RELATIONAL FUNCTIONING

As individuals' experiences form a collective picture of behaviors, perceptions, and relationships, a therapeutic dialogue develops in which the practitioner maintains a focus on the important and relevant relationships connected to either the problem itself or possible solutions. Specific interventions from pre-ferred models are part of this task. If a person is being seen individually, interac-tions should still maintain a focus on relationships, not behaviors or perceptions alone. As in problem defining, we recommend that systemic therapists ask about the experience of significant others not present. By including a variety of views in the discussion, the process remains tied to relational factors and maintains a broader view of the interactional context. In addition, the therapist should make it a routine practice to obtain a clear, close-up picture of family interactions that occur in relationship to the problem.

Tracking Interactional Sequences: The "Microscope" of Family Therapy

Regardless of the school of thought, much of the activity of a family therapist is focused on gathering interactional information about the family. Embedded in interactional sequences are thoughts, emotions, intentions, and behaviors that become targets for change within the relationship. This is why I use the analogy of the microbiologist: Tracking sequences is the "microscope" of the family therapist. Therapists should identify each element as a potential point of intervention in a relationship (see Chapter 7). In addition, focusing on these sequences begins to transform the description of the problem from an indi-vidual attribute (for example, "He's depressed") to an interactional definition ("When he's depressed, we don't agree on the solution").

Box 6.3 provides questions that illustrate how to track communication in interactional sequences. The approaches used in tracking a family's inter-personal patterns are similar to relationship techniques derived from client-centered therapy (Rogers, 1961). The therapist's open-ended questions, ability to reflect content and feelings, and attentive demeanor help establish a supportive relationship with the family. More complex techniques of track-ing center on the therapist's efforts to "listen with a third ear," that is, the therapist responds to thoughts and feelings that family members may be un-able to acknowledge. When family members begin to talk, they usually de-scribe the content of the problem. For example, a parent might say that a child "won't come home" or "won't do what I tell him." Therapists listen to what family members say about each other (content), but they are equally concerned about the process—how family members interact with each other. Do family members talk for each other? The therapist who focuses only on the content will not be able to assess the interactional pattern that con-tributes to the problem. Colapinto (1991) states:

> Following the content and the process of the family interaction, like the needle of a record player follows a groove, is the basic structural procedure to collect information on the family map. As the therapist listens to and encourages the con-tributions of family members, observes their mutual dances, and asks for clarifi-cations and expansions, he or she begins to draft first answers to structural ques-tions: Whether family members can converse without being interrupted, whether they tend to interact in age appropriate ways, how they organize each other's

| Box 6.3 | **Questions for Sequences, Meanings, and Messages** |

Interactional Sequences

Who did what when?

What did he or she actually say or do?

What was happening right before this?

When he or she said or did that, what happened next?

And then what happened?

Then what did they do?

While this was going on, where were _____, _____, _____ (other family or household members)?

When he or she does that, what happens next?

Meanings and Messages

What was actually said?

What were you thinking when he said that?

When you said _____, what were you thinking?

When you thought _____, how did you come to that conclusion? (Where did you get that idea?)

---

behaviors, how they deal with or avoid conflict, what alliances they tend to form. (pp. 431–432)

The therapist can also assess such patterns of interaction by asking Milan-style questions related to sequences (see Table 2.1 on page 32). When a family member begins to describe a problem, the therapist must explore with whom this problem exists and how the sequence unfolds. The following dialogue illustrates how this may be accomplished.

THERAPIST: Tell me what the problem is today.

MOTHER: He won't listen to me.

THERAPIST: Who won't listen to you?

MOTHER: My son, Eric.

THERAPIST: What does he do to indicate that he doesn't listen?

MOTHER: He just sits silently and watches TV when I tell him to do something.

THERAPIST: And what do you do when he does that?

MOTHER: Sometimes I go in and make him listen to me.

THERAPIST: How do you do that?

MOTHER: I go in and shut off the TV to get his attention.

THERAPIST: And then what happens?

MOTHER: He usually throws a tantrum.

THERAPIST: So what happens next? How does your husband get involved?

The important issue here is that the therapist is thinking about the pattern of interactions that surrounds the problem even if only one family member in the session. The interactional description of the problem tells us who should be talking to whom about it. For example, can a mother and stepfather discuss the problem in the presence of their child? Rather than reporting about the problem, the family therapist asks the present individuals to describe how the absent members would respond, thus gaining a picture of the interactional sequence before and after the problem. If the therapist cannot visualize exactly what happened, he should continue to ask more detailed questions. To successfully learn this skill, family therapists should practice using Box 6.3 and Table 2.1 in every session. Special attention should be given to repetitive behavioral sequences that occur around the problem and to the specific people involved. Family therapists can use this information to decide whether any important people are missing from the session.

Expanding the System: "There Is No Such Thing As a Person Without a Relationship"

Deciding whom to include in sessions is often difficult for the beginning family therapist. Whereas some pioneers were noted for their insistence upon seeing the entire family (Boszormenyi-Nagy & Framo, 1965; Napier & Whitaker, 1978), others were noted for seeing individuals (Bowen, 1978). We think it is important to remember Whitaker's (1986) assertion that "there is no such thing as a person without a relationship." To many in the profession, this is a central premise of all family therapy. However, in deciding on issues of inclusion, the expectations of the client must also be understood at the beginning of the therapeutic process to negotiate effectively *without coercion*. In most treatment settings, adult clients often come alone, without realization that the clincian wants contact with others. When the individual discovers the therapist's preference, some easily agree, some are surprised and have to think about it, and some definitely do not want others in attendance. The external parties may also be willing, surprised, or very reluctant to attend. A good rule of thumb is to assume the worst and *carefully explore, rather than suggest* any combination of people.

Regardless of who is in the room, the focus of family therapy also includes important relationships outside of formal family ties. For some, relationships between family and school may be targeted for intervention (Amatea & Sherrard, 1989). For others, nonblood kin may be more influential than the biological family (Boyd-Franklin, 1989). Therefore, any system or any set of relationships may be identified as the primary context for problem solving. As a relational network becomes the focus of the assessment, the family therapist develops an approach that fits with the nature of these relationships as they emerge through families, friendships, or various community ties. We believe beginning practitioners will develop greater effectiveness if they give careful thought to the sets of questions throughout this section. The first set concerns the influence of others.

1. **Who is defining the problem?** If it is a spouse or parent not in attendance, involving that person is a priority.
2. **Is the client living with significant others in the household or dependent on others in significant ways?** If so, involving them as sources of information and support should be strongly considered. Engaging spouses for such problems as depression, anxiety, and eating disorders is important. Many times, these individuals are willing to come, but coming simply did not occur to them. At other times, they may need to know they are not being blamed but, rather, are considered a therapeutic influence upon the healing process.
3. **Does the client explicitly name others as a legal, psychological, financial, or relational part of the presenting problem?** To ensure a peaceful resolution, the client must believe that the therapist can remain on his or her side while also engaging the other party. If convincing the client of this proves to be beyond the skill level of the clinician, working systemically may involve playing devil's advocate, developing interactional strategies, or asking questions that provide multiple points of view.
4. **Has a spouse definitely decided upon a divorce?** If not, when the therapist informed consent, provides the information could include that individual sessions may contribute to further distance in the marriage. Many times, one spouse who is reluctant to involve the other can clarify her or his own fears regarding including the husband or wife. Addressing these fears can become a preliminary goal until the person is assured that the therapist will be able to conduct conjoint therapy in a manner that is comfortable for the reluctant spouse. The skill level of the therapist may be a factor in this issue, and later chapters will address basic skills for conducting conjoint sessions.
5. **Are there significant others who appear to have ongoing knowledge of the day-to-day occurrence of the problem?** If so, a preliminary goal of gathering multiple points of view is important even if those other parties are unwilling to attend. Many times, however, parties who are involved but not necessarily perceived as part of the problem may be willing to attend as consultants. When expectations can be addressed and respected, it is possible to involve a number of people as sources of information or support, as long as the clinician respects their position as nonclient—people who are not asking for help or change.
6. **If others were involved in sessions, would the person seeking help become more or less alienated in the process?** Situations of violence, emotional abuse, and extreme alienation may be contraindications for involving

other parties on whom the client may be dependent. The clinician's skill level, the client's goals, and other contributing circumstances will have to be explored thoroughly to determine the most beneficial course to take.

Depending on who attends the first session, discussions might involve repeated references to significant people who are absent from the session. This is often the case when individuals come alone. These references should prompt the therapist to return to the possibility of including others in some way. Explore the client's ideas about what kind of service to expect and whether including others would conflict with the family's or individual's perception of help. Quite often it is only a general stereotype about psychotherapy that has led to a person's expectations. Because family therapy is different in scope and philosophy, clients deserve the opportunity to become educated about their options in seeking help. These questions can become the basis for therapist and client to negotiate an expanded system that is safe, productive, and supportive.

This second set of questions suggests an in-session exploration of concerns the clients have about process and specific feelings they may have about expanding the system.

1. How did you decide who would participate in today's session?
2. Maybe you are more comfortable without _____ here. Are there some reasons why you would prefer to leave them out?
3. What do you think might happen if _____ was invited?
4. If I encouraged you to invite them, would it be so uncomfortable that you might not return?

The answers to these questions help the family therapist find a starting point from which to explore important relational issues. For example, the therapist can learn about the person's sense of disempowerment in his or her relational network (for example, "I'm afraid you will side with my husband against me"). With this knowledge, the therapist can address each area of discomfort by following a plan that avoids the client's worst fears.

Certainly, in many situations a person's own framework for help would be violated and the inclusion of others would be inappropriate. Conversely, at other times a family therapist will consider the attendance of others to be essential to a positive therapeutic outcome. If the attendance of others seems imperative, before taking a strong position, the family therapist should conduct a self-evaluation. This third set of questions helps the therapist develop a careful, detailed, and respectful plan for expanding the system.

1. Have I elicited and acknowledged fears the client has about inviting others to join us?
2. Have I reassured the client that I can orchestrate a constructive outcome when others are included? Has my reassurance included detailed descriptions of what I will say and do?
3. Do I know enough about these other people, and do I have the skills necessary, to set goals that guarantee the outcome of such a meeting?

4. Am I ignoring messages (verbal or nonverbal) from the client about what is essential to him or her?
5. Am I operating out of a model that narrows my perception of how I can be helpful? Does the client have important information to which I should defer, and should I stop insisting on a certain structure?
6. Have we explored alternative ways of bringing the influence of the expanded system into our sessions, such as speaker phone calls, letters, or the use of empty chairs to represent important others?

The answers to these questions can help the practitioner weigh priorities and skills. In many cases, clients can be shown how the inclusion of others will be helpful. Of particular value is the work of a research project in which family therapists helped drug abusers involve their family of origin in therapy (Van Deusen, Stanton, Scott, Todd, & Mowatt, 1982). In these cases, the therapist might say something like this:

> There are many paths we could take to reach your goals. As a family therapist, I've found that some pathways may seem suitable to an individual at the time, only to find later that the spouse feels more alienated after an individual therapy experience or that the client wishes that friends could understand him the way the therapist does. Because of these situations, I always try to find the road that will be good for the person and good for the person's important relationships at the same time. The best way to find this balance is by involving those other people—in person, by telephone, or in some other way. Then we can look for a "win-win" direction that is good for everyone.

Sometimes, the invited people become motivated clients in their own right *if the therapist helps them to personalize what they can gain* from the process. At other times, they may come and provide helpful information without agreeing to further involvement. Still others may come and be successfully enlisted as consultants as long as the family therapist refrains from overt or covert attempts to turn them into clients. These possibilities for participation should be suggested to individuals in the first session. However, if a client is still opposed to inviting others after explaining his reluctance and being given reassuring explanations, the therapist must accept the client's position.

Once the position of the client is fully addressed, the next issue to address is how others may feel about being invited. Family members can often be reluctant to attend therapy sessions, especially if they fear being blamed for the problem. In particular, fathers and husbands characteristically are reluctant to discuss matters that they regard as private with someone outside the family. These problems can often be detected when a woman describes her perceptions of her husband's reluctance ("My husband would never talk to a therapist," or "He doesn't believe in counseling"). The beginning therapist must understand the protective nature of these responses and respond in a supportive manner. Asking permission to assume the husband's point of view in the relationship is often effective. Then, therapist and family member can gain empathy for another's position and develop a plan for addressing the husband's fears. Sometimes the client needs to know that the therapist will not criticize or blame those who are invited. At other times, the therapist needs to clarify that the purpose of including others is not to join the side of the client in some on-going conflict. Instead, the role of the therapist can be repeated: to develop a win-win experience for all sides.

Evidence-based approaches to adolescent drug abuse are now finding great success when this reluctance is used as the starting point for treatment (Cunningham & Henggeler 1999; Coatsworth, Santisteban, McBride, & Szapocznik, 2001). Instead of hoping that a family member, on his or her own, will persuade others, the therapist forms a partnership with the client and coaches that person on how to approach others. Sometimes, therapists support this process with a direct contact to the absent parties after permission is granted by the client. Such an approach evolved as service providers found that the individuals defining the problem and those crucial to the solution are as important as the client, especially when children and adolescents are involved.

In cases of adult substance abuse, David Treadway (1989) elaborates for the case in which the drinking husband is the reluctant partner. This strategy helps the therapist *gradually involve* the reluctant family member in therapy:

> The other way I elicit the husband's cooperation is by asking him if he cares about his wife's anxiety and distress and if he would like to be helpful to her. This defines my work as help to her rather than an attempt to change him. I want him to take the position of aiding her in getting help with her part of the problem. Many drinkers will go along with this idea, because at least for the moment it takes the heat off them. For once their wives are being challenged about their own behavior. Anticipating and blocking the drinker's reactivity are essential to effective inter-vention with the spouse. (p. 40)

At the very least, the family therapist can take the results of these discussions centering on reluctance as important information about specific challenges in significant relationships that can ultimately reveal the influence of the expanded system without the actual inclusion of additional parties. Identifying these obstacles can deepen the clinician's understanding of a client's personal reality. Accepting this reality enables the clinician to maintain a successful therapeutic alliance.

The exploration of these relationships greatly influences how assessment evolves into a treatment plan. All the information about these relationships can be summarized and organized by completing the GARF. The GARF will also guide the clinician during the goal-setting process.

Completing the GARF

Debates in family therapy are still common regarding the advantages, disad-vantages, values, and philosophies that underlie the medical model vs. a constructivist, nonlabeling approach (Hansen & Keeney, 1983; Kaslow, 1996). For example, all family therapists agree that assessing safety issues and follow-ing state laws related to the protection of others is important, but the issue of what *else* is important to assess is still under discussion. Some advocate for the

DSM-IV to include problematic relationship categories as legitimate targets of treatment (Wynne, 1987; Yingling, Miller, McDonald, & Galewater, 1998). These leaders have gained respect in the mental health field through developing the GARF mentioned in Chapter 1. This assessment tool appears in Appendix B of the DSM-IV and is the result of long and persistent efforts of the Group for the Advancement of Psychiatry Committee on the Family (1995). It represents an important step toward developing a common language in our profession that can be used to provide relational information for Axis IV of the DSM-IV (psychosocial and environmental problems). In this book, a copy of the instrument is in Appendix E.

The GARF provides three generic categories of relational functioning that can guide the practitioner in categorizing the *type* of psychosocial problem: *problem-solving, organization,* or *emotional climate.* These three dimensions help the practitioner describe important relationships in a manner that is brief, accurate, and informative. They also work well with any model of family therapy and can be used easily with either problem-based or strength-based perspectives. For example, in tracking interactional sequences, the therapist can obtain at least one description of a sequence in each of the three areas of the GARF.

M.R.I. questions from Chapter 1 illustrate how to explore problem-solving sequences and attempted solutions.

- How does the problem start?
- What is happening and who is doing what at the time?
- What happens next?
- What have you done to try to solve the problem?
- Who does what?
- What is the response from the other person when you try this?

Using family structure questions from Chapter 3, the clinician may explore organizational sequences with questions.

- How do you decide what gets accomplished within the family?
- What is the process of decision-making and who is involved?
- How do you decide the rules for your children?

Genogram questions from Table 7.x, page xxx help the clinician to explore emotional climate.

- How do you know when someone in the family is angry? Mom? Dad? Children? What do they do to let you know? How do you respond?
- How do you know when someone is feeling affectionate? What do they do to let you know? How do you respond?
- Who feels the most pain in the family? What signs tell you about their pain? What do they do? How do you respond?

In completing the GARF, the clinician chooses the scoring range that most closely describes observations of clients and then adjusts within that range for variations from the descriptions. For example, the Nelsons in Chapter 1 might have reported general relationship satisfaction (81–100 range), but therapist observation might have revealed "pain or ineffective anger or emotional deadness" (41–60 range). In cases with wide variations, the clinician can determine a score by taking the range of her observation and then adding up or down according to how a family appears in the other categories within the range. Thus, the clinician would give the Nelsons a score of 60, on the higher end of the range, because they have daily routines and structure as described in the 61–80 range, but because of the loss of the grandfather, their emotional climate is in the lower range. As this example shows, this GARF score and the corresponding description are an easy way to summarize relationships and set goals at the beginning of treatment.

The goal is to help the beginning practitioner find a pragmatic place from which to succeed *within* the current mental health service delivery system. Because research continues to show the benefits of using relational interventions with most mental health problems in children, adolescents, and adults (Sprenkle, 2002), there is little argument about its effectiveness and great demand for those who are trained to do the work.

DEVELOPING A SHARED DIRECTION

The therapist searches for language, metaphors, themes, or goals that unite family members as they move forward in treatment, build upon their strengths, and instill hope. Dialogues about direction with a client should consider client perceptions and summarize the therapist's perceptions. In the initial assessment, as the problem becomes described in relational terms, unifying goals for treatment are developed through an exploration of desired outcomes and processes. The family therapist searches with the family for phrases on which everyone can agree. At this point, the therapist should make recommendations about the process for working together. Does the family hope for a quick turnaround (such as in a crisis), or does the family prefer a period of exploration that helps to clarify the issues in a new way? Are the members of the family more pragmatic in their approach to problem solving, or do they value deliberation, education, and insight? As therapist and family decide on the course of action that best suits them, treatment goals state the desired outcome of therapy, and process goals state the desired procedures for accomplishing those goals. Thereafter, suggestions for the next sessions should be negotiated.

Setting Treatment Goals: Where Are You Going?

In the goal-setting stage, the therapist helps family members decide what they want changed. For example, the therapist might begin by asking:

1. How would you like things to be different in this family?
2. What would you like your son to be doing instead?

The responses eventually become goal behaviors ("If your husband doesn't pay attention to you, how would you like him to show that he cares?"). Later, when tracking the interactional sequence that is maintaining the problem, the therapist might say:

1. And when he yells at you, what would you like him to do instead?
2. It sounds like when he talks to you that way, you get angry and threaten him. How could he talk to you differently at that moment so that you wouldn't get angry with him?

Often, when tracking the interactional sequence, the therapist is asking family members to describe how they would like another family member to respond differently within the sequence of behavior preceding or following the identified problem. In earlier phases of the assessment, the clinician is requesting only that family members give a general statement of what they want to be different. Later, the therapist can help family members become more specific in formulating observable goals.

In most cases, client goals begin as abstract desires (for example, "I want help dealing with my low self-esteem," or "We want to communicate better"). The family therapist helps the family to clarify such desires until behavioral and perceptual elements of the problem are identified as specific goals ("I want to be able to go to a party and have something interesting to say," or "When we discuss finances, we'll be able to resolve the conflict to our satisfaction"). The treatment plan may include the assessment process, which clarifies the nature of the problem and outlines a subsequent plan of action, or it may consist only of the sequence of interventions set in motion as a result of the assessment process. In either case, the treatment plan should address the family's goals and hypotheses generated during the assessment process.

In some cases, the family's goals may be different from those of the therapist. A parent may wish to take care of a legal problem or illness, whereas the therapist may be concerned about the parent's relationship with the children. Parents often feel overwhelmed because they have multiple problems. The therapist should respond to the family's concern around these basic needs before inviting parents to consider an additional view about parent–child relationships. A good treatment plan requires the therapist to analyze hypotheses in order to (a) prioritize areas of change, and (b) make goals concrete and specific.

Prioritizing Areas of Change.   If the family presents several problem areas, the beginning therapist must start to set priorities for treatment. The therapist often establishes intermediate goals, each of which represents a step toward the final goal. This process helps make the family's problem more manageable. The following criteria are critical in making this determination:

1. Which problem is most pressing to the family?
2. Which problem has the greatest negative consequence if not handled immediately?
3. What forces (people, situations) stand in the way of problem resolution?
4. What are the consequences of change? Will anything get worse if the problem gets better? If so, should we develop a plan for coping with change?

It is often helpful for the therapist to brainstorm and write the family's responses on an easel for everyone to read. Once the options are explored, the therapist asks family members to decide on an order for the goals.

Making Goals Concrete and Specific.   Once goals are prioritized, they should be stated behaviorally so that everyone can agree when the goal has been reached. For example, if parents report that they want their child "to pay attention," the therapist must question the parent to determine what the child will be doing "to pay attention." Likewise, labels such as "unhappiness" and "anger" must be stated in such a way that they can be resolved. The following suggestions represent several different ways to help family members describe changes (goals) in more observable terms:

1. Ask each family member to describe how he or she would like things to be different. The therapist might ask, "What changes would you like to see in this family?" or "How would you like things to be different?"
2. Ask family members to describe changes in positive rather than negative terms. The therapist might comment, "I know you don't like the way your son said that. How would you like him to say it?"
3. Ask family members to be specific about what they want changed. The therapist might ask a question such as one of these: "What do you mean by _____?" "What would your son be doing to show you that he can be trusted?" "How would you know that your mother cares about you?" "What would be one way he could help you?" "How would she show you that she has an improved self-concept?"

Now let's look at Case 6 as an example of how a family therapist helps a client prioritize goals and become more specific and concrete when articulating them. Notice how each word is explored for further detail.

Case 6	**The Burns Family**

Mrs. Burns, a single parent, and her ten-year-old son, Keith, were referred by the school counselor because of Keith's fighting and poor grades. In the initial intake interview, Mrs. Burns indicated that she agreed with the school counselor and wanted the help that was recommended. She reported that since her divorce, she had to work nights and hadn't been able to spend enough time with Keith. Before that, Keith seemed to be doing fine. Mrs. Burns attended the first session alone because Keith was ill. The therapist makes a tentative hypothesis about problem severity as *situational,* and explores a pragmatic, behavioral assessment as a possible fit.

THERAPIST: I'm glad you could get off from work, and I'm sorry Keith is ill today.

MRS. BURNS: Well, I've been looking forward to talking with you. Keith has been very difficult for me to handle for a while but he seems to be getting even worse recently. He's just about too much for me to handle.

(Continued)

| Case 6 | The Burns Family (continued) |

THERAPIST: Tell me what you mean.

MRS. BURNS: You know, he just won't mind or do his schoolwork. I just don't know what to do with him.

THERAPIST: Sounds like you're really frustrated with him.

MRS. BURNS: That's for sure. Then I feel guilty about not wanting him home.

THERAPIST: Your feelings are mixed then. Although you know the house is more pleasant when he's not there, you think you should want him to be there.

MRS. BURNS: Yes. It doesn't make much sense, does it?

THERAPIST: What contact have you had with the school?

MRS. BURNS: Not much. I've talked with Mrs. Brown about his schoolwork. I've never talked with her alone, though. Do you think you could do that? I think you might get something out of her. She won't tell me why he does the things he does.

THERAPIST: Well, Mrs. Burns, I might call her just to get more information about Keith, but I'd prefer that you and I meet with his teacher to figure out how to get him to behave better.

MRS. BURNS: I've really tried everything I know. I can't imagine doing anything else with him.

THERAPIST: Are you willing to try some different things?

MRS. BURNS: Yes, but I can't think what.

During the sequence, the client gives some clues as to her expectation about the role of the therapist as advocate, go-between, and so on. The therapist helps to clarify the process by which he can fulfill such a role.

As the therapeutic relationship evolves, the therapist creates the expectation for change and asks for client cooperation in the process. "Trying some different things" becomes an informal description of the direction of therapy. Then, the therapist pursues a more specific definition of the problem.

THERAPIST: Well, I'm sure we'll think of some things. But first, I'd like to better understand what Keith does that you don't like.

MRS. BURNS: OK, I told you he won't mind and he does poorly at school.

THERAPIST: What do you mean when you say he doesn't mind?

MRS. BURNS: Just that. If I tell him to pick up his clothes or be home on time, he just doesn't do it. When I tell him to do his homework, he just ignores me.

THERAPIST: Does he tell you he's not going to do what you tell him or does he just act as though he will and then not follow through?

MRS. BURNS: Keith says things like, "OK, later," and then just doesn't do it.

(Continued)

Case 6 | **The Burns Family** (continued)

THERAPIST: When does this usually happen?

MRS. BURNS: Mostly right after school when he wants to watch TV.

THERAPIST: What happens when he doesn't do it?

MRS. BURNS: Sometimes I get mad and yell at him, but there's not much I can do.

THERAPIST: So you want Keith to do what you tell him. And you mentioned his poor schoolwork. Tell me more about that.

The therapist asks more questions to help define the problem in terms of interactional sequences on the assumption that behavioral patterns consist of circular repeating cycles. The problem is operationalized by means of questions that put the cycles in behavioral terms, with specific reports of what was actually done or said. The therapist helps the client to identify all problem areas before beginning to prioritize.

MRS. BURNS: Last grading period he got three Ds and he's always done well in school before. His teacher says he doesn't turn in his assignments and that he disrupts the class by talking out loud and talking to other students when they're supposed to be working. I've spoken to him about this and told him not to do it, but he denies that he talks to other students.

THERAPIST: You'd like to see him talk less, then, turn in more assignments, and get better grades.

MRS. BURNS: Right! That would certainly make life easier for all of us.

THERAPIST: We now have him minding you, completing assignments, and improving grades. Are there other things you're concerned about?

MRS. BURNS: Yes. Really, I'm bothered that Keith has so few friends. Well, really, he doesn't have any close friends. I think Keith just doesn't know how to act around other kids.

THERAPIST: How does he act?

MRS. BURNS: He's silly.

THERAPIST: What does he do that's silly?

MRS. BURNS: He hits people to get attention, or he will interrupt and talk very loudly. I don't know how he is at school.

THERAPIST: We could probably have a talk with his teacher sometime to find out.

MRS. BURNS: That would help. As I said, I just don't know what to do now.

THERAPIST: OK, you've mentioned three problem areas—Keith's failure to mind, his poor grades, and his peer relationships. Are there others?

MRS. BURNS: No, those about cover everything.

THERAPIST: Which of these problems is of most immediate concern to you? Which would you want to change first?

(Continued)

| Case 6 | **The Burns Family** (continued) |

MRS. BURNS: Getting him to mind. If he did that, it would help me.

THERAPIST: All right. Let's work on that one first. You've said he minds least right after school when he's watching TV. Is there a particular place where you have the biggest problem?

MRS. BURNS: Yes, usually in the TV room. For one thing, half the time he doesn't seem to hear me. When I tell him to do something, he may not respond at all.

THERAPIST: You mentioned before that he sometimes says, "OK, later."

MRS. BURNS: Yes, when I raise my voice, he makes a promise to do it later. If I talk in a tone of voice like I'm using with you now, he probably wouldn't even answer.

THERAPIST: How do you usually react when he doesn't answer?

MRS. BURNS: It depends on what I want him to do . . . or what kind of mood I'm in. Sometimes I just go on and do it myself. Other times I yell at him. Then he promises to do it later, and it usually turns into a yelling match, because he doesn't do it at all.

After exploring the areas of greatest concern to the client, the therapist and client explore other relationships, prioritize the problems, and clarify the issues regarding the most pressing of them.

THERAPIST: Does anyone else have difficulty getting him to mind?

MRS. BURNS: Primarily me. My boyfriend occasionally gets mad at him, but he actually asks Keith to do very few things. I think Keith does what he's told to do at school except for assigned work. Mrs. Brown says he isn't really a discipline problem, but that he just doesn't finish his work.

THERAPIST: You're the one who is mainly concerned about getting him to mind more then. What have you tried so far to get him to mind?

MRS. BURNS: Yelling. Threatening him.

THERAPIST: How has it worked?

MRS. BURNS: It hasn't. That's why I'm here.

THERAPIST: Let's work on it together. Now, are you satisfied with first working on getting Keith to mind and then attacking the other concerns?

MRS. BURNS: Fine.

THERAPIST: It would be important for Keith to be at our next session.

MRS. BURNS: Yes. He should be OK by then. So next week at this time?

THERAPIST: Yes, if that will work for you.

Therapist and client have a sense of direction with goals prioritized and stated in concrete, behavioral terms.

Setting Process Goals: How Will You Get There?

Breunlin (1985) notes that structural-strategic family therapists are comfortable intervening on the basis of a partial assessment of family functioning, whereas therapists using other models prefer a more thorough assessment before developing interventions. Both methods are of value and the choice should be guided by client expectations. In every initial session, it is important for the therapist to *assess the level of crisis* by asking these questions:

1. Do you feel so hopeless or desperate about this situation that you must see some change today, in this session?
2. What do you think will happen if you don't see some change occur from this meeting?

Once the level of crisis is assessed, options for agreeing upon a process can be explored. If clients are in a crisis, the therapist should focus on the person feeling the most desperation. Is the person in a position of leadership in the family? Will her or his position play a critical role in the outcome of therapy? If so, others should be enlisted to participate in a plan of crisis intervention that uses the earlier section on setting treatment goals to develop an immediate, short-term plan of action.

If clients are not in crisis, the therapist can have good results if he or she asks whether the clients prefer behavioral or perceptual changes related to their significant relationships. For example, when questioned about whether she preferred a therapy experience in which she was encouraged to make specific behavioral changes (through homework) or whether she preferred an experience in which she was able to reflect upon various aspects of her situation (insight), one woman chose the reflective mode. The therapist first used questions to reflect upon her family's genogram and then began making tentative suggestions about the possibility of discovering new patterns. After four weeks, the woman reported an incident of spontaneous behavior change at a routine family gathering. Thus, in the initial interview, if a client wants to work on certain interactional sequences or wants homework, the process goal may be *experimentation*. That would signal an emphasis on a quick strategic turnaround rather than on a longer developmental process.

When client expectations point toward a longer assessment, process goals are aimed at developing a more specific definition of the problem. These goals can be labeled as exploration or clarification. For example, if an individual states the goal as "I want to stop hating my father" or "I want to have a better relationship with men," the therapist may pursue present-oriented interactional information only to discover in later sessions the existence of childhood sexual abuse. Therefore, if the problem definition is still vague at the end of the initial interview, family therapists are encouraged to negotiate a process goal in order to maintain a sense of direction with the client. In this way, the therapist helps the client anticipate a two-step process of problem resolution: clarification of context, and development of strategies. An example of this follows:

Mary Ann, it sounds like there are many factors that enter into your desire to "stop hating" your father, and I want to make sure I fully understand your relationship with him before we develop more specific goals. You've been very helpful today, and I'm wondering if we could take another session to explore all of your feelings about this issue. If you decide to return, I would like to continue clarifying this situation until we are able to develop specific problem-solving strategies for you to try. How does this sound? After you've had some time to think about this, let me know next time if you would like to suggest anything different.

When the therapist interviews a family or couple, the process is similar. Families are usually so intent on getting results that they become oblivious to their own process, so in certain situations, families can benefit from a shift to process goals. Such goals can be explained to the family as a first step toward eventual problem resolution, to be followed by a second step in which strategies for change are developed. In the first step, focusing on the perspective of the family, the therapist can ask questions that begin to associate specific behaviors and perceptions with the description of the problem. This micro information can then be used to develop specific goals and strategies for change in the intervention phase of therapy. The family therapist might negotiate such a two-step agreement by stating the following:

> It sounds to me like you have an idea about what the problem is but are struggling with how to go about resolving it. In the past, I've found it useful to help people develop a very specific understanding of the behavior, thoughts, and feelings that they would like to change. After that, it's much easier to help them develop solutions. If you decide to return, I would like to explore more details about the problem [perceptual change], so that all of us can come to some agreement about what should change. After that, if you're satisfied with the direction we're heading [goals], we can pursue a specific plan of action [behavioral change].

If clients already have a clear set of behavioral goals when they enter family therapy, the negotiated goals may be easily determined to provide therapist and client with a clear sense of direction at the end of the first session. Because goals are tied to a certain sense of timing as the practitioner moves through the stages of family therapy (quick turnaround or slower exploration), goals also become closely tied to the type of treatment plan that the family and the family therapist develop.

Starting a Treatment Plan: Academia vs. Real World

As mentioned at the beginning of the chapter, most agencies require therapists to develop a treatment plan early in the therapeutic process. Personal services are most effective when families have the opportunity to take responsibility for the terms under which the services are rendered. Even in court-ordered cases, service delivery can be administered cooperatively. For example, a violent husband who has been ordered into treatment as part of a deferred-prosecution agreement may not have a choice about frequency or duration of sessions, but he might be able to choose some element of the content or process, such as the topics to be discussed (hopes, aspirations, goals, patterns, relationships), the role of the therapist (director, guide, consultant), and the therapy goals (behavioral change, perceptual change, or both). These elements can be included in the treatment plan.

An initial treatment plan might be a request to include certain people as sources of information during the assessment process, with the expectation that a different type of plan will emerge for later stages of treatment. Another plan could define the role of the therapist as a consultant rather than a referee in the case of a highly emotional couple. Still another plan with an individual seeking help for depression might formalize the client's choice regarding which topic to pursue: family-of-origin influences having a bearing on the client's depression, or strategies for day-to-day coping with the depression.

Each treatment plan must be individualized and fit the unique characteristics of the family and interactive culture. Most agency settings want the first goal in the plan to be related to symptom stabilization and role functioning. Return to Table 6.1, page 146 and review the lists of symptoms, goals and relational issues. As you review the table from left to right, you can see how symptoms and problems can become concrete goals related to relational problems and relational solutions. To use the table, take a presenting problem from your case load and decide what type of goal it suggests (physical, emotional, interpersonal, societal). Using the developmental framework presented in this book, I placed the goals according to a hierarchy of need, suggesting that clinicians should prioritize problems according to those most essential for survival (Weltner, 1985). Check to see whether one of the examples comes close to categorizing your case. Next, use the corresponding language of relational issues to develop hypotheses. Treatment plans should reflect these priorities. This is intended as a beginning guide that might take many possible forms. For instance, in some situations, one category might be cross-referenced with another. According to Hardy, sometimes physical goals are related to relational issues in the societal category (oppression, isolation, justice). As the table reflects, at other times, a number of problems might be related to the same relational issue, such as secure attachment. Also, symptoms from trauma may be manifest in all four categories.

Often, a problem will encompass more than one level, as in the case of Jerry in Chapter 2, page 39. Figure 6.1 is a genogram of Jerry's family and Box 6.4 is a treatment plan that shows how problems can overlap. For example, a suicidal client may present a situation in which the clinician must target safety issues and emotional issues simultaneously. In this way, the format can be used to develop a manageable order for complex problems. Reducing suicidality is listed first, but relational goals 2 and 3 can be addressed simultaneously.

Once family therapists shift the language of problems and goals to relational terms, treatment plans need to also include a description of how the goal will be addressed (intervention). To do this, Hanna (1997) first categorizes a problem according to its historical nature. Situational problems are new conflicts with a brief preexisting history (see Figure 6.1). Jerry's problem is situational. Transitional problems are those related to normative life stages or

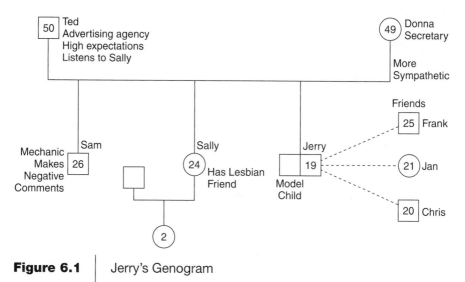

Figure 6.1 | Jerry's Genogram

nonnormative changes in families that have had successes in earlier stages but are unable to make the current adaptation. An example of a transitional problem is the Nelsons' in Chapter 1. (Box 6.5 shows a treatment plan for the Nelsons.) Chronic problems are those that can be traced to difficulties that may have started as situational in an earlier time frame but have persisted through a transitional time period, and now have such an extensive history that they have become an organizing influence on additional emerging problems. Ellie's problems in Chapter 5 are chronic (see Figure 5.1, page 128).

By placing the problem in its developmental context, the clinician can hypothesize about what therapeutic posture will be most successful with the family (direct or indirect). In general, the more chronic the problem, the more indirect the intervention should be, because chronic problems are often entwined in a sense of historical shame. Indirect interventions downplay client weaknesses, emphasize strengths, and focus on future possibilities. In this way, clients can "save face" while making changes in their lives. Success is more likely when the clinician can bypass the shame by lowering defenses as much as possible (White, 1983; Selvini Palazzoli, 1986). Chapter 8 reviews the interventions from major models of family therapy and explains how to determine which technique to use with particular goals. These interventions can be listed on treatment plans and revised as treatment progresses.

Box 6.5, which contains a treatment plan for the Nelson family from Chapter 1, illustrates how direct and indirect approaches relate to treatment goals. Using the GARF score of 60 and the descriptions listed for that scoring range, three goals are set with corresponding plans that include GARF concepts and the Initial Family Assessment that appears in Chapter 1, page 22. Following the developmental guidelines in this book, goals address individual functioning, relational functioning, and problem severity. Paul's depression is

Box 6.4 | **Treatment Plan for Jerry**

Date:　8-5-06
Goal #1:　Reduce depressive symptoms by 8-30-06
Steps To Achieve Goal:

　　　　　　　　　a) Client agrees to a 30-day no self-harm contract
　　　　　　　　　b) Client to consider inviting sister/friends/mother to
　　　　　　　　　　sessions by 8-30-06
　　　　　　　　　c) Therapist and client to complete genogram by
　　　　　　　　　　8-19-06 to understand family patterns of depression
　　　　　　　　　and facilitate self-expression

Client's Action:　_____
Type of Tx:　Individual　　　　　　　　**Freq.:**　Weekly for 30 days
Goal Met:　_____　**Extended On**　_____　**To**　_____

Date:　8-5-06
Goal #2:　Decrease family stress by 9-30-06 (problem solving and emotional climate)
Steps To Achieve Goal:

　　　　　　　　　a) Client to attend 3 conjoint sessions by 9-30-06
　　　　　　　　　b) Therapist, client, and support system to explore
　　　　　　　　　　options for overcoming depression and decreasing
　　　　　　　　　family conflict

Client's Action:　_____
Type of Tx:　Conjoint with friends, family　**Freq.:**　3 times by 9-30-06
Goal Met:　_____　**Extended On**　_____　**To**　_____

Date:　8-5-06
Goal #3:　Stabilize living arrangement by 10-30-06 (organization)
Steps To Achieve Goal:

　　　　　　　　　a) Client will make 1 call per day regarding job search
　　　　　　　　　　by 8-19-06
　　　　　　　　　b) Client and friends will contact associates who are
　　　　　　　　　　looking for a roommate by 8-12-06
　　　　　　　　　c) Client to explore church and family members for
　　　　　　　　　　temporary help by 8-19-06

Client's Action:　_____
Type of Tx:　Individual and conjoint　　**Freq.:**　2 times by 10-30-06
Goal Met:　_____　**Extended On**　_____　**To**　_____

_____　　_____

Client's Signature (Guardian Signature)　　　**Date**

_____　_____　_____　_____

Therapist Signature　　**Date**　　**Supervisor's Signature**　　**Date**

behavioral terms, and the process of problem resolution is straightforward. For example, if the family is seeking a consultation in order to decide on a strategy for the long-term care of an elderly parent, the goal might be to decide who will be responsible for which tasks, after some psychoeducational sessions regarding the impact of long-term care on families. If there are no pre-existing conflicts between family members, this direction could be decided in the initial session and described to the family as part of the therapeutic contract.

In another case, parents are seeking help for the long-standing behavioral problems of their daughter. Their goal might be for her to stop violent outbursts at school. A common treatment plan for such a presenting problem would be to explore the relationships between the family and the school, between the daughter and her peers, and between individual family members (MST). The family therapist, the family, and the school might form a collaborative team to address the relational issues (see Chapter 9 on collaborative teamwork). Then, the family therapist can facilitate cooperation among all parties in developing corrective strategies. This direction might develop over the first two assessment sessions. The treatment plan could be formalized once the family approves the treatment and process goals.

To account for the essential elements of a successful treatment plan, the clinician should review these questions:

1. Do I know what the client's original expectations were for the therapy process?
2. Have I provided a rationale if the process departs from those expectations?
3. Have we transformed symptoms and presenting problems into relational language?
4. Does the client have an understanding of the process goals, of what specifically will occur from session to session, and how these activities will address the presenting problem?
5. Have I enlisted each member in the process, clarified the role of each family member, and addressed any objections or questions?

Beginning practitioners sometimes try to maintain client commitment in indirect ways—by persuasion or lectures about why clients should return for treatment. At other times, therapists may expect clients to continue attending and paying for sessions in spite of lingering reservations. These situations can be avoided by thoroughly exploring and validating the concerns and reservations that clients express in the first session. By assuming a "one-down" position, the clinician is able to empower the client to feel a sense of entitlement when it comes to dictating the terms of therapy.

A practitioner's setting may influence whether a treatment plan is written or verbal. Fees, liability, releases of information, and other legal aspects of therapy are usually written in order to become legally binding. In some instances, clients are provided with statements regarding their rights to obtain records or to file grievances. It is empowering for clients to know that the therapist expects to renegotiate and evaluate the process on the basis of the client's personal experience. Too often, therapists develop expectations that clients will blindly participate in the process without holding therapists accountable for their part of the contract. When no-shows occur in clinical settings, usually, an unspoken concern has not been addressed. Many consumers are more compliant when they are in crisis, only to find later that they need to renegotiate but are too intimidated to do so. Dropping out of therapy becomes the most expedient option.

As this discussion has shown, a treatment plan is the result of sifting information related to the definition of the problem, the motivation to seek therapy, the likely participants, and their expectations for treatment. As this sifting takes place, the nature of the therapeutic process begins to evolve from the important elements that surface. The result is an agreement that specifies the role of the therapist, each family member's role, intermediate and long-range goals, and an initial plan for achieving the goals. The therapist can use Box 6.2 to summarize the process so that the end of the session covers important details of the future treatment plan. Although these first roles, goals, and plans may be changed many times throughout the therapeutic process, grappling with them in a systematic way during the initial assessment helps the family therapist begin the process in an organized manner.

SUMMARY

As beginning practitioners prepare for the first stage of treatment, reviewing Box 6.1 will help them decide what issues to address and when. Box 6.1 outlines the key issues reviewed in this chapter and in Chapter 5, with integrative notes to identify what model of family therapy has influenced each suggestion. This outline brings together key elements across models that have been reviewed thus far. The integration of these elements is based upon the belief that each first- and second-generation model of family therapy has strengths that can enhance the process at critical stages in the process. Box 6.1 suggests when these strengths can be most helpful within the initial stage of therapy. The order of the process assumes that the family therapist will exercise flexible leadership in which he or she assumes responsibility for organizing the treatment experience and for discovering the best fit for the client. The process is driven by the desire to individualize treatment for each family.

Problems are embedded in a multisystemic process that unfolds over time, just as a journey unfolds with many levels of process during a progression of events. Using these models of family therapy provides enough variety to find the right fit for the breadth of human experience. These models cover important elements of problems, relationships, and the process of change. Also, this integration of therapeutic approaches suggests that developing a polarized position with respect to modern and postmodern perspectives of therapy is unnecessary. Postmodernism is best considered as a refinement of therapeutic process, not a rejection of first-generation models. In this sense, both perspectives highlight a number of issues that help the practitioner with a smooth entry into the process. As these issues are addressed, the outline can serve as a guide for the practitioner to know when to move on to the middle stage of treatment, that of beginning and maintaining change.

Notice that Box 6.1 contains a session outline that can be used as a planning tool from session to session. In cases where both referral and intake information are gathered in the first session, the therapist might want to explain the first session of therapy as one of exploration leading to a definition of the problem. The second session can be used to address remaining topics leading to a treatment plan, or, the therapist can propose a plan that allows for an assessment period followed by recommendations. At the end of this assessment period (from one to four sessions), family members can decide whether they would like to continue.

Conducting an assessment, whether brief or thorough, should be considered an intervention in itself. However, bringing the exchange from mere conversation to the level of intervention requires the discipline and wisdom mentioned at the beginning of this chapter. Carefully chosen language and thoughtful questions must follow a deliberate order in the conversation. Chapter 7 discusses the assessment process in more detail and how its effectiveness is directly related to these skills. As beginning practitioners become acclimated to the process of therapeutic questions, they more fully understand the experience of those who have come seeking help.

7

Relational Assessments as Intervention: Exploring Client Experience

CHAPTER OUTLINE

Assessments as Intervention
Interactional Patterns: Content and Process
Temporal Patterns: Past, Present, Future
Genograms
Circular Questioning: In Relationship to What?
Tracking Interactional Sequences: Facts Versus Assumptions
Tracking Longitudinal Sequences: Narratives About Changes Over Time
Deconstruction
Developing a Rationale for the Timeline
Creating a Sense of Movement
Summarizing Details
Advantages of Timelines
Hypotheses
Developmentally Appropriate Treatment: Matching Intervention with Needs
The Process of Change
Summary

CORE COMPETENCIES

2.2.3 Perceptual Develop hypotheses regarding relationship patterns, their bearing on the presenting problem, and the influence of extra-therapeutic factors on client systems.

2.2.4 Perceptual Consider the influence of treatment on extra-therapeutic relationships.

2.3.6 Executive Assess family history and dynamics using a genogram or other assessment instruments.

2.3.7 Executive Elicit a relevant and accurate biopsychosocial history to understand the context of the clients' problems.

Chapter 6 reviewed ways to organize client information gleaned from the initial interview with the family so that the therapist can begin creating a treatment plan. Sometimes a clinical situation is straightforward and a plan can develop easily by the end of the first session. If the practitioner is able to match a treatment mode with a client's expectations, the first interview can be an initial assessment from which treatment is planned. However, because many agencies require the clinician to conduct initial mental health assessments, often not enough time exists to fully explore the relational aspects of the problem or to develop a corresponding strategy for intervention. In these cases, the family therapist can set the stage for an in-depth relational assessment by developing an initial treatment plan with the client that calls for the following:

1. Assessment of individual functioning (i.e., problem, symptoms, life stage, worldview)
2. Assessment of relational functioning (i.e., influences and impact of the problem, GARF scales)
3. Assessment of problem severity (situational, transitional, chronic)
4. Choice of a treatment mode and style that is developmentally appropriate, given the assessment information identified by the preceding questions

All problems have a relational component and all solutions have a relational component (Hanna, 1997). Thus, each of the steps just outlined can involve relational information in tandem with the necessary diagnostic information required in the therapist's workplace. As agency requirements are met, practitioners can gradually shift their focus to a more in-depth relational perspective, using *assessments as interventions*. Because the ability to use assessments in this way has always been one of the strengths of a systemic approach, the majority of this chapter is devoted to helping clinicians learn how to conduct assessments that create change. At the end of the chapter, suggestions for how to combine relational assessments with mental health assessments are provided.

ASSESSMENTS AS INTERVENTION

Often, the structured approach in agency practice provides a direction during the first stage of treatment. However, to make treatment plans an accurate representation of therapeutic practice, the clinician must think through a rationale for these assessments; otherwise, clients might say, "What does this have to do with my problem?" Thus, in family therapy, relational assessments have two important considerations.

First, information-seeking should complement the joining process by communicating interest, concern, creativity, and a desire to fully understand the experience of each family member. Gaining a sense of "systemic empathy" for each participant is an important goal. This sense of empathy must capture the *complexity* of each person's perspective, the *relationships* that have influenced that perspective, the *dilemmas* that may have evolved from these relationships, the unique *order of events* as they emerged in the family drama, and each person's stated *goal* or reason for participating in the session. If the case is not a crisis, a therapist can say,

> I'm a total stranger. If I were in your shoes, I would wonder how a stranger can help me. To be helpful, I need to know more detail about you as a person and what plan might fit best for you. I want you to be the judge of whether I understand you and your life the way you think I should. Can we start with a few sessions to look at the problem as it relates to the big picture of your life? Then, we'll brainstorm a detailed plan and put it into action.

The second important consideration in relational assessment is that whatever information the therapist seeks should be related to intervention—that is, to what will eventually bring about change. Change can take place within the levels of communication conceptualized by Bateson at M.R.I., namely, content and process. The content and process of interactions evolve over time, moving from the past to the present and into the future. In describing their problem, clients might place greater emphasis upon one of these time periods. Whereas structural, strategic, and behavioral family therapists emphasize the importance of staying in the here and now, intergenerational and experiential therapists often explore the emotional and developmental aspects of the problem in the past. Generally, second- and third-generation models of family therapy develop a balanced approach to the issue of history by taking an interest in narratives (narrative), comparative changes over time (Milan), exceptions in the past (solution-focused), and exploration of the context until the problem makes sense (MST). These methods of assessment help determine whether the problem is situational, transitional, or chronic.

Two dimensions of the assessment process capture the content and process of each person's relational journey, shedding light on past and present influences on the family that can encourage change in the future: *interactional* and *temporal* aspects of the family's story. Epston and White's (1992) narrative approach to family therapy refers to these dimensions as the *landscape of action* and the *landscape of meaning,* respectively. In general, the questions proposed in this chapter bring about discussions with the client that become a forum for shifts in emotion, thought, and behavior. Such changes are strengthened and amplified by additional interventions that reorganize key family relationships around these changes. In this chapter, specific concepts and methods involved in organizing the interactional and temporal levels of information obtained by the therapist are reviewed. Then, suggestions for incorporating these strategies into the initial stages of family therapy are illustrated.

Interactional Patterns: Content and Process

When family members come to therapy, they usually focus on the content of their concerns. Parents say their child does not come home on time or is hyperactive; a couple describes their relationship as empty. The therapist listens to what family members say about each other (content) and asks how family members interact when the problem arises (process). As explained throughout this book, a distinguishing characteristic of family therapists is their interest in relational process rather than content alone, so the beginning practitioner must begin to gather data on multiple levels. Through observation, in-session interactions can reveal the nature of intrafamilial relationships as well as the nature of the therapist-family relationship. Through questions and sequence tracking, the clinician also learns about out-of-session relationships and personal perceptions. As information is gathered regarding perceptions, behaviors, and relationships connected to the problem, the therapist begins to develop hypotheses about which area of change is the most appropriate to target.

Communication theorists at the Mental Research Institute (M.R.I.) often look for beliefs that can hinder problem resolution in the present. One of their concepts—the utopian syndrome—refers to problems that develop due to a client's idealistic view of how the world should be. For example, a widow hoping to cure her depression through therapy is invited to consider how her depression is a natural response to loss and not a problem to be solved. Her response to her own grief may actually be the problem. Only in a utopia would humans fail to feel the impact of death and loss. To integrate with other dimensions, the therapist can see that change might occur as a result of exploring the content of the client's thoughts and providing her with a new reality. This reality would then be a basis for helping her address her isolation from others.

Another M.R.I. concept—that the solution becomes the problem—suggests that some presenting problems grow out of a belief that "more is better." These problems escalate when an attempted solution has an exacerbating effect. The therapist can discover this phenomenon by tracking interactional sequences between people and gathering specific behavioral information about attempted solutions for the original problem. On the basis of these two M.R.I. concepts, therapists help the client analyze the content of thoughts and the process of problem-solving in the present, which leads to discovering alternative solutions that were previously overlooked.

The Milan team also balances attention to content and process. This team's approach is based on the Batesonian concept that bringing forth information regarding differences or comparisons within the family is the first step toward change in family life (e.g., the therapist might ask, "How are Mom and Dad different from each other?"). Some questions were designed as interventions to bring forth information (content) regarding the systemic functioning (process) of family members that would be new or different from the family's normal way of viewing the problem (i.e., to reframe the situation). Informational interventions can be thought of as eliciting *systemic insight* into the therapeutic arena so that a family can view itself from a distance. This metaperspective, as articulated by the Milan team, often includes questions regarding family roles, rules, and beliefs that can be related to the life of the presenting problem. This information becomes the basis for hypotheses and directives that affect out-of-session relational changes in a family.

Temporal Patterns: Past, Present, Future

Whereas the past and present provide background information regarding the context of the problem, the future becomes a stage for more flexible options. Haley (1980) and Minuchin (1974) recognized the importance of information regarding the family's current stage of life and focused their observations on present in-session behavior. Framo's (1981) approach seeks information about past interactions and perceptions to understand the development of current relationships. Boszormenyi-Nagy and Krasher (1986) gather information about past relationships between the child and his or her parents to understand the unconscious needs of parents. The Milan team is often interested in tracking the life of the problem from the past into the present, with interventions focused on the client's ability to impact the future (Boscolo et al., 1987).

Regardless of whether data gathering focuses on the past or the present, the therapeutic direction is always future-oriented; the therapist facilitates hopeful connections between the original problem and future solutions. Later in this chapter, illustrations will strike a balance between a focus on the past, working in the present, and the future. Ultimately, this balance must guide families into "forward thinking" (White, 1986) by gathering data about possible perceptions and behaviors in the future. Positive possibilities can be evoked by such questions as "What would you imagine your life to be like when you no longer have this problem?" or "What things would you like to be doing when this is no longer a problem?" These questions illustrate how the family therapist is required to think about multiple levels of experience and alternate between these levels to gather relevant information about the family system that contributes to positive change. Data gathering can be thought of as both an ongoing process that pervades all other stages of the therapeutic process and as an early formalized stage in some cases.

Most family therapists have been exposed to assessment techniques from a combination of first- and second-generation models. Bowen (1978) popularized the use of genograms for collecting family-of-origin information. Structural and strategic therapists engage in tracking interactional sequences as a way of learning about common relational patterns (Minuchin, 1974). Social constructionists inquire about the evolution of family issues over time as described in stories that the family relates (Boscolo et al., 1987; Sluzki, 1992; White & Epston, 1991). The way that each of these procedures can be systematically employed to gather microassessment and macroassessment data is described and illustrated in this chapter.

GENOGRAMS

In the early days of family therapy, Bowen began to diagram a person's family of origin by means of a three-generation family tree that came to be known as the *genogram*. (See Figure 7.1. Previous chapters contain genograms for the Nelsons, Ellie, and Jerry.) This diagram starts at the bottom with the identified patient's generation, including siblings, and moves up through the generations

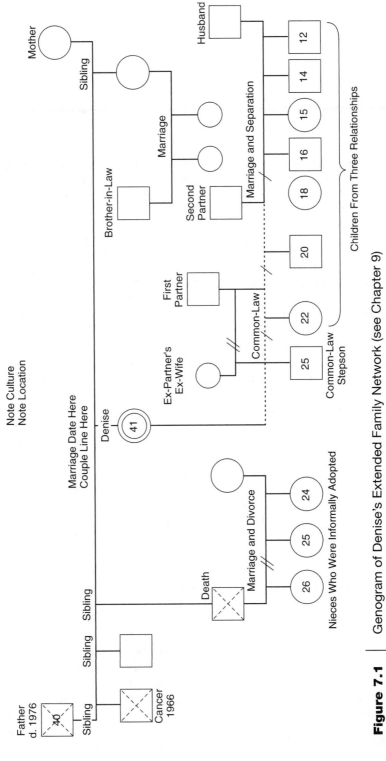

Figure 7.1 | Genogram of Denise's Extended Family Network (see Chapter 9)

177

to each parent's family of origin, including their parents and siblings. As the field has progressed, numerous practitioners from a variety of orientations have adapted the genogram for their own uses. As McGoldrick and Gerson (1985) note:

> In family therapy, genogram applications range from multi-generational mapping of the family emotional system using a Bowen framework, to systemic hypothesizing for Milan-style paradoxical interventions, to developing "projective" hypotheses about the workings of the unconscious from genogram interviews, to simply depicting the cast of characters in the family. (p. 4)

Kuehl (1995) has also used the genogram to concentrate on solution-focused material such as exceptions that manifest as the breaking of an undesirable pattern across generations (e.g., "You seem to have decided not to repeat your grandfather's mistakes. How did that happen?"). He has also used genograms to normalize current behavior by depathologizing it in the context of generational influences (e.g., "It's understandable that you are coping in this way, given the family challenges surrounding you"). Hardy and Laszloffy (1995) use the genogram to explore influences of the therapist's culture. Such influences as race, class, and gender are explored to highlight "pride-shame" issues that can impede a balanced therapeutic posture ("What aspects of your culture of origin do you have the most comfort 'owning' and the most difficulty 'owning'?"). (p. 234)

Figure 7.1 is an example of a genogram that uses common notations. It includes family members (and their relationships to one another); ages; dates of marriage, death, divorce, and adoption; and places of residence. Women are symbolized by circles and men by squares. Horizontal lines are used for couples and dates. Marriages are noted by solid lines; common-law unions are noted by dotted lines. Vertical lines extending down from couple lines connect parents and children. For further instructions on the conventions of genograms, consult McGoldrick and Gerson (1985) or Carter and McGoldrick (1989a).

In Figure 7.1, note that the client experienced untimely deaths of males and assumed child-rearing responsibilities for an entire network. In Figure 7.2, note that the father is 56 and the mother is 54. They were married in 1978 and both had previous marriages. Divorces are indicated by the double slash on the line joining marital pairs. The two-generation family can be expanded to include grandparents on each side. The birthplace of each person is listed. Also listed are the birth year; death year and cause of death (when applicable); marriage year; and ages of living and ages at time of death. These dates help to track sequences. The dotted circle indicates who was in the household prior to the divorce and before the *launching stage* began. The therapist can reflect on whether the history of losses on both sides or the racial issues are relevant to the divorce, especially because of the race issue attached to the abortion. Cultural issues may enter in, given the different locations represented intergenerationally. In addition, the nature of the client's remarried family, the effects of a child's Down syndrome, and actual causes of death are relevant to explore.

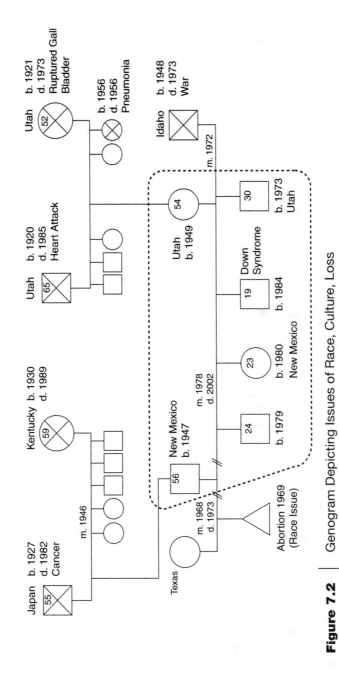

Figure 7.2 | Genogram Depicting Issues of Race, Culture, Loss

Table 7.1 presents a summary of suggested questions that can provide the family therapist with information at both the microlevel and macrolevel of family functioning.

Genograms can be constructed with participation of the family as a type of public note-taking that will help the family begin visualizing its own system. Because a family therapy model seeks to expand the area of focus regarding the presenting problem, a genogram is helpful in expanding the interpersonal area of focus from individual to family and from family to extended family. As the family therapist becomes aware of certain relationships that are important to the client, relevant areas of discussion can be determined through the construction of a genogram, and potential sources of family support are usually identified. In family sessions, the genogram helps family members consider where the presenting problem fits into the larger context of their three-generation heritage. In individual sessions, the family therapist learns to understand clients through a knowledge and understanding of their families. When the practitioner wants to know "where a client is coming from," the genogram becomes a vehicle for such an understanding in a most literal way, because most clients come from a family with a tradition and a history.

To use a genogram successfully, the family therapist must be able to articulate a rationale for its construction that is meaningful and reassuring to the client. In cases where the presenting problem seems unrelated to family or extended family, practitioners can explain that a diagram of the family helps the family members understand significant relationships that might be a resource in addressing the presenting problem. The therapist begins by posing the question, "What people are most helpful to you when this problem is bothering you?" As family members respond, the therapist can ask permission to diagram the relationship of these important people. In these instances, the genogram may be sketchy, because it reflects minimal information gathered in a short amount of time. However, if the questions elicit important information, the family therapist can ask if this line of questioning seems to be a useful direction for understanding the client's experience. Nonverbal behavior of family members often suggests whether they are engaged in the process.

The therapist can provide other rationales for the genogram, as well, based on the particular direction of therapy. The following are examples of certain approaches and the rationales that can be used by the therapist for constructing genograms:

- **Problem-solving approach** "By mapping your family, I can explore the ways you have solved other problems and see what types of solutions are most comfortable for you."
- **Solution-oriented approach** "When I draw a family tree, I look for ways that other people in your family have solved similar problems. This may give us some new ideas" (Kuehl, 1995).
- **Cultural or family-of-origin approach** "It sounds like part of your difficulty is related to a clash between two worlds, the world of _____ and the world of _____. I'd like to diagram these influences and see how we can begin to change these problems."

Table 7.1 | Circular Questions and Guidelines for Genograms

Questions	Directions for Therapists	Explanation
How is your family different from other families you know?	Begin writing brief words on the genogram that represent the responses to this question. Construct the genogram in front of the family and use public note-taking as a form of acknowledging each person's comments.	Explores family members' sense of difference from others in general and from others in their reference group (e.g., if Asian, the family can be asked, "How is your family different from other Asian families?"). This provides a window into the family's macroculture and microculture.
How are Mom and Dad different from each other?	List adjectives near the corresponding person on the genogram. When negative labels are given, try to reframe in a neutral, positive, or empathic way. Use these questions as an opportunity to tease, joke, and set people at ease. Many people will be privately fearing judgment, criticism, and psychological analysis; therefore, the less "therapeutic" the environment, the better.	Explores perceptions of parental interactional styles, provides clues as to whether there is polarization or cohesion between parents, and reveals the roles each may assume.
How is (each child) different from everyone else in the family?	List adjectives near the name of each person. As the interview continues, take notes and diagram any information that will help in answering the general assessment questions of this section.	Siblings (even twins) always have a sense of uniqueness from each other. This uniqueness provides clues to family roles, issues of fairness, and various alignments.
Who is most like Dad? Who is most like Mom? What makes you say that?	Encourage story telling. Jot a few words summarizing the story beside the name of the person mentioned.	Examples of comparisons lead to narratives about individual differences, strengths, possible coalitions, and beliefs.

(Continued)

Table 7.1   Circular Questions and Guidelines for Genograms (continued)

Questions	Directions for Therapists	Explanation
How does your family express affection?	Ask how they communicate positive feelings to one another. Ask how they know when a given family member is feeling positive toward them.	Specific examples of how affection is demonstrated provide a window into the family's affectional and communicational style.
Who gets the most angry? How do you know when that person is mad?	Reframe anger as pain, fear, or feeling overwhelmed. Ask who else gets angry besides _____. Ask what they get angry about. Whenever the family characterizes any member as being extreme in any way, follow up the comment with. "Who is the next most _____?"	Narratives about anger identify pain in the family. Expanding to "who else" prevents scapegoating and traces the pattern of pain that may often go unacknowledged (alternate story).
Who runs the family? Who gets the last word? Is there anyone outside the family who has a great deal of influence on members?	Use humor and pace the questions to suggest a sense of normalcy, not pathology. Give each member a chance to respond.	Perceptions of overt and covert power are critical to know and understand. Then the leadership of the family can be more fully engaged in treatment.

Source: Adapted from Hiebert (1980).

Boyd-Franklin (1989) notes that African American families or others may be anticipating judgmental views from the therapist when a genogram is constructed. Thus, before the genogram is made, a period of joining should occur so that the family is reassured that the genogram will not invite criticism of diverse extended-family structures. With these concerned families, prefacing the genogram with an explanation is best, such as:

THERAPIST: To help you, it's important for me to understand something about the significant people in your life and what they mean to you. It's my usual practice to diagram family and personal relationships so that I can get the big picture of a person's life. I think all families have unique strengths and a variety of relationships. Family members often have survived some hard times together. Would you be willing to let me get acquainted with the members of your family by putting them on a diagram?

In cases where clients were adopted or transferred through many foster placements, the genogram can be adapted with dotted lines, arrows, or other specific symbols to depict the multiple settings and relationships that have become the norm for the development of those clients. However, even with early disruptions, some clients still have a desire to know and understand their family roots. Thus, the main objective of a genogram can be either to chart biological patterns of behavior and relatedness, or to discover and diagram any relationships that shaped the development of family members, including thoughts, behaviors, and values that were embedded in those relationships. In either case, the result is a visual representation of important relationships in which similarities and differences are identified. These patterns are used to pinpoint attitudes or behaviors that might be involved in perpetuating or solving the presenting problem. Often, such details are elicited through the use of circular questions.

Circular Questioning: In Relationship to What?

Although the Milan team was the first to speak of circular questions, family therapists from a wide range of models now use the term generically in referring to questions that make "connections among actions, beliefs, and relationships of individuals within the system" (Campbell, Draper, & Crutchley, 1991, p. 346). Table 7.1 offers examples of circular questions that seek out perceptions of difference in family life. Systemic therapists find that circular questions elicit a broad range of information about family dynamics, including: individual roles that make family members unique; marital patterns of power, communication, and intimacy; and coalitions among subsystems within the family. This "information about differences," as Bateson (1972) once labeled it, becomes the family therapist's foundation for understanding the family as a social system. As this understanding evolves, the therapist formulates hypotheses and interventions.

The important focus for the family therapist is to gather information that compares one piece of information about perceptions, roles, and relationships with another (information about differences). As clients make statements, the therapist processes the information according to relationships, contrasts, and comparisons. The following sample dialogue illustrates this:

MOTHER: Becky is driving me crazy! I can't go on this way!

THERAPIST: (seeking a comparison) I can see this is very upsetting for you. Is there anyone else who is upset by Becky's behavior?

MOTHER: Yes. My mother is very concerned.

THERAPIST: (seeking a relationship) How does she become affected by Becky? Tell me about their relationship.

MOTHER: She tends Becky every day after school while I'm at work. By the time I pick Becky up, my mother's at the end of her rope.

THERAPIST: So, something happens between the two of them that leaves your mother upset. (seeking a contrast) Was there a time in the past when things were different?

MOTHER: Not recently. We've had trouble with her for a long time.

THERAPIST: (still seeking a contrast in time) What about in the *distant* past? How far back in time do we have to go to find a time when things were different?

MOTHER: Oh, my! (thinking) I guess when she was tiny—2 or 3 years old—she was so cute, and she loved her grandma. I guess things changed when she started school.

THERAPIST: How were the three of you getting along then?

Each piece of information about relationships, comparisons, and contrasts can be explored more fully in a real interview. This example illustrates how to begin using therapeutic conversations to develop a broad view of those who have some relationship to the problem, an understanding of differences and similarities related to the problem, and a preliminary hypothesis about how the problem developed.

Fleuridas, Nelson, and Rosenthal (1986) provide guidelines for teaching circular questions at each stage of the therapeutic process:

> This form of questioning serves as an efficient process for soliciting information from each member of the family regarding their experience of: (a) the family's presenting concern; (b) sequences of interactions, usually related to the problem; and (c) differences in their relationships over time. This provides the family and the therapist with a systemic frame of the problem, thereby enabling the therapist to generate hypotheses and design interventions (or additional questions) which interrupt dysfunctional cycles of interrelating and which challenge symptom-supporting myths or beliefs (cf. Minuchin & Fishman, 1981; Papp, 1983; Selvini Palazzoli et al., 1978, 1980b). (p. 114)

In addition, circular questions do the following:

- Compare people across generations ("Who is most/least like the identified patient?"), developmental time periods ("Has it always been this way? When did things change? What was it like before?"), and meanings ("Who agrees/disagrees that this is the problem?")
- Explore differences in perceptions of relationships ("Who is closer to Mom—your brother or your sister?") or differences of degree ("On a scale of 1 to 10, how well were you able to solve problems this week?")
- Focus on before and after distinctions ("Did she get angry before you told her or after you told her?")
- Pose hypothetical possibilities ("How would things be different if you spent more time together?") (Boscolo et al., 1987).

These questions help track family members as they evolve through different experiences and develop beliefs and attitudes about family life.

As shown in Table 7.1, the circular questions used with genograms focus on contrasts in the interviewee's perceptions of family relationships, roles, and the emotional climate. The first question, "How is your family different from other families you know?", gives respondents an opportunity to provide information about the interface between this family and the outside world. If certain obvious differences exist (e.g., a child with Down syndrome, racially different, religiously different), the therapist can make the question more specific to elicit the most useful information. For example, a family who has a child with Down syndrome has different experiences and a different identity from other families. However, all families with such a child do not seek family therapy, and many cope with their sense of difference in creative and insightful ways. If a family answers with the obvious difference first, it may also be important to ask, "Compared with other families affected by Down syndrome, how is your family different?" or "Compared with other Amish families you know, how is your family different?" These questions elicit clues about the client's sense of difference at personal, familial, and cultural levels. They often generate interesting information that acquaints the family therapist with themes and unique factors relevant to treatment planning.

The other questions in Table 7.1 follow a similar pattern of comparison, proceeding to smaller and more intimate levels of observation. As these questions about difference outline each family member's unique perceptual blueprint, the therapist can explore how these perceptions and beliefs impact behavior on both a microlevel and macrolevel, using questions that focus on sequences of immediate interaction and sequences of important changes through time.

Tracking Interactional Sequences: Facts Versus Assumptions

As an assessment proceeds, the family therapist discovers certain relationships at the microlevel that seem to have ultimate importance in the client's mind. For example, in the previous dialogue with the mother of Becky, the therapist could ask this mother which relationship (i.e., Mother-Becky, Grandmother-Becky, Mother-Grandmother) seems most relevant to the problem at hand. When these relationships are discussed, the therapist must gain a description of facts, not merely assumptions (O'Hanlon & Weiner-Davis, 1989), by tracking interactional sequences that occurred during important moments in the relationship:

THERAPIST: How would you describe your relationship with your father?

CLIENT: I'd say it's strained.

THERAPIST: (draws a line on the genogram between father and daughter and writes "strained") How is it strained?

CLIENT: Oh, it goes way back. He always tries to make me feel guilty. I can never do anything right.

THERAPIST: (writes "guilty" on the genogram next to daughter) When you say he always tries to make you feel guilty, what does he do or say that gives you that impression?

CLIENT: Well, when we talk on the phone, he'll say something like, "I sure would like to see you more often," implying that I don't visit him enough. Then, if I do come to visit, he complains that I haven't stayed long enough.

THERAPIST: (writes "wants to see her" on the genogram next to father) So, when you're on the phone with him and he says he wants to see you more often, what do you say back?

CLIENT: I try to explain to him that I'm busy and can't just pick up any ol' time to travel all that way.

THERAPIST: And then what does he say?

CLIENT: He usually starts to lecture me about how families ought to be close.

THERAPIST: And then what do you say?

CLIENT: I don't say anything. I just let him go on and on.

THERAPIST: So you clam up.

CLIENT: Yeah.

THERAPIST: And you're probably thinking to yourself—what?

CLIENT: Here we go again!

THERAPIST: Okay. So this is a familiar pattern with the two of you.

CLIENT: Oh, yes!

THERAPIST: Well, let's backtrack for a minute. When he first says he'd like to see you, what is going on right before that part of the conversation? Anything in particular?

CLIENT: Mmm. Usually just talk about what he's doing and what I'm doing.

THERAPIST: So in the earlier part of the discussion, you're talking and interacting with him, telling him about yourself, and then it changes when he makes his statements.

CLIENT: Yes. It usually starts out okay and then goes downhill.

In this discussion, the client is making an assumption about her father's intention based on what he says to her. The therapist does not challenge her assumption at this point, but seeks only to illuminate the facts—in this case, what her father actually says to her. Then, as the facts become known, they are put in sequence with her responses, and the entire sequence is placed in the larger context of their conversation and the way it evolved over time. In the same interaction, the therapist could also follow up on the client's statement that her father complains when she comes to visit. The word *complain* could be written on the genogram and explored in the same way because it connotes a negative intent on the part of the father. By gaining microinformation about what is actually said and what happens before and after the father's statement, the facts and assumptions begin to separate.

As the facts are described, the clinician can start to identify patterns of thinking and assumptions that may be hindering the development of a new pattern. The daughter believes that her father wants her to feel guilty. If the therapist has developed a supportive relationship, it might be appropriate to begin challenging her assumption during this phase of an assessment (e.g., "Is it possible that your father is trying to send you a different message besides wanting you to feel guilty?"). On the other hand, the client may have more concrete evidence through other experiences with her father that it is his intent to induce guilt. In this case, behavior patterns can be challenged as attempted solutions that have become unsuccessful ("When you clam up, does this solution give you the result that you want?"). In any event, the decision to intervene must be based on what the presenting problem is and whether the client perceives the intervention as relevant to stated goals. If the presenting problem was a child-focused problem, genogram discussions and the tracking of interactional sequences may provide information to help the clinician develop a broad understanding of the client's relational patterns, but interventions should be related to the problem (e.g., "Do you ever find that your son tries to make you feel guilty like your father does? How does he do that?"). Then, as similarities and differences are identified, the client's responses can be indicators of whether she is ready to consider alternative views.

If the presenting problem is directly related to the father-daughter relationship, the therapist might still want to complete the genogram, learning about the nature of other family relationships and tracking other important sequences before deciding on a treatment strategy. Sometimes, clients respond to the genogram with their own ideas about the best way to address the problem or who in their three-generation system could be most helpful with the problem. At other times, more developmental information may be needed to put a presenting problem into the context of family process over time. This may be done by tracking longitudinal sequences.

TRACKING LONGITUDINAL SEQUENCES: NARRATIVES ABOUT CHANGES OVER TIME

When gathering information about developmental progress across different stages of family life, it is often helpful to diagram a horizontal timeline that illustrates the family's story during significant time periods or that provides a chart of the family's history at the macrolevel of observation. Hiebert, Gillespie, and Stahmann (1993) use a timeline for marital and premarital counseling as a means of tracking the interpersonal "dance" of each couple and identifying the developmental roots of their presenting problem. Stanton (1992) uses a timeline to discover clues about what might have triggered the family's problem. Hanna (1997) uses a timeline to dissect the accumulation of stresses over time that have brought a family to the point of crisis.

In transitional family therapy, Suddaby and Landau (1998) make use of consecutive timelines in which they explore the progression of hardships followed by the progression of successes and positive stories. They suggest that this technique allows the family to construct a perspective of normal response to stress, rather than viewing themselves as failures across time. This is an excellent example of *gift giving,* which was mentioned in Chapter 4. When helping the family to see this positive, transitional perspective, the therapist should not simply implement a strategic maneuver, but, rather, show his or her own heartfelt respect for how the family has dealt with the repetitive stress and trauma. (p. 289)

The approaches previously noted adopt the premise that the identification of developmental patterns of interaction is an important step in developing hypotheses that are born out of client experience and that address nodal events related to key patterns. These events and patterns give rise to significant thoughts and beliefs which continue beyond the event and lead to subsequent difficulties. As these difficulties unfold, they might appear unrelated to previous events. However, the therapist often discovers that they are bound in relevance by certain patterns which originated with a prior nodal event. To change the patterns, it is helpful to discover how they originated and the meaning that is related to an important event.

Other family therapists also emphasize assessments with a historical element. Hargrave and Anderson (1992) conduct life reviews based on questioning to validate an older person's life history, but without the use of a visual chart. Fleuridas et al. (1986) provide examples of time-oriented circular questions exploring changes and transitions in the past that may be affecting the present. In these cases, the focus on historical information helps family members reflect on significant experiences that may stimulate their own natural abilities to heal or change.

The advantages of using a visual timeline are similar to those of using a genogram. Because families often feel stuck in a problem when they enter family therapy, a chronological account of important transitions can restore an element of movement and flow to the family's self-perception. After constructing a genogram, a logical transition is to take the recorded information and begin putting the significant events in sequence. This in-session process transforms awareness from the family as a system to the family as a larger story that extends beyond the presenting problem. Marriages, births, deaths, illnesses, job changes, graduations, and other significant events often cluster at certain points in a family's life story. These clusters might indicate transitions during which important themes in the family emerged. By tracking the sequences of these events through time, the therapist is able to broaden the family members' perception of how they came to be "stuck" and to summarize important information in a graphic manner. Consider the following example.

Case 7 | **Randy and Betty**

Randy, 48, and Betty, 42, were rebuilding their relationship after Randy served a jail sentence for drug dealing. They had both been married previously and met at a 12-Step meeting while Randy was in recovery from substance abuse. A review of their early relationship revealed his sobriety and exemplary recovery as an important attraction for Betty. She was attending Al-Anon after having been married first to an emotionally distant, autocratic man, and second to an alcoholic. Randy was attracted to Betty because of her strength and determination. They dated for over a year. However, the month before their wedding, Randy began using prescription drugs again. Betty was unaware of his relapse until their wedding day when he offered her drugs on the way to their honeymoon. She was devastated.

Figure 7.3 is a timeline of Randy and Betty's early relationship. As it was constructed, the therapist highlighted strengths of the couple (spiritual talks, flexibility), tracked

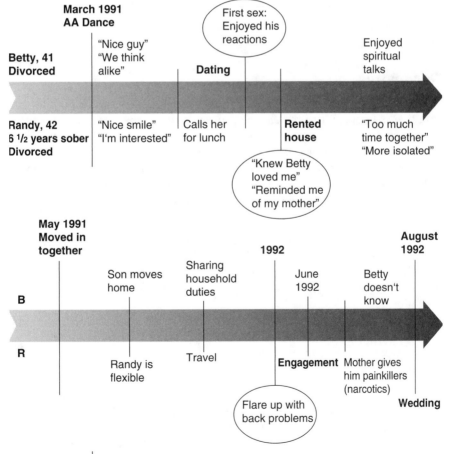

Figure 7.3 | Timeline of Randy and Betty

(Continued)

Case 7	**Randy and Betty** (continued)

interactional sequences, and explored each person's evolving perceptions of the other during courtship. As discussion of the relationship progressed beyond engagement toward marriage, the therapist asked the couple about whether they thought anything should have been different. Randy acknowledged that they became isolated. Betty reported not knowing about the pain medication.

As the timeline brought the therapist and family up to the present day, the clinician had the opportunity to reflect on this couple's courage and endurance as important qualities needed to overcome obstacles in the future. Because a timeline shows progression over time, it becomes an unspoken voice for the inevitability of change. These narratives about strengths and resilience in the face of adversity are important outcomes that therapists should pursue when constructing timelines. In this case, the therapist could empathize with Betty and Randy's pain, highlight their strengths, and puzzle with them about how to address the problems they identified.

Deconstruction

Dissecting microprocesses in the family also provides developmental information that is important to the change process. Just as when tracking sequences of behavior, when family therapists track sequences of thought and emotion, they are putting relationships under the microscope. White (1990) suggests a process of *deconstruction* in which a client's core belief (e.g., "I'm no good," "She's lazy," "We can't go on together") is addressed through careful and detailed questioning of how that belief developed. Questions might follow this sequence:

1. When you say _____, I'm wondering how you came to that conclusion.
2. Who are the people who have influenced your thinking on this?
3. What experiences have led you to think in this way?
4. Would you be interested in comparing your point of view with that of others?
5. If you began to think differently, would there be a backlash from important people?
6. How would you cope with such a backlash?

Each question might evolve into a lengthy conversation. People and experiences can be noted on a timeline. Future projections about coping can be noted beyond the present time. In this way, perceptions, behavior, and relationships are identified as part of the problem. These elements are dissected to develop opportunities for relational change as part of the solution. In some cases, treatment will paradoxically involve a plan to cope with change before actually addressing the original problem. (See Chapter 8 for more discussion on paradox.)

Developing a Rationale for the Timeline

Clinicians must provide a rationale for the timeline that emphasizes their neutral point of view and their desire to understand how the family came to be in its present position. The following sample rationale can be used in an initial interview to develop the contract.

> **THERAPIST:** Listening to your account of the problem that brings you here, I have been impressed by your sincere desire to solve it. In spite of your best efforts, things have not changed, and you seem to be stuck. When people try as hard as you have to solve a problem, but to no avail, there is usually something missing in their understanding of what the problem is. I can usually help people solve this puzzle by reviewing the experiences they have been through together, each person's point of view (content), and how they have come to this point (process). By looking at the big picture of their life, we are able to discover some new direction that proves successful. I would like to propose a few sessions in which you give me the chance to review important experiences with you. Then, we can see what solutions will best fit for you in view of your unique experience.

As with genograms, other rationales can be presented based on the therapist's chosen perspective, whether problem-solving, solution-focused, or cultural. If a person is deconstructing a client's beliefs, a timeline might become a natural extension of noting important experiences. In such cases, a rationale might need only to explain a reason for extending the timeline into other conversations. The most important task for the beginning therapist is learning how to relate this process to the presenting problem in a meaningful way. Chapter 6 suggests possible strategies for setting goals and developing therapeutic contracts. These strategies might also be helpful in developing a rationale for genograms and timelines. When the initial goal is clarification or exploration, these assessment procedures provide a sense of direction that has a concrete beginning and end. When the goal is experimentation, these tools are used to gather ideas about previous successes and behavioral sequences.

Creating a Sense of Movement

For the beginning practitioner, creating a sense of chronological movement along the continuum is the primary goal. Develop a different rhythm for each family or individual that captures the uniqueness of their interpersonal patterns through time; in some cases, lengthy discussions occur at some points along the timeline, and only superficial coverage is necessary at other points. The clinician must make sure that certain emotional points in time do not derail the discussion before it reaches the present; otherwise, a sense of movement toward the future may not be achieved. As significant events are explored but left unresolved, the therapist can develop a list of themes and experiences that family members identify as most influential. After the timeline is complete, the identified issues can be explored more fully using questions from the various themes in Chapter 3, such as gender, race, and organization. This list of issues noted by clients can form the foundation of additional goals in the treatment plan.

Summarizing Details

Boxes 3.2 and 3.3 give examples of questions in developmental interviewing that elicit microinformation, but writing details or complete sentences on a timeline isn't necessary. Key words, themes, or events with the month and year are adequate. Too many details clutter the family members' visual perception of their movement over time and leave them feeling overwhelmed. For example, a clinician who is helping a couple have a lengthy discussion about a misunderstanding that occurred 15 years earlier when the couple's first child was born needs only to note the misunderstanding and important reframings, questions, or alternative views that emerge.

Hanna (1997, p. 112) uses the following questions to assess the relationship between events, behaviors, and perceptions. This information can be summarized on a timeline.

1. What was the first (or next) significant event in your life (as a person, couple, family)?
2. When this happened, how did each of you react? What was the sequence of these reactions? (track interactional sequences for each event)
3. After it ended, what conclusions did you draw about yourself and others?

For couples and families, the usual starting point for a timeline is when the couple first meets, with progression from left to right through courtship to the birth of each child and so on. For individuals, the usual starting point is at birth, unless the presenting problem is child-oriented or work-related, in which case the timeline starts at some significant marker in the sequence of a person's life—college graduation, divorce or marriage, or some other important change.

Advantages of Timelines

One advantage of a timeline is that it helps the family therapist keep a sense of direction during stages of exploration when emotional issues are raised before a therapeutic direction is explicitly defined. Both the therapist and family understand, through constructing the timeline, that they are moving forward from past toward future. The timeline allows an emotional issue to be explored in its original context as a point along a continuum rather than as an end in itself. In this way, microinformation through deconstruction generates empathy; macroinformation through mapping nodal events generates perspective. The following case study illustrates how the timeline can be used with genograms and circular questions by providing an opportunity for these in-depth explorations.

Case 8	The Wilsons

The Wilsons were a white, middle-class family who sought family therapy after their son, Bob, 15, was caught smoking at school twice and was subsequently dropped from the basketball squad at school. Bob's parents were John, 42, and Kristin, 39. Bob also had a sister, Sue, 14, who attended the first session. John was a hospital social worker, and Kristin was a nurse. They had been married for 19 years. Both were raised in small rural communities. They met and married while attending college.

Figure 7.4 shows a genogram of the Wilsons. It summarizes information gathered in the initial sessions of family therapy with all members present. Figure 7.5 is a timeline of the Wilson's family story, noting transitions that have affected the family. Family members reminisced about happier times in the past. They were able to compare earlier stages with current circumstances.

First Session: Intake and Initial Interview

Defining the Problem
Everyone is asked to comment, but the therapist notices that Kristin is the most verbal and Bob is the least verbal during this stage of the process. After some initial small talk, the therapists asks, "What brings you here?" The family responds by giving various accounts of Bob's recent problems at school and by noting how each family member feels about the recent progression of events. Bob was caught smoking at school twice, was suspended for three days, and was dropped from the basketball team after playing in the first two games. John and Kristin express their concern and state that they wish Bob would "open up."

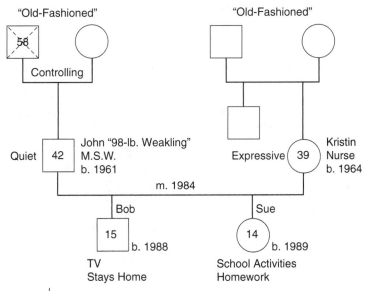

Figure 7.4 | Genogram of the Wilsons

(Continued)

Case 8	The Wilsons (continued)

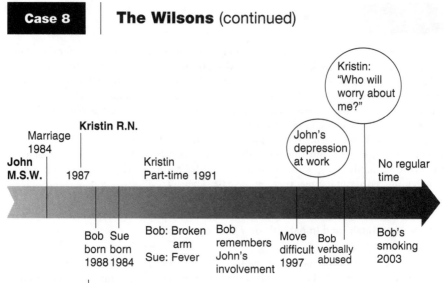

Figure 7.5 | Timeline of the Wilsons

Tracking Interactional Sequences

With the focus on present events, the therapist investigates interactional patterns of the family as the problem developed. "How did you find out about Bob's smoking?" "What did you do when you found out?" "Bob, what did you do when your mother confronted you?" "Sue, where were you and what were you doing while all this was going on?" "John, how did you find out and what did you do?" Information comes forth about Bob's tendency to withdraw, John's tendency to lecture, Kristin's tendency to interrogate, and Sue's tendency to stay busy when there is conflict.

Precipitating Events

Attention is shifted away from the topic of "What did Bob do?" (present-oriented) to the topic of "What has been happening to Bob?" (recent past). This shift diminishes his shame and provides a developmental perspective on how problems evolve from a sequence of events. Because Bob appears reserved and uncomfortable during this part of the discussion, the therapist decides to engage him in conversation that might be less threatening.

"It seems unusual for a guy of 15 to already be starting on the basketball team. How were you able to do this?" At this point, Bob opens up and tells the story of how the coaches noticed his unusual height and coordination while he was still in middle school. Anxious to have him play, they began to encourage him to try out for the team the summer before he started high school. He began attending practices and easily made the team. However, as the season approached, he began to feel bad although he couldn't explain why.

His parents state that they do not understand why he would be feeling bad when things seemed to be going so well. However, they believe that he has negative feelings about himself and quote him as saying, "Things don't matter. I wish I could fry my brains out."

(Continued)

Case 8 | # The Wilsons (continued)

Goals

All members are able to agree on the same goals. This is acknowledged by the therapist as a strength. The therapist asks what the family would like to see happen. The parents state their goals for therapy as wanting Bob to feel better about himself and wanting to improve communication and intimacy in the family. Bob and Sue both agree that these are good goals.

Contract

At this point, the family therapist responds to the family's story by describing the assessment process and clarifying expectations for change: "It sounds as if all of you care about each other and want to solve the puzzle of how to help Bob. It also sounds as if no one is certain about what the real problem might be. In view of this, one possible direction is to take a couple of sessions to explore the problem in greater detail. Once we have a definition of the problem that we all feel comfortable with, our efforts at developing solutions will be more effective and we can move on to developing a plan of action. How does that sound as a starting place?" The family agrees to a plan for three assessment sessions, after which subsequent sessions would be devoted to developing a plan for helping Bob.

Because, at this point, the family's goals are abstract (intimacy and communication) rather than concrete (change in behavior), the therapist suggests an interim process goal of exploration, which will produce more concrete goals to work on during the intervention stage.

Data-Gathering Phase (Genogram)

The members of the family are invited to shift their attention away from the immediate problem in the present to a discussion about general family relationships and extended-family influences. With time left in the first interview, the therapist explains that it would be helpful to understand the family relationships most important to the family members as a group and to see the way grandparents may have solved similar problems.

Using John and Kristin's marriage as the central relationship, the therapist proceeds to sketch a skeleton genogram that includes Bob and Sue as the youngest generation and shows both sides of the extended family. Listing only the names, ages, deaths, and home-towns of parents, the therapist has time afterward to ask circular questions about individual differences in the nuclear family and about the parents' experiences in their own families of origin (see Figure 7.4).

1. How are family members different from each other? John is quiet and Kristin is more expressive, suggesting a possible complementary marital relationship. She states, "We have a hard time expressing gut feelings." Bob watches a lot of TV and stays home more. Sue is immersed in school activities and homework.
2. What was each parent's experience in his or her family of origin? Kristin expresses regret that her own family did not care more about her and tells the story from her younger years of how her family, hardworking farmers, never came to see her perform when she was a cheerleader. John describes his family as very controlling of him and recounts an important experience: his decision to finally assert himself with his parents and change majors in college.

(Continued)

| Case 8 | The Wilsons (continued) |

As Kristin and John share their experiences, Bob expresses surprise at his father's account of standing up to the grandparents. Bob and Sue describe their grandparents on both sides as "old-fashioned." John also explains how he had been a "98-pound weakling" as a youth and therefore can't understand why Bob is not enjoying his enviable athletic ability; John would have given anything to have had Bob's height and strength. At this point, Bob is silent, eyes looking at the floor.

At the end of the session, the family therapist thanks the family members for their openness in sharing information and indicates that the next session will be an opportunity to explore the development of their family and the events that might be related to Bob's current feelings.

Second Session: Tracking Longitudinal Sequences

Timeline
The rationale for tracking longitudinal sequences (Figure 7.5) is that Bob's difficulties could possibly be related to various changes—recent or past—that might have affected him in ways no one was aware of. Thus, it would help the therapist if the family members could describe the various transitions they had been through together. What do the members of the family consider to be the major changes they have experienced together in the areas of personal development, job experience, and family roles?

The parents report success as a beginning young family: They were happy with each other, John's work, and their young children. From 1989 to 1991, there was some stress in the family. Sue developed a serious fever as a baby, Bob broke his arm when he fell off his bicycle, and Kristin began to work part-time so that they could buy their first home. The family weathered these challenges through hard work and sacrifice.

Marking and Discussing Time Periods
The horizontal timeline is divided into major time periods and labeled as the family discusses each stage (e.g., "Move difficult: 1997"). Short descriptions note important issues as the chart moves from left to right, from past to present. Family members are included by placing parents' experience above the line (e.g., "John's depression at work") with children's experience below the line (e.g., "Bob verbally abused"). The therapist uses the visual diagram to stimulate a reflection and reconceptualization of the problem as developmental-interactional in nature.

In 1997, John got a better job offer, and the family contemplated a major relocation. Soon, the members of the family were reestablishing themselves in a new city, with new jobs for the parents and a new school for the children. From this time forward, life proved more difficult. John's job required many more hours, and he was assigned patients with terminal illnesses. In addition, the salary increase he was promised after three months was put on hold because of the financial instability of the hospital. He became depressed and sought individual counseling for his depression. After two years, rumors were prevalent about the hospital's continued financial difficulties. John reports that his main way of coping was to tell himself that things would get better if he could only work harder and get a promotion. He found himself trying harder, but with no results.

In the meantime, Kristin was hired at a different hospital and was assigned to a critical care ward. Bob remembers his mother talking about her work and how anxious she

(Continued)

Case 8 | **The Wilsons** (continued)

felt about the stresses there, but he was completely unaware of his father's depression. Sue also indicates that she was unaware of her father's depression. Kristin reports that John talked a great deal to her about his depression, to the point that she remarks, "I wish someone would worry about me once in a while." In the last four years, the children had become more involved in school activities: Bob played hockey and basketball in middle school, and until recently played basketball in high school; Sue developed her hobbies and musical abilities. The parents state that time spent with the children now is usually after dinner and on some weekends when Kristin is not working. John and Kristin also say that their time together is usually when the children are busy or early in the morning. It has been years since they have scheduled any regular time for themselves.

Comparing Life Stages
What are the main differences between various life stages for this family? Asked how their past had been different, all the family members agree that the period before 1997 had been much happier for everyone. The therapist notes nonverbal cues that indicate the impact of the assessment process on Bob, who has become more verbal and involved. Bob is very active in this discussion, reminiscing that his dad had been more involved with the family during those days. He also defends John in some surprising ways, given the fact that Bob has had a great aversion to his father's lectures. The family agrees that Kristin is more involved with the children during the week, and John is home on the weekends but uninvolved with the children while Kristin works.

Using, Identifying, and Emphasizing Family Strengths
The therapist points out the family's strengths while externalizing the problem away from Bob. Life got hard. Patients at the hospital were struggling with life-and-death issues, and everyone at home began to feel the effects of each parent's stress. Now assessment begins to overlap with intervention. The therapist ends the session by commenting extensively on the transitions, reflecting for this family a picture of itself that includes many successes, the family's closeness and caring, the unexpected stresses after 1997, and the unintended consequences of these stresses as John's depression and Kristin's anxiety began to shape family interactions.

Third Session: A Return to the Presenting Problem
An exploration of cultural issues, interaction patterns, family structure, and the meaning of the symptom begins with a discussion about the symptom: Bob's smoking. It emerges that Bob had started smoking during the summer that the coaches began recruiting him for the team. When asked about the summer practices, Bob relates experiences in which he felt verbally abused by the coaches and thought about quitting. When asked what he thought might have happened if he had quit, Bob says he knew his dad would have been disappointed. John indicates that he had no idea that Bob was feeling this way.

Cultural Issues and Family Values
How do the parents feel about smoking in general? The parents are emphatically against Bob's smoking. John smoked earlier in his life and quit for health reasons. The family is

(Continued)

Case 8 | The Wilsons (continued)

very religious and has firm values about living a temperate life. This is an area where John frequently lectured Bob, and he had made many attempts to get Bob to stop smoking.

Family Interaction and Structure
How does the family handle other issues? By this time, Bob is much more comfortable discussing his relationship with his parents directly. He complains about how his mother "nags and interrogates" him about his schoolwork when he comes home. In response, he retreats and goes to his room or becomes distant by "vegging in front of the TV."

Transforming Assessment to Intervention Through Reframing
By the end of the third session, the therapist moves further into formal interventions by beginning to make implicit family processes more explicit: "It seems that some things are going on in the family that have been invisible until now. One is that Bob was struggling and feeling overwhelmed by the coaches, but no one in the family knew. Another is that John has been depressed at work, but only Kristin knew, and she has become overwhelmed by his depression and the stress of her work. Even though Dad envies Bob's size and ability, I wonder if Bob is really more like Dad on the inside, sensitive and caring, which makes it harder to tolerate harsh treatment from the coaches. At the risk of being called a quitter at school and disappointing Dad at home, maybe getting caught smoking was the best way for him to change the direction of his life. By the same token, it sounds like Kristin has needed more support than she has been able to get in the family, and she has dealt with her struggle by trying to get Bob to do things that would be more helpful to her. When we meet next time, I would like to get your reactions to these ideas and see if you're ready to develop a plan of action for meeting your goals."

The formal assessment for which the family had contracted concludes with the third session. As the process unfolds, the session becomes an opportunity for the family members to shift their focus from the immediate intensity of the presenting problem to a more reflective focus on their life together. In addition, the therapist is able to continue the joining process, to identify strengths, and to experiment with reframing to determine the clients' cognitive flexibility. The degree to which they are open to the reframing is information used in developing a treatment plan. Would direct or indirect interventions be more useful with this family? Would perceptual change, behavioral change, or both be needed for this family to achieve its goals?

Hypotheses

To adopt a pragmatic approach, the beginning clinician must understand something about how different hypotheses relate to the change process. In the case of the Wilsons, the therapist made the following tentative hypotheses:

Gender-Related

1. Bob might have felt trapped into playing basketball by the expectations of the coaches and his father. His lack of self-esteem could be related to interactions with other males and his resulting feelings of inadequacy.
2. Bob's mother might also have expectations of him that he perceives as overwhelming.

3. Because Kristin stated, "I wish someone would worry about me once in a while," she might be a catalyst for change in the area of gender patterns if her feelings are a manifestation of disempowerment in her marriage.

Culture-Related

4. The Wilsons both come from rural, religious backgrounds. Conformity to parental authority is expected. Bob may be breaking with tradition and feeling the effects of parental disapproval; however, both parents seem firm about adherence to family traditions.
5. Both parents have jobs in the helping professions. They believe in the values of respect, empathy, and promotion of self-esteem within their family. These values may become catalysts for change in their relationship with Bob.

Intergenerational

6. Bob's grandparents have not been resources for this family. Both parents report a lack of closeness with their families of origin. Lingering conflict over their own disengagement may make it difficult for them to be comfortable with Bob's individuation.
7. John's adolescent image of himself as a 98-pound weakling may prevent him from empathizing with his son and could thus contribute to Bob's discouragement. The pain that John still experiences over his inadequacies as a youth could become a catalyst for resolving personal beliefs that complicate his relationship with Bob.
8. There are cross-generational similarities in the temperament of Kristin and Sue, John and Bob. Perhaps Bob's low self-esteem is related to John's style of coping.

Transitions

9. The family successfully completed early stages of development but experienced overwhelming discomfort after 1997 as a result of job stress that precipitated a change in lifestyle and a significant sense of disengagement among all members. Bob's low self-esteem might have developed during this period of stress, in which his parents had little energy to address the tasks of families with adolescents. His depression is also an indication that he might be grieving the losses brought on from the move in 1997.

Family Structure

10. There may be a *complementarity* in the marital and parental subsystem that leaves Kristin overfunctioning for John and Bob but underfunctioning for herself. Her sense of overresponsibility for Bob may be the force behind her "interrogations" of Bob that leave him feeling criticized and suffocated. John's underinvolvement may leave Bob feeling abandoned.
11. There may be an imbalance between Bob's need for understanding and the family's need for accomplishment. The interaction pattern that surrounds Bob's depression usually runs as follows: Bob comes home from school.

Mother becomes involved by questioning Bob's homework. Bob retreats. Father becomes involved by lecturing. Bob retreats. Sue returns from school activities, and the family focuses on her accomplishments.

Individual Development

12. Bob is different from his father athletically, but similar to him in temperament. Bob's aversion to the subculture of male competition could be looked on as a strength and as a way in which he is loyal to his father's humanitarian values.
13. Bob's intent is to please his father. However, he feels abused by coaching strategies, embarrassed with his friends, and misunderstood within his family. Seen in this context, his actions (smoking and withdrawal) could be regarded as resources in that they served to help him out of his dilemmas at school with the coaches and at home with his mother and father.

DEVELOPMENTALLY APPROPRIATE TREATMENT: MATCHING INTERVENTION WITH NEEDS

Because some of the hypotheses were related to resources for change and some were not, it is appropriate for the therapist to ask herself which of these hypotheses fits best with the family's goals. The presenting problem was Bob getting caught smoking and being suspended from the basketball team. The parents stated that they wished Bob would open up and discuss his problems. Because of the parents' background (i.e., their expectation of conformity to parental authority) and disengagement from their family of origin, the therapist might hypothesize that they do not have a model for encouraging Bob to open up. This may be exacerbated by the pain that the father still carries from his adolescence. Acting on this hypothesis, the therapist might explore the parents' family of origin to understand how the past gets played out in the present. What current beliefs and new frames of meaning from the culture and family of origin can the therapist find to assist the Wilsons in resolving the problem? On the other hand, the therapist might also hypothesize that unrealistic gender expectations are contributing to the problem. This might lead the therapist to emphasize Kristin's desire to get help as a strength or to explore alternative ways in which Bob can meet his masculine needs or his mother's expectations.

The therapist can also view Bob's problem as a metaphor for the parents' job stress and may wish to explore some alternative ways to cope with that stress. Or the therapist may hypothesize that the problem is structural—that if Kristin curbed her impulse to be helpful, Bob could learn to be more responsible; or it may be that Mr. and Mrs. Wilson need to work together and help Bob become more responsible. The therapist must also consider individual strengths, such as Bob's loyalty to his father, and internal resources when choosing an intervention.

Knowing the parents' stated goals for therapy—wanting Bob to feel better about himself and wanting to improve communication and intimacy in the family—the therapist reviews the list of hypotheses to see which ones might relate to the family's stated goals. Hypotheses 3, 5, 7, 12, and 13 all recognize potential resources and strengths that might lead to change. Because intimacy and communication are often blocked by problematic interactional sequences, the therapist used Hypotheses 3, 5, and 6 to motivate the family to accept some tasks that would indirectly address Hypotheses 10 and 11.

By appealing to the parents' strengths and good intentions, the therapist made an assignment for Kristin to refrain from asking Bob about his homework at all times during a two-week experiment. In the meantime, during those two weeks, Bob could decide what he would initiate and talk about on his own regarding his progress in school. The parents were asked to find one night a week that was exclusively reserved for themselves and to set aside time in which Kristin was given a chance to vent her feelings and John would be willing to listen to her more.

In addition, the therapist decided to address Hypotheses 12 and 13 directly by reframing Bob's behavior, his reason for smoking, the dilemma he had found himself in, and the strength that he had been exhibiting. After two weeks, the family reported Bob's depression was lifting, and he and Kristin had no conflicted encounters about homework. Bob had successfully initiated conversation on his own about school progress, and Kristin was relieved and satisfied with this. Family members desired to continue with the current experiment and were also asked to add another dimension to their plan: John was asked to find some time to talk with Bob about how John felt as a young man when he began smoking. He was to share his memory of his feelings toward parents, peers, and others at the time he started smoking. Then he was to share his feelings and thoughts about when, as an older man, he decided to quit smoking on his own. The parents agreed to maintain their plan and asked if they could attend the next session alone. During this final session (the sixth), they reported continuing improvement in their relationship with Bob and used the time to discuss their own relationship—the imbalance and disempowerment that Kristin had been feeling and ways that they as a couple could restructure their lives for improved satisfaction. The Wilsons reported success in accomplishing their goals; there were no further school problems with Bob.

The next case provides a contrast to the white, middle class Wilsons. Ellie's case (first discussed in Chapter 5) is another illustration of how the construction of a timeline helps the therapist to assess problem severity and to engage the client in therapeutic dialogues about nodal events. With this single, African American mother, timeline diagraming provided structure to the session and showed the client that the therapist was able to comprehend the full picture of her life.

| Case 5 | A Return to Ellie |

Ellie's genogram and case introduction are in Chapter 5 on page 128. Figure 7.6 illustrates a timeline of Ellie's history. The therapist draws a large diagram for display in the therapy room so that the client can review it and reflect on it. This longitudinal perspective of Ellie's life shows how a sequence of events provides meaning to her current behavior. Each entry on the timeline signifies a nodal event or an important story. Sometimes notes are metaphors that become part of a therapeutic intervention to join, reframe, or remove blame from a situation, such as the shipwreck metaphor when Ellie's father had an affair and abruptly divorced her mother. Although the affair and divorce signified a turning

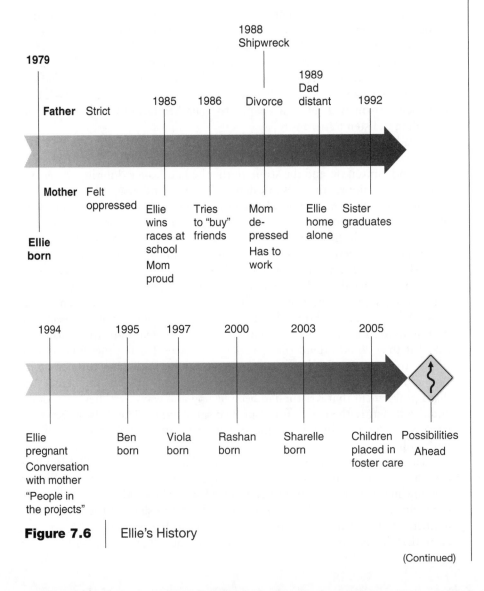

Figure 7.6 | Ellie's History

(Continued)

| Case 5 | A Return to Ellie (continued) |

point in Ellie's family, Ellie also had challenges with her father's oppressive leadership prior to the divorce. During elementary school, she enjoyed some successes in school, but would find ways to give money to her friends so that they would like her. Her mother's depression left her with only her older sister for support. As Ellie entered adolescence, her mother remarried, and her sister left home making Ellie even more isolated at home. Due to this cascade of events in Ellie's childhood, her case is considered chronic.

During Ellie's first pregnancy, while still in high school, her middle-class mother expressed fears about her daughter: "If you're not careful, you'll end up like those people in the projects!" Ellie felt compassion for people in the projects. She set out to prove to her mother that people in the projects were worthwhile human beings. During her childbearing years, she surrounded herself with people whom she considered to live in the projects. A more detailed timeline included important friends and partners, and its creation was accompanied by a discussion of how they affected her life. One timeline discussion was particularly poignant, as the therapist (the book author) heard the fears of Ellie's mother and Ellie's reaction:

THERAPIST: (asking the miracle question) "Ellie, suppose we could wave a magic wand and tomorrow you woke up and discovered that your mom had decided to devote her life to helping people in the projects, because she believed that they deserved to have a better life. What affect would that have on you?"

ELLIE: (long pause) Oh, Dr. Hanna, that's deep! (long pause) That would never happen. . . . I'm tellin' ya, that would not. . . . Oh no no no!

THERAPIST: I know it would seem like a miracle, but I wonder what you would do if this mission that you've taken on were to change. You're a woman on a mission . . . right?

ELLIE: Yes, ma'am, that's right. You know I am!

THERAPIST: I know you are, Ellie! And I just want to help you with that mission . . . to see if there are some other ways you could get through to your mom. I'd like to help you with that. . . .

ELLIE: You know, you're the only one that's ever been on my side. . . .

THERAPIST: Now, tell me the truth. What about the fact that I didn't recommend that you get your kids back. . . .

ELLIE: No, I'm not messin' with ya. All these people that have been against me . . . I knew you guys here [at the clinic] were always on my side and I wanna thank you for that.

THERAPIST: I appreciate that. I'm sorry that court couldn't go better. I know you worked hard, and I know it'll pay off for you in some other ways. When I hear you talk about how you and your mom are doin' better, I wonder what other things may be in store for you. I think she sees how much progress you've made. I could see how proud she was when she told me about you goin' to the Black Expo.

ELLIE: (smiles) Yes, ma'am. I think she was.

(Continued)

Case 5 | **A Return to Ellie** (continued)

When problem severity is chronic, indirect interventions are effective because they explore potential meanings surrounding the problem, validate strengths, and bypass shame. These interventions encourage change in small, gradual steps. When the past is used to elicit appropriate empathy from the therapist, the arrow of the timeline is like a road sign, pointing to future possibilities on the road ahead.

THE PROCESS OF CHANGE

All family therapy models share certain assessment procedures that make them effective in facilitating change. They each enable the therapist to gather certain information about the family in the form of stories and nodal events that families relate to the therapist. Regardless of whether the therapist's theme is transitions, intergenerational relationships, or nuclear family structure, the therapist takes the family's story and begins to evolve an alternate story. Any assessment from any model of family therapy is a plausible foundation for the remainder of the change process.

In the two preceding cases, an analysis of how change actually occurred must take into consideration the impact of the structured assessment process and the in-session interventions embedded in the questions and dialogue that took place during the genogram and through tracking the family's longitudinal sequences. For the Wilsons, the change process included tasks and assignments that helped members of the family modify their behavior between sessions. For Ellie, the process addressed her view of others and herself through reflection and exploration. The assessment was an opportunity for family members to tell their stories and have an audience in the form of the therapist, who could reflect their story with only slight modifications (e.g., through reframing). The intervention stage was an opportunity for behavior change to start and, if successful, stabilize during the last weeks of the treatment period.

The entire therapeutic process evolved through several stages, each with its own mystery about what the family would bring to it. With experience, the practitioner can develop good timing and rhythm, moving comfortably from one stage of therapy to the next. After narratives provide the therapist with an understanding of each person's predicament and the family's transitions over time, the salient issues for therapy can be organized and addressed as relational issues.

The case of the Wilsons can illustrate how the suggestions for treatment planning in Chapter 6 and the dimensions from the GARF fit together. Return to Table 6.1, and note that the family's goals were emotional (Bob's self-esteem) and interpersonal (intimacy). An analysis of problem severity suggests that the problem was transitional. The therapist makes this judgment because the family had a number of strengths, and they reported earlier life stages in which they overcame challenges together and enjoyed a positive emotional climate. However, since several family members reported a gradual erosion of positive emotion, the problem seemed more than situational, because a history of the erosion developed over a period of years (see Chapter 9 for a discussion of *pile-up*). The problem was not viewed as chronic because there was a significant history in which the problem did not exist. From the models of family therapy outlined in Chapter 1, the therapist chose strategic, experiential, and intergenerational family therapies. Experiential concepts were the basis for exploring Bob's sense of self-esteem in the family. Intergenerational information was used to understand beliefs and attitudes and to address issues of loss and transition. Both of these approaches are direct. Strategic interventions, which were more indirect, were used to reframe meanings, change interactions, and direct new patterns of relating. Because the problem was considered transitional, a mix of direct and indirect interventions was used. Indirect interventions are often more comfortable for adolescents. John and Kristin shared the same goals and level of motivation for help, which made many direct interventions appropriate.

Using the GARF, the therapist gave the family an initial rating of 68, based upon their strong sense of organization, their lack of satisfaction with reported problem solving (attempted solutions), and the inconsistency in their emotional climate. Regarding these dimensions, the family made great progress with Bob and his sense of well-being. They were exploring additional progress within the marital dyad, but had not completed those changes when therapy ended. Thus, the initial rating suggested a *somewhat unsatisfactory* experience for the majority of family members, but that experience improved in relationship to how the family related to Bob. The therapist gave them a closing rating of 78. We can guess that if John and Kristin made the progress they desired in their marriage, the rating would move into the *satisfactory* range (80 and above).

Table 7.2 shows which hypotheses from the Wilson case are likely to be relevant to GARF areas. As clinicians develop their hypotheses, they can summarize them according to GARF concepts for case records and treatment planning. Arguments can easily be made for the relevance of all possible combinations of concepts with GARF categories. This is one strength of the instrument: Because it doesn't limit clinicians from a wide range of perspectives, it helps them organize the breadth of information for brief summaries and progress reports.

Table 7.2 | Wilson Case Hypotheses and the GARF

Problem Solving	Organization	Emotional Climate
Transitions	Gender	Gender
Family structure	Culture	Culture
	Family structure	Intergenerational relationships
		Individual development

SUMMARY

To summarize, family therapy assessment is a series of interactional processes that are guided by flexible, strength-based clinicians who observe content and process; track sequences that span past, present, and future interactions; deconstruct the development of thoughts, emotions, intentions, and behaviors in relationships. Like all other relationships, the therapeutic relationship evolves through developmental stages as clinician and family discover new definitions of the problem and corresponding solutions. The family therapist organizes the structure of therapy, joins with each family member, and gathers information that focuses on the family's potential for change. Initial treatment plans combine relational and mental health information. As new information emerges, the therapist develops interventions that match the history of the problem, the family's developmental level, and the therapist's skill level. These interventions are often chosen from a collection of early and second-generation family therapy practices. They provide a foundation from which to begin and maintain the process of change.

Chapter 8 instructs practitioners how to implement a variety of common family therapy techniques. By this stage in the therapeutic process, the therapist has focused on how interpersonal dynamics relate to the problem by eliciting descriptions of client experience. These descriptions are the basis by which participants begin to see that all problems have behavioral, perceptual, emotional, and relational components. In family therapy, relationships are sometimes the background of a problem and sometimes the foreground. As the clients' experience becomes known and understood, the clients become more open to a change in the story or to a change in their perceptions of relevant relationships. Their understanding of the problem evolves into one in which they see that certain relational aspects need to change. To help them, the therapist can devote a group of sessions to a number of pragmatic processes that encourage relational change.

Interventions for Beliefs, Behaviors, and Emotions

CHAPTER OUTLINE

CORE COMPETENCIES

1.3.9	**Executive**	Manage session interactions with individuals, couples, families, and groups.
4.3.1	**Executive**	Match treatment modalities and techniques to clients' needs, goals, and values.
4.3.2	**Executive**	Deliver interventions in a way that is sensitive to special needs of clients (e.g., gender, age, socioeconomic status, culture/race/ethnicity, sexual orientation, disability, personal history, larger systems issues of the client).
4.3.6	**Executive**	Facilitate clients developing and integrating solutions to problems.

Family therapists must be facilitators of relational change. As explained in Chapter 7, asking carefully developed questions during assessment very often enables changes in thinking, feeling, and interaction. As a result of these reflective discussions, spontaneous behaviors emerge between sessions. As therapeutic process continues, the therapist becomes more action-oriented, encouraging new behaviors that help the family experiment and adopt new patterns and ultimately lead to competence with handling future life tasks. Such a process can take many forms. The result, however, should be *a developmentally appropriate strategy for a specific family in a specific culture at a specific stage in the family's life.* Let's review the recommended developmental scheme and examine what this means in a practical sense.

ASSESSING INDIVIDUAL FUNCTIONING

Assessment offers the therapist a chance to understand and reflect on three major aspects of a family's life. First, assessment should lead to certain hypotheses about an individual's life stage and about social functioning. Is each family member successful with the tasks for his or her life stage? Is the "emotional age" of a 40-year-old man really 12 because of sexual abuse at age 9 and substance abuse starting at 10? Although this man is a hard worker and reliable breadwinner, are his expectations for his wife and children coming from the fears and distrust he felt in childhood? If so, intervention will help him and his family take small steps that parallel those he missed in earlier times. For example, I ask clients to assess their own emotional age, given the life experiences that affect their development. They make their own conclusions and we proceed on that basis. They are relieved to be understood on their terms. A 12-year-old might be starting to experiment with independence, but still needs face-saving affirmation from parents. Thus, the therapist might want to be a coach that offers options, encouragement, and affirmation. At the same time, a wife might be emotionally 25 because of the way in which her parents and first husband influenced her choices and options. In helping her to address her marital conflict, the therapist might want to be a narrator that frames the repair of the marriage as a "courtship" in which each is exploring an earlier stage of the relationship through trial and error. She might need common sense suggestions like, "Pick your battles," "Negotiate the best time to address conflicts," and "Ask him for what you want."

Second, individual assessment should identify the stage of change for each family member. For example, if parents are saying, "Fix my child," perhaps they've exhausted their own solutions. In this case, the focus of change is their child, and they are in the *precontemplation* stage (they don't see options for changing their behavior). The examples from Chapter 2 and Chapter 4 illustrated three important strategies for parents when they are exhausted and see no options: *gift-giving* ("You're not alone. It's hard raising kids these days"), *systemic empathy* ("This is complicated, no wonder you're exhausted"), *and hope* ("Because of your good efforts so far, there are more steps we can take").

These strategies will prepare the parents to discover additional options without losing face as they move from precontemplation to contemplation.

Third, as described in Chapter 3, the worldview of clients includes beliefs about gender, race, emotion, help-seeking, relationships, traditions, politics, morals and religion. What are the symbols, ceremonies, customs, and beliefs in a family's background? Which of these aspects can be included in the therapist's questions, directives, and reflections, and have a positive effect on the course of family therapy? For example, consider a case in which the adult siblings, all successful professionals, were worried about the isolation and eccentricities of their youngest sister, a recent college graduate. They described unusual, irrational behavior and poor hygiene. They also described parents' responses to her behavior. The therapist and clients decided it that offering some help to their distraught parents would be important because their sister refused to seek counseling.

Prior to inviting the parents to join the therapy, the therapist asked siblings to read the chapter from McGoldrick, Pearce, and Giordano (1982) on Polish families. Given that their parents came from Polish immigrants, the therapist assumed this was an important influence. The siblings returned with many examples of how the chapter applied to their family. With this feedback, the therapist could plan an approach that fit with their reports. Therapy with the parents avoided direct attention to emotions and stayed with practical advice that came from structural-strategic ideas about taking back the parents' leadership roles and planning for their retirement, independent of their daughter. The siblings encouraged their parents and offered to help in various ways. Four months later, the oldest sister reported a significant change in her youngest sister's functioning. She applied for graduate school, was accepted, and moved into her own apartment.

From a developmental perspective, when working with a family from a different culture, exploring relational process from an emotional frame (Bowen, EFT, Experiential) might be more appropriate. However, thoughts about various approaches are always *tentative* hypotheses until the clinician explores the fit directly with family members. The fit of these elements also depends on aspects of relational functioning in the case.

ASSESSING RELATIONAL FUNCTIONING

As shown in Chapters 6 and 7, the GARF gives us three good starting places that guide assessment of relationships: problem solving, organization, and emotional climate. Do family members have skills and adaptability to solve their problems? Is there a system of leadership and balance that works? What is the ratio of harmony to disharmony? Each question suggests one aspect of functioning on the continuum between competence and dysfunction. The themes from Chapters 1 and 3 give ideas about what to look for and what questions to ask in each realm of a relationship (see Table 7.2).

Assessment can lead us to some hypotheses about strengths and challenges in relationships. Perhaps a family is high in emotional climate but low in organization. Although GARF scoring instructions do not address this variability, in many cases there is a mixture of competency across these areas. Thus, the therapist must choose a direction based on how he might use a family's strengths (emotional climate) to help the family overcome their challenges. For example, if a family has a good sense of humor and members are considerate of each other, I will *use* their humor and *label* their consideration when it's time for anxiety-provoking assignments or discussions. In addition, I ask myself, "What is needed to help this person or family improve their _____ (problem solving, organization, emotional climate)." "What intervention will help them learn or practice the skills and competence they need?" Is their relational functioning a result of situational, transitional, or chronic conditions?

ASSESSING PROBLEM SEVERITY

As discussed in Chapter 6, the life of a problem may be short or long by the time families come for help. This history gives us some clues as to whether it is better to take a *direct* or an *indirect* approach to working with a client. The approach refers to the style of the clinician in session and whether the focus stays on the client's initial view of the problem or whether other aspects of the problem take center stage first. Some examples can illustrate these two strategies.

Consider a *situational problem* in which parents seek counseling because their son was molested by an older cousin and they want to help him overcome the effects and receive help for themselves in coping. There are no prior events and their individual and extended family relational functioning is stable and competent. The therapist takes a direct, psychoeducational approach to providing the resources they seek. The focus is on immediate problem solving and prevention of lingering effects.

Suppose the same case had different circumstances—maybe the abuse happened a year prior, their son has serious problems at school, hostility exists among the extended family, and parents talk openly about their resentments toward others. This would be a *transitional case* in which the clinician would need to take an indirect approach to address the developmental needs of adults separate from the children and explore what each person needs to overcome the sustained effects of the situation. The therapist must look at what steps will help resolve the problem for each person. Developmentally, the clinician must be a nonblaming healer who helps the family tap their unused resources, a stage manager who can help the family reorganize their coping patterns, and a detective who uncovers and addresses historical conflicts that existed prior to the abuse. These treatment strategies combine indirect approaches that diplomatically shift the focus from the son and direct approaches that provide positive support to each family member, as well as address the presenting problem.

What if the same family members are seeking help for their substance-abusing son? He is now 17 and it has been years since the abuse took place. Perhaps other stressors such as job losses, illnesses, and deaths have added more complexity to the picture, and parents are stalmated in their disagreement about how to handle their son. Now, the problem is *chronic*. The individual and relational functioning of family members is likely to be low and the therapist will have to chart a course that addresses the substance use by helping the family prioritize their problems. Developmentally, each person needs a face-saving way to move ahead without being blamed or criticized. This problem might require an indirect approach—a "recovery from shipwreck" strategy—that downplays blame, responsibility, and failure.

As the therapist reviews client responses in these discussions, she makes some early hypotheses about individual and relational functioning. Then, the therapist determines the level of problem severity and matches certain interventions with the family's situation. Table 8.1 summarizes problem severity

Table 8.1 | Matching Direct and Indirect Interventions to Problem Severity

Problem History	Focus of Therapy	Possible Interventions	Systemic Outcome
Situational "Things have recently changed."	Family structure Individual experience Solutions	Psychoeducation Coach communication Assign tasks Explore options Give support, empathy	Successful problem solving
Transitional "It's been coming on for a while."	Family transitions Intergenerational themes Attachment issues	Address grief/loss Find rituals for healing Engage in conflict resolution Discover hidden emotions Explore meaning Make the covert overt Use metaphors	Improved organization and emotional climate
Chronic "It's always been this way."	Individual development Intergenerational themes Shame/blame	Communicate positve connotations Use paradox Find rituals for restructuring Deconstruct beliefs and the message in the symptom Coauthor new stories of hope and heroism Lower defenses	Improved emotional climate Restructured organization More effective problem solving

and possible approaches for each level. In general, the longer the circumstances have existed, the greater the need to match treatment with earlier developmental needs. Although a variety of strategies are available, the following sections describe some general categories of interventions. Within each, the practitioner can find skills for direct and indirect treatment that will match individual needs of the client: (a) managing in-session process, (b) reconstructing belief systems, (c) experimenting with new behaviors, and (d) discovering hidden emotions.

MANAGING IN-SESSION PROCESS

All families evolve interactional patterns that vary in degree of flexibility and permeability. Some family patterns are too rigid (inflexible), and therefore family members find it difficult to adjust to new situations. As Chapter 1 mentioned, the *permeability of a family pattern* or subsystem pattern refers to the amount of access family members have across *boundary* lines (e.g., children's access to parents). Some families' patterns are too permeable and allow too much access (or interference by other family members or society). In that case, the therapist must block such patterns to permit new, more functional patterns to evolve.

As the therapist begins to accommodate the family system, he or she observes behavioral or transactional clues to areas of difficulty or competence. The therapist might then want to focus on these areas and formulate hypotheses for testing. For example, to explore parental interactions, the therapist might focus on the behavior of one of the children, who is interrupting the parents' conversation. Accordingly, the therapist suggests that the parents "get the child to behave" so that the discussion can continue. If the child continues to interrupt the parental interaction, the therapist intervenes with a variety of techniques (Minuchin & Fishman, 1981). The therapist may wish to focus on a particular topic, build intensity by lengthening the time of interaction, or limit participation to specific members as a way of boundary marking. Other conditions might require the therapist to *unbalance the system* or to *make the covert overt* to alter family interactional patterns. Each of these options is considered in turn.

Focusing

Focus refers to the therapist's selection of an area to explore from the vast quantity of information presented by the family. Initially, the therapist focuses on the content of family communication—what the family is saying. Soon, though, the focus shifts to the process—how the family members interact with each other. For example, parents may report that their child is "out of control" or that Dad is "always on my back." These messages provide information about content and process. The therapist may expand on this and explore how family members interact with each other: Do family members speak for each other? When the child begins to speak, does Mom or Dad interrupt? Do parents argue about how to solve the problem? By focusing on the process, the therapist helps the family function better as a system. The following techniques are helpful in focusing:

- **Look for areas of content that might illustrate how family members typically interact with each other.** Some problems are too small or too large; that is, some problems are of such little concern or so severe that family members are unwilling to discuss them. It is sometimes important to look for recurring themes such as "Mom doesn't trust me" or "Dad has to make the decision." These areas often say the most about the family's interaction pattern.
- **Avoid jumping from one area of content to another.** Beginning therapists often make the mistake of searching for the area that resolves the family's problem. Consequently, they may move from area to area and never focus on what the family gives them to understand the family's process. However, if the family moves from one subject to another, the therapist can look for a pattern that ties the areas together, such as a theme of loyalty, pain, or loss.
- **Ask permission before focusing on a specific area.** By asking the family's permission, the therapist ensures that the family has control over the content, and the therapist can observe useful clues to the family's interaction pattern.

As an illustration of focusing, consider the case of a family who comes to therapy because the daughter is so "disagreeable." The mother and father present themselves as perfectly happy and compatible, except for their daughter's behavior. Early in the session, the therapist begins to notice that each parent's description of how he or she responds to the daughter's unpleasantness appears to displease the other parent. The parents' expression of disagreement is a detail that does not fit with the content level of their report. The therapist slowly expands the conversation about how they disagree. As the session unfolds, the therapist develops a hypothesis: This family doesn't know how to express disagreement. By focusing the therapy on this theme, the therapist can work to change the family structure by reframing the family's beliefs about disagreements—that is, by persuading the family members that family disagreements are normal and even beneficial.

Increasing Intensity

Intensity is a term used to describe the degree to which an emotion is being felt in the session. Family systems have coping styles that evolve to reduce anxiety by absorbing or deflecting outside intrusions. These protective mechanisms become dysfunctional when the system's boundaries are so impenetrable that information necessary for change is deflected, or when the family's boundaries are so permeable that individual boundaries must compensate for the lack of system security. Either way, some families have a low threshold for experiencing anxiety and attempt to modify the therapist's message by fitting it into their preestablished response patterns.

It is important to emphasize that transmission of a message to the family by the therapist does not mean that the members of the family are ready to act on the message. They may have heard the message and responded to it in a positive manner but failed to make any changes. Therapists, therefore, should cultivate a personal style that accommodates intensity by widening the range of potential therapeutic responses beyond those that are deemed appropriate by cultural norms. Drama, timing, and intensity are not part of daily discourse, and a family therapist must be comfortable with the tension such behaviors can create. Techniques for building intensity include (Minuchin & Fishman, 1981):

- **Use a simple repetition of the message.** Simple repetition creates intensity because the therapist focuses on one theme, resisting the family's attempts to avoid the message. The therapist may continue to repeat the question or highlight the same message in a variety of ways until he or she gets the desired response. The therapist may also create intensity by repeating messages that appear to be different yet focus on a single direction for change.

- **Encourage continuation of the interaction beyond the family's usual stopping point.** This pushes the family past the regulatory threshold that usually warns members they are entering an area of discomfort. In some cases, the extension elicits the necessary conflict or yields access to normally unavailable family resources (e.g., warmth and tenderness). In either case, the family breaks out of its predictable path and experiences new patterns of relating.

- **Avoid accepting the family's expectation of how the therapist should relate to the family.** For example, the therapist may insist that all family members attend the session even though some family members insist they cannot come; or in some cases, the therapist may appear confused when the family requests an expert opinion.

- **Manipulate the physical space of the therapy session.** By moving closer to a family member or moving two members closer to each other, the therapist is able to take advantage of the emotional response inherent in a change in personal boundaries. Because family members grow up learning the comfortable distance to maintain with other members, closer proximity creates momentary tension. If the tension is similar to the therapeutic message, the therapist is able to increase intensity.

To illustrate how a therapist might utilize these techniques, consider a parent with a teenager who doesn't get to school on time. The therapist might repeat the message by (a) letting the child wake himself and (b) letting him walk to school if he misses the bus. These messages are different, but both send the message that the parent needs to encourage the teenager's responsibility. The therapist might encourage the mother and child to move closer together when they discuss the issue, thereby violating the normal comfort zone. The therapist continues to keep the parent and teenager on the problem despite their attempts to avoid the issue.

Marking Boundaries

Boundary marking comprises a series of operations with the common goal of changing the family's structural boundaries. As the therapist begins to accommodate to the family system, he or she observes behavioral and transactional clues that aid in identifying the existing boundary structure of the family. Sometimes the therapist will block interruptions by family members so that transactions can be completed. In some cases, individuals or subsystems (parents or children) might participate in a separate session with the therapist to strengthen this behavior. For example, in multidimensional family therapy (MDFT) a therapist may meet with an adolescent boy to help him understand his mother's concerns and discuss some ways he can respond to these concerns. Likewise, the therapist may meet with the mother to help her recognize the son's needs for autonomy. Once individual sessions are completed, a conjoint session could be held to discuss these issues. The therapist can mark boundaries in the following ways:

- **Rearrange the seating.** The therapist can rearrange the seating to allow family members to carry out their functions. If a child is sitting between her parents, the therapist might move her further away so that the parents can discuss their issues without interruption.
- **Reframe the problem.** When therapists reframe or reinterpret a family's view, they are reconstructing reality. Families often get locked into problems because they see the problem from only one perspective. A discussion of how to reframe the problem is included in the next section.
- **Block interaction patterns.** The therapist can block inappropriate interactions by (a) moving closer to the family member, (b) raising a hand to stop the interaction, and (c) giving a directive. Staying in close proximity to family members permits the family therapist to disrupt an interaction by physical contact (a touch of the hand).
- **Encourage new subsystem development.** If a son and his mother have drawn together in a coalition because of Dad's moods, husband and wife may be assigned a date night and Dad and son may be asked to go to the hockey game together. While there, Mom is asked to spend time with friends. These assignments encourage the formation of new relationships within each subsystem.

In another example, a family consisting of a single mother, 20-year-old twin daughters, and a 15-year-old daughter who had been truant from school was referred to a family service agency. In the initial session, the therapist turned to the 15-year-old and inquired whether she had trouble waking up in the morning. At this point, the twins began to complain how difficult it was to wake her and how they had to use extreme measures to pull her out of bed. Assuming a weak parental and sibling subsystem, the therapist changed the seating arrangement by putting the mother and the 15-year-old next to each other, with one twin next to the 15-year-old and the other next to the therapist. He suggested that the twins were taking over the mother's job and neglecting their responsibilities. When the therapist asked about the mother's expectations, the mother was interrupted by one of the twins. At that point, the therapist raised his hand to block the twin and reframed the interruption as a need to avoid her own responsibilities by helping the mother.

Unbalancing

In family therapy, unbalancing comprises those operations by which the therapist attempts to tip the balance of power within a subsystem or between subsystems. Specifically, the therapist uses unbalancing techniques purposefully to align or affiliate with a particular family member who is in a position of low power. By asking for help, the family grants power (or influence) to the therapist, who then uses that power therapeutically. The only time that this power may not exist is when the family is externally ordered to therapy, as by a court referral.

The family members often grant power under the assumption that the power will be exercised equally or that they personally will not feel its weight—that is, only the "sick" member will be asked to change. On the contrary, in therapy, the therapist's power is often used to support one family member at the expense of the others in an attempt to alter the family structure, thus creating new alternatives that allow for greater complexity and flexibility in the family system. The therapist can unbalance the family system in the following ways:

- **Align with a family member who has less power.** The therapist aligns with a family member not because he or she necessarily agrees with that member's position but because he or she wants to lend power to a family member to modify the structure. The therapist might say, "I can see why you would feel that way," or "She needs to be convinced of your position."

- **Align with the vulnerability of the member who has more power.** The therapist can say to that person (about the other), "If she speaks up more, it may feel strange at first. That's to be expected. It's always a little unsettling when someone starts to speak up. You're doing a good job of listening." By doing this, the therapist reduces the backlash of unbalancing. In another situation, the therapist might ask permission to side with the less powerful person, thereby still recognizing the current balance of power, "I think it would help if she talks more about her position. Do you mind if I encourage her to speak up?"

- **Refuse to recognize a family member.** This technique is extremely powerful because it challenges the excluded family member's need to belong. A disengaged, oppositional, or controlling member of the family may begin to fight the therapist for a way back into the family. Because therapists control the interaction, they can influence how a family member comes back in; that is, the price of admission may be participation or tolerance or whatever facilitates an improved system.

An example of unbalancing can be found in the case just noted—of the single mother, twin daughters, and 15-year-old "troublemaker." The therapist used his power to unbalance the inappropriate parental subsystem. He empowered the mother to fire the twins from their parental role, even though the action and resulting loss of role placed temporary stress on the twins. He also did not let up on the pressure when the twins tried to reinvolve themselves. The family therapist is able to maneuver in this manner because the treatment plan focuses on the whole family system or organism and not on its individual members.

When the therapist sides with a family member—saying, in effect, "I agree with you; they need to be convinced of your position"—the content of the interaction matters less than the structural issues; that is, the therapist aligns with a family member simply as a means of modifying the family structure. For instance, the therapist may align with a depressed wife in her complaints about her husband's work habits not because the therapist also objects to the work habits, but because the therapist hopes to unbalance the marital subsystem.

Making the Covert Overt

Families seeking help are often characterized by vague communication and unclear role expectations. When a problem arises, the family often adheres to the same old rules and customs. Satir (1972) describes dysfunctional families as closed systems "in which every participatory member must be very cautious about what he or she says" (p. 185). Honest self-expression is discouraged and considered deviant by these families. Such families often reach an impasse during a life-cycle transition. When passing through this transition, interactions become more rigid, and symptomatic behavior may develop. If therapists are to be effective with these families, they must make the covert messages overt.

Satir (1972) suggests several ways to encourage honest and open communication:

- **Ask family members to speak in the first person singular and take the "I position."** When a family member uses referents such as "we" or "they" (e.g., "We don't like to go to Father's house"), the therapist should ask the family member to speak for himself or herself ("Tell me what you want to do"). "I" statements are a good indication of whether family members are taking responsibility for themselves. The therapist can often encourage the family member to take an "I position" by first saying, "I feel . . ." and then allowing the family member to complete the sentence with his or her own feelings (e.g., "I feel unhappy"). Family members who are able to state their own feelings are taking responsibility for themselves.
- **Ask family members to level with each other.** When family members level with each other, their tone of voice matches their words and bodily

expression. The therapist can get family members to level with each other by asking them to be specific ("Be specific and tell him what you want him to do").

- **Help family members sculpt the structure of the family.** Family sculpture may be used throughout the therapeutic process to increase family members' awareness of perception and thereby alter family relationships. To implement this technique, the therapist positions each family member in a composite living sculpture as other members see him or her. Satir (1972) also asks family members to express feelings through exaggerated facial expressions such as extreme smiling or frowning at each other. Family members may also be encouraged to express the way things are or the way they would like them to be. In some cases, family members may be asked to role-play their feelings.

These techniques help the therapist raise the family's self-awareness to a new level. When clients are helped to address issues that they normally observe but do not discuss, they begin to *metacommunicate* (Watzlawick et al., 1967)—to communicate about their own interpersonal process. As this occurs, individual family members begin to accept the reality that each family problem involves more than their own singular points of view.

As practitioners attend to in-session process through directive structural interventions, families are helped to develop more order in their interactions and a clearer understanding in their communication. They begin to develop more self-control (e.g., to refrain from interrupting others), and parents begin to see effective leadership modeled by the therapist. These interventions address the microprocess of the family on a behavioral level; the therapist may also assess the need to address the microprocess on a perceptual level. This entails addressing the language and beliefs that the members of the family incorporate into their understanding of the problem.

RECONSTRUCTING BELIEF SYSTEMS

The influence of social constructionists on traditional structural-strategic models of family therapy has prompted an increased interest in how beliefs, values, myths, and perceptions restrain family members from choosing alternative behaviors and solutions (Bateson, 1972; Selvini Palazzoli, et al., 1978; White, 1986). Selekman and Todd (1991) noted the limitations of their structural-strategic approach with a certain subgroup of adolescent substance abusers. Generally, when these individuals experienced multigenerational drug abuse or past treatment failures, the researchers found indirect interventions to be more effective. Interventions that address perceptions and beliefs are generally more indirect than structural interventions. In this section, we review a few basic interventions that help the beginning practitioner address problematic aspects of the family's belief system and language patterns. The strategic use of language affords a new understanding of family problems.

Identifying Current Belief Systems

Several family therapy models emphasize the importance of belief systems in contributing to the problems that families bring to therapy (Hargrave & Hanna, 1997). Indeed, self-defeating thoughts typically lead to feelings of self-pity, anger, and blame. None of these reactions are constructive. Rather, they lead a person to feel that things should not be as they are because he or she doesn't like them that way, or they make the person feel inadequate or incapable. In either case, the anxiety, depression, or feelings of inadequacy prevent family members from behaving in a constructive fashion to change the situation. Different family members process cognitions or beliefs in different ways. For example, suppose that a person walks across the room, trips over someone's foot, and falls to the floor. One person's first reaction may be extreme anger. Another person may feel little or no anger. The different reactions are due to different belief systems. The first person probably thought something like, "That rude, inconsiderate clod! He has the nerve to trip me! I know he did that purposely." On the other hand, the second person may have thought, "Oops, I'd better start watching where I'm going. He didn't mean to trip me. It was an accident." The therapist should be sensitive to these differences and respond accordingly.

Family members' belief systems are often at the core of the problem. Snider (1992) discusses this issue as follows:

> Some clients present themselves with a symptom such as depression or anxiety. After evaluation, it becomes clear that their agenda is to change someone else's behavior to get them into therapy. I saw one woman who presented symptoms of depression. After reviewing her situation, it became clear that she thought her husband should be in therapy. Her presumption was that if he changed then she would not have any problems. . . . Sometimes people seek therapy because they are alone and lonely. I saw an elderly widow whose children lived in other parts of the country. She had a successful experience in therapy many years earlier. She presented symptoms around a difficulty in relationship with her children. After discussion, she acknowledged that there was nothing wrong with her relationship to them except the distance between them. She needed to talk and felt that this would be an appropriate entree. Her fantasy was that I would help her find a way to get her children to move back to the same city. (p. 145)

Understanding the family members' belief systems helps the therapist to understand the underlying problems and formulate goals for future interventions. Tying interventions to a person's belief system will enhance cooperation. In identifying current belief systems, the therapist should explore the presence of constructive and nonconstructive beliefs related to the problem. The therapist can identify current belief systems in the following ways:

- **Identify beliefs that contribute to the problem.** Helpful questions include: "What do you think when _____ is going on?" "What makes it better?" "What makes it worse?" "What goes through your mind during this time?"

- Ask family members to complete incomplete sentences. Such sentences might begin: "I think . . ."; "I believe . . ."; "I should . . ."; "My husband thinks I want . . ."; "When my wife comes in the door, I think . . ."
- Identify family members' self-talk. Everyone engages in some kind of internal dialogue. This dialogue, or self-talk, expresses the family members' belief system. The therapist can identify self-talk through the following questions: "What do you say to yourself at this time?" "When she uses that tone of voice, what do you tell yourself?" "What are you telling yourself before this happens?" By identifying current beliefs and thoughts that contribute to the problem, the therapist can identify thought patterns that must change before constructive action can be taken to correct the problem.
- Look for themes. As information accumulates during a person's life, that person's beliefs might be related to certain themes. "It sounds like you've had some disappointments the last few years. Do you think they're related in any way?" "What do you make of these experiences coming along like this?" Clients may respond with beliefs about themselves, the others involved, or the patterns in general.

Reframing the Meaning of Symptoms

Reframing—sometimes known as *relabeling*—refers to a change or modification in the family members' thoughts or views of the problem. When therapists reframe a family's view, they are suggesting a change in the family's definition of the problem. Reframing often shifts the focus from the identified patient or scapegoat to the family system in which each family member is an interdependent part (Watzlawick et al., 1974). Thus, reframing alters the way the family thinks about the problem.

In reframing, the therapist must first alter the family's view of reality. By using the technique of focusing, the therapist takes bits and pieces of what the family supplies and provides information that forms a new perspective. The therapist attempts to create a therapeutic reality from a family reality. For example, parents may describe their son as "defiant" or "hard to control," whereas the therapist may view the son as "independent" or "discriminative." By voicing these alternative descriptions, the therapist helps the parents see their son in another way. Such a reconstruction is only possible, however, if the family has a worldview that includes such a possibility. For example, the therapist may reframe a child's tantrums or uncontrollable behavior as a signal that the parents have taught their child how to express independence, but this may be ineffective if it is too far from family or societal norms.

The therapist can also accomplish reframing by giving the symptom universal qualities. For example, a child who is having difficulty following rules may be redefined as "having difficulty growing up." If a therapist is working with a family whose religious culture emphasizes a dominant patriarchal order, the therapist might challenge the image of a distant, emotionally controlled father by saying, "Surely you realize that it is only the courageous leader who is able to show tenderness to his family." By drawing on universal symbols, the therapist is able to pair a dysfunctional family belief with a universal belief that offers a new frame or view of the problem. In addition to these strategies, the therapist can also reframe the meaning of the symptom in the following ways:

- **Relabel problem behaviors to give them more positive meanings.** Giving new labels often provides family members with a new way of thinking about the problem so that it can be resolved. For example, therapists can relabel "jealousy" as "caring" and "anger" as "desiring attention."
- **Relabel deficits as strengths.** All behavior can be viewed positively and negatively depending on the person's perspective. For example, a child who has trouble getting things done may be viewed as a "thinker" or a "perfectionist" depending on the circumstances. Family members are more likely to accept a reframing if their strengths are emphasized.
- **Reframe the context of the problem.** Reframing the context of the problem permits the family to decide with whom a given problem behavior is appropriate (Cormier & Cormier, 1991). Every behavior has costs and benefits. Thus, when a wife complains that her husband abandons her when he leaves during their arguments, the therapist might help the couple identify those situations (contexts) where leaving is useful (e.g., when there is a threat of violence). In addition, every behavior has a function. If the husband leaves because he feels helpless and he's trying to regain his composure, the therapist can help the couple negotiate a pattern that allows him to regain his composure. Addressing behavior as an attempted solution to a secondary problem provides a focus on those developmental elements that need addressing (his emotional arousal) before tackling the main issue (their ability to resolve a conflict).
- **Give homework to reinforce new beliefs.** Cormier and Cormier (1991) believe that homework helps family members practice aspects of the problem that go undetected. For example, a husband and wife might be required to observe those times when the husband attempts to walk away from a situation. What was going on? What was each thinking at the time? What happened afterward? The therapist can then discuss this information to help the family discover new beliefs and perceptions of the problem.

Reframing helps family members get unstuck from rigid thought patterns that contribute to the problem. A new perspective invites family members to look for alternate solutions to their dilemma.

Stressing Complementarity

The therapist often finds it useful to help family members understand that they are interconnected in ways that make one member's actions complementary to another's. For example, a therapist might underline a couple's complementarity by congratulating the wife for the husband's change in behavior. The therapist in this case is teaching the couple that they do affect each other and that they have the potential to do so constructively. This intervention also allows the husband to reconnect with his wife by encouraging him to praise her for helping him express his feelings. Complementarity also helps the members of the family understand their relationship over time. During an assessment, if family members begin to describe each other as opposites in some way, the therapist should note these as potential examples of complementarity. Some common examples occurring in most families are shy versus outgoing, dominant versus submissive, stable versus unstable, and emotional versus rational. Even though these labels may need to be reframed for the family, the dynamic of complementarity can still be addressed. Jorge Colapinto (1991) describes the process of complementarity as follows:

> Family rules develop primarily through a process of correlated differentiation: The behaviors of any two family members mutually accommodate in such a way that one develops selective aspects of himself or herself, while the other develops a complementary trait. Typical examples are the harsh and soft parents, the active and passive spouses, the left brain and the right brain siblings. When all the members of the family are considered, the resulting image is like a jigsaw puzzle, where the irregular borders of the various pieces fit—complement—each other. Carrying the metaphor further, the salient borders of each piece represent the traits expected from each member (harshness, passivity, left brain) while the concave sections represent traits not expected. In well-functioning families, complementarity takes the form of effective teamwork. (pp. 422–423)

Complementary relationships become a problem when they fail to provide flexibility for individual members. Traditional fixed male and female roles often have costs that lead to problems. A father who insists on making all the decisions may take away the mother's executive role when she is home with the children. At the same time, the father may feel overly responsible, which doesn't permit him to enjoy or play with the children. When these patterns become fixed, families experience problems in moving through developmental transitions. The therapist can emphasize complementary roles in the following ways:

- **Ask a family member to relate his or her behavior to what another family member is doing.** For example, a husband who describes himself as "jealous" may be asked what he is noticing about his wife when he begins to feel jealous ("What things do you see or hear her doing when you begin to feel jealous?").
- **Congratulate a family member for another member's accomplishments.** For example, a wife may be congratulated for helping her husband express his feelings. Here it is important to look for small changes in a family member's behavior that contribute to another family member's behavior (e.g., a smile that another family member notices and reacts to).

Attending to complementarity broadens the family's perceptual framework by emphasizing the interpersonal nature of the problem. Thus, rather than focusing on a problem residing within the individual (e.g., jealousy), the therapist focuses on current interactions that contribute to the problem (e.g., the husband's behavior). Moreover, the therapist can emphasize complementarity to punctuate interactions that alleviate the symptomatic behavior (e.g., the therapist congratulates the husband for the wife's change in behavior). The therapist is thus teaching the family members that they do affect each other and that they have the potential to do so constructively.

Using Metaphors

A metaphor is a word or phrase that represents another condition by analogy. Metaphors characterize family relationships or conditions, such as symptoms. They illustrate how family process can mirror natural processes in other realms of living. In some instances, the therapist may use metaphors to represent patterns of communication. The therapeutic use of metaphor helps reframe a family's reality by simply tracking the family's communication from the content to the process level. Minuchin (Minuchin & Fishman, 1981) is a master of such tracking skills, using metaphors for family process as diverse as "You're his alarm clock," or "You're her memory bank." Often, he will derive a metaphor from a family member's occupation. With a nurse (content), he might say, "Your relationship needs first-aid" (process); with a teacher, "You need a lesson plan in discipline." If there is a point of family pride, as with a family whose policy is "never a late payment," he might say, "You are indebted to each other." When illustrating a family rule, as with a family that has a strong work ethic, he might say, "Playtime should never be done slipshod!"

Using metaphors is a form of accommodation because it is effective only when therapists are able to tune themselves in to the family language rather than imposing their own. Clients often provide their own metaphors. Once the clinician becomes attuned to listening for these metaphors, enlarging upon them is an excellent way to match a client's worldview. Some therapists use structured exercises to draw out metaphors. Box 8.1 outlines a metaphor game that Rickert (1995) uses with couples.

This game can be adapted for many other relationships and situations. For example, White uses metaphor in most cases where a child is the client of record. A small boy who is anorexic may be invited to "feed the tiger," after he identifies his favorite animal or chooses the tiger as a symbol for himself. He presents awards to children for their triumph over some sinister influence like the "monster," for nightmares or "sneaky poo," for encopresis (White & Epston, 1991).

Here are some steps for designing appropriate metaphors (Cormier & Cormier, 1991):

- **Select words in the metaphor that match the family member's visual, auditory, and kinesthetic frame of reference.** For example, you might suggest to an electrician and his wife that their marriage needed to be "rewired." Similar metaphors could be used with a mechanic ("Your marriage needs a tune-up") or a doctor ("You need a new prescription").
- **Expand or embellish the character to promote behavioral change.** For example, a therapist may explore characteristics of a client's metaphor. "Is this a good beast or a bad beast? I know of some beasts who changed into princes."
- **Develop a story that includes an element of mystery.** For example, the therapist may tell a story of a character who miraculously overcame a disease and went through a transformation that brought a new meaning to her life.

Box 8.1 | The Metaphor Game

1. Ask each spouse to close his or her eyes and reflect on his or her current mood.

2. As they reflect on their current moods, ask each to think of himself or herself in terms of an object, symbol, or picture of some kind. Tell them that "anything will do and it is usually the first thing that pops into you mind." Ask them to nod their heads when they have selected the images. Instruct them not to talk.

3. Ask each person to think of his or her partner in the same way and to nod his or her head when the image is selected.

4. Ask the couple to imagine the two objects together in some motion or physical placement that will form a relationship and again nod their heads when complete. Once complete, ask the couple to open their eyes.

5. Ask each spouse to describe the images without interpreting, analyzing, explaining, reasoning, or apologizing.

6. Asked whether they would like to perform an experiment that will help them to learn more about each other. They usually say yes. If they say, "No," skip to Step 9. Otherwise, describe this experiment: Ask one person to go first and become the object he or she selected and to use creativity to shape the scene. (For example, if the object was a cloud hovering over a rock, one spouse might stand on a chair over the other who is rolled into a ball on the floor; if it was a bulldozer rolling toward a tree, one might pose as a tree while the other lunges forward in that direction.)

7. During each person's turn, once that scene is completed, address him or her as the object and ask whether the scene is satisfactory. Usually, the answer is "no." Ask him or her to improve upon the scene using "magical powers." With each effort to improve the picture, ask "Are you completely satisfied?" The couple continues to experiment until each is completely satisfied with the final scene as each has arranged it. While they experiment, ask each partner to refrain from helping. Discourage talking.

8. Upon completion, ask each to describe his or her emotional reaction to the experiment without interpreting, analyzing, or reasoning. Help them identify their emotions (sad, mad, afraid, hurt, puzzled, happy, relieved, amused, etc.).

9. Send the couple home and set another appointment for the following week. Do not discuss the meaning or interpretation of the metaphors. This has a strategic effect in that it gives the couple a lot to talk about.

10. In the next session, ask the couple about how the experiment affected their experience with each other during the week. Use the metaphors to arrive at practical solutions for their relationship problems (e.g., "How can a rock and a cloud get closer together?"). In future sessions, use the metaphors to anchor solutions (e.g., "Is it possible for a tree to hold back a bulldozer?").

*Adapted by Rickert (1995) from training at the Family Institute of Chicago and Papp (1982).

EXPERIMENTING WITH NEW BEHAVIORS

Generating Alternative Solutions

Generating alternative solutions is central to the problem-solving process; the goal is to identify as many potential solutions as possible. This process is based on the following three assumptions: (a) There are a number of potentially effective ways to handle a problem; (b) families are often aware of some alternative ways to alter a problem; and (c) generating solutions increases the likelihood of selecting a manageable solution to the problem. Families are more likely to implement a solution if they suggest it. When the family generates alternative solutions, the family takes greater ownership of the solution and works collaboratively with the therapist.

In generating alternative solutions, the therapist uses a brainstorming procedure. There are three basic rules for good brainstorming: (a) If the therapist or family member suggests an alternative solution (e.g., "Maybe I need to set a time aside for homework"), each party refrains from critiquing the other; (b) the therapist and family can take an idea and improve on it; and (c) all parties should attempt to generate as many solutions as possible. The more solutions generated, the more likely it is that an effective solution will be found. The therapist can generate alternative solutions in the following ways:

- **Explore possible solutions to the problem.** The therapist might say, "Let's think of some ways you could handle this situation," or "What are some things you could do now to handle this problem?"
- **Encourage family members to improve on another member's idea.** The therapist might say, "What do you think about John's suggestion? Do you have anything you want to add to it?"
- **Ask family members how two or more ideas can be combined to form a better idea.** In some cases, two suggestions can readily be combined into a better idea ("So, Mary, you want to wait to talk about the problem after dinner. And, John, you want to be relaxed. What might be a good time and place to talk this issue over?").
- **Rehearse the new solution.** Once family members have decided to try something new, review the sequence: who will do what, when, where and how. Each person can recite what their part will be in the new solution.
- **Explore exceptions.** Chapter 2 mentions the miracle question that is often posed by solution-focused therapists. This question is, "Suppose you wake up tomorrow and this problem is resolved through a spontaneous miracle. What would you be doing differently?" The clinician can explore the same details of who, what, when, where, and how, and ask the family to brainstorm ways they might implement this "vision," regardless of whether the problem still exists ("I'm depressed," "He's flunking eighth grade," "I'm on probation"). By enacting these patterns, additional solutions emerge that help the family move forward and develop hope and competence.

Resolving Conflict

A set of well-developed strategies for dealing with disagreements when they arise comprise skills in conflict resolution (Stuart, 1980). Conflict resolution has proved effective in treating marital conflict (Jacobson & Margolin, 1979). The process has two distinct phases: problem definition and problem resolution. In the problem definition phase, the critical issue or problem—for example, "You don't care about me"—is defined in operational terms. An operational definition of the problem is much more likely to lead to an effective response.

The problem resolution phase emphasizes behavior change rather than insight. It is best to choose a solution that can be implemented by the family with minimal help. Solutions should be kept simple; complex plans often fail because the costs (in time and energy) outweigh the benefits (say, parenting skills). A therapist can use several strategies to help families choose the best solution:

1. **Choose a solution that is acceptable to family members.** Once the family generates alternative solutions, the therapist can help the family select one of them. Family members have the option of striking out any that are unacceptable. The remaining solutions can be subjected to a cost-benefit analysis for all family members. The best solution is selected from the most promising alternatives. Note that the best solution will produce an outcome that requires some accommodation from all family members.

2. **Decide how the solution will be implemented.** How will the solution be put into practice, and who will work with the family to carry it out? Because specificity and consistency are essential to success here, it is often helpful to prepare a written plan or contract listing what procedures will be followed and where the plan is to be implemented; as well as conditions, resources (both personal and material), and the amount of time that the plan will be in effect. The plan ensures that the family and therapist follow the agreed-upon steps and do not change their practices midway through the program. It also reminds the family members which resources they will need. The following questions can be used to develop a written plan:

   What is the chosen solution?

   What are the steps to carry out the solution?

   Who will work with the family members to help them carry out the plan?

   When will the plan begin and end?

   Who else should be involved in this plan?

   When do we meet again?

3. **Evaluate the proposed solution.** How will family members carry out their agreed-upon responsibilities? Are responsibilities or tasks being carried out according to the specifications in the contract? These questions can best be answered through data such as self-reports, collateral reports from

social workers or teachers, and so on. Once information is collected, the therapist should hold a meeting with the family to discuss progress toward the adopted goals.

4. **Renegotiate the contract if necessary.** The evaluation may suggest that the contract should be renegotiated. Do the results meet the desired level of satisfaction for the family? If not, are more cost-effective solutions available to reach the goals? What have the members of the family learned from the attempted solution that can help them find a better way to resolve their problem? What adjustments (changes in behavior) must be made to reach the desired goals? In some cases, the family's level of satisfaction may not increase as the goals are attained. Here the therapist should help family members decide whether negotiated agreements—what they will talk to each other about and under what conditions—will be more satisfying over time, or whether the family should set new goals.

Coaching Communication

Regardless of the therapist's orientation, coaching communication is a key element of family therapy change strategies. Coaching communication is effective for couples (Gottman and Notarius, 2002), parents and adolescents (Liddle and Schwartz, 2002), and divorced parents (Gottman and Levenson, 1999). Related programs often last from 3 to 15 weeks and contain the following core components.

Modeling.   The first step in helping a couple communicate more effectively is to demonstrate, or model, the appropriate communication skill; that is, the family therapist shows each spouse what the response looks like or how it sounds. Therapists themselves model behavior throughout the treatment process. Modeling has been effective in teaching information-seeking behavior (Krumboltz, Varenhorst, & Thoresen, 1967), reducing feelings of alienation (Warner & Hansen, 1970), and improving attitudes toward drug abuse (Warner, Swisher, & Horan, 1973).

Another common practice is to provide live or symbolic models (e.g., on audiotapes or videotapes) who show, in sequential steps, the specific behaviors necessary to solve the problem (Hosford & de Visser, 1974). Taped or filmed models have been used successfully (Hansen, Pound, & Warner, 1976). The models only demonstrate the desired behaviors; there is no opportunity for interaction between the models and family members. However, the taped models may help stimulate discussion, which is important to prevent rote imitation by family members. If new behaviors are to be effective, family members need to learn a variety of responses for a particular problem situation.

The therapist may also wish to develop models for each of several sessions. For example, the therapist could develop tapes that teach each spouse to (a) listen, (b) express a compliment, (c) express appreciation, (d) ask for help, (e) give feedback, and (f) express affection (Goldstein, 1973). Each skill could be modeled and practiced during a session if family members' skill levels allow. Each modeling sequence could thus represent a closer approximation of the final behavior. Effective modeling includes the following procedures:

1. **Model a clear delineation of the desired behavior.** The behavior must be identified clearly so that family members know precisely what the therapist is actually modeling. If the modeling sequence is too vague, learning is highly unlikely to take place. For example, rather than trying to model "awareness" to a family member, the therapist should operationalize this behavior by identifying and labeling emotions. To teach relationship skills, the therapist might break the relationship down into "expressing" and "responding." These areas might be broken down further into subskills such as responding to anger and affection. Operationalizing the skill to be learned is always beneficial; that is, the skill should be such that it can be seen and heard. After operationalizing the skill, the therapist explains what the model (in this case, the therapist) will be saying or doing and tells family members what they should look for. For example, if a family member is having difficulty asking for help, the therapist might say, "John, I need you to _____ when I'm feeling down."

2. **Model behaviors that hold the family members' attention.** Familiar and relevant experiences are more likely to hold attention and facilitate learning. In addition, models are generally most effective when they are the same sex as a family member and similar in appearance, age, and so on. Because of this, the therapist may want the family to identify personal resources (friends) who could serve as models. If the family member is having difficulty entering a social situation, a friend who is accepted in that situation and who is similar to the family member might be asked to model or demonstrate how to get involved. The therapist might say, "I would like you to show Mary what to do when she wants to have a conversation with others." A model who verbalizes his or her own uncertainty (e.g., "I'm not sure, but here is one way to try it") and offers subsequent problem-solving or coping strategies can be helpful in eliciting the family members' attention. Another useful technique is to emphasize those behaviors to be modeled. The therapist might ask the model to speak more loudly during the relevant responses or to repeat a key passage ("Would you repeat that, please"). Tone of voice and mannerisms can also be used to gain the family members' attention.

3. **Ask family members to discuss what they have observed.** Unless family members are able to understand and retain the essential characteristics of the model's behavior, the intervention is of no avail. When the modeled behavior is particularly abstract, retention may be facilitated if either the model or therapist discusses the important features of the model's performance. For example, a model demonstrating how to express affection to a family member could discuss different ways to show affection. The therapist could evaluate the family members' understanding by asking them to summarize the main features or general rules of the model's performance.

4. **Reinforce the modeled behavior.** The therapist must provide incentives that encourage family members to perform the modeled behavior. When modeled behavior is not reinforced, imitation does not occur. The likelihood that imitative behavior will occur increases with the probability of receiving reinforcement. To reinforce the modeled behavior, the therapist might respond to the model's statements with positive comments ("That's an interesting point," or "That's a thoughtful idea"). By observing that the model is reinforced for expressing an opinion or solving a problem, the family members learn the most effective response in that situation.

Instruction.   Once the family has attended to and understood the model's behavior, the therapist should provide instructions before the family begins practicing the new behavior. The therapist can focus attention on the relevant and essential aspects of the model's performance. The instructions may be spoken or written by the therapist or be provided in the form of an audiotape or videotape. The therapist might say, "Watch how I show appreciation to your wife," and then model the appropriate behavior, adding, "Now I want you to show appreciation for something your wife has done recently." Instructions can be provided in the following ways:

1. **Prompt specific behaviors for family members to try.** The therapist is now essentially serving as a coach who prompts specific behavior for the family to try. Instructions generally may be positive (do this) or negative (don't do that). The therapist gives numerous specific examples. Instructing a wife to give feedback to her husband, the therapist might say, "Look directly at your husband and tell him how it makes you feel when he doesn't call to say he won't be home. Don't just accuse him of being inconsiderate."
2. **Help family members decide when to give feedback to each other.** The therapist might discuss when to give feedback—for example, "when you have time to sit down" or "when you are not so angry"—because family members might know what to say but not when to say it. By going over the demonstration, the therapist can pinpoint behaviors by the model (therapist, friend) and discuss why such behaviors can serve as a cue to a family member to perform a specific behavior.

Practice.   Having received instructions for what to say and do, the family is ready to practice the behavior; practice is an essential part of the learning process because people learn by doing. Family members role-play new relationships or problem-solving behaviors. If a person shows resistance to this idea, the therapist can provide examples of the usefulness of practice. The crucial point is that each family member must feel that he or she is not just learning a role that is artificial and unusable. Consequently, the role-playing situations should be as realistic as possible and should include verbal responses with which each family member feels comfortable. The following are important guidelines:

1. **Prepare the family member for practice.** The family must accept the idea that practice is an appropriate way to develop new coping or problem-solving behaviors. If the family shows some resistance to this idea, the therapist can provide examples where practice has proved useful. Experience, drills, rehearsal, recitation, homework, and exercises all involve practice. The therapist might say, "Maybe we could practice expressing appreciation to your son. I'll role-play your son, and we'll see how it goes. If you have trouble thinking of something to say, I'll help you."

2. **Start with a situation that the family can perform with little difficulty.** Practice is more successful when the initial situation is familiar to the family. For example, in a parent-adolescent conflict, the therapist might ask both parties to start by "talking about something that happened at school today." If they are unable to do this, the therapist might ask them to engage in less threatening activities such as sitting next to each other. Regardless of the activity, the therapist should begin with a nonthreatening situation.

3. **Break the behavior down into small steps.** These steps should range in complexity from simple (e.g., giving a compliment) to the complete new behavior (e.g., asking for help). In this case, the social interaction varies according to the level of difficulty.

4. **Prompt family members when they can't think of what to say or do.** The therapist can provide a sentence that fits within the context of the interaction (e.g., "It's important to me to know how you feel"). It is essential that the prompt occur only when the family member pauses or hesitates (generally for about five seconds). In addition, the therapist can use hand signals to raise or lower the family member's voice or to signal to come closer. Prompts should be faded as family members become able to practice the behavior unaided. At this point, the therapist should praise the family members for expressing the desired behavior in their own words.

Feedback.   When family members have practiced the skills, each must receive feedback on her or his performance. Such feedback provides an incentive for improvement. Information received about poor performance can be potentially as helpful as knowledge regarding positive performance. The following guidelines are important in providing feedback:

1. **Solicit the family's ideas about feedback prior to practice.** The therapist might say, "I'll observe you and try to give you some helpful hints." When a family member denies or disagrees with feedback from the therapist ("That's not the way it sounded to me") or attempts to justify a response ("The reason I said that was . . ."), feedback was probably not solicited or agreed on prior to practice.

2. **Describe rather than evaluate the family members' behaviors.** For example, the therapist might replay a videotape of what a family member said and comment, "Here you say 'My mother thinks I should. . . .' Do you

remember we agreed you would say, 'I think I should . . .'?" The therapist's feedback statements should avoid blame. Statements such as "That just doesn't sound right" or "I don't know why you can't do that" fail to provide helpful information.

3. **Reinforce a family member's response and at the same time prompt similar responses.** For example, the therapist might say, "That's a good question to get him to talk to you. Sometimes, however, your husband may not want to talk about his job. Can you think of some other questions you could ask him?" By prompting additional questions, the therapist not only helps reinforce the spouse's use of questions in a practice session but also facilitates its generalization to other situations and people.

The therapist should provide opportunities for the family members to practice their skills at home and should supply guidelines or worksheets to facilitate such practice. Therapy is more effective when family members are able to practice skills successfully in everyday interactions.

Assigning Tasks

Tasks attempt to change the sequence of interaction in the family. They may help a family become more organized, establish operational boundaries, set rules, or establish family goals (Madanes, 1981). Tasks might include (a) advice, (b) explanations or suggestions, or (c) directives to change the interactional sequence in the family (Papp, 1980). For example, in the case of a family with a mother and daughter who are overinvolved and a father who is peripheral, the therapist might give the following explanation to the mother: "Your daughter needs to treat you with respect. She will be able to do that when you have your husband's support. Right now, he gets called on as the bad guy when you aren't able to deal with her. This is a critical time when your daughter needs to spend more time with her father." Unfortunately, advice may not be successful because family members often know what to do but don't know how to do it.

In many cases, the therapist must convince the family to follow the directive or task. This may be difficult unless each family member sees some payoff. Persuading a family to perform a task depends on the type of task, the family, and the kind of relationship the therapist has with the family (Haley, 1976). For example, adolescents might not see a payoff for talking in a session if they aren't certain that their parents care about them or if they can get their way without talking. In this case, the therapist's directive must provide some benefits (e.g., more privileges or parental concern) for the adolescent as well as for other members of the family. Haley (1976) offers several suggestions to therapists for finding the tasks and directives that fit for each family:

1. **Discuss everything the family has done to try to solve the problem.** In this way, the therapist can avoid making suggestions that have already been tried. The therapist should lead the family to the conclusion that everything has been tried but nothing has worked. At this point, the therapist is in a position to offer the family something different.

2. **Ask family members to discuss the negative consequences if their problem is not handled now** (i.e., "What is going to happen if this problem is not resolved?"). Aversive consequences are probably different for different members of the family. Nevertheless, examining the negative consequences of the problem for each family member emphasizes the intensity of the problem. A mother and her adolescent daughter, for instance, get into conflicts; both cry and are unhappy, and neither gets her way. The mother doesn't get the kind of respect she deserves, and the daughter doesn't get any privileges. It is important for the therapist to emphasize these consequences and to project what might happen if the problem is not resolved.

3. **Assign a task that is reasonable and easily accomplished.** To ensure that the family members can complete the task at home, getting them to complete the task in the session is often necessary. For example, the therapist may want an adolescent daughter to have a conversation with her mother without interruptions by her father. Therefore, the therapist may ask the daughter to talk with her mother in session while the father reads a magazine. The therapist might suggest an activity that both of them might enjoy doing together. If the father interrupts before the mother and daughter complete the task, the therapist may wish to devise something else for the father to do, such as running an errand, so as to improve the chances that he does not interrupt when mother and daughter attempt to complete a conversation at home. The therapist can also ensure that the task is accomplished by providing adequate instructions. In this instance, the therapist focuses attention on the relevant and essential aspects of each family member's performance. Before the family begins the task, the therapist might instruct the father that staying out of it will be difficult for him and that he needs to occupy himself in some other way.

4. **Assign a task to fit the ability and performance level of the family members.** In the film *Family With a Little Fire* (Minuchin, 1974), the task is focused on the scapegoated child's fire setting. The therapist, Braulio Montalvo, asks the mother to spend five minutes each day teaching her daughter how to light matches correctly. He also instructs the parental child who stands between mother and child to watch the other children while the mother is teaching the child. This task is suited to each family member's level of ability.

5. **Use authority to get the family to follow the directive or task.** Sometimes the therapist must use his or her knowledge and expertise to get the family to comply. It is important for the therapist to accept the role of expert rather than asking the members of the family what they think they should do. The therapist might say, for example, "From my experience, I'd say that this is a critical time for your son, and he needs time with his father." The therapist is really saying, "On the basis of my expertise, I believe that it is important for you to do this." Sometimes the therapist may ask whether the family or family member trusts him or her. If the family or family member says yes, the therapist might say, "Good. Then I want you to do this because it is important. Trust me." Here the therapist uses trust to gain control of the interview.

6. **Give clear instructions to each member of the family.** Everyone should know what his or her responsibilities are. If a therapist asks a father and daughter to do something together, exact dates and times should be specified. By deciding in advance on a time, the father and daughter make a commitment to perform the task. Establishing a time also decreases the likelihood of interference by something else, such as work or TV. The therapist and the family should also decide who will take care of the other children and what the mother will be doing during that time. The therapist might ask family members to describe what they will be doing so that they are all clear about their roles. Family members should be encouraged to discuss anything that might interfere with the completion of the task.

Developing Rituals

Rituals can address a number of therapeutic goals related to rigid family rules and omitted developmental tasks in the life cycle. The Milan team (Selvini Palazzoli et al., 1978) designed specific strategic instructions in the form of family rituals. The ritualized prescriptions were designed for "breaking up those behaviors through which each parent disqualifies and sabotages the initiatives and directions of the other parent in his relationship with the children" (Selvini Palazzoli et al., 1978, p. 3). Such prescriptions can be repeated with the same format for any type of family. Rituals are used instead of interpretation, which is often ineffective in altering the rules of the system. At the end of an assessment period, the therapist helps the family develop a ritual. The following is a common Milan-style prescription:

> On even days of the week—Tuesdays, Thursdays, and Saturdays—beginning from tomorrow onwards until the date of the next session and fixing the time between X o'clock and Y o'clock (making sure that the whole family will be at home during this time), whatever Z does (name of patient, followed by a list of his symptomatic behaviors), father will decide alone, at his absolute discretion, what to do with Z. Mother will have to behave as if she were not there. On odd days of the week—Mondays, Wednesdays, and Fridays—at the same time, whatever Z may do, mother will have full power to decide what course of action to follow regarding Z. Father will have to behave as if he were not there. On Sundays, everyone must behave spontaneously. Each parent, on the days assigned to him or her, must record in a diary any infringement by the partner of the prescription according to which he is expected to behave as if he were not there. (In some cases the job of recording the possible mistakes of one of the parents has been entrusted to a child acting as a recorder or to the patient himself if he is fit for the task). (Selvini Palazzoli et al., 1978, p. 5)

Selvini Palazzoli et al. (1978) note that the ritualized prescription operates at several levels. First, the rules of the game are changed to prevent interferences from occurring. Second, parents are blocked from competing for the therapist's approval because their efforts serve only to deflect attention from the problem (relationship). Finally, the therapist gains information regardless of whether the family follows the prescription. This information can be used to design subsequent interventions. The following guidelines are helpful in designing rituals:

1. **Prescribe one or more aspects of the problem.** Those problematic thoughts and behaviors then form the content of the ritual. For example, a boy who threw frequent "out-of-control" temper tantrums was asked to continue having his tantrums but to have them in a special place at home and only after school when he really had time to throw one.

2. **Provide a rationale for the ritual to increase the likelihood of compliance.** For example, the therapist might suggest to the family that structuring the temper tantrums in this way helps family members gain control of the problem or helps the therapist better understand the problem.

Another type of ritual, suggested by Imber-Black, Roberts, and Whiting (1988), helps families address unresolved developmental issues by grieving traumatic losses, completing developmental milestones, or celebrating and stabilizing progress. Such rituals form a part of many religious and societal traditions, but may have been overlooked as a family's problem was developing. For example, if families have suffered a traumatic death or loss, the therapist may develop special grieving rituals for the family to facilitate the further healing necessary to break a dysfunctional pattern. These rituals are most effective when the influence of the loss on the presenting problem has been recognized and the family becomes the author of the ceremony, determining the participants and the desired meaning of the ritual.

Sometimes, families skip important developmental milestones that later become metaphors for the presenting problem. For example, when couples elope or forgo a honeymoon, family therapists may use this as a metaphor for skipping some important developmental task, such as creating a strong marital attachment. As the couple identifies elements of the marriage that were skipped and need to be developed, the planning of a honeymoon or special anniversary celebration can symbolize the completion of relationship tasks facilitated during the course of therapy.

Other rituals celebrate the completion of therapy as a rite of passage (Epston & White, 1992); for example, a triangulated child may be helped to disengage from the position of "marital therapist" and be given a new position as "liberated sixth grader," free to explore how children grow up when they don't have to worry about their parents' marriage. A concluding ritual then allows the family to celebrate such achievements in the company of significant others. Thus, the culmination of therapy is not seen as being a private termination or as implying loss of the therapeutic relationship (Epston and White, 1992). Rather, such rituals help families to stay focused on the changes they have made. These rituals also normalize therapy by incorporating societal traditions into the process.

Introducing Paradox

In the early stages of family therapy history, the use of paradox generated much controversy. Hanna (1995) suggests that the paradox associated with strategic models of family therapy often had elements that could be perceived as manipulation and dishonesty. Such strategies were considered by some to be disrespectful of clients. However, as the field has progressed, paradox has become a way of understanding the change process with all its complexities. For example, Weeks (1991) suggests that much of psychotherapy in general has the following paradoxical elements:

1. The therapist takes charge by placing the client in charge.
2. The therapist maintains a positive view of symptoms through accepting and understanding the client.
3. Change is not directly attributed to the therapist but to the interaction with clients, inviting them to attribute the change to themselves.
4. Clients are encouraged to "work through" a problem, not flee from it. They are asked to move toward the symptom and examine it. "Don't change quickly. Be who you are."
5. Responsibility for change is put back on the client, either directly or indirectly.
6. What was once uncontrollable eventually becomes controllable.

Contemporary family therapists make use of paradox as an element that encourages perceptual changes in subtle ways. For example, a number of strategic models encourage families to "go slow" with the change process. The therapist explains that there can be "side effects" to the change process and so approaching change cautiously is sometimes helpful to properly prepare for any of its negative effects (Lewis et al., 1991). The deconstruction process of White (1990) also follows this direction (see Chapter 7). The person is invited to explore the backlash that might occur in significant relationships if change occurs. The process then turns to an exploration of how one might cope with change rather than continuing to focus on the change itself.

These recent applications of paradox suggest that change sometimes happens in *indirect* or "slow" ways because there are, in fact, some disadvantages to change. My rule of thumb is that when some things get better, other things might get worse. I have watched many clients become animated and engaged in a discussion of the possible disadvantages of change. These disadvantages, such as a change in the way people view a person, the uncertainty of one's self-perception, or even depression (e.g., in the case of substance abuse recovery), constitute *real dilemmas* that should be taken seriously as a precursor to the presenting problem. This illustrates why some interventions are termed indirect. When family therapists encourage discussion of these legitimate dilemmas, such a paradoxical direction can be seen as a deeper form of respect and empathy for the client's unique drama (Hanna, 1995). These discussions also help change beliefs about the problem for both therapist and client.

An example of the respectful use of paradox came during work with a 28-year-old woman who was obese. She wanted to lose weight and had tried for many years but to no avail. A genogram and time line were effective in explaining how her weight problem emerged shortly after her parents' divorce and how conflict with her mother began to center on her pattern of overeating at that time. However, when the family therapist began asking about the disadvantages of losing weight, more specific information came forth about how her friends might consider her a threat in vying for certain men and how the messages her weight was sending to each parent might be silenced. At this point, the therapist helped her compensate for these projected effects of change by developing strategies to maintain a secure circle of friends and by communicating more directly with her parents about her needs. She began to see that her weight problem was a relational problem, not merely a problem of "willpower."

As our clients practice any new behavior, they experience relief in seeing conflicts diminish, hope that they can successfully solve their problems, and confidence that their leadership skills are growing. However, sometimes, the developmental aspects of emotional climate continue to inhibit greater progress. As the GARF indicates, sometimes attachment issues underlie the quality of a relationship. When this happens, the clinician may find it necessary to help family members overcome emotional restraints to their progress.

DISCOVERING HIDDEN EMOTIONS

A focus on emotional process in relationships often results in the discovery that *primary emotions* exist that have never been labeled or affirmed. In emotionally focused couples therapy (EFT), Johnson (1996) describes primary emotions that go unrecognized, even though they are the foundation of our emotional world. These emotions are those that relate to the continuum between a secure and insecure attachment. She suggests that the central questions related to attachment issues are, "Can I count on this person to be there for me, if I need them?" "Are others trustworthy and responsive?" "Am I lovable and able to elicit caring?" (Hazan & Shaver, 1994). The answers are usually, respectively, "yes," "no," and "maybe." These commonly invoke six basic attachment emotions: anger, sadness, surprise/excitment, disgust/shame, fear, or joy. As the therapist raises awareness of these common emotions, the emotions are framed as normal and human, and partners in the relationship are invited into new dialogues that help them respond safely to each other. EFT shares a number of elements with experiential, structural, and narrative family therapies.

Review Table 2.7. These are the nine steps of EFT. A number of these correspond to the skills outlined in other chapters. Beginning clinicians are advised to begin with these skills. Then, as the emotional bond emerges as a problem area, use the following steps as a guide to help clients discover their core attachment emotions:

Validating Attachment Patterns

EFT is based upon the notion that all people develop *adaptive* responses to their environment. Thus, they are not sick or developmentally delayed, they are simply stuck in *previously useful* patterns. Patterns such as withdrawal or pursuit are labeled as understandable and useful, given the person's experience. The patterns become understandable in light of a person's attachment history, as their function may have been to prevent hurt, disappointment, or abuse. The therapist builds a strong alliance with each person related to their adaptive pattern and the purpose for it. As each person's attachment journey is known and accepted, the therapist might say:

> I can see how you came to a pattern of coping where you think that if you don't pursue her, she'll never approach you on her own. Is it possible that your experience tried to convince you that the only love you could have was what you tried to get on your own? It must be lonely to always be on your guard. It shows how much courage you have to keep trying.

Introducing Attachment Needs

As the therapist tracks interactional sequences (Chapter 7), each partner is asked about his or her emotions in the sequence (see the Awareness Wheel, Chapter 3). These emotions are framed as each person's desire for caring and love. When clients mention anger or an emotion other than one of the six core emotions, the therapist may say,

> I'm wondering if your hurt feelings have some shame or sadness attached to them. Is it possible you're also feeling sad that he can't be there for you?

If clients draw a blank or disagree, the therapist accepts all responses as the person's current adaptive position. The therapist may say,

> It's normal to want to depend on someone. We all have the desire to have someone who will be there for us. It must be painful when you feel let down again. I can imagine that your anger may come from your awareness that you deserve to be loved, but it's sad when you're rejected.

Promoting Acceptance of Attachment Needs

Each partner is invited to accept his or her own and the other's attachment needs. This exploration happens slowly to avoid either partner becoming critical or negative toward the other during times of vulnerability.

> Can you say to yourself that it's alright to want your partner to be there for you? What do you think will happen if you tell her what you need? Can you get past your fear to hear what she's saying?

The therapist is careful to reframe any negative emotion aimed at the other within one of the six core emotions.

> When you say that you don't believe that he cares about you, is there some (fear, shock/surprise) that he would really feel that? Is it hard to believe because you've been disappointed so many times in the past?

Gradually, as each person is affirmed for their vulnerable feelings of distrust and those feelings are accepted by the therapist who models acceptance for each person, the nonjudgmental environment in the session promotes safety for each person, allowing them to begin acceptance of the other's needs. This begins the growth of new trust.

Inviting Responsiveness to Attachment Needs

Each partner is encouraged to respond to the new feelings that emerge.

> June, Rob is saying he wants to be there for you. Can you tell him what you need from him when he wants to be there for you? Tell him what would make it safe for you. Rob, can you reassure June that you won't criticize her, now that you are learning more about your own coping patterns?

As the therapist coaches and guides a couple through an understanding of their previous coping responses, their healthy attachment needs and the new responses that can build a secure base, the couple grows together with a "corrective emotional experience." The therapist's job is to elicit a series of successful dialogues during sessions that enable trust to evolve into a secure base. Then, this base becomes solid as couples are able to replicate these times of intimacy at home as relevant situations occur.

The movement in family therapy toward attachment interventions does not stop with EFT. MDFT has demonstrated specific interventions that address parent-adolescent attachment. Contrary to some stereotypes, adolescents need a number of things from their parents. One of these is a secure base and reassurance that parents are still there during times of challenge. Liddle & Schwartz (2002) use enactments as attachment interventions that address the same issues as EFT, but with adolescents and their families.

Enacting Attachment Dialogues.   *Enactments* are interventions orchestrated by the therapist that enable family members to effectively communicate with each other. Typically, the therapist suggests that two people discuss an issue of mutual importance. However, the intervention is often superficially conducted and beginning therapists may give up for lack of proper coaching through the process. Allen-Eckert, Fong, Nichols, et al. (2001) provide an excellent guide for implementing enactments that is based on their research. They suggest that families have different levels of comfort with talking directly to each other. Because of this, successful enactments are often related to how carefully the therapist is able to execute each of four stages. Table 8.2 outlines the four stages and what therapists can do during each stage to enhance the attachment bond between family members. In addition, the following characteristics of successful enactments are important criteria for evaluating success:

- Both parties expressed their observations, thoughts, feelings, and intentions.
- Clients agreed to work toward a resolution, or someone acknowledged his or her part of the problem.
- Something new or important happened with either the content or the process of the dialogue.

Table 8.2	Four Stages of Enactments

Pre-enactment	• Ask about issues of attachment and choose one that has importance to both parties (e.g., disappointment, criticism, abandonment, fear of intimacy). • Explore the nature of discussions that have occurred within the family about the attachment issue. • Emphasize the importance and benefits of communication and understanding between the people involved.
Initiation	• Specify the topic, who should talk, and who should listen. • Ask people to turn their chairs toward each other. • Direct them to begin talking about the concern.
Facilitation	• Don't interrupt unless clients become hostile, give up, stop talking, or change the subject. • Encourage them to keep trying, listen to each other, describe more of their feelings, and focus on each other rather than on the therapist.
Summary	• Praise participants for their efforts in communication. • Provide an overview of the emotional process they just experienced and model acceptance of their attachment needs. • Point out strengths and barriers. • Make suggestions for how each person might overcome the barriers.

SUMMARY

This chapter explored a number of suggestions for facilitating relational change in families. One of the concepts from general systems theory is that the whole is greater than the sum of its parts. In family therapy, this means that a family is more than just a collection of people. Instead, a family is a unique group of people with a dynamic, evolving history together that creates organizational complexity and includes elements of content and process in its communication. This communication, in turn, leads to interpersonal patterns that include thoughts, behaviors, emotions, and intentions. These interpersonal patterns can be deconstructed into the various themes from Chapter 3 (gender, race, culture, structure, intergenerational relationships, individual experience). These are a few of the many elements that constitute our concept of relationships.

Similarly, the process of relational change is much greater than the sum of the suggestions offered in this chapter. These suggestions provide beginning clinicians with some basic techniques, but the interplay of the themes from these interventions make the whole process complex. For example, assigning successful tasks requires that the therapist have credibility with clients and that the task is appropriate to the unique culture of the family. Increasing intensity also requires a solid and positive therapeutic alliance and a climate of safety felt by clients. Thus, it is helpful to remember that suggestions from this chapter will not be successful unless the therapist is developing competent relational skills such as those described in Chapter 4.

Another level of complexity also makes therapeutic work challenging and rewarding. When clinicians think of themselves as made up of separate parts, they might miss the creative energy that often contributes to their greatest successes. For example, in Chapter 2, I noted a growing trend that recognizes the importance of emotion and attachment in relationships. If therapists place these basic skills alongside this growing emphasis in the field, they can see a number of ways in which first- and second-generation family therapies impact emotion, even though the writing from a particular author might not have made the link explicit—for example, when some intergenerational tasks are assigned to a client and the therapist witnesses a transformation of the troubled relationship with an aging parent. This transformation will include the new emotions that develop from this change.

When therapists speak of changing behaviors, beliefs, or communication, they are really encouraging the beginning therapist to see these elements as inseparable from emotions. These elements form the web of interpersonal process, and good therapeutic plans impact all these factors in some way. (Remember the Awareness Wheel in Chapter 3?). A successful therapist has the ability to know what might be the most relevant entry point, given the unique contexts of family members. For example, some families are comfortable speaking directly about their feelings, and others are not. Given these differences, one plan may call for behavioral interventions that delay speaking about difficult emotions until the therapist ascertains a feeling of safety from family members. A different situation might prompt the therapist to immediately confront the strong emotion in a conflicted marriage before the relationship deteriorates further. Finding a balance within this range of possibilities is my goal for the developing, creative family therapist. To enhance an understanding of these direct and indirect options, review Table 8.1, which illustrates how each skill fits along this continuum. You may find this helpful in treatment planning as you assess a family and match the problem and people with certain interventions.

To continue with the metaphor of driving a car, the therapist is in first gear during referral, intake, and initial session (the process is deliberate and careful); and shifted into second gear during assessment, treatment planning, and initial interventions (the speed picked up, but the therapist is far from settled). If the therapist has a direction that produces a good fit with the client, she might be ready to shift into third or fourth gear. As the therapeutic process continues, the nature of the journey will call up the involvement of other influences. Weather and traffic conditions may require stop-and-go driving. Gas stations and restaurants challenge the ability to park and maneuver in small spaces. There may even be times when others ask to drive. These challenges help the therapist develop more flexibility and confidence when trying to understand the range of experience that encompasses family therapy. Chapter 9 examines some additional challenges.

Family Therapy Collaborations

CORE COMPETENCIES

1.3.8	**Executive**	Develop and maintain collaborative working relationships with referral resources, other practitioners involved in the clients' care, and payers.
4.3.8	**Executive**	Empower clients and their relational systems to establish effective relationships with each other and larger systems.
4.3.9	**Executive**	Provide psychoeducation to families whose members have serious mental illness or other disorders.
4.5.1	**Professional**	Respect multiple perspectives (e.g., clients, team, supervisor, practitioners from other disciplines who are involved in the case).
4.5.2	**Professional**	Set appropriate boundaries, manage issues of triangulation, and develop collaborative working relationships.

Marriage and family therapists work in many different settings. When the therapist understands and practices the basic elements from Chapters 1 through 8, he or she can apply them to a host of problems as the foundation of many problem solving strategies. Although the field of family therapy began as the study of family relationships and the practice of relational change, it now encompasses cybernetics, communication, human development, and intimate relationships, and the therapist can use his or her knowledge of these areas to help other professionals who experience problems in various organizations, including those in the medical organizations/settings, educational fields, and public social service fields.

As Core Competency 4.5.1 suggests, it is important for family therapists to understand other professional cultures and cooperate with service providers who contribute important expertise that can enhance success. For example, in working with children, art therapists have been especially helpful to family therapists because children may not have verbal skills to fully communicate their experience. When family therapists and art therapists work together, children's needs can be fully addressed at individual and family levels. Also, two evidence-based models outlined most extensively in Chapters 2 and 8 build bridges of understanding and communication between professionals who work together on each case (teachers, probation officers, case manager). This chapter uses all these approaches as a roadmap to help clinicians achieve successful collaborations.

EVIDENCE-BASED FAMILY THERAPY MODELS AND COLLABORATION

In multisystemic therapy (MST), Henggeler et al. (1998) train their clinicians to work with any system in which the adolescent is a member. Thus, in addition to home sessions, clinicians work with teachers, attend social service case meetings, and may even visit a work site. Their goal is to influence each system to participate in a coordinated plan for the youth. Now, the beginning clinician (and maybe her supervisor) will rightly say, "Whew! How can I do all that?" First, explore the entire project, and then pick just one area in one case. Don't try to do it all. MST research projects receive federal funding to provide state-of-the-art training to clinicians who have carefully controlled caseloads and intensive supervision. Even though the new clinician likely doesn't have those luxuries, she can still learn from the researchers' process and experiment with different components of a larger project. You can use their state-of-the-art process, but adapt it to your clients.

For example, in the other collaborations listed in this chapter, I took the beginning intervention described by Henggeler and applied it to the respective setting. You can start small with just one case and one experiment of your own. Decide what system outside the family is the next most important (school, peers, church, etc.). Work with parents to develop a plan for collaboration and then act as their coach and a facilitator for conjoint meetings. Join with the other system by visiting as an observer and a consultant (see examples later in this chapter). Once those goals are achieved, you can decide whether addressing the next most important system is important. If you feel it is, each system can be addressed one by one rather than simultaneously. At the end of the chapter are some general guidelines for team-building. You can use those to get started and then apply what you learn to additional cases. Now let's look at the MST collaboration process.

Multisystemic Therapy and Overarching Goals

MST begins even before the clinician starts working with the family. A meeting of all stakeholders (court, family, adolescent, caseworker, etc.) provides a forum for discussing goals for the youth. The MST clinician *expects* disagreement among the parties. It is common for the family to have one goal and the teen or court to have another. The main objective of the meeting is to reach an agreement between the participants about one overarching goal, such as "keep Allen out of trouble." The clinician facilitates the discovery of this goal to begin the process of unified collaboration. As work with the family proceeds, the clinician keeps communication open between parties and organizes the best way for each participant to contribute. For example, the case worker may agree to review the positive aspects of progress before a court appearance so that legal meetings are less adversarial. A teacher may agree to provide regular reports when the parent calls.

One of the assumptions of this model is that the family has multiple stressors and thus, parents are often overwhelmed and discouraged. (Remember the joining suggestions in Chapter 4). Rather than adding to their burden, clinicians help each party develop a plan that leads to increased cooperation with schools, courts, and so on. They may coach, prompt, and encourage a family member who is withdrawn or intimidated by authorities (developmentally appropriate). Once the parent gains some confidence, the practitioner can support parents' effort and suggest that they take the lead. These interventions increase collaboration *between* systems in an adolescent's life. Because they target chronic cases, the successes of this program are impressive.

Multidimensional Family Therapy and Juvenile Justice

Likewise, multidimensional family therapy (MDFT) provides guidelines for collaboration that keep the practitioner in a similar position. However, multidimensional family therapists' work with substance abusers makes the juvenile justice system one of their prime targets.

MDFT often seeks cooperation with probation officers. The need for this is obvious, given that these professionals have authority to place teens outside the home or order treatment from a variety of sources. They can also influence the timing of events. Clinicians in MDFT programs work deliberately to gain cooperation with these officers. They often "buy time" with the officer to forestall a placement that would disrupt therapeutic gains. The following are steps in the MDFT process with probation officers (Liddle, 2000). The therapist does the following:

1. Contacts the officer at the start of a case.
2. Asks about the officer's experience and knowledge of the teen.
3. Explores any insights about what has happened to the teen in the family.
4. Expresses a desire to collaborate, acknowledging the time constraints and burdens of the officer.
5. Asks about practical matters, officer's busy schedule, best time to contact, etc.
6. States what the program can and will do in practical, non-jargon terms.
7. Assures officer that the goal of therapy is to meet requirements of the juvenile justice system.
8. Emphasizes the practical aspects where there is common ground between the two systems (i.e., better parent monitoring, best interest of the teen).
9. Encourages teen and family to see officer as a resource, not adversary.
10. Shares contacts, information, resources with officer.
11. Makes direct requests for cooperation: "Can I count on your support of our program's efforts? Is it okay with you if I call you and check in regularly, so we can share information and make sure we're on the same page?" (p. 147).

MDFT is an excellent example of a program that fosters "multiple therapeutic alliances." The distinguishing factor here is in the amount of time the clinician spends fostering increased understanding between these entities. For example, when teens and their parents have long-standing resentments toward authority, these practitioners attend to the family's distress, offer sympathy and empathy, provide a sounding board, encourage problem solving, and advocate for them. As discussed in Chapter 8, the emotion-focused approach of MDFT practitioners seeks to address the underlying emotion that may inhibit new patterns of behavior and thought. Because of this, the program is very innovative in the way the model addresses the family–juvenile justice relationship. In addition, both MST and MDFT address school problems for children and adolescents. This is an area of increasing interest for a number of family therapists.

COLLABORATION WITH SCHOOLS

Historically, family therapists have been keenly interested in promoting healthy family systems that will meet the needs of children. As mental health services become needed by more and more children, settings for mental health practice are growing to include educational systems. Mental health work with children is taking family therapists out of the office and into the school. In addition to the needs of children, teachers are finding a need for innovative interpersonal strategies to reach students and parents. Family therapists are excellent resources for helping children make the transition from home to school and for helping teachers and parents work together. Boyd-Franklin and Bry (2000) document the need for diversity in family therapy practice based upon cultural, racial, and socioeconomic differences that are found among many mental health consumers. School-based family therapy is a good example of culturally sensitive practice that teaches the family therapist how to honor the different cultures of family and community. This is particularly important when the welfare of children is at stake.

Family therapists often encounter school problems directly, when schools recommend to parents that they seek help for themselves or their children. Family therapists may also encounter school problems indirectly, when families seek help for one problem and happen to mention that school issues are a problem for one of their children. In American society, where education is compulsory, school problems can become dominating factors that influence family life in important ways. Thus, it is important for family therapists to address these issues and offer school consultation services as part of treatment. When referrals are made from schools, it is important to explore how the family views the problem. Does the family agree or disagree with the referral process (see Chapter 5)? When families disagree with the school assessment, clinicians can offer to be mediators between schools and families. Therapists can maintain a balance between the two sides by defining their role as one of seeking a win-win solution—a solution that includes the desires of both sides in the final plan. Once this role definition is clear, asking the family's permission to discuss and understand the school's position will not be seen as taking sides. Many times, families will agree with the school because they have been struggling at home. In these cases, therapists can define their role as that of consultant to both sides, helping families and schools discover ways of working together with shared strategies.

If the family indicates that it would like help with school problems, the therapist should assess relationships at multiple levels to gain a full picture of the problem in context. In addition to family relationships (student and parents, student and siblings), these multiple levels may be between:

- Student and teacher
- Student and peers
- Teacher and parent
- Parent and administrators

In assessing these relationships, Henggeler et al. (1998) suggest that attention be given to resources and concerns in order to build on existing strengths in the problem solving process (i.e., the student is in conflict with peers but likes her teacher). As suggested in Chapters 5 and 6, these additional relationships might be important resources and expanding the system can often accelerate improvement when other professionals become part of the team.

If the family therapist is recruited by the school or referring agency, it is best to adopt the role of consultant and clarify with the school and family that a problem solving consultation need not carry the stigma of mental health treatment (Hanna, 1997). This approach encourages school personnel to

Table 9.1 | Common Attitudes Taken by Parents and Teachers

Parents	Teachers
I don't have a problem with my child at home.	I'm concerned about this child, but I don't need help in the classroom.
I don't want help at home with my child.	I think the problem is best solved at home.
I want help at home with my child.	I'm unsure if I should respond to family issues, the child's feelings, etc.
I have the same problem at home with my child.	I need help in the following area: _____.
I want help at home with issues other than my child.	I want the family to help more.
I want the teacher to have more help with my child at school.	I think the problem is best solved in the classroom.

reframe the problem in simple terms and reassures the family that the consultant is not rushing to judgment about the severity of the problem.

Involving the Network

It is important to understand that the cultures of schools often place great pressure on teachers because of trends that emphasize test scores and on administrators because of increasing school violence. Although consultants often know that psychosocial influences weigh heavily on the development of any given problem, they must also understand that educators might not view a problem through the same lens. A common problem of beginning therapists is trying to persuade or convince other professionals to adopt their position. But as explained in Chapter 4, a successful working relationship comes from assessing another's worldview, respecting the other's culture, building rapport and trust, instilling hope, emphasizing the professional's strengths, and allowing for disagreements without becoming judgmental. Table 9.1 presents examples of common attitudes adopted by parents and teachers when a problem arises at school.

As Table 9.1 shows, the potential for agreement and disagreement between parent and teacher varies according to the particular situation. The top two rows in the table represent levels in which the greatest conflict may occur. In these cases, the consultant must adopt a win-win goal with both sides. Multi-directed partiality, as discussed in Chapter 1, is an important skill in showing empathy and understanding for all sides. When therapists can truly place themselves in the position of the other, therapists can sympathize with both sides and pursue explorations that may include a strength-based and solution-focused approach to solving the problem.

Case 9	Gary

Gary was a nine-year-old European American boy who was having a hard time paying attention in his fourth grade class, and the teacher and parents reached a heated impasse. The consultant joined with both sides and used direct classroom observation to explore ways in which Gary's strengths at home could be incorporated into the culture of the classroom. His father described his amazing ability to remember the smallest details about the solar system. By suggesting that everyone's position was legitimate (multidirected partiality), the therapist redirected each side's blame of the other and moved toward a mode of creative experimentation that was based upon the strengths of Gary, the teacher, and parents. A new plan of communication between home and school was developed, and the parents began providing materials for the teacher to use that brought Gary's strengths into the classroom.

As Gary's case illustrates, a starting point is to work with all relevant parties on their terms. For example, if consultants want a positive working relationship with teachers, they can review Chapter 4, with a teacher in mind, to develop a positive and respectful foundation for problem solving. Many teachers feel rushed and exhausted just trying to keep up with the day-to-day pressures of instruction. Phone consultations and on-site observations (for children ages three to ten) by the therapist are more convenient for many teachers. The following points can help clinicians begin the process:

1. In all cases, make sure releases of information are signed by family members in order to communicate freely with school personnel.
2. Contact the teacher and ask about the possibility of a consultation, an on-site observation, or both.
3. If an on-site observation occurs, report to the main office and identify yourself. Many schools require that visitors sign in at this point.
4. When feasible, negotiate with the teacher to conduct the observation first and then discuss and consult with the teacher afterward.

Once initial contacts are made, the consultant should review the position of each member of the system to decide on an intervention strategy.

Implementing Intervention Strategies

When referrals involve a request for behavior modification plans at school, structured worksheets are helpful in guiding a classroom observation. Box 9.1 is a guide for gathering information about school-related behavior. Adopt a behavioral perspective, looking for antecedents and consequences of behavior (see Chapter 1). Behavioral management plans are common in educational settings, and these can form a common language for consultants, parents, and schools to use. Box 9.2 outlines a behavioral management plan. Such a plan might evolve from consultations with all relevant parties. Although all relevant parties

Box 9.1	**Teacher Consultation**

1. Describe the primary/targeted behavior.

   Is the behavior observed today different from that observed other days? If so, how? Better? Worse?

2. In what situations does the behavior occur?

Location	Time	Person	Instructional context
__ Class	__ Arrival to school	__ Teacher	__ Entire group/mealtime
__ Hallways	__ Morning	__ Resource	__ Small group
__ Cafeteria	__ Lunch	__ Assistants	__ Individual
__ Special classes	__ Afternoon	__ Bus driver	__ Experiential learning
__ Bus	__ Recess/ break	__ Other children	__ Field trips
__ Other____	__ Other____	__ Other____	__ Other____

3. How intense is the behavior?

   __ No problem __ Low   __ Moderate

   __ High   __ Very high __ Catastrophic

4. How long does the behavior last?

   __ <2 min   __ 2–6 min   __ 6–12 min   __ 12–20 min   __ >20 min

5. When the behavior occurs, what happens right <u>before</u> that might be influencing the behavior?

   __ Child was involved in activity he or she enjoyed

   __ Child was being given direction by an adult

   __ Child was alone performing a task

   __ Child was in transition from one activity to the next

   __ Child was given a lot of praise

   __ Child was given more attention by adults

   __ Child was interacting with peers

   __ Other _____

6. What do people do right <u>after</u> the behavior?

   Child in question _____

   Other children _____

   Teachers _____

   Others _____

(Continued)

Box 9.1	**Teacher Consultation** (continued)

7. What interventions has the teacher tried?

___ Redirect   ___ Verbal reprimand/warning   ___ Ultimatum   ___ Time out

___ Ignore   ___ Taking something away   ___ Office referral   ___ Other ___

Comments: _____

8. What was tried to help the child settle down? _____

9. What are the child's strengths? _____

10. What are his or her strongest interests? _____

11. What time of the day is the most positive for the child in the classroom?

_____

12. How is the child doing academically?   IEP in place?: Y/N

13. How is the child doing with other services?

a. Other service providers: _____

b. Teacher's knowledge of any history of services (consultations with providers):

14. What are your thoughts about the causes of the child's misbehavior?

15. Do you have any thoughts about the best course of action?

16. Would you be interested in hearing other suggestions about this issue in addition to the ones you have offered?

17. What could be changed in the classroom environment that would make it easier for the child to have better behavior?

Box 9.2	**Behavior Management Plan**

Name of Child: _____   Age of Child: _____   Today's Date: _____

Child's Interests and Strengths (which can be used in increasing desired behavior or decreasing undesired behavior):

_____

_____

_____

Desired Behavior (behavior that the team would like to see the child develop, both in the short term and the long term):

Short term:

_____

_____

_____

(Continued)

Box 9.2	**Behavior Management Plan** (continued)

Long term:

_____
_____
_____

Short term:

_____
_____
_____

Long term:

_____
_____
_____

Who will do what, when, and where?

Who	What	When and Where
_____	_____	_____
_____	_____	_____
_____	_____	_____
_____	_____	_____

Evaluation:

Date _____ Progress made/changes needed: _____

Date _____ Progress made/changes needed: _____

meeting together is ideal, it is not necessary if school personnel are under extreme time pressures and the consultant establishes positive rapport with them.

The following two cases illustrate how consultants provided home and school consultations using the guidelines shown in Box 9.1. In case of Sara, parents and teacher were amenable to meeting together and developing teamwork.

Case 10	**Sara**

A first grade teacher was concerned about Sara's pattern of lying and stealing from other children. Sara was blonde, blue-eyed, small for her age, and the oldest of three children. The therapist first helped the parents explore family circumstances related to the problem. The parents were able to recognize that the father's travel schedule had left the mother with added burdens at home. When he returned, he would inadvertently indulge his children because he missed them and wanted to enjoy them. The mother was

(Continued)

Case 10	**Sara** (continued)

perceived as the "bad guy," and Sara developed beliefs that she wasn't important from interactions in which her mother was under pressure and was trying to maintain order at home. The therapist helped the parents to design a series of experiences in which the father took a more active role in disciplining all the children and the mother planned some errands in which Sara could join her and they could "steal" some time together. At the same time, the concerned teacher was invited to develop an understanding with Sara that when she wanted something that wasn't hers, she could talk with her teacher and they would plan a way for her to have something special that was rightfully hers. The teacher allowed her class to check out special books and take them home. This became a way for Sara to have nice things without stealing.

During the teacher consultation, the teacher reported that she overlooked Sara's lies because she was small for her age and very endearing (consequence). In addition, the consultant discovered that Sara was quiet and would often get lost in the crowd, a result of her size and lack of assertiveness (antecedent). This information helped the therapist to understand Sara in both contexts and to draw some parallels between the two. A multisystems approach such as that practiced by Boyd-Franklin (2000) helped the clinician to develop and test hypotheses about Sara's emotional development and about the way each side could foster her growth. This is a good example of how many teachers and parents go the extra mile to benefit the children in their care.

In the case of Jeff (Case 11), tensions were extreme between parent and teacher. However, the consultant was able to enlist the help of additional school personnel to bring about a new agreement between the school and family.

Case 11	**Jeff**

Jeff was an African American boy in third grade when he set a fire that destroyed his family's apartment. This was the third fire in two years that led to another relocation for his family. He lived with his grandmother for a year before the fires started. During his transition back to his mother's care, conflict developed between his grandmother and mother. His grandmother wanted him returned to her custody. She had friends who worked at his school, and they supported her position. As a result, Jeff's mother felt outnumbered and powerless when interacting at his school. Reports about Jeff from his teacher were inconsistent with those from other teachers who had been in the classroom with him. The consultant found Jeff to be competent and capable in completing class assignments. She also observed that he would often finish ahead of the other children and begin looking around the room for something else to do. However, the teacher insisted that a report should be filed to child social services indicating that Jeff was a danger to himself and others. An investigation ensued that united the grandmother and mother. During this process, the role of the consultant was initially to foster trust with the mother, who believed everyone was against her. As that alliance developed, the investigation ironically became an opportunity for the consultant to enlist the grandmother's

(Continued)

| Case 11 | **Jeff** (continued) |

support of her family. The mother and grandmother began to reconcile during consultations with the consultant, and all three developed a plan for helping Jeff change
schools. The consultant discovered that student services personnel were willing to be
advocates for change within the system. They provided a counterpoint with the family
that led to a satisfactory change in which Jeff was transferred into a small classroom
with one of the few male teachers in the district. This proved beneficial for Jeff, and his
family continued to call upon the consultant for help with nonschool issues. At this
point, the clinician negotiated with the family to provide "family therapy."

One of the keys to success in this case was the therapist's ability to expand
the system to include helpful school personnel who were outside the immediate conflict. As the issues of crisis waned and Jeff's family began to settle their
differences to help him, the therapist enlisted the family in new ways of helping Jeff with any problematic behaviors that remained. The grandmother was
affirmed for her importance in his life. The mother was complimented for her
courage in advocating for her son. The therapist helped them form a team by
suggesting parenting strategies that they could learn together. Box 9.3 contains
principles of child behavior change that were used with the family to promote
prosocial behavior from a strengths' perspective. These are adapted from
Adlerian parent education materials (Dinkmeyer, McKay et al., 1997).

| Box 9.3 | **Steps to Individual Behavior Management** |

1. **Determine the purpose of the target behavior.**

   Keep a journal for several days.

   What happens right before the behavior occurs? With whom?

   What happens after? With whom?

   What is the result of the behavior? Attention? Control? Revenge? Dependency?

   How might the aftermath be a reinforcement?

2. **Divert the child from the problem situations by increasing positive reinforcement in other areas.**

   What are the child's strong points? Where lies potential? Begin a systematic
   campaign to convince the child of his or her strengths.

   When the child comes close to doing something right, call attention to the
   child as if he or she had already done it. ("Good job, Jerry, you almost kept
   your hands to yourself. I can see that you were trying. I bet next time you'll
   be able to keep your hands quiet.")

   For competitive children, "dare" them to do what is right. ("I bet you can't walk
   all the way to the cafeteria! Let me see if you can!")

(Continued)

| Box 9.3 | **Steps to Individual Behavior Management** (continued) |

3. Remove reinforcements from the old behavior.

Use nonverbal communication as much as possible.

For attention seekers, use a pat on the shoulder or nonverbal signals.

Avoid power struggles. Walk away from tantrums. Explain to other children that Maria is upset, but she will learn how to calm herself down. Reassure Maria that she can learn to calm herself.

Acknowledge that aggression can be an expression of hurt feelings.

Ask if something made the child feel bad. Show empathy. Brainstorm new ways to handle the child's hurt feelings in the future.

Encourage children who display helplessness. Allow them to have natural consequences.

Such collaborations with schools, families, and family therapists are a growing innovation in the profession. Family therapists bring the strength of their interactional perspective with the wisdom of relational interventions to address conflicts and problems that drain energy from homes and schools. One of the ways therapists gain trust and credibility in these situations is by proving how their services can make everyone's job easier and more successful. Thus, a win-win situation is brought about by addressing the needs of each member in the system (teacher, parent, child, etc.) and by finding a way for the tension between competing needs to lead into creative problem solving that is developmentally appropriate for everyone. This approach is equally effective when family therapists bring their skills to medical settings and health problems.

COLLABORATION WITH HEALTH CARE PROFESSIONALS

As health care continues to change, the need for lower costs, better patient care, and improved health outcomes continues to grow. Family therapists have been active in developing methods of consultation that are directed at these goals. In this role, they promote a coordinated partnership between (a) psychosocial providers and biomedical providers and (b) provider systems and family systems. Rolland (1994) suggests that the family can be an important part of the health care team. Often family therapists facilitate the involvement of family members in the treatment and recovery of medical patients for better health outcomes. McDaniel, Hepworth, and Doherty (1992) suggest that family therapists in medical settings have a unique and important role because of the:

> attention to medical illness and its role in the personal life of the patient and the interpersonal life of the family . . . family therapists are trained to work with difficult cases in an intense and sometimes prolonged manner. . . . In the current

healthcare system . . . the family, if it is involved at all, is likely to be viewed as an adjunctive aid in treating the patient, not as a group of people who need help in their own right. (pp. 4–5)

Research continues to improve understanding of the human body and the impact of health and illness on individuals and their relational networks is of increasing relevance. For example, providing services that address these linkages is an important role for the family therapist working in health care settings.

Medical Family Therapy: Is This the Best Term?

Although McDaniel, Hepworth, and Doherty (1992) used the term *medical family therapy,* with the passage of time, the term has become problematic in the context of interacting with patients, families, and health care professionals. This is because the referral process and the precipitating circumstances are often related to illness or stress, and families do not think of themselves as candidates for mental health treatment, even though they may want help in coping or problem solving (Hanna, 1997). Walsh and Rolland (2003) also find the term confusing. They suggest that "medical" implies physician involvement. "Family therapy" implies either relational or mental health treatment. None of these may be part of the process. For these and the reasons mentioned in working with schools and families, I label the activity as a *problem solving consultation* until there is some indication that family and clinician are entering into a "traditional" client-therapist relationship. Walsh and Rolland (2003) also use the term *psychoeducational family consultation.* This term is useful in emphasizing how important education is to the empowerment of families in health care settings.

Problem solving consultations can be helpful in a variety of ways, and the well-being of the family can be preserved or restored, depending upon the level of need. Some of these needs are those of the family, whereas others are those of the physician or other health care professional. For example, doctors are often concerned about how well a patient can follow medical directives. Consider diabetes: the demands to manage insulin levels at home can be difficult for some patients. Age of patients, pharmaceutical costs, quality of life, and severity of the disease can be factors in what doctors call *compliance,* or following the doctor's orders. Social isolation or family conflict over some part of the medical directives (as with adolescents with diabetes) can become added problems if not addressed. Using the same win-win approach that is successful in schools, the consultant can assess important relationships related to the problem of compliance and look for practical solutions that include a recognition of each person's needs.

From an educational perspective, the consultant's role can also complement that of the health educator. Often, nurses assume the role of health educator, that of providing information to families about an illness and its management. A psychoeducational family consultant can provide time to the family members to help them problem-solve how they can adapt and cope with life changes that are brought about from a medical condition. These changes range from traumatic (i.e., spinal cord injury and paralysis) to inconvenient (i.e., broken leg that will take a few months to heal). They may also range in prognosis from good to poor, or even fatal (i.e., metastasized cancer).

McCubbin (1980) found that families can cope best with the challenges of illness when they have information about why an event happened, how it happened, and what they can do to cope successfully. The psychoeducational consultant can help them gain access to this information by using knowledge of family structure and family development (Chapter 3). Using the familiar metaphor of driving a car, becoming a helpful consultant to a family is like being a tour guide who helps a group of people find their way when life brings them to a foreign land. The consultant can help by doing some of the driving while the visitors become oriented to the new situation. They can provide information about common challenges that illnesses pose to family relationships and personal well-being. Engaging these visitors in discussions about how they might prevent their own health breakdown while coping with that of a family member can be useful. Another part of being a helpful consultant should involve providing these directions as options and exploring which directions would be most relevant for them at a given time.

LaVoie (1985) offers seven important points to keep in mind when providing help to families facing illness or loss:

1. The practitioner must be sensitive to the life cycle phase of the individual and family. The family life cycle, age, and sex are more sensitive indicators of abnormal conditions than age and sex alone (Medalie, 1979).
2. Family treatment of an individual's health breakdown should be considered. Family medical practitioners are moving in the direction of treating the family as a unit. Family therapists can consult with physicians regarding the family dynamics that led to the breakdown.
3. The chronic crisis-ridden family must be identified early so that intervention procedures can be initiated before major problems appear (Rainsford & Schulman, 1981).
4. Where possible, family coping strategies should be assessed; if found to be deficient, coping techniques should be introduced and practiced.
5. Families should be made more aware of their stage in the life cycle and of future events.
6. The social network of the family should be examined, because support systems are important buffers in coping with stress.
7. Individuals and families must learn to recognize stress build-up and to initiate stress reduction strategies as necessary, because stress appears to have a negative impact on the immune system. (pp. 65–66)

This emphasis on the family's stage of life is especially important because it often provides an explanation for conflict that normalizes or removes blame from family members. Especially during times of normal transition when illness may complicate the family's normal adaptation process, explaining how life stage affects family interactions can provide the family with a road map that includes coping with the illness and fostering the healthy development of its members.

These suggestions form the basis of my own approach to consultations for health issues. The spectrum of this work will range from prevention for the patient and family members to actual treatment in cases where research shows that interpersonal interventions can impact the recovery and management of an illness. For example, if a family member is diagnosed with Alzheimer's disease, the consultant may meet to help members of the family consider their own unique type of loss (Boss, 1999), to help them reorganize family roles when the patient has been central to their organizational scheme, and to help them develop strategies to cope with stress and promote optimal functioning of the family (Long, 1997). Psychoeducational interventions bring together elements of mind, body, spirit, and relationship that are needed to bring about the best possible health outcomes.

Mind, Body, Spirit, and Relationship: A Framework for Health Care Interventions

Medical problems can sometimes bring shocking and life-changing circumstances into family life. These often prompt family members to reflect upon the spiritual aspects of coping with illness and of those losses associated with death. When we ask families to talk about how they have coped with challenges in the past, they often share unique aspects about their faith and spirituality. These are important resources to mobilize during times of challenging illnesses. Often, spiritual resources are intergenerational gifts that are passed down through generations. As discussed in Chapter 3, exploring intergenerational strengths and legacies can be an important starting point in mobilizing hope and courage for families in pain. The family's future may be uncertain, but they appreciate being reminded of traditions and values that help them to endure adversity.

Case 12	Denise

Denise was a 40-year-old African American woman who had become severely depressed after she discovered that she was HIV positive. She was the victim of a rape and later learned that her assailant had died of AIDS. She had a history of seizures, and her compromised immune system was discovered during a hospitalization two years later. Upon discharge, she was referred to an outpatient clinic to begin management of her HIV. Her depression was understandable, and the nurse suggested that she speak to the family consultant at the clinic. Often, medical cases are referred in this way. When family therapists work in health care settings, client contact is most often made during routine medical visits. Consultants may speak with patients in the exam room before or after the doctor's visit and then follow up with home or office-based work according to the needs of the patient.

Denise's genogram is Figure 7.1 in Chapter 7. The consultant listened sympathetically to Denise's story and explored her current support system. Her closest supports

(Continued)

Case 12	**Denise** (continued)

were her niece and a friend, nicknamed "Big Mama," who was a nurse. They shared her grief and vowed to stay close to her during this ordeal. Big Mama explained what she knew about HIV medications, and Denise's niece was willing to become the guardian for her children if the need arose. The consultant used the genogram and a timeline to explore areas of strength and vulnerability with Denise and her family. In this case, the complexity of past history was important to know and understand. Also, the timeline extended into the future to note Denise's most important goals. She had important dreams that her children would finish high school.

During initial consultations, medical history contained the story that Denise had been seizure-free for the past two years after she felt compelled to stop her medication. In her words, the Lord had protected her, and she had accomplished this through a miracle from faith and prayer. She attended her church weekly and in the midst of her current challenge had kept her faith in God. The consultant agreed that she was a "miracle woman" and that this history of miracles and faith could help her address the problems at hand (spirit). Initial consultations focused upon information about the disease because new drugs were helping HIV patients to live longer. She no longer needed to fear an immediate death. Her condition could be considered a chronic illness that needed safe management, rather than a fatal disease from which she would soon die. This education (mind) helped Denise's depression to lift, and she began to see how she could disclose her diagnosis to her four children and reassure them that she would not die immediately (relationships). She resolved to follow the doctor's directives in the management of her disease (body) so that she could live to see her youngest son, age 14, graduate from high school. The consultant helped her develop strategies for disclosing her condition to her family, for improving her mental health, and for using her support system as part of her "management" team.

As in this case of Denise, strengths and vulnerabilities may encompass mental, physical, spiritual, or relational functioning. Mind, body, and spirit each have a strong impact upon the nature of relationships during times of coping and problem solving. Conversely, the strength of relationships through intimacy, commitment, sacrifice, and nurturing can greatly enhance the functioning of mind, body, and spirit. Schwenk and Hughes (1983) found that the incidence of chronic illness increases in family members of those families with chronic illness. Thus, it is important to conduct a careful assessment of family strengths that can be highlighted as protective factors against this increased risk. Chapter 4 provides suggestions for exploring and identifying family strengths.

Chapter 3 outlined aspects of individual experience that are important to track during medical crises. Genograms can be used to note personal resources, family strengths, patterns of illness, and causes of death in the intergenerational family. Timelines are particularly important when tracking the sequence and timing of multiple stressors that may have besieged a family in a short period of time. This is called *pile-up* and is an important factor in explaining how severe the effects of the most recent stressor may be (McCubbin, Dahl & Hunter, 1976). For example, consider family members who have already exhausted their emotional and spiritual resources because of a serious automobile accident and then learn three months later that a member of the family has been diagnosed with cancer. This knowledge would be critical to know before health care providers could develop a true appreciation of a family's stress and corresponding strengths. In addition, important encounters with health care providers can be explored on timelines to understand medical histories as sequential and interactive.

Often, individuals with medical problems are older, and they become more retrospective in their focus: They appreciate the opportunity to review their past strengths and accomplishments. Butler (1963) suggested that *life review* should be a primary mental health intervention for older clients, and I have found it therapeutic to organize the telling of narratives around a structured timeline with the entire family of an older client, to facilitate shared coping and problem solving. Hanna and Hargrave (1997) have suggested that many models of family therapy are present-oriented and should be modified to meet the needs of persons in later life. Thus, constructing a genogram and timeline on a large easel in front of the family lends itself to the role of a consultant who is exploring strengths and problem solving strategies from the past as a starting point for addressing present difficulties. Younger families also appreciate the opportunity for the consultant to learn about them before they were affected by a life-changing illness.

In these cases, the timeline can be used to map grief and loss issues. By keeping questions focused on strengths and methods of coping, consultants can control the level of intimacy in the interview. If families want the consultation to include a focus on historical conflicts, past misunderstandings, and long-standing symptoms, a formal therapeutic relationship can be negotiated. Otherwise, a positive, affirming, pragmatic problem solving relationship should be maintained by the consultant.

Case 3 | **Return to Harvey**

Let's return to the case of Harvey, described in Chapter 4 as a 65-year-old man with a 20-year history of paranoia and schizophrenia. His case illustrates how the consultant's role must be balanced between that of a therapeutic relationship and that of a psychoeducational consultant. Harvey had been steadfast in his refusal of any mental health or physical health service. He was referred by a local social service agency when volunteers with the Meals on Wheels program tried to deliver his meals and became intimidated by his behavior. They refused to return, and intervention was sought through a home-based service program to mediate this conflict. The consultant found Harvey to have many medical complaints, one of which was trouble breathing. However, he was well-known in the social service community, and other providers considered his report of symptoms to be part of his mental illness.

The consultant negotiated a plan with Harvey to help others understand his needs. In the process, she found a family doctor at the university clinic who was willing to work with Harvey's complex interpersonal patterns in order to provide his medical care. The consultant did not try to treat Harvey's mental health issues. Instead, based upon his

(Continued)

Case 3	**Return to Harvey** (continued)

most consistent complaints, she worked to gain Harvey's trust, and he considered going with the consultant under certain conditions to the doctor's office. The initial appointment brought Harvey to the waiting room, but he was unable to tolerate sitting long enough to keep the appointment. However, on the second visit, Harvey found that he could tolerate the threat of confinement, and he allowed the doctor to examine him. Some simple, noninvasive procedures revealed a significant oxygen shortage in his blood, and he was immediately provided with ongoing oxygen for his lung disease. With this success, Harvey remained open to the consultations, which eventually led to a reunion with one of his seven children after ten years of no contact.

In health care consultations, traditional family therapy skills are initially used to solve immediate and practical problems. However, when the medical condition has a strong influence on the family, the trusting relationship that is developed over practical matters often becomes the foundation for careful work related to grief and loss, life stage transitions, intergenerational conflict, and family reorganization (Chapter 3). The key to being a successful consultant in medical settings is to go slowly and let the family members dictate their goals. In addition, the relationships developed with health care professionals must be built upon the same principles of understanding discussed in working with teachers and students in school settings. As consultants, the "clients" are often other professionals who want help addressing difficult problems. They deserve the same careful empathy and trust that given to clients who seek traditional mental health services. The following section further illustrates how family therapists can develop these collaborations, with art therapists to provide innovative mental health services.

COLLABORATION WITH ART THERAPISTS

Along the continuum of behavioral and mental health practice, various allied health disciplines contribute to cutting-edge practice. Research shows that many innovative approaches from family therapy and art therapy are successful with groups who underutilize traditional clinic-based mental health services (Campbell, Liebmann, Brooks, Jones, & Ward, 1990; Henggeler et al., 1998; McGoldrick & Giordano, 1996). For example, family therapists address mental health problems such as mental illness and substance abuse from a pragmatic relational approach (Anderson, Reiss, & Hogarty, 1986; McFarlane, 2002; Stanton & Todd, 1982; Todd & Selekman, 1991b). Art therapists successfully address numerous problems including bereavement, domestic violence, antisocial behavior, and medical trauma (Wadeson, Durkin, & Perach, 1989; Koplewiez & Goodman, 1999). This section explores some of the characteristics of another mental health profession and illustrates how family therapists can collaborate to develop innovative services for groups who are uncomfortable with traditional mental health services.

Because psychotherapy developed within the white, middle-class, industrialized world, and family therapy has been influenced by this historical context, many people still do not come to office-based counseling with the same goals, values, traditions, or worldviews as those of the therapists themselves. Often, people living in economically impoverished conditions are sent to counseling by someone with authority over them or their family (medical, educational, legal, or governmental). These referral sources often adopt goals for the family that are not adopted by the family. Thus, knowing how to address this unspoken disparity and knowing when nonverbal communication should become the preferred mode of conducting therapy is important. Because art is a universal language found on a neighborhood wall or in a posh, upper-class gallery, it transcends many of the barriers that are constructed from differences in class, race, politics, or sexual orientation.

Art therapy is a human service profession using art, images, the creative process, and patient responses to reflect an individual's development, abilities, personality, interests, concerns, and conflicts. The practice is based on theories of human development and psychology to treat emotional conflicts, foster self-awareness, develop social skills, manage behavior, solve problems, reduce anxiety, aid reality orientation, and increase self-esteem (American Art Therapy Association, 2001).

As a profession, art therapy has a national association and promotes board certification. In addition, a number of states are becoming aware of the value of art therapy and have adopted certification or licensure regulations. The profession's history has a similar pattern to that of family therapy, in that art therapy sprang from a number of people who were innovators in a variety of fields such as education, medicine, and psychology in the 1940s (Rubin, 1999). One of these pioneers was a sculptor from Poland, Hanna Yaxa Kwiatkowska, who developed a method of family art therapy and evaluation at the National Institute of Mental Health in 1958 (Kwiatkowska, 1978; 1967). There, she developed a close friendship with family therapy pioneer Lyman Wynne and his wife Adele (see Chapter 1).

Achieving success in multidisciplinary collaboration depends on the clinician's ability to value the contributions of other professionals and to look for win-win solutions when professional disagreements occur. The case of art therapy and family therapy is an example of how family therapists discovered the value of other professions and how they addressed points of potential disagreement. The preceding definition of art therapy reveals that art therapy focuses more on individual growth and phenomenology; family therapy focuses more on relational growth and family process. Whereas family art therapy combines both perspectives, many art therapists are trained in traditional individual and group theories of counseling, whereas family therapists are departing more from those traditions and adopting nontraditional lenses that do not focus upon pathology (diagnoses), defense mechanisms (denial, rationalization), or the attribution of certain intentions (avoidance, control, ego).

In spite of these conceptual and language differences, the two professions often share similar goals, especially in school-based settings. Thus, staying focused on common goals is useful in developing collaborations. In addition, family therapy and art therapy share a number of values such as putting an emphasis on the client's narrative; deconstructing client experience; and creating a safe, accepting, and nurturing environment. The language of these values is also useful in creating a respectful and innovative collaboration. The welfare of clients provide a unifying framework around which each professional can make his or her unique contribution. This can happen through in-service meetings in which individual professionals have the opportunity to teach others about the perspectives and interventions from their practice (Robbins, 1994), or through case management meetings in which team members share information and accept assignments related to their area of expertise (Ronaldson & Hanna 2001). These same forms of collaboration also exist in the medical activities outlined earlier. If beginning clinicians do not find these activities in existence at their practice sites, they may suggest these and even volunteer to lead them if need be. Many people are receptive to new ideas that have a mutual benefit to all the stakeholders.

In collaborative projects for children, art therapy and family therapy can easily become a synergistic combination, that is, they can be combined to produce better results than either activity in isolation. For example, there is a distinction between *multidisciplinary* (many professionals sharing a case but working independently) and *interdisciplinary* (many professionals working together and developing a common treatment plan while maintaining separate roles that occasionally overlap). Because synergy is a concept from general systems theory, it is a notion that lies at the center of successful interdisciplinary work. Synergy involves the process of interprofessional education in which each learned about the other. Family therapists preparing for such collaboration can benefit from some basics in art therapy that provide enhancements to their own practice. These include some elementary concepts from the field and foundational art activities that are relevant for family therapists.

Understanding Expressive Communication

Art therapy rests on the premise that all people are inherently creative and that the creative process mirrors the natural world and evokes processes that promote growth and balance. Rubin (1999) suggests that the practice combines "involved doing" and "relaxed reflection" together. Further, the combination of these two elements is more powerful than either alone. Lusebrink (1992) established the *expressive therapies continuum* (ETC), outlining levels of individual experience in dynamic interaction that can be used to guide the practitioner's work. These levels are placed on a continuum of complexity that corresponds with human development: kinesthetic-sensory, perceptual-affective, and cognitive-symbolic. The author uses the principles of systems theory to explain the relationships between these levels, similar to how a family therapist would use systems theory to explain relationships between family members. Ronaldson and Peacock (2001) have suggested the following principles in conducting successful art therapy:

1. The process and content of an individual's self-expression is valued over the aesthetic quality of the visual product.

2. The expressive therapies continuum provides a framework for establishing continuity between media, self-expression, and communication with others.
3. Nonverbal expression using visual images related to internal experience provides a catalyst for self-reflection, insight, and verbal response.

In addition to these principles, Box 9.4 lists corresponding outcomes to assess client satisfaction with the process. These outcomes assume that the process also involves joining with the client, explaining the value of the art process in therapy, and engaging the client in meaningful creativity and reflection.

Although art therapists are noted for their innovative work with all ages and all types of psychosocial problems, collaborations began over work with children in school settings. These projects showed great value in combining family therapy and art therapy. The field of family therapy has often relied too much on "talk therapy," with too little attention paid to involving children in ways that match their attention span and developmental level. Art therapy has had much to add to the family therapy process.

Developmentally Appropriate Practice

As mentioned in Chapter 1, early childhood educators are already very familiar with the term *developmentally appropriate practice*. With the exception of

---

Box 9.4 | **Desired Outcomes in Art Therapy**

Self-expression is valued over aesthetic quality.

1. I felt comfortable with making art.
2. The therapist was very accepting of my artwork.
3. I was able to talk easily about my artwork.
4. The therapist respected my artwork and what I had to say about it.
5. My process of making art was pleasurable and satisfying.
6. I gained new information about myself and my problems from the artwork.

The expressive therapies continuum (ETC) integrates levels of media, self-expression, and communication.

1. I had an opportunity to explore a variety of art materials.
2. I was able to understand myself and my family better after making art together.
3. Using a variety of art materials and techniques helped me to look at my problems in different ways.
4. The therapist was knowledgeable about how to use different art materials.

The art process evokes self-reflection, insight, and verbal response.

1. The artwork stimulated my thinking about my problems.
2. The therapist did not interpret my artwork for me.
3. The artwork helped me to see things differently.

Michael White's playful interventions for children, current models of family therapy fail to consider how a family therapy session can privilege children's voices in a developmentally appropriate way. Most often, children are asked adult questions and are expected to give well-formed verbal answers. However, Koppitz (1968) suggests that children can express their experience through images long before they can verbalize them. One way to overcome this shortcoming in family therapy is through family art therapy.

In a pioneering program that embraced both family therapy and art therapy, Robbins (1994) found that families and schools became better collaborators through a program called Family Builders in which family therapists and art therapists worked together to provide school-based services. In another project, Ronaldson and Hanna (2001) reported that reluctant parents often became more engaged in problem solving regarding their preschool child when the child's art was shown and discussed. These projects used the concept of developmentally appropriate practice to unify professionals around the needs of children and to respect the wishes of parents to provide help to their child. The following suggestions present beginning therapists with an example of how a creative process from art therapy can give children and their families a concrete experience that provides a framework for communication and problem solving.

Accessing Relationships Through the Creative Process

A common art intervention is known as the *kinetic family drawing,* or KFD (Burns & Kaufman, 1970). This intervention can be used when art therapists see children in individual sessions or when family therapists have sessions that include children. Box 9.5 provides directions for conducting a family session

---

Box 9.5 | **Instructions for Kinetic Family Drawing**

1. Provide the directive: "I'd like you each to draw a picture of your family *doing something together.*"

2. Limit your observations to permissive phrases such as "You can make your drawing any way you want," "Whatever you decide to draw will be just fine," "No one will be judging your work," or "Take your time."

3. Wait until all family members are finished before beginning a discussion. At that time, ask: "Who would like to start telling about their picture?"

4. "Tell me about the picture. Who is each person and how old is each one?"

5. "What is the family doing (it may be a past event, distant memory, or daily activity)?" "What is the best part of the activity for you?" "Do you have any other favorite memories about the activity?"

6. "What do other family members remember about this activity?"

7. Rotate descriptions and reflections until all the members have described and discussed their drawings.

using the KFD. When parents are anxious for treatment to be directed toward the identified child, the KFD, as an introductory activity in which all members can participate, reassures parents that treatment will focus upon the child's needs. Because family life is often filled with child-centered activities, stories, and goals, the KFD can help a family therapy session mirror the natural environment and set the family at ease. Here are some suggestions for incorporating into a session.

1. Explain to parents that children can often gain new skills and insights through art activities. To help their children, the clinician would like family members to do an activity together, and then they will all discuss how this activity can contribute to some problem solving strategies.
2. If adults are reluctant to participate with their children, offer analogies such as coaches in sports using diagrams to discuss their team's strategies, or fashion designers sketching their future plans. In some cases, the therapist may need to give some examples of events, memories, or daily routines.
3. Encourage all the participants to draw their own pictures independently and reassure them that the nonverbal process of communication is more important than the appearance of their drawing. The game Pictionary is an example of how families can use drawings for fun and recreation.
4. Limit the media to blank paper and pencils or crayons for young children to simplify the process and to emphasize that the activity is more about creating a positive experience together. Usually, pencils are ordinary enough to avoid posing a threat for adults. The erasers are also important to help people feel comfortable with the process. Children are generally more familiar with crayons and might find pencils to be too formal.
5. Once the KFDs are complete, discuss the process as an example of how family members provide different perspectives about their life together. These perspectives can often generate more potential solutions to a problem.

Beginning clinicians should not make interpretations from the drawings. If the drawings are of concern to parents or the clinician, consultation should be sought from a registered art therapist who is board certified (ATR-BC). Art therapists are required to meet strict standards of practice and assessment to become board certified. Family therapists can locate an ATR-BC through the American Art Therapy Association website (www.AATA.org).

Instead of using the drawings as a platform for interpretation, use these activities as a developmentally appropriate catalyst for discussion. From a narrative perspective, the KFD elicits each person's story about the family. The KFD can be followed by a similar exercise in which family members are asked to draw the presenting problem from their perspective. Thereafter, each member can discuss how she or he sees the problem. Drawings can communicate perceptions and feelings in ways that are symbolic and less threatening than stating them verbally. The clinician's role is that of reflection. Families are often so fraught with stress that they have little time for reflection. That single element is an asset to the therapeutic experience. Clinicians can model reflection by highlighting strengths, similarities, and differences in a nonjudgmental way and by asking rhetorical questions that incorporate the images and metaphors from the drawings (refer to Chapter 8 for more discussion of metaphors). These activities become the basis for assignments and interventions that use the material that the child and family have presented. Case 13 illustrates this process as part of a collaborative team.

Case 13 | Ray

Ray was a five-year-old African American boy who was living with his grandparents. He had come to the attention of his teacher and the school because of his angry outbursts. The most concerning event was when he struck another child's lunch tray, sending the dishes and food crashing to the floor. An art therapy-family therapy team was assigned to work with the boy and his family. On alternating weeks, the art therapist saw Ray at school and focused on drawings that would access his kinesthetic-sensory level, because his problems were described in terms of physical action. Using this level for art interventions provided a way to learn about Ray's perceptual-affective level of functioning. The therapist used Ray's drawings to discuss his feelings about his school relationships, the specific events leading up to his outbursts (antecedents), and eventually his feelings of loss, because he was not allowed contact with his mother due to her drug use. During other weeks, the family therapist met with the grandparents, highlighted their strengths, and helped them explore strategies that would help Ray with transitions in the family.

The art therapist explored Ray's drawings and learned that remarks were made before he hit the tray that left him with the impression that someone was criticizing him. The therapist helped Ray with other ways to express his hurt feelings. The teacher was also concerned with his lack of concentration in class, so the art therapist consulted with the teacher regarding strategies for helping Ray stay focused. They discovered that Ray's worst times occurred in the later morning, right before lunch. Box 9.1 illustrates how a consultant can obtain this information. The consultant helped the teacher brainstorm strategies for scheduling certain assignments for Ray during that time of day, such as help her with a task or go with her assistant to get supplies. However, the teacher expressed dismay at spending so much time on Ray when other children also deserved her attention. She had tired of the extra work he required and was not open to changes that would take more of her time. The consultant respected her position and explored what desired change would give her the most relief. They decided that delegating an assignment to her assistant during the later morning would be a compromise that could help her and Ray (win-win solution).

DEVELOPING A COLLABORATIVE TEAM

The preceding examples of collaboration came about because (a) physicians, educators, art therapists, and family therapists all recognized the value of working together on behalf of those who needed their services, and (b) the professionals were willing to change the way they practiced to improve clinical outcomes. Whereas good intentions and sacrifice are important to the success of collaboration, additional skills and abilities are also critical to cultivate. Here are some suggestions for successful collaborations:

- The therapist must develop good relationships with larger systems such as schools, hospitals, and social service agencies. A beginning therapist might call to make an appointment in order to learn more about the organization. In some special cases, it might be helpful for the therapist to offer a free workshop or consultation.
- Therapists should provide feedback to referral sources (school counselors, social workers, and so on) about current cases when clients have given their permission.
- Therapists should ask other professionals (collaborators) for their suggestions and ideas about cases. Would they be willing to provide assistance if asked?

In many settings (schools, hospitals, social service agencies, and mental health centers), the family is assigned to a case manager or team. Although the therapist treats the family, the case manager or team determines the nature of treatment. In these settings, the therapist might not have access to all family members nor have control over the welfare of the child. For example, in a school setting, the therapist does not have control over the educational plan for the child. The important issue here is how the therapist works with the team or network to empower the family.

A critical consideration is how the therapist can establish a collaborative relationship with team members to protect the boundaries of individual roles. Collaborative relationships are predicated largely on the problem solving process. Team members (teachers, social workers, ministers, friends, and others) are encouraged to identify specific problems and generate solutions. The therapist facilitates full participation from all team members. Working with team members as mutual partners within their prescribed roles, the therapist establishes mutual trust with the collaboration team. Finally, positive changes in the family are more likely to be maintained when team members are fully involved. Given the importance of collaboration, practitioners should become aware of potential barriers before organizing a collaborative team. The list in the following section will prepare practitioners to address these possibilities in a proactive way.

Obstacles to Collaboration

In preparing for collaboration, the beginning practitioner is advised to anticipate as many potential problems as possible (Amatea & Sherrard, 1989). Amatea and Sherrard (1991, p. 6) list the following obstacles to collaboration in school settings. Their original words appear in italics.

- *Educators and therapists are engaged in different systems and traditions, which often makes communication and team work problematic.* For example, educators often handle the needs of the school and community, which requires them to develop rules and expectations for that group. By contrast, therapists deal with the specific beliefs and patterns depicted by the family members before them.

- *Therapists can often become triangulated in the pattern of blaming and counter blaming between adults at home and school.* The school can often blame the therapist because the school perceives she or he is allied with the family. This may serve as an obstacle to working cooperatively with school personnel.

- *Many therapists are unfamiliar with school contexts and learning/schooling issues.* Unless they are willing to become active learners about the realities of school life and educational practice from educators, they will not be able to collaborate effectively.

- *The engagement of school personnel in addition to family members in the resolution of a child's problem requires a redefinition of traditional notions of family confidentiality and parameters as to what information is to be shared and with whom.*

- *Insurance reimbursement is not organized to fund collaborative team efforts between family therapists and school personnel.* Collaborative team efforts often require additional time that does not get reimbursed by the insurance carrier.

When these obstacles are overcome, the collaboration process may become an intervention that effects change on its own. At other times, the collaboration sets the stage for other interventions that relate to specific hypotheses formulated by the family therapist through ongoing assessment.

Guidelines for the Collaboration Team Interview

The collaboration team interview has evolved from the ecostructural model of Harry Aponte (1994a) and has been described more recently by O'Callaghan (1988) and Boyd-Franklin (1989). Brown and Vaccaro (1991) have developed a set of guidelines for the collaboration team based on these models (Box 9.6). The collaboration team interview is implemented currently with at-risk children and their families at public schools, social service agencies, and mental health centers.

The most essential consideration for the therapist in conducting the collaboration team interview is to remain neutral. Whether the therapist is inside or outside the system (school, social service agency, hospital, and so on), the therapist should not be identified too closely with any particular part of the team. For example, if a therapist is too close to the staff in a school, the therapist may have difficulty in remaining neutral and side with the school against the family. The position of neutrality allows the therapist the greatest latitude for effecting change. The family therapist can do several other things to maintain a collaborative relationship with team members:

- Try to understand the family problem and the way each team member perceives it. Inherent in this understanding is some discussion of the extent to which the problem is affecting the individual team members, as well as each

| Box 9.6 | Guidelines for Conducting a Family-School Collaboration Meeting |

1. Establish a positive climate for change by acknowledging each person's good intentions, contribution, and significance.

2. Summarize the purpose of the meeting.

3. Ask each participant to tell how he or she sees the problem.

4. Discuss the strengths of the child.

5. Suggest that participants tell what results they hope to see.

6. Decide how this can be accomplished. Who will do what? When?

7. Decide if other people need to be involved in the intervention.

8. Discuss obstacles to the intervention (e.g., lack of transportation, schedule conflicts).

9. Define how the participants will know if the intervention has been successful.

10. Determine if a follow-up meeting needs to be scheduled. If so, when?

team member's expectations for the family. In this context, the therapist can clarify the team members' biases and unrealistic expectations.

- Use the word "we" as consensus develops among the team members. The word *we* helps to build a sense of cooperation and support among team members. The therapist should avoid criticizing fellow team members.

- Suggest attempted solutions on the part of team members. Team members might want to refer the family to the family therapist without doing anything about the problem. For example, a school counselor might refer a child to a family therapist without attempting to address the problem itself. Unless the counselor has tried to solve the problem, the therapist might be unaware of its severity and uncertain of the school's commitment to do something about it. Moreover, if the counselor has intervened, the therapist needs to know the results of the attempted solution.

- Work with individuals within their prescribed roles. For example, classroom problems should be handled by the classroom teacher, behavior problems at home should be handled by the parents, and so on. Friends should be asked to provide support without usurping the executive role of parents. Respecting roles will help to establish a collaborative relationship with team members and avoid triangles and coalitions that interrupt the treatment plan.

Occasionally, the therapist might choose to shift to the role of advocate for a family if the family is having difficulty obtaining services or needs the weight of an expert to effect a change in the system. Sometimes therapists need to act as advocates for families, primarily around issues of educational placement, when appropriate procedures are not being followed or testing data are not being interpreted accurately to parents (similar to Case 11 in this chapter). But moving back to a more neutral stance as quickly as possible is preferable. In this way, parents can retain their sense of power and competence. Sometimes too much advocacy restricts the range of therapy and polarizes the therapist's role with school personnel.

SUMMARY

The increased emphasis on family preservation and home-based services has led to therapeutic practices characterized by collaboration between families and community organizations (schools, churches, and other agencies). The therapist must help families become aware of resources and support. Moreover, the therapist must move beyond simply making families aware of services and programs to helping them become effective and successful in accessing them. Using the metaphor of therapist as tour guide, as the family becomes more empowered with information and confidence to take action on its own behalf, the therapist can shift from driving the car to simply going along for the ride. Usually, this signals it is time to terminate therapeutic services.

As the beginning practitioner starts to implement assessment, treatment, and collaboration skills, confusion and anxiety inevitably set in, just as they do when you first learned to drive a car. This is a normal part of the learning process. However, when practitioners accumulate in-session experience, they are able to review their own therapeutic behavior, assessing what parts of the process might need attention—the therapeutic process is complex and fast-paced, and sometimes only in retrospect can we make sense of it. Professional growth often depends upon the therapists' willingness to reflect on the therapeutic process, which doesn't always conform to a step-by-step recipe. Instead, therapists must identify missing elements or possible options for improving the therapeutic experience. Though the elements of effective therapeutic practice discussed in this book have been reviewed as separate skills, these elements are rarely so distinct in practice.

I hope the developmental framework presented in this book will give you some starting points for examination of your own practice. After the basics are mastered, the territory differs from trip to trip. Many times, the driver must consider the needs of passengers in deciding how each adventure is approached, how each challenge is addressed, and what meaning will ultimately be given to the relationships that are encountered along the way. Other times, the therapist will be the passenger and not the driver. Still other times, the vehicle may be towed, ferried, or repaired as part of the experience. Just as the driver eventually arrives at some desired destination, the clinician enters the room, takes his or her best intentions, discovers the family's best intentions, and forms a partnership in which each side helps the other to travel their road just a little further. I hope your journey as a family therapist is filled with courage to enter the unknown, hope to believe in positive possibilities, and compassion to find value in the uniqueness of all people. Bon voyage!

> We shall not cease from exploration, and the end of all our exploring will be to arrive where we started and know the place for the first time.
>
> T.S. Eliot (1971)

A

APPENDIX | **AAMFT Code of Ethics**

Effective July 1, 2001

© *2002 American Association for Marriage and Family Therapy.* Reprinted with permission.

112 South Alfred Street, Alexandria, VA 22314

Phone: (703) 838-9808 - Fax: (703) 838-9805

The Board of Directors of the American Association for Marriage and Family Therapy (AAMFT) hereby promulgates, pursuant to Article 2, Section 2.013 of the Association's Bylaws, the Revised AAMFT Code of Ethics, effective July 1, 2001. The AAMFT strives to honor the public trust in marriage and family therapists by setting standards for ethical practice as described in this Code. The ethical standards define professional expectations and are enforced by the AAMFT Ethics Committee. The absence of an explicit reference to a specific behavior or situation in the Code does not mean that the behavior is ethical or unethical. The standards are not exhaustive. Marriage and family therapists who are uncertain about the ethics of a particular course of action are encouraged to seek counsel from consultants, attorneys, supervisors, colleagues, or other appropriate authorities.

Both law and ethics govern the practice of marriage and family therapy. When making decisions regarding professional behavior, marriage and family therapists must consider the AAMFT Code of Ethics and applicable laws and regulations. If the AAMFT Code of Ethics prescribes a standard higher than that required by law, marriage and family therapists must meet the higher standard of the AAMFT Code of Ethics. Marriage and family therapists comply with the mandates of law, but make known their commitment to the AAMFT Code of Ethics and take steps to resolve the conflict in a responsible manner. The AAMFT supports legal mandates for reporting of alleged unethical conduct. The AAMFT Code of Ethics is binding on Members of AAMFT in all membership categories, AAMFT-Approved Supervisors, and applicants for membership and the Approved Supervisor designation (hereafter, AAMFT Member). AAMFT members have an obligation to be familiar with the AAMFT Code of Ethics and its application to their professional services. Lack of awareness or misunderstanding of an ethical standard is not a defense to a charge of unethical conduct.

The process for filing, investigating, and resolving complaints of unethical conduct is described in the current Procedures for Handling Ethical Matters of the AAMFT Ethics Committee. Persons accused are considered innocent by the Ethics Committee until proven guilty, except as otherwise provided, and are entitled to due process. If an AAMFT Member resigns in anticipation of, or during the course of, an ethics investigation, the Ethics Committee will complete its investigation. Any publication of action taken by the Association will include the fact that the Member attempted to resign during the investigation.

CONTENTS

PRINCIPLE I: RESPONSIBILITY TO CLIENTS

Marriage and family therapists advance the welfare of families and individuals. They respect the rights of those persons seeking their assistance, and make reasonable efforts to ensure that their services are used appropriately.

1.1 Marriage and family therapists provide professional assistance to persons without discrimination on the basis of race, age, ethnicity, socioeconomic status, disability, gender, health status, religion, national origin, or sexual orientation.

1.2 Marriage and family therapists obtain appropriate informed consent to therapy or related procedures as early as feasible in the therapeutic relationship, and use language that is reasonably understandable to clients. The content of informed consent may vary depending upon the client and treatment plan; however, informed consent generally necessitates that the client: (a) has the capacity to consent; (b) has been adequately informed of significant information concerning treatment processes and procedures; (c) has been adequately informed of potential risks and benefits of treatments for which generally recognized standards do not yet exist; (d) has freely and without undue influence expressed consent; and (e) has provided consent that is appropriately documented. When persons, due to age or mental status, are legally incapable of giving informed consent, marriage and family therapists obtain informed permission from a legally authorized person, if such substitute consent is legally permissible.

1.3 Marriage and family therapists are aware of their influential positions with respect to clients, and they avoid exploiting the trust and dependency of such persons. Therapists, therefore, make every effort to avoid conditions and multiple relationships with clients that could impair professional judgment or increase the risk of exploitation. Such relationships include, but are not limited to, business or close personal relationships with a client or the client's immediate family. When the risk of impairment or exploitation exists due to conditions or multiple roles, therapists take appropriate precautions.

1.4 Sexual intimacy with clients is prohibited.

1.5 Sexual intimacy with former clients is likely to be harmful and is therefore prohibited for two years following the termination of therapy or last professional contact. In an effort to avoid exploiting the trust and dependency of clients, marriage and family therapists should not engage in sexual intimacy with former clients after the two years following termination or last professional contact. Should therapists engage in sexual intimacy with former clients following two years after termination or last professional contact, the burden shifts to the therapist to demonstrate that there has been no exploitation or injury to the former client or to the client's immediate family.

1.6 Marriage and family therapists comply with applicable laws regarding the reporting of alleged unethical conduct.

1.7 Marriage and family therapists do not use their professional relationships with clients to further their own interests.

1.8 Marriage and family therapists respect the rights of clients to make decisions and help them to understand the consequences of these decisions. Therapists clearly advise the clients that they have the responsibility to make decisions regarding relationships such as cohabitation, marriage, divorce, separation, reconciliation, custody, and visitation.

1.9 Marriage and family therapists continue therapeutic relationships only so long as it is reasonably clear that clients are benefiting from the relationship.

1.10 Marriage and family therapists assist persons in obtaining other therapeutic services if the therapist is unable or unwilling, for appropriate reasons, to provide professional help.

1.11 Marriage and family therapists do not abandon or neglect clients in treatment without making reasonable arrangements for the continuation of such treatment.

1.12 Marriage and family therapists obtain written informed consent from clients before videotaping, audio recording, or permitting third-party observation.

1.13 Marriage and family therapists, upon agreeing to provide services to a person or entity at the request of a third party, clarify, to the extent feasible and at the outset of the service, the nature of the relationship with each party and the limits of confidentiality.

PRINCIPLE II: CONFIDENTIALITY

Marriage and family therapists have unique confidentiality concerns because the client in a therapeutic relationship may be more than one person. Therapists respect and guard the confidences of each individual client.

2.1 Marriage and family therapists disclose to clients and other interested parties, as early as feasible in their professional contacts, the nature of confidentiality and possible limitations of the clients' right to confidentiality. Therapists review with clients the circumstances where confidential information may be requested and where disclosure of confidential information may be legally required. Circumstances may necessitate repeated disclosures.

2.2 Marriage and family therapists do not disclose client confidences except by written authorization or waiver, or where mandated or permitted by law. Verbal authorization will not be sufficient except in emergency situations, unless prohibited by law. When providing couple, family, or group treatment, the therapist does not disclose information outside the treatment context without a written authorization from each individual competent to execute a waiver. In the context of couple, family, or group treatment, the therapist may not reveal any individual's confidences to others in the client unit without the prior written permission of that individual.

2.3 Marriage and family therapists use client and/or clinical materials in teaching, writing, consulting, research, and public presentations only if a written waiver has been obtained in accordance with subprinciple 2.2, or when appropriate steps have been taken to protect client identity and confidentiality.

2.4 Marriage and family therapists store, safeguard, and dispose of client records in ways that maintain confidentiality and in accord with applicable laws and professional standards.

2.5 Subsequent to the therapist moving from the area, closing the practice, or upon the death of the therapist, a marriage and family therapist arranges for the storage, transfer, or disposal of client records in ways that maintain confidentiality and safeguard the welfare of clients.

2.6 Marriage and family therapists, when consulting with colleagues or referral sources, do not share confidential information that could reasonably lead to the identification of a client, research participant, supervisee, or other person with whom they have a confidential relationship unless they have obtained the prior written consent of the client, research participant, supervisee, or other person with whom they have a confidential relationship. Information may be shared only to the extent necessary to achieve the purposes of the consultation.

PRINCIPLE III: PROFESSIONAL COMPETENCE AND INTEGRITY

Marriage and family therapists maintain high standards of professional competence and integrity.

3.1 Marriage and family therapists pursue knowledge of new developments and maintain competence in marriage and family therapy through education, training, or supervised experience.

3.2 Marriage and family therapists maintain adequate knowledge of and adhere to applicable laws, ethics, and professional standards.

3.3 Marriage and family therapists seek appropriate professional assistance for their personal problems or conflicts that may impair work performance or clinical judgment.

3.4 Marriage and family therapists do not provide services that create a conflict of interest that may impair work performance or clinical judgment.

3.5 Marriage and family therapists, as presenters, teachers, supervisors, consultants and researchers, are dedicated to high standards of scholarship, present accurate information, and disclose potential conflicts of interest.

3.6 Marriage and family therapists maintain accurate and adequate clinical and financial records.

3.7 While developing new skills in specialty areas, marriage and family therapists take steps to ensure the competence of their work and to protect clients from possible harm. Marriage and family therapists practice in specialty areas new to them only after appropriate education, training, or supervised experience.

3.8 Marriage and family therapists do not engage in sexual or other forms of harassment of clients, students, trainees, supervisees, employees, colleagues, or research subjects.

3.9 Marriage and family therapists do not engage in the exploitation of clients, students, trainees, supervisees, employees, colleagues, or research subjects.

3.10 Marriage and family therapists do not give to or receive from clients (a) gifts of substantial value or (b) gifts that impair the integrity or efficacy of the therapeutic relationship.

3.11 Marriage and family therapists do not diagnose, treat, or advise on problems outside the recognized boundaries of their competencies.

3.12 Marriage and family therapists make efforts to prevent the distortion or misuse of their clinical and research findings.

3.13 Marriage and family therapists, because of their ability to influence and alter the lives of others, exercise special care when making public their professional recommendations and opinions through testimony or other public statements.

3.14 To avoid a conflict of interests, marriage and family therapists who treat minors or adults involved in custody or visitation actions may not also perform forensic evaluations for custody, residence, or visitation of the minor. The marriage and family therapist who treats the minor may provide the court or mental health professional performing the evaluation with information about the minor from the therapist's perspective as a treating marriage and family therapist, so long as the marriage and family therapist does not violate confidentiality.

3.15 Marriage and family therapists are in violation of this Code and subject to termination of membership or other appropriate action if they:

(a) are convicted of any felony; (b) are convicted of a misdemeanor related to their qualifications or functions; (c) engage in conduct which could lead to conviction of a felony, or a misdemeanor related to their qualifications or functions; (d) are expelled from or disciplined by other professional organizations; (e) have their licenses or certificates suspended or revoked or are otherwise disciplined by regulatory bodies; (f) continue to practice marriage and family therapy while no longer competent to do so because they are impaired by physical or mental causes or the abuse of alcohol or other substances; or (g) fail to cooperate with the Association at any point from the inception of an ethical complaint through the completion of all proceedings regarding that complaint.

PRINCIPLE IV: RESPONSIBILITY TO STUDENTS AND SUPERVISEES

Marriage and family therapists do not exploit the trust and dependency of students and supervisees.

4.1 Marriage and family therapists are aware of their influential positions with respect to students and supervisees, and they avoid exploiting the trust and dependency of such persons. Therapists, therefore, make every effort to avoid conditions and multiple relationships that could impair professional objectivity or increase the risk of exploitation. When the risk of impairment or exploitation exists due to conditions or multiple roles, therapists take appropriate precautions.

4.2 Marriage and family therapists do not provide therapy to current students or supervisees.

4.3 Marriage and family therapists do not engage in sexual intimacy with students or supervisees during the evaluative or training relationship between the therapist and student or supervisee. Should a supervisor engage in sexual activity with a former supervisee, the burden of proof shifts to the supervisor to demonstrate that there has been no exploitation or injury to the supervisee.

4.4 Marriage and family therapists do not permit students or supervisees to perform or to hold themselves out as competent to perform professional services beyond their training, level of experience, and competence.

4.5 Marriage and family therapists take reasonable measures to ensure that services provided by supervisees are professional.

4.6 Marriage and family therapists avoid accepting as supervisees or students those individuals with whom a prior or existing relationship could compromise the therapist's objectivity. When such situations cannot be avoided, therapists take appropriate precautions to maintain objectivity. Examples of such relationships include, but are not limited to, those individuals with whom the therapist has a current or prior sexual, close personal, immediate familial, or therapeutic relationship.

4.7 Marriage and family therapists do not disclose supervisee confidences except by written authorization or waiver, or when mandated or permitted by law. In educational or training settings where there are multiple supervisors, disclosures are permitted only to other professional colleagues, administrators, or employers who share responsibility for training of the supervisee. Verbal authorization will not be sufficient except in emergency situations, unless prohibited by law.

PRINCIPLE V: RESPONSIBILITY TO RESEARCH PARTICIPANTS

Investigators respect the dignity and protect the welfare of research participants, and are aware of applicable laws and regulations and professional standards governing the conduct of research.

5.1 Investigators are responsible for making careful examinations of ethical acceptability in planning studies. To the extent that services to research participants may be compromised by participation in research, investigators seek the ethical advice of qualified professionals not directly involved in the investigation and observe safeguards to protect the rights of research participants.

5.2 Investigators requesting participant involvement in research inform participants of the aspects of the research that might reasonably be expected to influence willingness to participate. Investigators are especially sensitive to the possibility of diminished consent when participants are also receiving clinical services, or have impairments which limit understanding and/or communication, or when participants are children.

5.3 Investigators respect each participant's freedom to decline participation in or to withdraw from a research study at any time. This obligation requires special thought and consideration when investigators or other members of the research team are in positions of authority or influence over participants. Marriage and family therapists, therefore, make every effort to avoid multiple relationships with research participants that could impair professional judgment or increase the risk of exploitation.

5.4 Information obtained about a research participant during the course of an investigation is confidential unless there is a waiver previously obtained in writing. When the possibility exists that others, including family members, may obtain access to such information, this possibility, together with the plan for protecting confidentiality, is explained as part of the procedure for obtaining informed consent.

PRINCIPLE VI: RESPONSIBILITY TO THE PROFESSION

Marriage and family therapists respect the rights and responsibilities of professional colleagues and participate in activities that advance the goals of the profession.

6.1 Marriage and family therapists remain accountable to the standards of the profession when acting as members or employees of organizations. If the mandates of an organization with which a marriage and family therapist is affiliated, through employment, contract or otherwise, conflict with the

AAMFT Code of Ethics, marriage and family therapists make known to the organization their commitment to the AAMFT Code of Ethics and attempt to resolve the conflict in a way that allows the fullest adherence to the Code of Ethics.

6.2 Marriage and family therapists assign publication credit to those who have contributed to a publication in proportion to their contributions and in accordance with customary professional publication practices.

6.3 Marriage and family therapists do not accept or require authorship credit for a publication based on research from a student's program, unless the therapist made a substantial contribution beyond being a faculty advisor or research committee member. Coauthorship on a student thesis, dissertation, or project should be determined in accordance with principles of fairness and justice.

6.4 Marriage and family therapists who are the authors of books or other materials that are published or distributed do not plagiarize or fail to cite persons to whom credit for original ideas or work is due.

6.5 Marriage and family therapists who are the authors of books or other materials published or distributed by an organization take reasonable precautions to ensure that the organization promotes and advertises the materials accurately and factually.

6.6 Marriage and family therapists participate in activities that contribute to a better community and society, including devoting a portion of their professional activity to services for which there is little or no financial return.

6.7 Marriage and family therapists are concerned with developing laws and regulations pertaining to marriage and family therapy that serve the public interest, and with altering such laws and regulations that are not in the public interest.

6.8 Marriage and family therapists encourage public participation in the design and delivery of professional services and in the regulation of practitioners.

PRINCIPLE VII: FINANCIAL ARRANGEMENTS

Marriage and family therapists make financial arrangements with clients, third-party payors, and supervisees that are reasonably understandable and conform to accepted professional practices.

7.1 Marriage and family therapists do not offer or accept kickbacks, rebates, bonuses, or other remuneration for referrals; fee-for-service arrangements are not prohibited.

7.2 Prior to entering into the therapeutic or supervisory relationship, marriage and family therapists clearly disclose and explain to clients and supervisees: (a) all financial arrangements and fees related to professional services, including charges for canceled or missed appointments; (b) the use of collection agencies or legal measures for nonpayment; and (c) the procedure for obtaining payment from the client, to the extent allowed by law, if payment is denied by the third-party payor. Once services have begun, therapists provide reasonable notice of any changes in fees or other charges.

7.3 Marriage and family therapists give reasonable notice to clients with unpaid balances of their intent to seek collection by agency or legal recourse. When such action is taken, therapists will not disclose clinical information.

7.4 Marriage and family therapists represent facts truthfully to clients, third-party payors, and supervisees regarding services rendered.

7.5 Marriage and family therapists ordinarily refrain from accepting goods and services from clients in return for services rendered. Bartering for professional services may be conducted only if: (a) the supervisee or client requests it, (b) the relationship is not exploitative, (c) the professional relationship is not distorted, and (d) a clear written contract is established.

7.6 Marriage and family therapists may not withhold records under their immediate control that are requested and needed for a client's treatment solely because payment has not been received for past services, except as otherwise provided by law.

PRINCIPLE VIII: ADVERTISING

Marriage and family therapists engage in appropriate informational activities, including those that enable the public, referral sources, or others to choose professional services on an informed basis.

8.1 Marriage and family therapists accurately represent their competencies, education, training, and experience relevant to their practice of marriage and family therapy.

8.2 Marriage and family therapists ensure that advertisements and publications in any media (such as directories, announcements, business cards, newspapers, radio, television, Internet, and facsimiles) convey information that is necessary for the public to make an appropriate selection of professional services. Information could include: (a) office information, such as name, address, telephone number, credit card acceptability, fees, languages spoken, and office hours; (b) qualifying clinical degree (see subprinciple 8.5); (c) other earned degrees (see subprinciple 8.5) and state or provincial licensures and/or certifications; (d) AAMFT clinical member status; and (e) description of practice.

8.3 Marriage and family therapists do not use names that could mislead the public concerning the identity, responsibility, source, and status of those practicing under that name, and do not hold themselves out as being partners or associates of a firm if they are not.

8.4 Marriage and family therapists do not use any professional identification (such as a business card, office sign, letterhead, Internet, or telephone or association directory listing) if it includes a statement or claim that is false, fraudulent, misleading, or deceptive.

8.5 In representing their educational qualifications, marriage and family therapists list and claim as evidence only those earned degrees: (a) from institutions accredited by regional accreditation sources recognized by the

United States Department of Education, (b) from institutions recognized by states or provinces that license or certify marriage and family therapists, or (c) from equivalent foreign institutions.

8.6 Marriage and family therapists correct, wherever possible, false, misleading, or inaccurate information and representations made by others concerning the therapist's qualifications, services, or products.

8.7 Marriage and family therapists make certain that the qualifications of their employees or supervisees are represented in a manner that is not false, misleading, or deceptive.

8.8 Marriage and family therapists do not represent themselves as providing specialized services unless they have the appropriate education, training, or supervised experience.

B
APPENDIX | # NASW Code of Ethics

Approved by the 1996 NASW Delegate Assembly and revised by the 1999 NASW Delegate Assembly

© 1999 National Association of Social Workers, Inc., NASW Code of Ethics.

PREAMBLE

The primary mission of the social work profession is to enhance human well-being and help meet the basic human needs of all people, with particular attention to the needs and empowerment of people who are vulnerable, oppressed, and living in poverty. A historic and defining feature of social work is the profession's focus on individual well-being in a social context and the well-being of society. Fundamental to social work is attention to the environmental forces that create, contribute to, and address problems in living.

Social workers promote social justice and social change with and on behalf of clients. "Clients" is used inclusively to refer to individuals, families, groups, organizations, and communities. Social workers are sensitive to cultural and ethnic diversity and strive to end discrimination, oppression, poverty, and other forms of social injustice. These activities may be in the form of direct practice, community organizing, supervision, consultation, administration, advocacy, social and political action, policy development and implementation, education, and research and evaluation. Social workers seek to enhance the capacity of people to address their own needs. Social workers also seek to promote the responsiveness of organizations, communities, and other social institutions to individuals' needs and social problems.

Source: Codes of Ethics for the Helping Professions 2007, Thomson, ISBN: 0495187178

The mission of the social work profession is rooted in a set of core values. These core values, embraced by social workers throughout the profession's history, are the foundation of social work's unique purpose and perspective:

- Service
- Social justice
- Dignity and worth of the person
- Importance of human relationships
- Integrity
- Competence

This constellation of core values reflects what is unique to the social work profession. Core values, and the principles that flow from them, must be balanced within the context and complexity of the human experience.

PURPOSE OF THE NASW CODE OF ETHICS

Professional ethics are at the core of social work. The profession has an obligation to articulate its basic values, ethical principles, and ethical standards. The *NASW Code of Ethics* sets forth these values, principles, and standards to guide social workers' conduct. The *Code* is relevant to all social workers and social work students, regardless of their professional functions, the settings in which they work, or the populations they serve.

The *NASW Code of Ethics* serves six purposes:

1. The *Code* identifies core values on which social work's mission is based.
2. The *Code* summarizes broad ethical principles that reflect the profession's core values and establishes a set of specific ethical standards that should be used to guide social work practice.
3. The *Code* is designed to help social workers identify relevant considerations when professional obligations conflict or ethical uncertainties arise.
4. The *Code* provides ethical standards to which the general public can hold the social work profession accountable.
5. The *Code* socializes practitioners new to the field to social work's mission, values, ethical principles, and ethical standards.
6. The *Code* articulates standards that the social work profession itself can use to assess whether social workers have engaged in unethical conduct. NASW has formal procedures to adjudicate ethics complaints filed against its members.* In subscribing to this *Code,* social workers are required to cooperate in its implementation, participate in NASW adjudication proceedings, and abide by any NASW disciplinary rulings or sanctions based on it.

The *Code* offers a set of values, principles, and standards to guide decision making and conduct when ethical issues arise. It does not provide a set of rules

---

*For information on NASW adjudication procedures, see *NASW Procedures for the Adjudication of Grievances.*

that prescribe how social workers should act in all situations. Specific applications of the *Code* must take into account the context in which it is being considered and the possibility of conflicts among the *Code*'s values, principles, and standards. Ethical responsibilities flow from all human relationships, from the personal and familial to the social and professional.

Further, the *NASW Code of Ethics* does not specify which values, principles, and standards are most important and ought to outweigh others in instances when they conflict. Reasonable differences of opinion can and do exist among social workers with respect to the ways in which values, ethical principles, and ethical standards should be rank ordered when they conflict. Ethical decision making in a given situation must apply the informed judgment of the individual social worker and should also consider how the issues would be judged in a peer review process where the ethical standards of the profession would be applied.

Ethical decision making is a process. There are many instances in social work where simple answers are not available to resolve complex ethical issues. Social workers should take into consideration all the values, principles, and standards in this *Code* that are relevant to any situation in which ethical judgment is warranted. Social workers' decisions and actions should be consistent with the spirit as well as the letter of this *Code*.

In addition to this *Code*, there are many other sources of information about ethical thinking that may be useful. Social workers should consider ethical theory and principles generally, social work theory and research, laws, regulations, agency policies, and other relevant codes of ethics, recognizing that among codes of ethics social workers should consider the *NASW Code of Ethics* as their primary source. Social workers also should be aware of the impact on ethical decision making of their clients' and their own personal values and cultural and religious beliefs and practices. They should be aware of any conflicts between personal and professional values and deal with them responsibly. For additional guidance social workers should consult the relevant literature on professional ethics and ethical decision making and seek appropriate consultation when faced with ethical dilemmas. This may involve consultation with an agency-based or social work organization's ethics committee, a regulatory body, knowledgeable colleagues, supervisors, or legal counsel.

Instances may arise when social workers' ethical obligations conflict with agency policies or relevant laws or regulations. When such conflicts occur, social workers must make a responsible effort to resolve the conflict in a manner that is consistent with the values, principles, and standards expressed in this *Code*. If a reasonable resolution of the conflict does not appear possible, social workers should seek proper consultation before making a decision.

The *NASW Code of Ethics* is to be used by NASW and by individuals, agencies, organizations, and bodies (such as licensing and regulatory boards, professional liability insurance providers, courts of law, agency boards of directors, government agencies, and other professional groups) that choose to adopt it or use it as a frame of reference. Violation of standards in this *Code* does not automatically imply legal liability or violation of the law. Such determination can only be made in the context of legal and judicial proceedings.

Alleged violations of the *Code* would be subject to a peer review process. Such processes are generally separate from legal or administrative procedures and insulated from legal review or proceedings to allow the profession to counsel and discipline its own members.

A code of ethics cannot guarantee ethical behavior. Moreover, a code of ethics cannot resolve all ethical issues or disputes or capture the richness and complexity involved in striving to make responsible choices within a moral community. Rather, a code of ethics sets forth values, ethical principles, and ethical standards to which professionals aspire and by which their actions can be judged. Social workers' ethical behavior should result from their personal commitment to engage in ethical practice. The *NASW Code of Ethics* reflects the commitment of all social workers to uphold the profession's values and to act ethically. Principles and standards must be applied by individuals of good character who discern moral questions and, in good faith, seek to make reliable ethical judgments.

ETHICAL PRINCIPLES

The following broad ethical principles are based on social work's core values of service, social justice, dignity and worth of the person, importance of human relationships, integrity, and competence. These principles set forth ideals to which all social workers should aspire.

Value: *Service*
Ethical Principle: Social workers' primary goal is to help people in need and to address social problems.

Social workers elevate service to others above self-interest. Social workers draw on their knowledge, values, and skills to help people in need and to address social problems. Social workers are encouraged to volunteer some portion of their professional skills with no expectation of significant financial return (pro bono service).

Value: Social Justice
Ethical Principle: Social workers challenge social injustice.

Social workers pursue social change, particularly with and on behalf of vulnerable and oppressed individuals and groups of people. Social workers' social change efforts are focused primarily on issues of poverty, unemployment, discrimination, and other forms of social injustice. These activities seek to promote sensitivity to and knowledge about oppression and cultural and ethnic diversity. Social workers strive to ensure access to needed information, services, and resources; equality of opportunity; and meaningful participation in decision making for all people.

Value: Dignity and Worth of the Person
Ethical Principle: Social workers respect the inherent dignity and worth of the person.

Social workers treat each person in a caring and respectful fashion, mindful of individual differences and cultural and ethnic diversity. Social workers promote clients' socially responsible self-determination. Social workers seek to enhance clients' capacity and opportunity to change and to address their own needs. Social workers are cognizant of their dual responsibility to clients and to the broader society. They seek to resolve conflicts between clients' interests and the broader society's interests in a socially responsible manner consistent with the values, ethical principles, and ethical standards of the profession.

Value: Importance of Human Relationships
Ethical Principle: Social workers recognize the central importance of human relationships.

Social workers understand that relationships between and among people are an important vehicle for change. Social workers engage people as partners in the helping process. Social workers seek to strengthen relationships among people in a purposeful effort to promote, restore, maintain, and enhance the well-being of individuals, families, social groups, organizations, and communities.

Value: Integrity
Ethical Principle: Social workers behave in a trustworthy manner.

Social workers are continually aware of the profession's mission, values, ethical principles, and ethical standards and practice in a manner consistent with them. Social workers act honestly and responsibly and promote ethical practices on the part of the organizations with which they are affiliated.

Value: Competence
Ethical Principle: Social workers practice within their areas of competence and develop and enhance their professional expertise.

Social workers continually strive to increase their professional knowledge and skills and to apply them in practice. Social workers should aspire to contribute to the knowledge base of the profession.

ETHICAL STANDARDS

The following ethical standards are relevant to the professional activities of all social workers. These standards concern (1) social workers' ethical responsibilities to clients, (2) social workers' ethical responsibilities to colleagues, (3) social workers' ethical responsibilities in practice settings, (4) social workers' ethical responsibilities as professionals, (5) social workers' ethical responsibilities to the social work profession, and (6) social workers' ethical responsibilities to the broader society.

Some of the standards that follow are enforceable guidelines for professional conduct, and some are aspirational. The extent to which each standard is enforceable is a matter of professional judgment to be exercised by those responsible for reviewing alleged violations of ethical standards.

1. Social Workers' Ethical Responsibilities to Clients

1.01 Commitment to Clients. Social workers' primary responsibility is to promote the well-being of clients. In general, clients' interests are primary. However, social workers' responsibility to the larger society or specific legal obligations may on limited occasions supersede the loyalty owed clients, and clients should be so advised. (Examples include when a social worker is required by law to report that a client has abused a child or has threatened to harm self or others.)

1.02 Self-Determination. Social workers respect and promote the right of clients to self-determination and assist clients in their efforts to identify and clarify their goals. Social workers may limit clients' right to self-determination when, in the social workers' professional judgment, clients' actions or potential actions pose a serious, foreseeable, and imminent risk to themselves or others.

1.03 Informed Consent

(a) Social workers should provide services to clients only in the context of a professional relationship based, when appropriate, on valid informed consent. Social workers should use clear and understandable language to inform clients of the purpose of the services, risks related to the services, limits to services because of the requirements of a third-party payer, relevant costs, reasonable alternatives, clients' right to refuse or withdraw consent, and the time frame covered by the consent. Social workers should provide clients with an opportunity to ask questions.

(b) In instances when clients are not literate or have difficulty understanding the primary language used in the practice setting, social workers should take steps to ensure clients' comprehension. This may include providing clients with a detailed verbal explanation or arranging for a qualified interpreter or translator whenever possible.

(c) In instances when clients lack the capacity to provide informed consent, social workers should protect clients' interests by seeking permission from an appropriate third party, informing clients consistent with the clients' level of understanding. In such instances social workers should seek to ensure that the third party acts in a manner consistent with clients' wishes and interests. Social workers should take reasonable steps to enhance such clients' ability to give informed consent.

(d) In instances when clients are receiving services involuntarily, social workers should provide information about the nature and extent of services and about the extent of clients' right to refuse service.

(e) Social workers who provide services via electronic media (such as computer, telephone, radio, and television) should inform recipients of the limitations and risks associated with such services.

(f) Social workers should obtain clients' informed consent before audiotaping or videotaping clients or permitting observation of services to clients by a third party.

1.04 Competence

(a) Social workers should provide services and represent themselves as competent only within the boundaries of their education, training, license, certification, consultation received, supervised experience, or other relevant professional experience.

(b) Social workers should provide services in substantive areas or use intervention techniques or approaches that are new to them only after engaging in appropriate study, training, consultation, and supervision from people who are competent in those interventions or techniques.

(c) When generally recognized standards do not exist with respect to an emerging area of practice, social workers should exercise careful judgment and take responsible steps (including appropriate education, research, training, consultation, and supervision) to ensure the competence of their work and to protect clients from harm.

1.05 Cultural Competence and Social Diversity

(a) Social workers should understand culture and its function in human behavior and society, recognizing the strengths that exist in all cultures.

(b) Social workers should have a knowledge base of their clients' cultures and be able to demonstrate competence in the provision of services that are sensitive to clients' cultures and to differences among people and cultural groups.

(c) Social workers should obtain education about and seek to understand the nature of social diversity and oppression with respect to race, ethnicity, national origin, color, sex, sexual orientation, age, marital status, political belief, religion, and mental or physical disability.

1.06 Conflicts of Interest

(a) Social workers should be alert to and avoid conflicts of interest that interfere with the exercise of professional discretion and impartial judgment. Social workers should inform clients when a real or potential conflict of interest arises and take reasonable steps to resolve the issue in a manner that makes the clients' interests primary and protects clients' interests to the greatest extent possible. In some cases, protecting clients' interests may require termination of the professional relationship with proper referral of the client.

(b) Social workers should not take unfair advantage of any professional relationship or exploit others to further their personal, religious, political, or business interests.

(c) Social workers should not engage in dual or multiple relationships with clients or former clients in which there is a risk of exploitation or potential harm to the client. In instances when dual or multiple relationships are unavoidable, social workers should take steps to protect clients and are responsible for setting clear, appropriate, and culturally sensitive boundaries.

(Dual or multiple relationships occur when social workers relate to clients in more than one relationship, whether professional, social, or business. Dual or multiple relationships can occur simultaneously or consecutively.)

(d) When social workers provide services to two or more people who have a relationship with each other (for example, couples, family members), social workers should clarify with all parties which individuals will be considered clients and the nature of social workers' professional obligations to the various individuals who are receiving services. Social workers who anticipate a conflict of interest among the individuals receiving services or who anticipate having to perform in potentially conflicting roles (for example, when a social worker is asked to testify in a child custody dispute or divorce proceedings involving clients) should clarify their role with the parties involved and take appropriate action to minimize any conflict of interest.

1.07 Privacy and Confidentiality

(a) Social workers should respect clients' right to privacy. Social workers should not solicit private information from clients unless it is essential to providing services or conducting social work evaluation or research. Once private information is shared, standards of confidentiality apply.

(b) Social workers may disclose confidential information when appropriate with valid consent from a client or a person legally authorized to consent on behalf of a client.

(c) Social workers should protect the confidentiality of all information obtained in the course of professional service, except for compelling professional reasons. The general expectation that social workers will keep information confidential does not apply when disclosure is necessary to prevent serious, foreseeable, and imminent harm to a client or other identifiable person. In all instances, social workers should disclose the least amount of confidential information necessary to achieve the desired purpose; only information that is directly relevant to the purpose for which the disclosure is made should be revealed.

(d) Social workers should inform clients, to the extent possible, about the disclosure of confidential information and the potential consequences, when feasible before the disclosure is made. This applies whether social workers disclose confidential information on the basis of a legal requirement or client consent.

(e) Social workers should discuss with clients and other interested parties the nature of confidentiality and limitations of clients' right to confidentiality. Social workers should review with clients circumstances where confidential information may be requested and where disclosure of confidential information may be legally required. This discussion should occur as soon as possible in the social worker-client relationship and as needed throughout the course of the relationship.

(f) When social workers provide counseling services to families, couples, or groups, social workers should seek agreement among the parties involved concerning each individual's right to confidentiality and obligation to preserve the confidentiality of information shared by others. Social workers should inform participants in family, couples, or group counseling that social workers cannot guarantee that all participants will honor such agreements.

(g) Social workers should inform clients involved in family, couples, marital, or group counseling of the social worker's, employer's, and agency's policy concerning the social worker's disclosure of confidential information among the parties involved in the counseling.

(h) Social workers should not disclose confidential information to third-party payers unless clients have authorized such disclosure.

(i) Social workers should not discuss confidential information in any setting unless privacy can be ensured. Social workers should not discuss confidential information in public or semipublic areas such as hallways, waiting rooms, elevators, and restaurants.

(j) Social workers should protect the confidentiality of clients during legal proceedings to the extent permitted by law. When a court of law or other legally authorized body orders social workers to disclose confidential or privileged information without a client's consent and such disclosure could cause harm to the client, social workers should request that the court withdraw the order or limit the order as narrowly as possible or maintain the records under seal, unavailable for public inspection.

(k) Social workers should protect the confidentiality of clients when responding to requests from members of the media.

(l) Social workers should protect the confidentiality of clients' written and electronic records and other sensitive information. Social workers should take reasonable steps to ensure that clients' records are stored in a secure location and that clients' records are not available to others who are not authorized to have access.

(m) Social workers should take precautions to ensure and maintain the confidentiality of information transmitted to other parties through the use of computers, electronic mail, facsimile machines, telephones and telephone answering machines, and other electronic or computer technology. Disclosure of identifying information should be avoided whenever possible.

(n) Social workers should transfer or dispose of clients' records in a manner that protects clients' confidentiality and is consistent with state statutes governing records and social work licensure.

(o) Social workers should take reasonable precautions to protect client confidentiality in the event of the social worker's termination of practice, incapacitation, or death.

(p) Social workers should not disclose identifying information when discussing clients for teaching or training purposes unless the client has consented to disclosure of confidential information.

(q) Social workers should not disclose identifying information when discussing clients with consultants unless the client has consented to disclosure of confidential information or there is a compelling need for such disclosure.

(r) Social workers should protect the confidentiality of deceased clients consistent with the preceding standards.

1.08 Access to Records

(a) Social workers should provide clients with reasonable access to records concerning the clients. Social workers who are concerned that clients' access to their records could cause serious misunderstanding or harm to the client should provide assistance in interpreting the records and consultation with the client regarding the records. Social workers should limit clients' access to their records, or portions of their records, only in exceptional circumstances when there is compelling evidence that such access would cause serious harm to the client. Both clients' requests and the rationale for withholding some or all of the record should be documented in clients' files.

(b) When providing clients with access to their records, social workers should take steps to protect the confidentiality of other individuals identified or discussed in such records.

1.09 Sexual Relationships

(a) Social workers should under no circumstances engage in sexual activities or sexual contact with current clients, whether such contact is consensual or forced.

(b) Social workers should not engage in sexual activities or sexual contact with clients' relatives or other individuals with whom clients maintain a close personal relationship when there is a risk of exploitation or potential harm to the client. Sexual activity or sexual contact with clients' relatives or other individuals with whom clients maintain a personal relationship has the potential to be harmful to the client and may make it difficult for the social worker and client to maintain appropriate professional boundaries. Social workers—not their clients, their clients' relatives, or other individuals with whom the client maintains a personal relationship—assume the full burden for setting clear, appropriate, and culturally sensitive boundaries.

(c) Social workers should not engage in sexual activities or sexual contact with former clients because of the potential for harm to the client. If social workers engage in conduct contrary to this prohibition or claim that an exception to this prohibition is warranted because of extraordinary circumstances, it is social workers—not their clients—who assume the full burden of demonstrating that the former client has not been exploited, coerced, or manipulated, intentionally or unintentionally.

(d) Social workers should not provide clinical services to individuals with whom they have had a prior sexual relationship. Providing clinical services to a former sexual partner has the potential to be harmful to the individual and is likely to make it difficult for the social worker and individual to maintain appropriate professional boundaries.

1.10 Physical Contact.   Social workers should not engage in physical contact with clients when there is a possibility of psychological harm to the client as a result of the contact (such as cradling or caressing clients). Social workers who engage in appropriate physical contact with clients are responsible for setting clear, appropriate, and culturally sensitive boundaries that govern such physical contact.

1.11 Sexual Harassment.   Social workers should not sexually harass clients. Sexual harassment includes sexual advances, sexual solicitation, requests for sexual favors, and other verbal or physical conduct of a sexual nature.

1.12 Derogatory Language.   Social workers should not use derogatory language in their written or verbal communications to or about clients. Social workers should use accurate and respectful language in all communications to and about clients.

1.13 Payment for Services
(a) When setting fees, social workers should ensure that the fees are fair, reasonable, and commensurate with the services performed. Consideration should be given to clients' ability to pay.
(b) Social workers should avoid accepting goods or services from clients as payment for professional services. Bartering arrangements, particularly involving services, create the potential for conflicts of interest, exploitation, and inappropriate boundaries in social workers' relationships with clients. Social workers should explore and may participate in bartering only in very limited circumstances when it can be demonstrated that such arrangements are an accepted practice among professionals in the local community, considered to be essential for the provision of services, negotiated without coercion, and entered into at the client's initiative and with the client's informed consent. Social workers who accept goods or services from clients as payment for professional services assume the full burden of demonstrating that this arrangement will not be detrimental to the client or the professional relationship.
(c) Social workers should not solicit a private fee or other remuneration for providing services to clients who are entitled to such available services through the social workers' employer or agency.

1.14 Clients Who Lack Decision-Making Capacity.   When social workers act on behalf of clients who lack the capacity to make informed decisions, social workers should take reasonable steps to safeguard the interests and rights of those clients.

1.15 Interruption of Services.   Social workers should make reasonable efforts to ensure continuity of services in the event that services are interrupted by factors such as unavailability, relocation, illness, disability, or death.

1.16 Termination of Services

(a) Social workers should terminate services to clients and professional relationships with them when such services and relationships are no longer required or no longer serve the clients' needs or interests.

(b) Social workers should take reasonable steps to avoid abandoning clients who are still in need of services. Social workers should withdraw services precipitously only under unusual circumstances, giving careful consideration to all factors in the situation and taking care to minimize possible adverse effects. Social workers should assist in making appropriate arrangements for continuation of services when necessary.

(c) Social workers in fee-for-service settings may terminate services to clients who are not paying an overdue balance if the financial contractual arrangements have been made clear to the client, if the client does not pose an imminent danger to self or others, and if the clinical and other consequences of the current nonpayment have been addressed and discussed with the client.

(d) Social workers should not terminate services to pursue a social, financial, or sexual relationship with a client.

(e) Social workers who anticipate the termination or interruption of services to clients should notify clients promptly and seek the transfer, referral, or continuation of services in relation to the clients' needs and preferences.

(f) Social workers who are leaving an employment setting should inform clients of appropriate options for the continuation of services and of the benefits and risks of the options.

2. Social Workers' Ethical Responsibilities to Colleagues

2.01 Respect

(a) Social workers should treat colleagues with respect and should represent accurately and fairly the qualifications, views, and obligations of colleagues.

(b) Social workers should avoid unwarranted negative criticism of colleagues in communications with clients or with other professionals. Unwarranted negative criticism may include demeaning comments that refer to colleagues' level of competence or to individuals' attributes such as race, ethnicity, national origin, color, sex, sexual orientation, age, marital status, political belief, religion, and mental or physical disability.

(c) Social workers should cooperate with social work colleagues and with colleagues of other professions when such cooperation serves the well-being of clients.

2.02 Confidentiality. Social workers should respect confidential information shared by colleagues in the course of their professional relationships and transactions. Social workers should ensure that such colleagues understand social workers' obligation to respect confidentiality and any exceptions related to it.

2.03 Interdisciplinary Collaboration

(a) Social workers who are members of an interdisciplinary team should participate in and contribute to decisions that affect the well-being of clients by drawing on the perspectives, values, and experiences of the social work profession. Professional and ethical obligations of the interdisciplinary team as a whole and of its individual members should be clearly established.

(b) Social workers for whom a team decision raises ethical concerns should attempt to resolve the disagreement through appropriate channels. If the disagreement cannot be resolved, social workers should pursue other avenues to address their concerns consistent with client well-being.

2.04 Disputes Involving Colleagues

(a) Social workers should not take advantage of a dispute between a colleague and an employer to obtain a position or otherwise advance the social workers' own interests.

(b) Social workers should not exploit clients in disputes with colleagues or engage clients in any inappropriate discussion of conflicts between social workers and their colleagues.

2.05 Consultation

(a) Social workers should seek the advice and counsel of colleagues whenever such consultation is in the best interests of clients.

(b) Social workers should keep themselves informed about colleagues' areas of expertise and competencies. Social workers should seek consultation only from colleagues who have demonstrated knowledge, expertise, and competence related to the subject of the consultation.

(c) When consulting with colleagues about clients, social workers should disclose the least amount of information necessary to achieve the purposes of the consultation.

2.06 Referral for Services

(a) Social workers should refer clients to other professionals when the other professionals' specialized knowledge or expertise is needed to serve clients fully or when social workers believe that they are not being effective or making reasonable progress with clients and that additional service is required.

(b) Social workers who refer clients to other professionals should take appropriate steps to facilitate an orderly transfer of responsibility. Social workers who refer clients to other professionals should disclose, with clients' consent, all pertinent information to the new service providers.

(c) Social workers are prohibited from giving or receiving payment for a referral when no professional service is provided by the referring social worker.

2.07 Sexual Relationships

(a) Social workers who function as supervisors or educators should not engage in sexual activities or contact with supervisees, students, trainees, or other colleagues over whom they exercise professional authority.

(b) Social workers should avoid engaging in sexual relationships with colleagues when there is potential for a conflict of interest. Social workers who become involved in, or anticipate becoming involved in, a sexual relationship with a colleague have a duty to transfer professional responsibilities, when necessary, to avoid a conflict of interest.

2.08 Sexual Harassment.

Social workers should not sexually harass supervisees, students, trainees, or colleagues. Sexual harassment includes sexual advances, sexual solicitation, requests for sexual favors, and other verbal or physical conduct of a sexual nature.

2.09 Impairment of Colleagues

(a) Social workers who have direct knowledge of a social work colleague's impairment that is due to personal problems, psychosocial distress, substance abuse, or mental health difficulties and that interferes with practice effectiveness should consult with that colleague when feasible and assist the colleague in taking remedial action.

(b) Social workers who believe that a social work colleague's impairment interferes with practice effectiveness and that the colleague has not taken adequate steps to address the impairment should take action through appropriate channels established by employers, agencies, NASW, licensing and regulatory bodies, and other professional organizations.

2.10 Incompetence of Colleagues

(a) Social workers who have direct knowledge of a social work colleague's incompetence should consult with that colleague when feasible and assist the colleague in taking remedial action.

(b) Social workers who believe that a social work colleague is incompetent and has not taken adequate steps to address the incompetence should take action through appropriate channels established by employers, agencies, NASW, licensing and regulatory bodies, and other professional organizations.

2.11 Unethical Conduct of Colleagues

(a) Social workers should take adequate measures to discourage, prevent, expose, and correct the unethical conduct of colleagues.

(b) Social workers should be knowledgeable about established policies and procedures for handling concerns about colleagues' unethical behavior. Social workers should be familiar with national, state, and local procedures for handling ethics complaints. These include policies and procedures created by NASW, licensing and regulatory bodies, employers, agencies, and other professional organizations.

(c) Social workers who believe that a colleague has acted unethically should seek resolution by discussing their concerns with the colleague when feasible and when such discussion is likely to be productive.

(d) When necessary, social workers who believe that a colleague has acted unethically should take action through appropriate formal channels (such as contacting a state licensing board or regulatory body, an NASW committee on inquiry, or other professional ethics committees).

(e) Social workers should defend and assist colleagues who are unjustly charged with unethical conduct.

3. Social Workers' Ethical Responsibilities in Practice Settings

3.01 Supervision and Consultation

(a) Social workers who provide supervision or consultation should have the necessary knowledge and skill to supervise or consult appropriately and should do so only within their areas of knowledge and competence.

(b) Social workers who provide supervision or consultation are responsible for setting clear, appropriate, and culturally sensitive boundaries.

(c) Social workers should not engage in any dual or multiple relationships with supervisees in which there is a risk of exploitation of or potential harm to the supervisee.

(d) Social workers who provide supervision should evaluate supervisees' performance in a manner that is fair and respectful.

3.02 Education and Training

(a) Social workers who function as educators, field instructors for students, or trainers should provide instruction only within their areas of knowledge and competence and should provide instruction based on the most current information and knowledge available in the profession.

(b) Social workers who function as educators or field instructors for students should evaluate students' performance in a manner that is fair and respectful.

(c) Social workers who function as educators or field instructors for students should take reasonable steps to ensure that clients are routinely informed when services are being provided by students.

(d) Social workers who function as educators or field instructors for students should not engage in any dual or multiple relationships with students in which there is a risk of exploitation or potential harm to the student. Social work educators and field instructors are responsible for setting clear, appropriate, and culturally sensitive boundaries.

3.03 Performance Evaluation. Social workers who have responsibility for evaluating the performance of others should fulfill such responsibility in a fair and considerate manner and on the basis of clearly stated criteria.

3.04 Client Records

(a) Social workers should take reasonable steps to ensure that documentation in records is accurate and reflects the services provided.
(b) Social workers should include sufficient and timely documentation in records to facilitate the delivery of services and to ensure continuity of services provided to clients in the future.
(c) Social workers' documentation should protect clients' privacy to the extent that is possible and appropriate and should include only information that is directly relevant to the delivery of services.
(d) Social workers should store records following the termination of services to ensure reasonable future access. Records should be maintained for the number of years required by state statutes or relevant contracts.

3.05 Billing. Social workers should establish and maintain billing practices that accurately reflect the nature and extent of services provided and that identify who provided the service in the practice setting.

3.06 Client Transfer

(a) When an individual who is receiving services from another agency or colleague contacts a social worker for services, the social worker should carefully consider the client's needs before agreeing to provide services. To minimize possible confusion and conflict, social workers should discuss with potential clients the nature of the clients' current relationship with other service providers and the implications, including possible benefits or risks, of entering into a relationship with a new service provider.
(b) If a new client has been served by another agency or colleague, social workers should discuss with the client whether consultation with the previous service provider is in the client's best interest.

3.07 Administration

(a) Social work administrators should advocate within and outside their agencies for adequate resources to meet clients' needs.
(b) Social workers should advocate for resource allocation procedures that are open and fair. When not all clients' needs can be met, an allocation procedure should be developed that is nondiscriminatory and based on appropriate and consistently applied principles.
(c) Social workers who are administrators should take reasonable steps to ensure that adequate agency or organizational resources are available to provide appropriate staff supervision.

(d) Social work administrators should take reasonable steps to ensure that the working environment for which they are responsible is consistent with and encourages compliance with the NASW Code of Ethics. Social work administrators should take reasonable steps to eliminate any conditions in their organizations that violate, interfere with, or discourage compliance with the Code.

3.08 Continuing Education and Staff Development. Social work administrators and supervisors should take reasonable steps to provide or arrange for continuing education and staff development for all staff for whom they are responsible. Continuing education and staff development should address current knowledge and emerging developments related to social work practice and ethics.

3.09 Commitments to Employers
(a) Social workers generally should adhere to commitments made to employers and employing organizations.
(b) Social workers should work to improve employing agencies' policies and procedures and the efficiency and effectiveness of their services.
(c) Social workers should take reasonable steps to ensure that employers are aware of social workers' ethical obligations as set forth in the NASW Code of Ethics and of the implications of those obligations for social work practice.
(d) Social workers should not allow an employing organization's policies, procedures, regulations, or administrative orders to interfere with their ethical practice of social work. Social workers should take reasonable steps to ensure that their employing organizations' practices are consistent with the NASW Code of Ethics.
(e) Social workers should act to prevent and eliminate discrimination in the employing organization's work assignments and in its employment policies and practices.
(f) Social workers should accept employment or arrange student field placements only in organizations that exercise fair personnel practices.
(g) Social workers should be diligent stewards of the resources of their employing organizations, wisely conserving funds where appropriate and never misappropriating funds or using them for unintended purposes.

3.10 Labor-Management Disputes
(a) Social workers may engage in organized action, including the formation of and participation in labor unions, to improve services to clients and working conditions.
(b) The actions of social workers who are involved in labor-management disputes, job actions, or labor strikes should be guided by the profession's values, ethical principles, and ethical standards. Reasonable differences of opinion exist among social workers concerning their primary obligation as

professionals during an actual or threatened labor strike or job action. Social workers should carefully examine relevant issues and their possible impact on clients before deciding on a course of action.

4. Social Workers' Ethical Responsibilities as Professionals

4.01 Competence

(a) Social workers should accept responsibility or employment only on the basis of existing competence or the intention to acquire the necessary competence.

(b) Social workers should strive to become and remain proficient in professional practice and the performance of professional functions. Social workers should critically examine and keep current with emerging knowledge relevant to social work. Social workers should routinely review the professional literature and participate in continuing education relevant to social work practice and social work ethics.

(c) Social workers should base practice on recognized knowledge, including empirically based knowledge, relevant to social work and social work ethics.

4.02 Discrimination. Social workers should not practice, condone, facilitate, or collaborate with any form of discrimination on the basis of race, ethnicity, national origin, color, sex, sexual orientation, age, marital status, political belief, religion, or mental or physical disability.

4.03 Private Conduct. Social workers should not permit their private conduct to interfere with their ability to fulfill their professional responsibilities.

4.04 Dishonesty, Fraud, and Deception. Social workers should not participate in, condone, or be associated with dishonesty, fraud, or deception.

4.05 Impairment

(a) Social workers should not allow their own personal problems, psychosocial distress, legal problems, substance abuse, or mental health difficulties to interfere with their professional judgment and performance or to jeopardize the best interests of people for whom they have a professional responsibility.

(b) Social workers whose personal problems, psychosocial distress, legal problems, substance abuse, or mental health difficulties interfere with their professional judgment and performance should immediately seek consultation and take appropriate remedial action by seeking professional help, making adjustments in workload, terminating practice, or taking any other steps necessary to protect clients and others.

4.06 Misrepresentation

(a) Social workers should make clear distinctions between statements made and actions engaged in as a private individual and as a representative of the social work profession, a professional social work organization, or the social worker's employing agency.

(b) Social workers who speak on behalf of professional social work organizations should accurately represent the official and authorized positions of the organizations.

(c) Social workers should ensure that their representations to clients, agencies, and the public of professional qualifications, credentials, education, competence, affiliations, services provided, or results to be achieved are accurate. Social workers should claim only those relevant professional credentials they actually possess and take steps to correct any inaccuracies or misrepresentations of their credentials by others.

4.07 Solicitations

(a) Social workers should not engage in uninvited solicitation of potential clients who, because of their circumstances, are vulnerable to undue influence, manipulation, or coercion.

(b) Social workers should not engage in solicitation of testimonial endorsements (including solicitation of consent to use a client's prior statement as a testimonial endorsement) from current clients or from other people who, because of their particular circumstances, are vulnerable to undue influence.

4.08 Acknowledging Credit

(a) Social workers should take responsibility and credit, including authorship credit, only for work they have actually performed and to which they have contributed.

(b) Social workers should honestly acknowledge the work of and the contributions made by others.

5. Social Workers' Ethical Responsibilities to the Social Work Profession

5.01 Integrity of the Profession

(a) Social workers should work toward the maintenance and promotion of high standards of practice.

(b) Social workers should uphold and advance the values, ethics, knowledge, and mission of the profession. Social workers should protect, enhance, and improve the integrity of the profession through appropriate study and research, active discussion, and responsible criticism of the profession.

(c) Social workers should contribute time and professional expertise to activities that promote respect for the value, integrity, and competence of the social work profession. These activities may include teaching, research, consultation, service, legislative testimony, presentations in the community, and participation in their professional organizations.

(d) Social workers should contribute to the knowledge base of social work and share with colleagues their knowledge related to practice, research, and ethics. Social workers should seek to contribute to the profession's literature and to share their knowledge at professional meetings and conferences.

(e) Social workers should act to prevent the unauthorized and unqualified practice of social work.

5.02 Evaluation and Research

(a) Social workers should monitor and evaluate policies, the implementation of programs, and practice interventions.

(b) Social workers should promote and facilitate evaluation and research to contribute to the development of knowledge.

(c) Social workers should critically examine and keep current with emerging knowledge relevant to social work and fully use evaluation and research evidence in their professional practice.

(d) Social workers engaged in evaluation or research should carefully consider possible consequences and should follow guidelines developed for the protection of evaluation and research participants. Appropriate institutional review boards should be consulted.

(e) Social workers engaged in evaluation or research should obtain voluntary and written informed consent from participants, when appropriate, without any implied or actual deprivation or penalty for refusal to participate; without undue inducement to participate; and with due regard for participants' well-being, privacy, and dignity. Informed consent should include information about the nature, extent, and duration of the participation requested and disclosure of the risks and benefits of participation in the research.

(f) When evaluation or research participants are incapable of giving informed consent, social workers should provide an appropriate explanation to the participants, obtain the participants' assent to the extent they are able, and obtain written consent from an appropriate proxy.

(g) Social workers should never design or conduct evaluation or research that does not use consent procedures, such as certain forms of naturalistic observation and archival research, unless rigorous and responsible review of the research has found it to be justified because of its prospective scientific, educational, or applied value and unless equally effective alternative procedures that do not involve waiver of consent are not feasible.

(h) Social workers should inform participants of their right to withdraw from evaluation and research at any time without penalty.

(i) Social workers should take appropriate steps to ensure that participants in evaluation and research have access to appropriate supportive services.

(j) Social workers engaged in evaluation or research should protect participants from unwarranted physical or mental distress, harm, danger, or deprivation.

(k) Social workers engaged in the evaluation of services should discuss collected information only for professional purposes and only with people professionally concerned with this information.

(l) Social workers engaged in evaluation or research should ensure the anonymity or confidentiality of participants and of the data obtained from them. Social workers should inform participants of any limits of confidentiality, the measures that will be taken to ensure confidentiality, and when any records containing research data will be destroyed.

(m) Social workers who report evaluation and research results should protect participants' confidentiality by omitting identifying information unless proper consent has been obtained authorizing disclosure.

(n) Social workers should report evaluation and research findings accurately. They should not fabricate or falsify results and should take steps to correct any errors later found in published data using standard publication methods.

(o) Social workers engaged in evaluation or research should be alert to and avoid conflicts of interest and dual relationships with participants, should inform participants when a real or potential conflict of interest arises, and should take steps to resolve the issue in a manner that makes participants' interests primary.

(p) Social workers should educate themselves, their students, and their colleagues about responsible research practices.

6. Social Workers' Ethical Responsibilities to the Broader Society

6.01 Social Welfare. Social workers should promote the general welfare of society, from local to global levels, and the development of people, their communities, and their environments. Social workers should advocate for living conditions conducive to the fulfillment of basic human needs and should promote social, economic, political, and cultural values and institutions that are compatible with the realization of social justice.

6.02 Public Participation. Social workers should facilitate informed participation by the public in shaping social policies and institutions.

6.03 Public Emergencies. Social workers should provide appropriate professional services in public emergencies to the greatest extent possible.

6.04 Social and Political Action

(a) Social workers should engage in social and political action that seeks to ensure that all people have equal access to the resources, employment, services, and opportunities they require to meet their basic human needs and to develop fully. Social workers should be aware of the impact of the political arena on practice and should advocate for changes in policy and legislation to improve social conditions in order to meet basic human needs and promote social justice.

(b) Social workers should act to expand choice and opportunity for all people, with special regard for vulnerable, disadvantaged, oppressed, and exploited people and groups.

(c) Social workers should promote conditions that encourage respect for cultural and social diversity within the United States and globally. Social workers should promote policies and practices that demonstrate respect for difference, support the expansion of cultural knowledge and resources, advocate for programs and institutions that demonstrate cultural competence, and promote policies that safeguard the rights of and confirm equity and social justice for all people.

(d) Social workers should act to prevent and eliminate domination of, exploitation of, and discrimination against any person, group, or class on the basis of race, ethnicity, national origin, color, sex, sexual orientation, age, marital status, political belief, religion, or mental or physical disability.

C APPENDIX | Ethics At-Risk Test for Marriage and Family Therapists

Ever wonder how close you are to blundering over the ethics edge and possibly harming your clients, yourself, and/or the profession? The At-Risk Test may tell you. Of course, you must answer honestly. Add up your score and compare the total with the key at the end.

1. Is it true that you have *never* taken an academic course on MFT practice ethics? — No = 0 — Yes = 1

2. Honestly, are you *unfamiliar* with some parts of the latest version of our Ethics Code? — No = 0 — Yes = 1

3. Do you think our Ethics Code *interferes* somewhat with the quality of your therapy, research, or supervision? — No = 0 — Yes = 1

4. Have you *ever* sent a false bill for therapy to an insurance carrier? — No = 0 — Yes = 1

5. Do you feel sexually attracted to any of your *present* clients? — No = 0 — Yes = 1

6. Do you fantasize about kissing or touching a *present* client? — No = 0 — Yes = 1

7. Do you comment to a *present* client how attractive he or she is or make positive remarks about his or her body? — No = 0 — Yes = 1

8. Are you tempted to ask out an ex-client even though less than 2 years have passed since termination? — No = 0 — Yes = 1

9. Do you commonly take off your jewelry, remove shoes, loosen your tie, or otherwise become more informal during therapy sessions? — No = 0 — Yes = 1

10. *Presently,* do you meet a client for coffee or meals or for socializing outside of therapy? — No = 0 — Yes = 1

11. Has a *present* client given you an expensive gift or frequently given you inexpensive gifts? No = 0   Yes = 1

12. Are you stimulated by a *current* client's description of sexual behavior or thoughts? No = 0   Yes = 1

13. Are you in the midst of a difficult personal or family crisis yourself? No = 0   Yes = 1

14. During the past 2 months, have you seen clients while you were hung over or under the influence of drugs, even if only a little? No = 0   Yes = 1

15. Does your personal financial situation cross your mind when considering whether to terminate therapy or to refer a client? No = 0   Yes = 1

16. Do you feel manipulated by a *current* client such that you are wary of him/her or are angry and frustrated by him/her? No = 0   Yes = 1

17. Do you provide therapy to a *current* student, supervisee, or employee? No = 0   Yes = 1

18. Have you wanted to talk to a colleague about a *current* case but feared doing so would show your lack of skill or might lead to an ethics case against you? No = 0   Yes = 1

19. Are you behind on case notes? No = 0   Yes = 1

20. Do you talk about clients with other clients or gossip about clients with colleagues? No = 0   Yes = 1

0   Excellent, you are nearly risk free.

1–2   Review your practice. Read and follow the Ethics Code.

3–4   Review your practice for problem areas. Consider needed changes.

5–7   Consult a supervisor. You are engaging in high-risk behavior.

8+   Probably you are harming your clients and/or yourself. Seek therapy and supervision. Come to terms with your situation by making immediate changes.

Table by Gregory Brock

The items making up the Ethics At-Risk Test come from research and from Ethics Committee case experience. Send your comments and questions to Gregory Brock, PhD, 315 Funkhouser Building, University of Kentucky, Lexington, KY 40506-0054, U.S.A. Permission is granted to copy, distribute, or publish the At-Risk Test with credit given for authorship.

APPENDIX

Films of Interest to Students of Family Therapy

Some films have several themes. Those are listed in more than one category due to the complexity of the plot and characters.

AGING/DEATH
About Schmidt
Avalon
Beyond Rangoon
Brian's Song
Cocoon
Cocoon: The Return
Dad
Dying Young
Folks
Fried Green Tomatoes
Harry & Tonto
Iris
Life Is Beautiful
Moonstruck
My Life
On Golden Pond
Shadowlands
Steel Magnolias
Stepmom
The Straight Story
Strangers in Good
   Company
Terms of Endearment
The Doctor
The War
With Honors

ADOLESCENTS
Back to the Future
Billy Jack
Edge of America
Lucas
Ordinary People
Running on Empty
Sixteen Candles
Smoke Signals
Stand and Deliver
Swing Kids
The Great Santini
The Karate Kid
Thirteen
To Sir With Love
With Honors

CHILDREN
Grand Canyon
The Hours
Mr. Mom
My Life as a Dog
The Parent Trap
Shadowlands
The Education of Little
   Tree
The Sandlot

Stand By Me
The War
To Kill a Mockingbird
What's Eating Gilbert
   Grape

CULTURE
About Schmidt
American Me
A Stranger Among Us
Avalon
Beyond Rangoon
Billy Jack
Girl, Interrupted
Get On the Bus
Edge of America
The Joy Luck
   Club
Moonstruck
October Sky
Real Women Have
   Curves
Smoke Signals
Sophie's Choice
The Education of Little
   Tree
The Chosen

To Sir With Love
Tortilla Soup

DIVORCE
Kramer vs. Kramer
Music of the Heart
Mr. Mom
Mrs. Doubtfire
The Parent Trap
The Squid and the
  Whale
The War of the Roses

GENDER
Brian's Song
Fried Green Tomatoes
The Full Monty
Lakota Woman: Siege
  at Wounded Knee
Moonstruck
Nuts
Ordinary People
Real Women Have
  Curves
Shallow Hal
Strangers in Good
  Company
Terms of Endearment
This Boy's Life
Waiting to Exhale

INTERGENERA-
TIONAL
Autumn Sonata
Avalon
Born on the Fourth
  of July
Catch Me If You Can
Divine Secrets of the
  Ya-Ya Sisterhood
Joy Luck Club
Nixon
Nuts
Shine
Smoke Signals

Soul Food
This Boy's Life
Tortilla Soup
What's Eating Gilbert
  Grape
You Can Count On Me

LAUNCHING
About Schmidt
Betsy's Wedding
Father of the Bride
Guess Who's Coming
  to Dinner?
Moonstruck
October Sky
Steel Magnolias

MARRIAGE
A Beautiful Mind
Barefoot in the Park
Best Intentions
Chapter 2 (Remarriage)
Enchanted April
Goodbye Girl
Hannah & Her Sisters
The Hours
Prelude to a Kiss
Scenes from a Marriage
Shadowlands
The Story of Us
Who's Afraid of
  Virginia Woolf?

MENTAL ILLNESS
A Beautiful Mind
Girl, Interrupted
The Hours
Nuts
Ordinary People

STEP-FAMILIES &
REMARRIAGE
Chapter Two
Emmy & Alexander
Shadowlands

Stepmom
This Boy's Life
Tortilla Soup
With Six You Get
  Eggroll
Yours, Mine & Ours

RACE
American Me
A Soldier's Story
Beloved
Beyond Borders
Billy Jack
Brian's Song
Boyz N the Hood
Crash
Cry Freedom
Devil's Arithmetic
Do the Right Thing
Guess Who's Coming
  to Dinner?
Jungle Fever
Lakota Woman: Siege
  at Wounded Knee
Malcolm X
Roots
School Ties
Swing Kids
To Kill a Mockingbird
Waiting to Exhale

UNATTACHED
ADULTS
An Officer & A
  Gentleman
Autumn Sonata
Bull Durham
Frankie & Johnny
Pretty Woman
Stanley & Iris
The Graduate
Waiting to Exhale
When Harry Met
  Sally
You've Got Mail

E

Global Assessment of Relational Functioning (GARF)

INSTRUCTIONS

The GARF Scale can be used to indicate an overall judgment of the functioning of a family or other ongoing relationship on a hypothetical continuum ranging from competent, optimal relational functioning to a disrupted, dysfunctional relationship. It is analogous to Axis V (Global Assessment of Functioning Scale) provided for individuals in DSM-IV. The GARF Scale permits the clinician to rate the degree to which a family or other ongoing relational unit meets the affective or instrumental needs of its members in the following areas:

A. *Problem solving*—skills in negotiating goals, rules, and routines; adaptability to stress; communication skills; ability to resolve conflict
B. *Organization*—maintenance of interpersonal roles and subsystem boundaries; hierarchical functioning; coalitions and distribution of power, control, and responsibility
C. *Emotional climate*—tone and range of feelings; quality of caring, empathy, involvement, and attachment/commitment; sharing of values; mutual affective responsiveness, respect, and regard; quality of sexual functioning

In most instances, the GARF Scale should be used to rate functioning during the current period (i.e., the level of relational functioning at the time of the evaluation). In some settings, the GARF Scale may also be used to rate functioning for other time periods (i.e., the highest level of relational functioning for at least a few months during the past year).

Note: Use specific, intermediate codes when possible, for example, 45, 68, 72. If detailed information is not adequate to make specific ratings, use midpoints of the five ranges, that is, 90, 70, 50, 30, or 10.

81–100 OVERALL

Relational unit is functioning satisfactorily from self-report of participants and from perspectives of observers.

Agreed-on patterns or routines exist that help meet the usual needs of each family/couple member; there is flexibility for change in response to unusual demands or events; and occasional conflicts and stressful transitions are resolved through problem-solving communication and negotiation.

There is a shared understanding and agreement about roles and appropriate tasks, decision making is established for each functional area, and there is recognition of the unique characteristics and merit of each subsystem (e.g., parents/spouses, siblings, and individuals).

There is a situationally appropriate, optimistic atmosphere in the family; a wide range of feelings is freely expressed and managed within the family; and there is a general atmosphere of warmth, caring, and sharing of values among all family members. Sexual relations of adult members are satisfactory.

61–80 OVERALL

Functioning of relational unit is somewhat unsatisfactory. Over a period of time, many but not all difficulties are resolved without complaints.

Daily routines are present, but there is some pain and difficulty in responding to the unusual. Some conflicts remain unresolved but do not disrupt family functioning.

Decision making is usually competent, but efforts at control of one another quite often are greater than necessary or are ineffective. Individuals and relationships are clearly demarcated but sometimes a specific subsystem is depreciated or scapegoated.

A range of feeling is expressed, but instances of emotional blocking or tension are evident. Warmth and caring are present but are marred by a family member's irritability and frustrations. Sexual activity of adult members may be reduced or problematic.

41–60 OVERALL

Relational unit has occasional times of satisfying and competent functioning together, but clearly dysfunctional, unsatisfying relationships tend to predominate.

Communication is frequently inhibited by unresolved conflicts that often interfere with daily routines; there is significant difficulty in adapting to family stress and transitional change.

Decision making is only intermittently competent and effective; either excessive rigidity or significant lack of structure is evident at these times. Individual needs are quite often submerged by a partner or coalition.

Pain or ineffective anger or emotional deadness interferes with family enjoyment. Although there is some warmth and support for members, it is usually unequally distributed. Troublesome sexual difficulties between adults are often present.

21–40 OVERALL

Relational unit is obviously and seriously dysfunctional; forms and time periods of satisfactory relating are rare.

Family/couple routines do not meet the needs of members; they are grimly adhered to or blithely ignored. Life cycle changes, such as departures or entries into the relational unit, generate painful conflict and obviously frustrating failures of problem solving.

Decision making is tyrannical or quite ineffective. The unique characteristics of individuals are unappreciated or ignored by either rigid or confusingly fluid coalitions.

There are infrequent periods of enjoyment of life together; frequent distancing or open hostility reflects significant conflicts that remain unresolved and quite painful. Sexual dysfunction among adult members is commonplace.

1–20 OVERALL

Relational unit has become too dysfunctional to retain continuity of contact and attachment.

Family/couple routines are negligible (e.g., no mealtime, sleeping, or waking schedule); family members often do not know where others are or when they will be in or out; there is little effective communication among family members.

Family/couple members are not organized in such a way that personal or generational responsibilities are recognized. Boundaries of relational unit as a whole and subsystems cannot be identified or agreed on. Family members are physically endangered or injured or sexually attacked.

Despair and cynicism are pervasive; there is little attention to the emotional needs of others; there is almost no sense of attachment, commitment, or concern about one another's welfare.

0

Inadequate information.

Marriage and Family Therapy Core Competencies

The marriage and family therapy (MFT) core competencies were developed through a collaborative effort of the American Association for Marriage and Family Therapy (AAMFT) and interested stakeholders. In addition to defining the domains of knowledge and requisite skills in each domain that comprise the practice of marriage and family therapy, the ultimate goal of the core competencies is to improve the quality of services delivered by marriage and family therapists (MFTs). Consequently, the competencies described herein represent the minimum that MFTs licensed to practice independently must possess.

Creating competencies for MFTs and improving the quality of mental health services was considered in the context of the broader behavioral health system. The AAMFT relied on three important reports to provide the framework within which the competencies would be developed: *Mental Health: A Report of the Surgeon General*; the President's New Freedom Commission on Mental Health's *Achieving the Promise: Transforming Mental Health Care in America*; and the Institute of Medicine's *Crossing the Quality Chasm*. The AAMFT mapped the competencies to critical elements of these reports, including IOM's 6 Core Values that are seen as the foundation for a better health care system: 1) Safe, 2) Person-Centered, 3) Efficient, 4) Effective, 5) Timely, and 6) Equitable. The committee also considered how social, political, historical, and economic forces affect individual and relational problems and decisions about seeking and obtaining treatment.

The core competencies were developed for educators, trainers, regulators, researchers, policymakers, and the public. The current version has 128 competencies; however, these are likely to be modified as the field of family therapy develops and as the needs of clients change. The competencies will be reviewed

Source: American Association for Marriage and Family Therapy.
http://www.aamft.org/resources/MFT_Core_Competencies/CC_Intro_NM.asp

and modified at regular intervals to ensure the competencies are reflective of the current and best practice of MFT.

The core competencies are organized around 6 primary domains and 5 secondary domains. The primary domains are:

1. **Admission to Treatment** – All interactions between clients and therapist up to the point when a therapeutic contract is established.
2. **Clinical Assessment and Diagnosis** – Activities focused on the identification of the issues to be addressed in therapy.
3. **Treatment Planning and Case Management** – All activities focused on directing the course of therapy and extra-therapeutic activities.
4. **Therapeutic Interventions** – All activities designed to ameliorate the clinical issues identified.
5. **Legal Issues, Ethics, and Standards** – All aspects of therapy that involve statutes, regulations, principles, values, and mores of MFTs.
6. **Research and Program Evaluation** – All aspects of therapy that involve the systematic analysis of therapy and how it is conducted effectively.

The subsidiary domains are focused on the types of skills or knowledge that MFTs must develop. These are: a) Conceptual, b) Perceptual, c) Executive, d) Evaluative, and e) Professional.

Although not expressly written for each competency, the stem "Marriage and family therapists . . ." should begin each. Additionally, the term "client" is used broadly and refers to the therapeutic system of the client/s served, which includes, but is not limited to individuals, couples, families, and others with a vested interest in helping clients change. Similarly, the term "family" is used generically to refer to all people identified by clients as part of their "family system," this would include fictive kin and relationships of choice. Finally, the core competencies encompass behaviors, skills, attitudes, and policies that promote awareness, acceptance, and respect for differences, enhance services that meet the needs of diverse populations, and promote resiliency and recovery.

Domain 1 | Admission to Treatment

Number	Subdomain	Competence
1.1.1	Conceptual	Understand systems concepts, theories, and techniques that are foundational to the practice of marriage and family therapy.
1.1.2	Conceptual	Understand theories and techniques of individual, marital, couple, family, and group psychotherapy.
1.1.3	Conceptual	Understand the behavioral health care delivery system, its impact on the services provided, and the barriers and disparities in the system.

(Continued)

Domain 1 | Admission to Treatment (continued)

Number	Subdomain	Competence
1.1.4	Conceptual	Understand the risks and benefits of individual, marital, couple, family, and group psychotherapy.
1.2.1	Perceptual	Recognize contextual and systemic dynamics (e.g., gender, age, socioeconomic status, culture/race/ethnicity, sexual orientation, spirituality, religion, larger systems, social context).
1.2.2	Perceptual	Consider health status, mental status, other therapy, and other systems involved in the clients' lives (e.g., courts, social services).
1.2.3	Perceptual	Recognize issues that might suggest referral for specialized evaluation, assessment, or care.
1.3.1	Executive	Gather and review intake information, giving balanced attention to individual, family, community, cultural, and contextual factors.
1.3.2	Executive	Determine who should attend therapy and in what configuration (e.g., individual, couple, family, extrafamilial resources).
1.3.3	Executive	Facilitate therapeutic involvement of all necessary participants in treatment.
1.3.4	Executive	Explain practice setting rules, fees, rights, and responsibilities of each party, including privacy, confidentiality policies, and duty to care to client or legal guardian.
1.3.5	Executive	Obtain consent to treatment from all responsible persons.
1.3.6	Executive	Establish and maintain appropriate and productive therapeutic alliances with the clients.
1.3.7	Executive	Solicit and use client feedback throughout the therapeutic process.
1.3.8	Executive	Develop and maintain collaborative working relationships with referral resources, other practitioners involved in the clients' care, and payers.
1.3.9	Executive	Manage session interactions with individuals, couples, families, and groups.
1.4.1	Evaluative	Evaluate case for appropriateness for treatment within professional scope of practice and competence.
1.5.1	Professional	Understand the legal requirements and limitations for working with vulnerable populations (e.g., minors).
1.5.2	Professional	Complete case documentation in a timely manner and in accordance with relevant laws and policies.
1.5.3	Professional	Develop, establish, and maintain policies for fees, payment, record keeping, and confidentiality.

Domain 2 | Clinical Assessment and Diagnosis

Number	Subdomain	Competence
2.1.1	Conceptual	Understand principles of human development; human sexuality; gender development; psychopathology; psychopharmacology; couple processes; and family development and processes (e.g., family, relational, and system dynamics).
2.1.2	Conceptual	Understand the major behavioral health disorders, including the epidemiology, etiology, phenomenology, effective treatments, course, and prognosis.
2.1.3	Conceptual	Understand the clinical needs and implications of persons with comorbid disorders (e.g., substance abuse and mental health; heart disease and depression).
2.1.4	Conceptual	Comprehend individual, marital, couple and family assessment instruments appropriate to presenting problem, practice setting, and cultural context.
2.1.5	Conceptual	Understand the current models for assessment and diagnosis of mental health disorders, substance use disorders, and relational functioning.
2.1.6	Conceptual	Understand the strengths and limitations of the models of assessment and diagnosis, especially as they relate to different cultural, economic, and ethnic groups.
2.1.7	Conceptual	Understand the concepts of reliability and validity, their relationship to assessment instruments, and how they influence therapeutic decision making.
2.2.1	Perceptual	Assess each clients' engagement in the change process.
2.2.2	Perceptual	Systematically integrate client reports, observations of client behaviors, client relationship patterns, reports from other professionals, results from testing procedures, and interactions with client to guide the assessment process.
2.2.3	Perceptual	Develop hypotheses regarding relationship patterns, their bearing on the presenting problem, and the influence of extra-therapeutic factors on client systems.
2.2.4	Perceptual	Consider the influence of treatment on extra-therapeutic relationships.
2.2.5	Perceptual	Consider physical/organic problems that can cause or exacerbate emotional/interpersonal symptoms.
2.3.1	Executive	Diagnose and assess client behavioral and relational health problems systemically and contextually.
2.3.2	Executive	Provide assessments and deliver developmentally appropriate services to clients, such as children, adolescents, elders, and persons with special needs.

(Continued)

Domain 2 | Clinical Assessment and Diagnosis (continued)

Number	Subdomain	Competence
2.3.3	Executive	Apply effective and systemic interviewing techniques and strategies.
2.3.4	Executive	Administer and interpret results of assessment instruments.
2.3.5	Executive	Screen and develop adequate safety plans for substance abuse, child and elder maltreatment, domestic violence, physical violence, suicide potential, and dangerousness to self and others.
2.3.6	Executive	Assess family history and dynamics using a genogram or other assessment instruments.
2.3.7	Executive	Elicit a relevant and accurate biopsychosocial history to understand the context of the clients' problems.
2.3.8	Executive	Identify clients' strengths, resilience, and resources.
2.3.9	Executive	Elucidate presenting problem from the perspective of each member of the therapeutic system.
2.4.1	Evaluative	Evaluate assessment methods for relevance to clients' needs.
2.4.2	Evaluative	Assess ability to view issues and therapeutic processes systemically.
2.4.3	Evaluative	Evaluate the accuracy and cultural relevance of behavioral health and relational diagnoses.
2.4.4	Evaluative	Assess the therapist-client agreement of therapeutic goals and diagnosis.
2.5.1	Professional	Utilize consultation and supervision effectively.

Domain 3 | Treatment Planning and Case Management

Number	Subdomain	Competence
3.1.1	Conceptual	Know which models, modalities, and/or techniques are most effective for presenting problems.
3.1.2	Conceptual	Understand the liabilities incurred when billing third parties, the codes necessary for reimbursement, and how to use them correctly.
3.1.3	Conceptual	Understand the effects that psychotropic and other medications have on clients and the treatment process.
3.1.4	Conceptual	Understand recovery-oriented behavioral health services (e.g., self-help groups, 12-step programs, peer-to-peer services, supported employment).

(Continued)

Domain 3 | Treatment Planning and Case Management (continued)

Number	Subdomain	Competence
3.2.1	Perceptual	Integrate client feedback, assessment, contextual information, and diagnosis with treatment goals and plan.
3.3.1	Executive	Develop, with client input, measurable outcomes, treatment goals, treatment plans, and after-care plans with clients utilizing a systemic perspective.
3.3.2	Executive	Prioritize treatment goals.
3.3.3	Executive	Develop a clear plan of how sessions will be conducted.
3.3.4	Executive	Structure treatment to meet clients' needs and to facilitate systemic change.
3.3.5	Executive	Manage progression of therapy toward treatment goals.
3.3.6	Executive	Manage risks, crises, and emergencies.
3.3.7	Executive	Work collaboratively with other stakeholders, including family members, other significant persons, and professionals not present.
3.3.8	Executive	Assist clients in obtaining needed care while navigating complex systems of care.
3.3.9	Executive	Develop termination and aftercare plans.
3.4.1	Evaluative	Evaluate progress of sessions toward treatment goals.
3.4.2	Evaluative	Recognize when treatment goals and plan require modification.
3.4.3	Evaluative	Evaluate level of risks, management of risks, crises, and emergencies.
3.4.4	Evaluative	Assess session process for compliance with policies and procedures of practice setting.
3.4.5	Professional	Monitor personal reactions to clients and treatment process, especially in terms of therapeutic behavior, relationship with clients, process for explaining procedures, and outcomes.
3.5.1	Professional	Advocate with clients in obtaining quality care, appropriate resources, and services in their community.
3.5.2	Professional	Participate in case-related forensic and legal processes.
3.5.3	Professional	Write plans and complete other case documentation in accordance with practice setting policies, professional standards, and state/provincial laws.
3.5.4	Professional	Utilize time management skills in therapy sessions and other professional meetings.

Domain 4 | Therapeutic Interventions

Number	Subdomain	Competence
4.1.1	Conceptual	Comprehend a variety of individual and systemic therapeutic models and their application, including evidence-based therapies and culturally sensitive approaches.
4.1.2	Conceptual	Recognize strengths, limitations, and contraindications of specific therapy models, including the risk of harm associated with models that incorporate assumptions of family dysfunction, pathogenesis, or cultural deficit.
4.2.1	Perceptual	Recognize how different techniques may impact the treatment process.
4.2.2	Perceptual	Distinguish differences between content and process issues, their role in therapy, and their potential impact on therapeutic outcomes.
4.3.1	Executive	Match treatment modalities and techniques to clients' needs, goals, and values.
4.3.2	Executive	Deliver interventions in a way that is sensitive to special needs of clients (e.g., gender, age, socioeconomic status, culture/race/ethnicity, sexual orientation, disability, personal history, larger systems issues of the client).
4.3.3	Executive	Reframe problems and recursive interaction patterns.
4.3.4	Executive	Generate relational questions and reflexive comments in the therapy room.
4.3.5	Executive	Engage each family member in the treatment process as appropriate.
4.3.6	Executive	Facilitate clients developing and integrating solutions to problems.
4.3.7	Executive	Defuse intense and chaotic situations to enhance the safety of all participants.
4.3.8	Executive	Empower clients and their relational systems to establish effective relationships with each other and larger systems.
4.3.9	Executive	Provide psychoeducation to families whose members have serious mental illness or other disorders.
4.3.10	Executive	Modify interventions that are not working to better fit treatment goals.
4.3.11	Executive	Move to constructive termination when treatment goals have been accomplished.
4.3.12	Executive	Integrate supervisor/team communications into treatment.
4.4.1	Evaluative	Evaluate interventions for consistency, congruency with model of therapy and theory of change, cultural and contextual relevance, and goals of the treatment plan.

(Continued)

Domain 4 | Therapeutic Interventions (continued)

Number	Subdomain	Competence
4.4.2	Evaluative	Evaluate ability to deliver interventions effectively.
4.4.3	Evaluative	Evaluate treatment outcomes as treatment progresses.
4.4.4	Evaluative	Evaluate clients' reactions or responses to interventions.
4.4.5	Evaluative	Evaluate clients' outcomes for the need to continue, refer, or terminate therapy.
4.4.6	Evaluative	Evaluate reactions to the treatment process (e.g., transference, family of origin, current stress level, current life situation, cultural context) and their impact on effective intervention and clinical outcomes.
4.5.1	Professional	Respect multiple perspectives (e.g., clients, team, supervisor, practitioners from other disciplines who are involved in the case).
4.5.2	Professional	Set appropriate boundaries, manage issues of triangulation, and develop collaborative working relationships.
4.5.3	Professional	Articulate rationales for interventions related to treatment goals and plan, assessment information, and systemic understanding of clients' context and dynamics.

Domain 5 | Legal Issues, Ethics, and Standards

Number	Subdomain	Competence
5.1.1	Conceptual	Know state, federal, and provincial laws and regulations that apply to the practice of marriage and family therapy.
5.1.2	Conceptual	Know professional ethics and standards of practice that apply to the practice of marriage and family therapy.
5.1.3	Conceptual	Know policies and procedures of the practice setting.
5.1.4	Conceptual	Understand the process of making an ethical decision.
5.2.1	Perceptual	Recognize situations in which ethics, laws, professional liability, and standards of practice apply.
5.2.2	Perceptual	Recognize ethical dilemmas in practice setting.
5.2.3	Perceptual	Recognize when a legal consultation is necessary.
5.2.4	Perceptual	Recognize when clinical supervision or consultation is necessary.
5.3.1	Executive	Monitor issues related to ethics, laws, regulations, and professional standards.

(Continued)

Domain 5 | Legal Issues, Ethics, and Standards (continued)

Number	Subdomain	Competence
5.3.2	Executive	Develop and assess policies, procedures, and forms for consistency with standards of practice to protect client confidentiality and to comply with relevant laws and regulations.
5.3.3	Executive	Inform clients and legal guardian of limitations to confidentiality and parameters of mandatory reporting.
5.3.4	Executive	Develop safety plans for clients who present with potential self-harm, suicide, abuse, or violence.
5.3.5	Executive	Take appropriate action when ethical and legal dilemmas emerge.
5.3.6	Executive	Report information to appropriate authorities as required by law.
5.3.7	Executive	Practice within defined scope of practice and competence.
5.3.8	Executive	Obtain knowledge of advances and theory regarding effective clinical practice.
5.3.9	Executive	Obtain license(s) and specialty credentials.
5.3.10	Executive	Implement a personal program to maintain professional competence.
5.4.1	Evaluative	Evaluate activities related to ethics, legal issues, and practice standards.
5.4.2	Evaluative	Monitor attitudes, personal well-being, personal issues, and personal problems to insure they do not impact the therapy process adversely or create vulnerability for misconduct.
5.5.1	Professional	Maintain client records with timely and accurate notes.
5.5.2	Professional	Consult with peers and/or supervisors if personal issues, attitudes, or beliefs threaten to adversely impact clinical work.
5.5.3	Professional	Pursue professional development through self-supervision, collegial consultation, professional reading, and continuing educational activities.
5.5.4	Professional	Bill clients and third-party payers in accordance with professional ethics, relevant laws and polices, and seek reimbursement only for covered services.

Domain 6 | Research and Program Evaluation

Number	Subdomain	Competence
6.1.1	Conceptual	Know the extant MFT literature, research, and evidence-based practice.
6.1.2	Conceptual	Understand research and program evaluation methodologies, both quantitative and qualitative, relevant to MFT and mental health services.
6.1.3	Conceptual	Understand the legal, ethical, and contextual issues involved in the conduct of clinical research and program evaluation.
6.2.1	Perceptual	Recognize opportunities for therapists and clients to participate in clinical research.
6.3.1	Executive	Read current MFT and other professional literature.
6.3.2	Executive	Use current MFT and other research to inform clinical practice.
6.3.3	Executive	Critique professional research and assess the quality of research studies and program evaluation in the literature.
6.3.4	Executive	Determine the effectiveness of clinical practice and techniques.
6.4.1	Evaluative	Evaluate knowledge of current clinical literature and its application.
6.5.1	Professional	Contribute to the development of new knowledge.

Reference List

Ackerman, N. (1981). The functions of the family therapist. In Green R.J. & J.L. Framo (Eds.), *Family therapy: Major contributions.* New York: International Universities Press.

Ackerman, N.W. (1958). *The psychodynamics of family life.* New York: Basic Books.

Allen-Eckert, H., Fong, E., Nichols, M.P., Watson, N., & Liddle, H.A. (2001). Development of the family therapy enactment rating scale. *Fam Process, 40*(4), 469–78.

American Art Therapy Association (2001). www.aata.org

American Psychiatric Association. (1994). *Diagnostic and statistical manual of mental disorders.* (4th ed.). Washington, D.C.: American Psychiatric Association.

Anderson, C., Reiss, D., & Hogarty, G. (1986). *Schizophrenia and the family: A practitioner's guide to psycho-education and management.* New York: Guilford Press.

Anderson, H. (1991). Opening the door for change through continuous conversations. In T.C. Todd & M.D. Selekman (Eds.), *Family therapy approaches with adolescent substance abuse.* (pp. 176–189). Needham Heights, MA: Allyn & Bacon.

Anderson, H. (1999). Reimagining family therapy: Reflections on Minuchin's invisible family. *Journal of Marital and Family Therapy, 25*(1), 1–8.

Anderson, S., & Bagarozzi, D. (1989). *Family myths: Psychotherapy implications.* New York: Haworth Press.

Aponte, H.J. (1994). *Bread & spirit: Therapy with the new poor: Diversity of race, culture and values.* New York: Norton.

Bateson, G. (1972). *Steps to an ecology of mind.* New York: Dutton.

Berg, I.K., & Gallagher, D. (1991). Solution focused brief treatment with adolescent substance abusers. In T.C. Todd & M.D. Selekman (Eds.), *Family therapy approaches with adolescent substance abusers.* (pp. 93–111). Boston: Allyn &Bacon.

Bergin, A.E., & Garfield, S.L. (1994). *Handbook of psychotherapy and behavior change.* (4th ed.). New York: Wiley.

Bernal, G., & Flores-Ortiz Y. (1991). Contextual family therapy with adolescent drug abusers. In T. Todd & M. Selekman (Eds.), *Family therapy approaches with adolescent substance abusers.* (pp. 70–92). Needham Heights, MA: Allyn & Bacon.

Bernal, G., & Ysern, E. (1986). Family therapy and ideology. *Journal of Marital and Family Therapy, 12*(2), 129–136.

Bertram, D. Walking the MFT walk while talking the DSM-IVTR talk. In Anonymous. Louisville, KY: University of Louisville.

Boscolo, L., Cecchin, G., Hoffman, L., & Penn, P. (1987). *Milan systemic family therapy: Conversations in theory and practice*. New York: Basic Books.

Boss, P. (1999). *Ambiguous loss*. Cambridge, MA: Harvard University Press.

Boszormenyi-Nagy, I. (1987). *Foundations of contextual therapy: Collected papers*. New York: Brunner/Mazel.

Boszormenyi-Nagy, I. (1966). From family therapy to a psychology of relationships; fictions of the individual and fictions of the family. *Comprehensive Psychiatry, 7*, 408–423.

Boszormenyi-Nagy, I., & Framo, J.L. (1965). *Intensive family therapy*. New York: Harper & Row.

Boszormenyi-Nagy, I., & Krasner, B. (1986). *Between give and take: A clinical guide to contextual therapy*. New York: Brunner/Mazel.

Boszormenyi-Nagy, I., & Spark, G.M. (1973). *Invisible loyalties: Reciprocity in intergenerational family therapy*. New York: Harper & Row.

Boszormenyi-Nagy, I., & Ulrich, D.N. (1981). Contextual family therapy. In A.S. Gurman & D.P. Kniskern (Eds.), *Handbook of family therapy*. (pp. 159–188). New York: Brunner/Mazel.

Bowen, M. (1978). *Family therapy in clinical practice*. New York: Aronson.

Bowlby, J. (1969). *Attachment and loss: Vol. 1. Attachment*. New York: Basic Books.

Boyd-Franklin, N. (1989). *Black families in therapy: A multisystem approach*. New York: Guilford Press.

Boyd-Franklin, N., & Bry, B.H. (2000). *Reaching out in family therapy: Home-based, school, and community interventions*. New York: Guilford Press.

Breunlin, D. (1985). Expanding the concept of stages in family therapy. In Anonymous, *States: Patterns of change over time*. (pp. 95–120). Rockville, MD: Aspen.

Breunlin, D., Schwartz, R.C., & Mac Kune-Karrer, B.M. (1992). *Metaframeworks: Transcending the models of family therapy*. San Francisco: Jossey-Bass.

Brock, G., & Barnard, C. (1988). *Procedures in family therapy*. Needham Heights, MA: Allyn & Bacon.

Brock, G.W. (1997). Reducing vulnerability to ethics code violations: An at-risk test for marriage and family therapists. *Journal of Marital and Family Therapy, 23*(1), 87–90.

Broderick, C.B., & Schrader, S.S. (1981). The history of professional marriage and family therapy. In A.S. Gruman & D.P. Kniskern (Eds.), *Handbook of family therapy*. (pp. 3–40). New York: Brunner/Mazel.

Bronfenbrenner, U. (1979). *The ecology of human development: Experiments by nature and design*. Cambridge, MA: Harvard University Press.

Brooks, G.R. (1998). Why traditional men hate psychotherapy. *Psychotherapy Bulletin, 33*(3), 45–49.

Brown, J., Brown, C., & Portes, P. (1991). *The families in transition program*. Louisville, KY: University of Louisville Press.

Brown, J.H., Eichenberger, S.A., Portes, P., & Christensen, D.N. (1991). Family functioning factors associated with the adjustment level of children of divorce. *Journal of Divorce and Remarriage, 17*, 81–95.

Brown, J.H., & Vaccaro, A. (1991). *A manual for resource and youth services coordinators*. Louisville, KY: University of Louisville and Cities in Schools.

Burns, R.C., & Kaufman, S.H. (1970). *Kinetic family drawings*. New York: Brunner/Mazel.

Butler, R. (1963). The life review: Interpretation of reminiscence in the aged. *Psychiatry, 26*, 65–76.

Campbell, D., Draper, R., & Crutchley, E. (1991). The Milan systemic approach to family therapy. In A.S. Gurman & D.P. Kniskern (Eds.), *Handbook of family therapy*. (pp. 324–362). New York: Brunner/Mazel.

Campbell, J., Liebmann, M., Brooks, F., Jones, J., & Ward, C. (1990). *Art therapy, race and culture*. London: Jessica Kingsley Publishers, Ltd.

Carter, B., & McGoldrick, M. (1989a). *The changing family life cycle: Framework for family therapy*. (2nd ed.). Needham Heights, MA: Allyn & Bacon.

Carter, B., & McGoldrick, M. (1989b). Forming a remarried family. In B. Carter & M. McGoldrick (Eds.), *The changing family life cycle: Framework for family therapy*. (pp. 399–432). Needham Heights, MA: Allyn & Bacon.

Carter, E.A., & McGoldrick, M. (1980). *The family life cycle: A framework for family therapy*. New York: Gardner Press.

Coatsworth, J.D., Santisteban, D.A., McBride, C.K., & Szapocznik, J. (2001). Brief strategic family therapy versus community control: Engagement, retention, and an exploration of the moderating role of adolescent symptom severity. *Family Process, 40*(3), 313–332.

Cocoran, J. (2000). *Evidence-based social work practice with families*. New York: Springer Publishing.

Colapinto, J. (1991). Structural family therapy. In A.S. Gurman & D.P. Kniskern (Eds.), *Handbook of family therapy*. (pp. 417–443). New York: Brunner/Mazel.

Coleman, S. (1985). *Failures in family therapy*. New York: Guilford Press.

Commission on Accreditation for Marriage and Family Therapy Education. (1997). Anonymous. Washington, D.C.

Cordova, J.V., Jacobson, N.S., & Christensen, A. (1998). Acceptance versus change interventions in behavioral couple therapy: Impact on couple's in-session communication. *Journal of Marital and Family Therapy, 24*(4), 437–456.

Cordova, J.V., Warren, L.Z., & Gee, C.B. (2001). Motivational interviewing as an intervenion for at-risk couples. *Journal of Marital and Family Therapy, 27*(3), 315–326.

Cormier, W.H., & Cormier, L.S. (1991). *Interviewing strategies for helpers: Fundamental skills and cognitive behavioral interventions*. (3rd ed.). Pacific Grove, CA: Brooks/Cole.

Crando, R., & Ginsberg, B.G. (1976). Communication in the father-son relationship: The parent-adolescent relationship development program. *The Family Coordinator, 4,* 465–473.

Cross, T.L. (1995). Understanding family resiliency from a relational world view. In H.I. McCubbin, E.A. Thompson, A.I. Thompson, & J.E. Fromer (Eds.), *Resiliency in ethnic minority families: Native and immigrant American families*. (pp. 143–157). Madison, WI: University of Wisconsin-Madison Center for Family Studies.

Cunningham, P.B., & Henggeler, S. (1999). Engaging multiproblem families in treatment: Lessons learned throughout the development of multisystemic therapy. *Family Process, 38*(3), 265–281.

De Shazer, S. (1985). *Keys to solution in brief therapy*. New York: Norton.

Diller, J.V. (1999). *Cultural diversity: A primer for the human services*. Belmont, CA: Brooks Cole/Wadsworth.

Dinkmeyer, D., McKay, G., Dinkmeyer, J.S., Dinkmeyer, D., & McKay, J. (1997). *Parenting young children*. Circle Pines, MN: American Guidance Service.

Duncan, B., & Parks, M.B. (1988). Integrating individual and systems approaches: Strategic-behavioral therapy. *Journal of Marital and Family Therapy, 14,* 151–161.

Dunst, C., Trivette, C., & Deal, A. (1988). *Enabling and empowering families: Principles and guidelines for practice*. Cambridge, MA: Brookline Books.

Durrant, M. (1988). Gwynne: A new recipe for life. *Case studies, [special edition].* 25–28.

Duvall, E. (1977). *Marriage and family development*. (5th ed.). Philadelphia: Lippincott.

Efran, J., Lukens, M., & Lukens, R. (1990). *Language, structure and change*. New York: Norton.

Eliot, T.S. (1971). *Four quartets*. New York: Harcourt, Inc.

Epston, D., & White, M. (1992). *Experience, contradiction, narrative and imagination: Selected papers of David Epston and Michael White, 1989–1991*. Adelaide, Australia: Dulwich Centre Publications.

Erickson, M., & Rossi, E. (1979). *Hypnotherapy: An exploratory casework*. New York: Irvington.

Ericson, P., & Rogers, L.E. (1973). New procedures for analyzing relational communication. *Family Process, 12*(3), 245–268.

Falicov, C. (1988). *Family transitions: Continuity and change over the lifecycle*. New York: Guilford Press.

Falloon, I.R. (1991). Behavioral family therapy. In A.S. Gurman & D.P. Kriskern (Eds.), *Handbook of family therapy*. (pp. 65–95). New York: Brunner/Mazel.

Feixas, G. (1990). Personal construct theory and systemic therapies: Parallel or convergent trends? *Journal of Marital and Family Therapy, 16*(1), 1–20.

Ferreira, A. (1963). Family myth and homeostasis. *Archives of General Psychiatry, 9,* 457–463.

Figley, C., & Nelson, T. (1989). Basic family therapy skills. I: Conceptualization and findings. *Journal of Marital and Family Therapy, 4*(14), 349–366.

Fleuridas, C., Nelson, T., & Rosenthal, D.M. (1986). The evolution of circular questions: Training family therapists. *Journal of Marital and Family Therapy, 12*(27), 113–128.

Fleuridas, C., Rosenthal, D.M., Leigh, G.K., & Leigh, T.E. (1990). Family goal recording: An adaptation of goal attainment scaling for enchancing family therapy assessment. *Journal of Marital and Family Therapy, 16,* 389–406.

Framo, J. (1976). Family of origin as a therapeutic resource for adults in marital and family therapy: You can and should go home again. *Family Process, 15,* 193–210.

Framo, J. (1981). The integration of marital therapy with sessions with family of origin. In A.S. Gurman & D.P. Kniskern (Eds.), *Handbook of family therapy.* (pp. 133–158). New York: Brunner/Mazel.

Gambino, R. (1974). *Blood of my blood: The dilemma of Italian-Americans.* New York: Doubleday.

Garcia-Preto, N. (1982). Family therapy with Puerto Rican families. In J. McGoldrick, J.K. Pearce, & J. Giordano (Eds.), *Ethnicity and family therapy.* (pp. 164–186). New York: Guilford Press.

Garfield, R. (1981). Mourning and its resolution for spouses in marital separation. In J.C. Hansen & L. Messinger (Eds.), *Therapy with remarriage and families.* (pp. 1–15). Rockville, MD: Aspen.

Garfield, S., & Bergin, A. (1978). *Handbook of psychotherapy and behavior change.* (2nd ed.). New York: Wiley.

Garfield, S.L. (1994). *Research on client variables in psychotherapy.* (4th ed.). New York: Wiley.

Garrett, J., Landau-Stanton, J., Stanton, M.D., Stellato-Kobat, J., & Stellato-Kobat, D. (1997). ARISE: A method for engaging reluctant alcohol- and drug-dependent individuals in treatment. *Journal of Substance Abuse Treatment, 14,* 235–248.

Gergen, K.J. (1994). *Realities and relationships.* Cambridge, MA: Harvard University Press.

Gergen, K.J. (1985). The social constructionist in modern psychology. *American Psychologist, 40,* 266–275.

Goldner, V. (1988). Generation and gender: Normative and covert hierarchies. *Family Process, 27,* 17–31.

Goldstein, A. (1973). *Structured learning therapy.* New York: Academic Press.

Gonzales, N.A., Hiraga, Y., & Cauce, A.M. (1995). Observing mother-daughter interaction in African-American and Asian-American families. In H.I. McCubbins, E.A. Thompson, A.I. Thompson, & J.A. Futrell (Eds.), *Resiliency in ethnic minority families: Aftrican-American families.* (pp. 259–286). Madison: University of Wisconsin-Madison Center for Family Studies.

Goolishian, H.A., & Anderson, H. (1992). Strategy and intervention versus nonintervention: A matter of theory? *Journal of Marital and Family Therapy, 18*(1), 5–15.

Gottman, J.M., & Levenson, R.W. (1999). Rebound from marital conflict and divorce prediction. *Fam Process, 38*(3), 287–92.

Gottman, J.M., & Notarius, C.I. (2002). Marital research in the 20th century and a research agenda for the 21st century. *Fam Process, 41*(2), 159–97.

Green, R.J., & Framo, J.L. (1983). *Family therapy: Major contributions.* New York: International Universities Press.

Greenberg, L.S., & Johnson, S.M. (1988). *Emotionally focused therapy for couples.* New York: Guilford Press.

Griffith, J.L., & Griffith, M.E. (1994). *The body speaks: Therapeutic dialogues for mind-body problems.* New York: Basic Books.

Group for the Advancement of Psychiatry Committee on the Family. (1995). Beyond DSM-IV: A model for the classification and diagnosis of relational disorders. *Psychiatric Services, 46,* 926–931.

Gurman, A.S., & Kniskern, D.P. (Eds.). (1981). *Handbook of family therapy.* New York: Brunner/Mazel.

Gurman, A.S., & Kniskern, D.P. (Eds.). (1991). *Handbook of family therapy.* New York: Brunner/Mazel.

Guttman, H.A., Feldman, R.B., Engelsmann, F., Spector, L., & Buonvino, M. (1999). The relationships between psychiatrists' couple and family therapy training experience and their subsequent practice profile. *Journal of Marital and Family Therapy, 25*(1), 31–42.

Haley, J. (1980). *Leaving home: The therapy of disturbed young people.* New York: McGraw-Hill.

Haley, J. (1976). *Problem-solving therapy.* San Francisco: Jossey-Bass.

Haley, J. (1967). Toward a theory of pathological systems. In G.H. Zuk & I. Boszormenyi-Nagy (Eds.), *Family theory and disturbed families.* (pp. 11–27). Palo Alto, CA: Science and Behavior Books.

Hanna, S.M. (1997). A developmental-interactional model. In T.D. Hargrave & S.M. Hanna (Eds.), *The aging family: New visions in theory, practice and reality.* (pp. 101–130). New York: Brunner/Mazel.

Hanna, S.M. (1995). On paradox: Empathy before strategy. *Journal of Family Psychotherapy, 6*(1), 85–88.

Hanna, S.M., & Hargrave, T.D. (1997). Integrating the process of aging and family therapy. In T.D. Hargrave & S.M. Hanna (Eds.), *The aging family: New visions in theory, practice and reality.* (pp. 19–38, 122). New York: Brunner/Mazel.

Hansen, J., & Keeney, B. (1983). *Diagnosis and assessment in family therapy.* Rockville, MD: Aspen.

Hansen, J., Pound, R., & Warner, R. (1976). Use of modeling procedures. *Personnel and Guidance Journal, 54,* 242–245.

Hardy, K.V., & Laszloffy, T.A. (1995). The cultural genogram: Key to training culturally competent family therapists. *Journal of Marital and Family Therapy, 21*(3), 227–237.

Hardy, K.V., & Laszloffy, T.A. (2005). *Teens who hurt: Clinical interventions to break the cycle of adolescent violence.* New York: Guilford.

Hare-Mustin, R. (1978). A feminist approach to family therapy. *Family Process, 17,* 181–194.

Hargrave, T.D., & Anderson, W. (1992). *Finishing well: Aging and reparation in the intergenerational family.* New York: Brunner/Mazel.

Hargrave, T.D., & Hanna, S.M. (Eds.). (1997). *The aging family: New visions in theory, practice and reality.* New York: Brunner/Mazel.

Hayes, J., & Wall, T. (1998). What influences clinicians' responsibility attributions? The role of problem type, theoretical orientation, and client attribution. *Journal of Social and Clinical Psychology, 17,* 69–74.

Hazan, C., & Shaver, P. (1994). Attachment as an organizational framework for research on close relationships: Target article. *Psychological Inquiry, 5,* 1–22.

Henggeler, S.W., Schoenwald, S.K., Borduin, C.M., Rowland, M.D., & Cunningham, P.B. (1998). *Multisystemic treatment of antisocial behavior in children and adolescents.* New York: Guilford Press.

Hiebert, W., Gillespie, J., & Stahmann, R. (1993). *Dynamic assessment in couples therapy.* New York: Lexington Books.

Hirschmann, M.J., & Sprenkle, D.H. (1989). The use of therapeutic paradox among members of the American Association for Marriage and Family Therapy. *American Journal of Family Therapy, 17*(4), 348–358.

Hoffman, L. (1983). A co-evolutionary framework for systemic family therapy. In J. Hansen & B. Keeney (Eds.), *Diagnosis and assessment if family therapy.* (pp. 35–62). Rockville, MD: Aspen.

Hoffman, L. (1981). *Foundations of family therapy.* New York: Basic Books.

Hoffman, L. (1998). Setting aside the model in family therapy. *Journal of Marital and Family Therapy, 24*(2), 145–156.

Holtzworth-Munroe, A., & Jacobson, N.S. (1991). Behavioral marital therapy. In Anonymous, *Handbook of family therapy.* (pp. 96–133). New York: Brunner/Mazel.

Hosford, R., & de Visser, C. (1974). *Behavioral counseling: An introduction.* Washington, D.C.: American Personnel and Guidance Press.

Howard, J. (1978). *Families.* New York: Simon & Schuster.

Hubble, M., Duncan, B., & Miller, S. (1999). *The heart and soul of change.* Washington, D.C.: APA Press.

Imber-Black, E. (1993). *Secrets in families and family therapy.* New York: Norton.

Imber-Black, E., Roberts, J., & Whiting, R. (1988). *Rituals in families and family therapy.* New York: Norton.

Jacobson, N.S. (1984). A component analysis of behavioral marital therapy: The relative effectiveness of behavior exchange and problem solving training. *Journal of Consulting & Clinical Psychology, 52,* 295–305.

Jacobson, N.S. (1991). Toward enhancing the efficacy of marital therapy and marital therapy research. *Journal of Family Psychology, 4*(4), 373–393.

Jacobson, N.S., & Christensen, A. (1996). *Integrative couple therapy.* New York: Norton.

Jacobson, N.S., Holtzworth-Monroe, A., & Schmaling, K.B. (1989). Marital therapy and spouse involvement in the treatment of depression, agoraphobia, and alcoholism. *Journal of Consulting & Clinical Psychology, 57,* 5–10.

Jacobson, N.S., & Margolin, B. (1979). *Marital therapy: Strategies based on social learning and behavior exchange principles.* New York: Brunner/Mazel.

Jenkins, A. (1991). *Invitations to responsibility: The therapeutic engagement of men who are violent and abusive.* Adelaide, Australia: Dulwich Centre Publications.

Johnson, L., Bruhn, R., Winek, J., Kreps, J., & Wiley, K. (1999). The use of child-encountered play therapy and filial therapy with Head Start families: A brief report. *Journal of Marital and Family Therapy, 25*(2), 169–176.

Johnson, S.M. (1998). Listening to the music: Emotion as a natural part of systems theory. *Journal of Systemic Therapies, 17,* 1–18.

Johnson, S.M. (1996). *The practice of emotionally focused marital therapy: Creating connection.* New York: Brunner/Mazel.

Johnson, S.M., Makinen, J.A., & Millikan, J.W. (2001). Attachment injuries in couple relationships: A new perspective on impasses in couples therapy. *Journal of Marital and Family Therapy, 27*(2), 145–156.

Johnson, S.M., & Whiffen, V. (1999). Made to measure: Attachment styles in couples therapy. *Clinical Psychology: Science & Practice, Special Edition on Individual Differences and Couples Therapy, 6,* 366–381.

Karpel, M. (1986). Questions, obstacles, and contributions. In M.A. Karpel (Ed.), *Family resources: The hidden partner in family therapy.* (pp. 3–64). New York: Guilford Press.

Kaslow, F.W. (1996). *Handbook of relational diagnosis and dysfunctional family patterns.* New York: Wiley.

Keith, D., & Whitaker, C. (1985). Failure: Our bold companion. In S. Coleman (Ed.), *Failures in family therapy.* (pp. 8–26). New York: Guilford Press.

Kelly, G.A. (1963). *A theory of personality: The psychology of personal constructs.* New York: Norton.

Kendall, P.C., & Braswell, L. (1993). *Cognitive-behavioral therapy for impulsive children.* New York: Guilford Press.

Kerr, M. (1981). Family systems theory and therapy. In A.S. Gurman & D.P. Kniskern (Eds.), *Hankbook of family therapy.* (pp. 226–266). New York: Brunner?Mazel.

Kinney, J., Haopala, P., & Booth, C. (1991). *Keeping families together: The home builders model.* New York: Aldine De Gruyter.

Kiser, D., Piercy, F., & Lipchik, E. (1993). The integration of emotion in solution-focused therapy. *Journal of Marital and Family Therapy, 19,* 233–242.

Knudson-Martin, C. (2000). Gender, family competence and psychological symptoms. *Journal of Marital and Family Therapy, 26*(3), 317–328.

Koplewicz, H.S., & Goodman, R.F. (1999). *Childhood revealed: Art expressing pain, discovery, hope.* New York: Abrams.

Koppitz, E.M. (1968). *Psychological evaluation of children's human figure drawings.* New York: Grune & Stratton.

Kowal, J., Johnson, S.M., & Lee, A. (2003). Chronic illness in couples: A case for emotionally focused couples therapy. *Journal of Marital and Family Therapy, 29*(3), 299–310.

Kramer, J. (1985). *Family interfaces: Transgenerational patterns.* New York: Brunner/Mazel.

Krumboltz, J., Varenhorst, B., & Thoresen, C. (1967). Nonverbal factors in effectiveness of models in counseling. *Journal of Couseling Psychology, 14,* 412–418.

Kuehl, B.P. (1995). The solution-oriented genogram: A collaborative approach. *Journal of Marital and Family Therapy, 21*(3), 239–250.

Kwiatkowska, H.Y. (1967). Family art therapy. *Family Process, 6*(1), 37–55.

Kwiatkowska, H.Y. (1978). *Family therapy and evaluation through art.* Springfield, IL: Charles C Thomas.

Lambert, M.J., & Bergin, A.E. (1994). The effectiveness of psychotherapy. In A.E. Bergin & S.L. Garfield (Eds.), *Handbook of psychotherapy and behavior change.* (pp. 143–189). New York: Wiley.

Landau-Stanton, J. (1986). Competence, impermanence, and transitional mapping: A model for systems consultation. In L.C. Wynne, S.H. McDaniel, & T.T. Weber (Eds.), *Systems consultation: A new perspective for family therapy.* (pp. 253–269). New York: Gardner Press.

Landau-Stanton, J., & Stanton, M.D. (1985). Treating suicidal adolescents and their families. In M.P. Mirkin & S. Koman (Eds.), *Handbook of adolescents and family therapy.* (pp. 309–328). New York: Gardner Press.

Lankton, S. (1988). *Ericksonian hypnosis application, preparation and research.* New York: Brunner/Mazel.

Lankton, S., & Lankton, C. (1983). *The answer within: A clinical framework of Ericksonian hypnotherapy.* New York: Brunner/Mazel.

Lankton, S., Lankton, C., & Matthews, W. (1991). Ericksonian family therapy. In A.S. Gurman & D.P. Kniskern (Eds.), *Handbook of family therapy.* (pp. 239–283). New York: Brunner/Mazel.

LaVoie, J. (1985). Health in the family life cycle. In J. Springer & R. Woody (Eds.), *Health promotion in family therapy.* (pp. 46–70). Rockville, MD: Aspen.

Lebow, J.L. (1987). Training psychologists in family therapy in family institute settings. *Journal of Family Psychology, 1,* 219–231.

Leitch, M.L., & Thomas, V. (1999). The AAMFT-Head Start training partnership project: Enhancing MFT capacities beyond the family system. *Journal of Marital and Family Therapy, 25*(2), 141–154.

Lewis, R., Piercy, F., Sprenkle, D., & Trepper, T. (1991). Family based interventions for helping drug abusing adolescents. *Journal of Adolescent Research, 5,* 82–95.

Multidimensional family therapy treatment manual. (2000). Rockville, MD: Center for Substnce Abuse Treatment.

Liddle, H.A., Rowe, C., Diamond, G.M., Sessa, F.M., Schmidt, S., & Ettinger, D. (2000). Toward a developmental family therapy: the clinical utility of research on adolescence. *Journal of Marital Family Therapy, 26*(4), 485–99.

Liddle, H.A., & Schwartz, S.J. (2002). Attachment and family therapy: clinical utility of adolescent-family attachment research. *Family Process, 41*(3), 455–76.

Lindblad-Goldberg, M., Dore, M.M., & Stern, L. (1998). *Creating competence from chaos: A comprehensive guide to home-based services.* New York: Norton.

Lipchik, E. (1987). Purposeful sequence for beginning the solution-focused interview. In E. Lipchik (Ed.), *Interviewing.* Rockville, MD: Aspen.

Locke, H., & Wallace, K. (1959). Short marital-adjustment and prediction tests: The reliability and validity. *Marriage and Family Living, 21,* 251–255.

Long, J. (1997). Alzheimer's disease and the family: Working with new realities. In T.D. Hargrave & S.M. Hanna (Eds.), *The aging family: New visions in theory, practice and reality.* (pp. 209–234). New York: Brunner/Mazel.

Lusebrink, V.B. (1992). A systems oriented approach to the expressive therapies: The expressive therapies continuum. *The Arts in Psychotherapy, 18*(4), 395–403.

Madanes, C. (1981). *Strategic family therapy.* San Francisco: Jossey-Bass.

Madsen, W.C. (1999). *Collaborative Therapy with Multi-stressed Families: From Old Problems to New Futures.* New York: Guilford Press.

Mahoney, M.J. (1991). *Human change process.* New York: Basic Books.

McCubbin, H.I. (1980). Family stress and coping: A decade review. *Journal of Marriage and the Family, 42,* 855–871.

McCubbin, H.I., Dahl, B., & Hunter, E. (1976). *Families in the military system.* Beverly Hills, CA: Sage.

McCubbin, H.I., Thompson, E.A., Thompson, A.I., & Fromer, J.E. (1995). *Resiliency in ethnic minority families: Native and immigrant American families.* Madison: University of Wisconsin-Madison Center for Family Studies.

McDaniel, S.H., Hepworth, J., & Doherty, W. (1992). *Medical family therapy: A biopsychosocial approach to families with health problems.* New York: Basic Books.

McDowell, T. (1999). Systems consultation and Head Start: An alternative to traditional family therapy. *Journal of Marital and Family Therapy, 25*(2), 155–168.

McFarlane, W. (2002). *Multifamily groups in the treatment of severe psychiatric disorders.* New York: Guilford Press.

McGoldrick, J., Pearce, J.K., & Giordano, J. (1982). *Ethnicity and family therapy.* New York: Guilford Press.

McGoldrick, M. (1982). Ethnicity and family therapy: An overview. In J. McGoldrick, J.K. Pearce, & J. Giordano (Eds.), *Ethnicity and family therapy.* (pp. 3–30). New York: Guilford Press.

McGoldrick, M., & Gerson, R. (1985). *Genograms in family assessment.* New York: Norton.

McGoldrick, M., & Giordano, J. (1996). Overview: Ethnicity and family therapy. In J. McGoldrick, J.K. Pearce, & J. Giordano (Eds.), *Ethnicity and family therapy.* (pp. 1–27). New York: Guilford Press.

Medalie, J.H. (1979). The family life cycle and its implications for family practice. *Journal of Family Practice, 9,* 47–56.

Menses, G., & Durrant, M. (1987). Contextual residential care: The application of the principles of cybernetic therapy to the residential treatment of irresponsible adolescents and their families. *Journal of Strategic and Systemic Therapies, 6,* 3–15.

Metcalf, L., Thomas, F., Duncan B.L., Miller, S.D., & Hubble, M.A. (1996). What works in solution-focused brief therapy: A qualitative analysis of client and therapist perceptions. In S.D. Miller, B.L. Duncan, & M.A. Hubble (Eds.), *Handbook of solution-focused brief therapy.* San Francisco: Jossey-Bass.

Miklowitz, D.J., & Goldstein, M.J. (1997). *Bipolar disorder: A family-focused treatment approach.* New York: Guilford Press.

Miller, S., Nunnally, E., Wackman, D., & Miller, P. (1988). *Connecting with self and others.* Littleton, CO: Interpersonal Communication Programs.

Miller, S.D., Duncan, B.L., & Hubble, M.A. (1997). *Escape from Babel: Toward a unifying language for psychotherapy practice.* New York: Norton.

Minuchin, S. (1974). *Families and family therapy.* Cambridge, MA: Harvard University Press.

Minuchin, S. (1984). *Family kaleidoscope.* Cambridge, MA: Harvard University Press.

Minuchin, S. (1987). My many voices. In J.K. Zeig (Ed.), *The evolution of psychotherapy.* (pp. 5–28). New York: Brunner/Mazel.

Minuchin, S., & Fishman, H.C. (1981). *Family therapy techniques.* Cambridge, MA: Harvard University Press.

Minuchin, S., Montalvo, B., Guerney, B., Rosman, B., & Schumer, F. (1967). *Families of the slums: An exploration of their structure and treatment.* New York: Basic Books.

Napier, A., & Whitaker, C. (1978). *The family crucible: The intense experience of family therapy.* New York: Harper & Row.

Nelson, T.S., & Johnson, L.N. (1999). The basic skills evaluation device. *Journal of Marital and Family Therapy, 25*(1), 15–30.

Newfield, N.A., Kuehl, B.P., Joanning, H., & Quinn, W.H. (1991). We can tell you about "psychos and shrinks": An ethnography of the family therapy of adolescent drug abusers. In T. Todd & M.D. Selekman (Eds.), *Family therapy approaches with adolescent substance abusers.* (pp. 277–316). Needham Heights, MA: Allyn & Bacon.

Nichols, M., & Schwartz, R. (1991). *Family therapy: Concepts and methods.* (2nd ed.). Needham Heights, MA: Allyn & Bacon.

Nichols, M.P., & Schwartz, R.C. (2001). *Family therapy: Concepts and methods.* (5th ed.). Boston, MA: Allyn and Bacon.

Nichols, W., & Everett, C. (1988). *Systemic family therapy: An integrative approach.* New York: Guilford Press.

O'Callaghan, J.B. Family school consultation, state of the art analysis and blueprint. In Anonymous.

O' Hanlon, B. (1999). *Evolving possibilities: Selected papers of Bill O'Hanlon.* Philadelphia: Brunner/Mazel.

O'Hanlon, W.H. Acknowledgement and possibility. 91. Louisville, KY, Family and Children's Agency. (GENERIC)

O'Hanlon, W.H. (1987). *Taproots.* New York: Norton.

O'Hanlon, W.H. (1982). Two generic patterns in Ericksonian therapy. *Journal of Strategic and Systemic Therapies, 1*(4), 21–25.

O'Hanlon, W.H., & Weiner-Davis, M. (1989). *In search of solutions: A new direction in psychotherapy.* New York: Norton.

Olson, D.H., Porter, J., & Ravee, Y. (1985). *FACES I.* St. Paul: Family Social Science, University of Minnesota.

Palazzoli, M.S., Cirillo, S., Selvini, M., & Sorentino, A.M. (1989). *Family games: General models of Psychotic processes in the family.* New York: Norton.

Papp, P. (1983). *The process of change.* New York: Guilford Press.

Papp, P. (1982). Staging reciprocal metaphors in a couples group. *Family Process, 21*(4), 453–467.

Papp, P. (1980). The use of fantasy in a couples group. In M. Andolfi & I. Zwerling (Eds.), *Dimensions of family therapy.* (pp. 73–90). New York: Guilford Press.

Patterson, G.R. (Ed.). (1975). *Families: Applications of social learning to family life.* Champaign, IL: Research Press.

Patterson, G.R. (1971). *Families: Applications of social learning to family life.* Champaign, IL: Research Press.

Paul, G.L. (1967). Strategy of outcome research in psychotherapy. *Journal of Consulting Psychology, 31,* 109–118.

Paul, N., & Paul, B.B. (1975). *A marital puzzle.* New York: Norton.

Penn, P. (1982). Circular questioning. *Family Process, 19,* 267–280.

Petker, S. (1982). The domino effect in a system with two or more generations of unresolved mourning. *The Family, 9*(2), 75–79.

Piaget, J. (1952). *The origins of intelligence in children.* New York: Norton.

Piercy, F., Laird, R., & Mohammed, Z. (1983). A family therapist rating scale. *Journal of Marital and Family Therapy, 9*(1), 49–59.

Piercy, F., & Sprenkle, D. (1986). *Family therapy sourcebook.* New York: Guilford Press.

Pinsof, W.M., & Catherall, D. (1986). The integrative psychotherapy alliance. *Journal of Marital and Family Therapy, 12,* 137–152.

Pittman, F. (1991). The secret passions of men. *Journal of Marital and Family Therapy, 177*(17), 17–23.

Pittman, F., DeYoung, C., Flomenhaft, K., Kaplan, D., & Langsley, D. (1966). Crisis family therapy. In J.H. Masserman (Ed.), *Current psychiatric therapies.* (pp. 187–196). New York: Grune & Stratton.

Prochaska, J.O., DiClemente, S.C., & Norcross, J.C. (1992). In search of how people change. *American Psychologist, 47,* 1102–1114.

Quinn, W., & Davidson, B. (1984). Prevalence of family therapy models: A research note. *Journal of Marital and Family Therapy, 10*(4), 393–398.

Rainsford, G.L., & Schulman, S.H. (1981). The family in crisis: A case study of overwhelming illness and stress. *Journal of the American Medical Association, 246,* 60–63.

Rappaport, A.F. (1976). Conjugal relationship enhancement program. In D.H.L. Olson (Ed.), *Treating relationships.* (pp. 41–66). Lake Mills, IA: Graphic Publishing.

Rickert, V. (1995). The metaphor game. *Unpublished manuscript.*

Rickert, V. (2006). Personal communication.

Robbins, T.D. (1994). *Family builders: A collaborative family/school initiative.* Louisville, KY: Archdiocese of Louisville.

Rogers, C. (1961). *On becoming a person.* Boston: Houghton Mifflin.

Rolland, J. (1994). *Families, illness and disability: An integrated treatment model.* New York: Basic Books.

Ronaldson, C.A., & Hanna, S.M. (2001). Opening borders between art therapy, family therapy and other mental health professions. American Art Therapy Association 32nd Annual Conference. Albuquerque, NM.

Ronaldson, C.A., & Peacock, M. (2001). Guiding principles for art therapy. *Unpublished manuscript.*

Rosen, S. (1988). What makes Ericksonian therapy so effective? In J.K. Zeig & S.R. Lankton (Eds.), *Developing Ericksonian therapy.* (pp. 5–29). New York: Brunner/Mazel.

Rubin, J. (1999). *Art therapy: An introduction.* Philadelphia: Brunner/Mazel.

Ruesch, J., & Bateson, G. (1951). *Communication: The social matrix of psychiatry.* New York: Norton.

Sager, C. (1981). Couples therapy and marriage contracts. In A.S. Gurman & D.P. Kniskern (Eds.), *Handbook of family therapy.* (pp. 85–132). New York: Brunner/Mazel.

Satir, V. (1972). *Peoplemaking.* Palo Alto, CA: Science and Behavior Books.

Scalise, J. (1992). Life or death: A family suicide watch. *GrassRoutes: Stories from family and systemic therapists, 1*(1), 22.

Schoenwald, S.K., Henggeler, S.W., Brondino, M.J., & Rowland, M.D. (2000). Multisystemic therapy: Monitoring treatment fidelity. *Family Process, 29*(1), 83–103.

Schwenk, T.L., & Hughes, C.C. (1983). The family as a patient in family medicine: Rhetoric or reality? *Social Science and Medicine, 17,* 1–16.

Segal, L., & Bavelas, J.B. (1983). Human systems and communications theory. In B.B. Wolman & G. Strickler (Eds.), *Handbook of family and marital therapy.* (pp. 11–27). New York: Plenum.

Selekman, M.D., & Todd, T. (1991). Major issues from family therapy research and theory: Implications for the future. In T. Todd & M.D. Selekman (Eds.), *Family therapy approaches with adolescent substance abusers.* (pp. 311–325). Needham Heights, MA: Allyn & Bacon.

Selvini Palazzoli, M. (1985). The problem of the sibling as the referring person. *Journal of Marital and Family Therapy, 11*(1), 21–34.

Selvini Palazzoli, M. (1978). *Self starvation.* New York: Aronson.

Selvini Palazzoli, M. (1986). Towards a general model of psychotic family games. *Journal of Marital and Family Therapy, 12,* 339–349.

Selvini Palazzoli, M., Boscolo, L., Cecchin, G., & Prata, G. (1980a). Hypothesizing, circularity, neutrality: Three guidelines for the conduct of the session. *Family Process, 19*(1), 7–19.

Selvini Palazzoli, M., Boscolo, L., Cecchin, G., & Prata, G. (1980b). Why a long interval between sessions? The therapeutic control of the family-therapist supersystem. In M. Andolfi & I. Zwerling (Eds.), *Dimensions of family therapy.* (pp. 161–169). New York: Guilford Press.

Selvini Palazzoli, M., Boscolo, L., Checchin, G., & Prata, G. (1978). *Paradox and counterparadox.* New York: Aronson.

Selvini Palazzoli, M., Cirillo, S., Selvini, M., & Sorrentino, A.M. (1989). *Family games: General models of psychotic processes in the family.* New York: Norton.

Selvini Palazzoli, M., & Prata, G. (1982). Snares in family therapy. *Journal of Marital and Family Therapy, 8*(4), 443–450.

Sheinberg, M. (1992). Navigating treatment impasses at the disclosure of incest: Combining ideas from feminism and social constructionism. *Family Process, 31*(3), 201–216.

Sheinberg, M., & Penn, P. (1991). Gender dilemmas, gender questions and the gender mantra. *Journal of Marital and Family Therapy, 17*(1), 33–44.

Siegel, D.J. (1999). *The developing mind: Toward a neurobiology of interpersonal experience.* New York: Guilford Press.

Simon, R. (1986). Behind the one-way kaleidoscope. *The Family Therapy Networker,*

Simon, R. (1992). *One on one: Conversations with the shapers of family therapy.* Washington, D.C.: The Family Therapy Networker.

Sluzki, C. (1992). Transformations: A blueprint for narrative changes in therapy. *Family Process, 31*(3), 217–230.

Snider, M. (1992). *Process family therapy.* Needham Heights, MA: Allyn & Bacon.

Spanier, G.B. (1976). Measuring dyadic adjustment: New scales for assessing the quality of marriage and similar dyads. *Journal of Marital and Family Therapy, 38,* 15–28.

Spiegel, J. (1982). An ecological model of ethnic families. In J. McGoldrick, J.K. Pearce, & J. Giordano (Eds.), *Ethnicity and family therapy.* (pp. 31–51). New York: Guilford Press.

Sprenkle, D. (2002). *Effectiveness research in marriage and family therapy.* Alexandria, VA: American Association for Marriage and Family Therapy.

Stanton, M.D. (1981). Strategic approaches to family therapy. In A.S. Gurman & D.P. Kniskern (Eds.), *Handbook of family therapy.* (pp. 361–402). New York: Brunner/Mazel.

Stanton, M.D. (1992). The time line and the "why now?" question: A technique and rationale for therapy, training, organizational consultation and research. *Journal of Marital and Family Therapy, 18*(4), 331–344.

Stanton, M.D., & Todd, T.C. (1982). *The family therapy of drug abuse and addiction.* New York: Guilford Press.

Steinglass, P., Bennett, L., Wolin, S., & Reiss, D. (1987). *The alcoholic family.* New York: Basic Books.

Stuart, R.B. (1980). *Helping couples change: A social learning approach to marital therapy.* Champaign, IL: Research Press.

Stuart, R.B. (1976). An operant interpersonal program for couples. In D.H.L. Olson (Ed.), *Treating relationships.* (pp. 119–132). Lake Mills, IA: Graphic Publishing.

Stuart, R.B., & Stuart, F. (1972). *Marital pre-counseling inventory.* Champaign, IL: Research Press.

Suddaby, K., & Landau, J. (1998). Positive and negative timelines: A technique for restoring. *Family Process, 37*(3), 287–298.

Sue, S., & Zane, N. (1987). The role of culture and cultural techniques in psychotherapy: A critique and reformulation. *American Psychologist, 42,* 37–45.

Szapocznik, J., & Coatsworth, J.D. (1999). An ecodevelopmental framework for organizing the influences on drug abuse: A developmental model of risk and protection. In M. Glantz & C.R. Hartell (Eds.), *Drug abuse: Origins and interventions.* (pp. 331–366). Washington, D.C.: American Psychological Association.

Thomas, V., McCollum, E.E., & Snyder, W. (1999). Beyond the clinic: In-home therapy with Head Start families. *Journal of Marital and Family Therapy, 25*(2), 177–190.

Todd, T.C. (1986). Structural-strategic marital therapy. In N.S. Jacobson & A.S. Gurman (Eds.), *Clinical handbook of marital therapy.* (pp. 71–106). New York: Guilford Press.

Todd, T.C., & Selekman, M.D. (1991a). Beyond structural-strategic family therapy: Integrating other brief systemic therapies. In T. C. Todd & M.D. Selkman (Eds.), *Family therapy approaches with adolescent substance abusers.* (pp. 241–274). Boston: Allyn and Bacon.

Todd, T.C., & Selekman, M.D. (Eds.). (1991b). *Family therapy approaches with adolescent substance abusers.* Needham Heights, MA: Allyn & Bacon.

Tomm, K.M. (1984). One perspective on the Milan systemic approach I: Overview of development, theory and practice. *Journal of Marital and Family Therapy, 10,* 113–125.

Tomm, K.M., & Wright, L.M. (1979). Training in family therapy: Perceptual, conceptual and executive skills. *Family Process, 18,* 227–250.

Treadway, D. (1989). *Before it's too late.* New York: Norton.

Van Deusen, J., Stanton, M.D., Scott, S., Todd, T., & Mowatt, D. (1982). Getting the addict to agree to involve his family of origin: The initial contact. In M.D. Stanton & T.C. Todd (Eds.), *The family therapy of drug abuse and addiction.* (pp. 39–59). New York: Guilford Press.

Wadeson, H., Durkin, J., & Perach, D. (1989). *Advances in art therapy.* New York: Wiley.

Waldegrave, C. (1990). Social justice and family therapy. *Dulwich Centre Newsletter, 1*, 6–45.

Walsh, F., & Rolland, J. Strengthening family resilience: Mastering the challenges of illness, disability and loss. In Anonymous. Workshop presented at Loma Linda University Department of Counseling and Family Sciences.

Wamboldt, F., & Wolin, S. (1989). Reality and myth in family life: Changes across generations. In S.B.D. Anderson (Ed.), *Family myths: Psychotherapy implications.* (pp. 141–166). New York: Haworth Press.

Warner, R., & Hansen, J. (1970). Verbal-reinforcement and model-reinforcement group counseling with alienated students. *Journal of Couseling Psychology, 14*, 168–172.

Warner, R.S.J., & Horan, J. (1973). Drug abuse prevention: A behavioral approach. *NAASP Bulletin, 372*, 49–54.

Watzlawick, P., Beavin, J., & Jackson, D. (1967). *Pragmatics of human communication.* New York: Norton.

Watzlawick, P., Weakland, J.H., & Fisch, R. (1974). *Change: Principles of problem formation and problem resolution.* New York: Norton.

Weakland, J., Fisch, R., Watzlawick, P., & Bodin, A. (1974). Brief therapy: Focused problem resolution. *Family Process, 13*, 141–168.

Weber, T., McKeever, J., & McDaniel, S. (1985). The beginning guide to the problem-oriented first family interview. *Family Process, 24*(3), 356–364.

Weeks, G.R. (1991). *Promoting change through paradoxical therapy.* New York: Brunner/Mazel.

Weeks, G.R., & Abate, L. (1982). *Paradoxical psychotherapy: Theory and technique.* New York: Brunner/Mazel.

Weiss, R.L., & Perry, B.A. (1979). *Assessment and treatment of marital dysfunction.* Eugene, Or: Marital Studies Program.

Weltner, J.S. (1985). Matchmaking: Choosing the appropriate therapy for families at various levels of pathology. In M. Pravder Mirkin & S.L. Koman (Eds.), *Handbook of adolescents and family therapy.* (pp. 39–49). New York: Gardiner Press.

Whitaker, C.A. (1976). Comment: Live supervision in psychotherapy. *Voices, 12*, 24–25.

Whitaker, C.A. (1982). The ongoing training of the psychotherapist. In J.R. Neill & D.P. Kniskern (Eds.), *From psyche to system: The evolving therapy of Carl Whitaker.* (pp. 121–138). New York: Guilford Press.

Whitaker, C.A. (1986). Personal communication.

Whitaker, C.A., & Keith, D.V. (1981). Symbolic-experiential family therapy. In A.S. Gurman & D.P. Kniskern (Eds.), *Handbook of Family Therapy.* (pp. 187–225). New York: Brunner/Mazel.

White, M. (1983). Anorexia nervosa: A transgenerational system perspective. *Family Process, 22*(3), 255–273.

White, M. Couple therapy and deconstruction. In Anonymous.

White, M. (1986). Negative explanation, restraint, and double description: A template for family therapy. *Family Process, 25*(2), 169–184.

White, M. (1995). *Re-authoring lives: interviews & essays.* Adelaide, Australia: Dulwich Centre Publications.

White, M., & Epston, D. (1991). *Narrative means to therapeutic ends.* New York: Norton.

Williamson, D. (1981). Personal authority via termaination of the intergenerational hierarchical boundary: A "new" stage in the family lifecycle. *Journal of Marital and Family Therapy, 7*, 441–452.

Wright, L., & Leahey, M. (1984). *Nurses and families: A guide to family assessment and intervention.* Philadelphia: Davis.

Wynne, L.C. (1987). A preliminary proposal for strengthening the multiaxial approach of DSM-III: Possible family-oriented revisions. In G. Tischler (Ed.), *Diagnosis and classification in psychiatry: A critical appraisal of DSM-III.* (pp. 477–488). Cambridge, England: Cambridge University Press.

Wynne, L.C., Shields, C.G., & Sirkin, M.I. (1992). Illness, family theory, and family therapy: I. Conceptual issues. *Family Process, 31*(1), 3–18.

Yingling, L., Miller, W., McDonald, A., & Galewater, S. (1998). *GARF assessment sourcebook: Using the DSM-IV Global Assessment of Relational Functioning.* New York: Brunner/Mazel.

Zeig, J.K., & Lankton, S. (1988). *Developing Ericksonian Therapy.* New York: Brunner/Mazel.

Name Index

Subject Index